REINVENTING THE AMERICAN THOROUGHBRED

THE ARABIAN ADVENTURES OF ALEXANDER KEENE RICHARDS

GARY A. O'DELL

LOUISIANA STATE UNIVERSITY PRESS
BATON ROUGE

Published with the assistance of the V. Ray Cardozier Fund

Published by Louisiana State University Press
lsupress.org

Manufactured in the United States of America

FIRST PRINTING

DESIGNER: Michelle A. Neustrom
TYPEFACE: Freight Text Pro
PRINTER AND BINDER: Sheridan Books, Inc.

JACKET IMAGE: Alexander Keene Richards in Arab garb with his imported Arabian stallion Mokhladi, 1854, by Edward Troye. Private collection.

Cataloging-in-Publication Data are available from the Library of Congress.

ISBN 978-0-8071-8369-4 (cloth: alk. paper) — ISBN 978-0-8071-8464-6 (pdf) —
ISBN 978-0-8071-8463-9 (epub)

CONTENTS

ACKNOWLEDGMENTS

The author of a historical work invariably must rely upon many others for advice and assistance during the various stages of a writing project. I cannot sufficiently express the gratitude I feel for those who have helped me in the long journey to illuminate the life and work of Alexander Keene Richards. Any errors of fact or interpretation are strictly my own.

I am, in particular, indebted to two direct descendants of William B. Keene, Keene Richards Kelley of New Orleans, Louisiana, who can trace his ancestry to Keene Richards's middle daughter, Emily, and Lowry Schneider of Monroe, Louisiana, who is a descendant of John Wallis Keene. These gentlemen opened up their family archives to me and provided many important documents as well as previously unpublished photographs of their ancestors. In addition, Palmer Ragsdale—a descendant of Keene Richards through his daughter Emily—was kind enough to supply me with photographs of some original Troye paintings in her possession, and her daughter Emily Ragsdale supplied copies of some previously unpublished Keene Richards letters. I am also very grateful for the encyclopedic knowledge possessed and shared by Ann Bolton Bevins, eminent historian of Scott County, Kentucky, who read successive drafts of the manuscript and offered many valuable suggestions for improvement. Ann has long been enthusiastic about this project and supportive in every way possible.

I owe a great deal to the expertise of equine historian Kathleen H. Kirsan, who, in some stimulating discussions, corrected some of my misunderstandings of the development of English and American Thoroughbreds. Kathleen was also kind enough to read the manuscript and offer suggestions for correction of errors of fact or interpretation. Brenda Jean

("B. J.") Gooch, Special Collections archivist (retired) at the Transylvania University library in Lexington, helped with information about the Keene family. Felicity Ruggiero, a retired curator of Historic Bethany, Bethany College, West Virginia, located many documents for me concerning Keene Richards's attendance at that institution, and Heather Ricciuti, also at Bethany, provided high-resolution scans of Troye's paintings. Dr. Terry Jones, of the University of Louisiana at Monroe, suggested many useful sources of information on the history of Carroll Parish. Dr. Ernest F. Bailey of the Maxwell H. Gluck Equine Research Center, University of Kentucky, read the chapter on the origin of the Arabian horse and offered valuable suggestions for improvement. Gus Cothran, emeritus professor at Texas A&M university, answered many of my questions on equine genetics. Sarah Gaddy, of the American Saddlebred Museum at the Kentucky Horse Park, investigated Keene Richards's contributions to the development of the modern Saddle horse for me and provided valuable information. Mohammad Safdar of the Tareq Rajab Museum in Kuwait City, Kuwait, kindly provided the image of the painting of Sheikh Medjuel housed in their collection, and also translated some Arabic phrases for me. David P. Manning, president of the Alexandria Historical and Genealogical Library and Museum, kindly provided a photograph of Thomas Jefferson Wells. Lawrence E. Babits, a fellow of the Company of Military Historians and editor of *Artilleryman Magazine,* evaluated Richards's portable cannon patent design and offered his assessment of its practicality. Denis Blake, a member of the Facebook discussion group "Growing the Texas Racing Industry," assisted in tracking down information about Keene Richards's horses in Texas during the Civil War. I am particularly grateful to Danny Thomas and his wife Deneb of Lawrenceburg, Kentucky, for allowing me to become acquainted with the splendid Arabian horses at their Belle Vista farm.

A historian cannot operate without libraries and archives, and too seldom is the assistance provided by the staff of such institutions properly acknowledged. This work would not have been possible without the outstanding staff and resources of the Keeneland Library at Lexington, certainly one of the finest specialty libraries to be found in the country. The staff at the Camden-Carroll Library at Morehead State University aided in locating and borrowing many rare books for my use, and the reference librarians at the British Library in London provided prompt and thorough responses to my email inquiries. In Fayette and Scott counties, respectively, staff at the county clerk's offices were instrumental in helping to locate many old documents. All these overworked and underappreciated persons deserve our gratitude for the invaluable services they provide. As always, my greatest appreciation must go to my spouse, Carol, for her unwavering love, support, and critical evaluation of this and all my projects.

REINVENTING THE AMERICAN THOROUGHBRED

INTRODUCTION

There can be little doubt that Keene Richards of Blue Grass Park in Scott County, Kentucky, along with his close friend Robert Alexander of Woodburn Farm in Woodford County, should be considered among the most influential Thoroughbred breeders of Kentucky during the nineteenth century, in a state and era marked by many celebrated equine luminaries. Each of these men had a talent for identifying superb horses, and they were responsible for importing superior Thoroughbred mares and stallions from England and thereby making an indelible impression on American bloodlines, as well as selecting some of the best American stock for their breeding programs. Despite their friendship, Richards and Alexander pursued quite different courses to become the leading turfmen of the region.

Keene Richards (1847–1881), who was born in Georgetown, Kentucky, became obsessed with horses at an early age. When sent on a Grand Tour of Europe with two trusted companions in 1851 after his college graduation, instead of visiting cultural icons, he turned this rite of passage into an investigation of the most famous equine centers of the Old World. His journey through Spain became a life-altering event. There he encountered some Arabian horses recently imported by Queen Isabella, and this experience cemented a desire that he must travel to the Near East to view these magnificent animals in their natural setting. In Syria, then part of the Ottoman empire, he purchased two Arabian stallions and a mare, which were shipped back to America while Richards and his friends continued their tour into central and eastern Europe. Young Keene Richards was the first westerner, of any nation, to journey into the desert lands to seek out pureblooded Arabians from Bedouin tribes, rather than be content with inferior specimens from Mediterranean coastal cities.

Upon his return to the United States in early spring 1853 and reunion with his new Arabian horses, Richards conceived of a plan that would become his driving passion for the remainder of his life. Prior to the Civil War, the racing of running horses was quite different from today's competitions, being as much a matter of endurance as of speed because horses raced in multiple heats, or events, that might total twenty or more miles in a single day. Arabian horses were legendary for their ability to run for long distances through a harsh desert environment, and Richards believed that a fresh infusion of Arabian blood might enhance the stamina of American racehorses. The English Thoroughbred was believed to have been developed more than a century before by breeding Arabian stallions to English mares. He launched his experiment by acquiring some first-rate American horses and English Thoroughbreds, and returned to the East for more Arabians to breed with these.

Richards's ability to pursue the lifestyle of an elite turfman was based on wealth derived from cotton plantations in the Deep South, along the Mississippi in northeast Louisiana, wealth bestowed at first by a doting grandfather and later inherited. The wealth of his friend Robert Aitcheson Alexander (1819–1867), unlike that of most Kentucky turfmen, was industrial in nature, like that of many of the northern turf magnates. Born at Midway, Kentucky, Robert A. Alexander was the son of Robert Alexander, who came to America from England in 1787 and obtained a large land grant in Virginia that would later become Woodburn Farm in Kentucky. At the age of thirteen, Robert A. was sent abroad to study in England, earning a degree from Trinity College. While a student, he inherited the estate of his uncle, Sir William Alexander, which included a number of large properties and a substantial income from iron mines. Robert returned to Kentucky in 1849 and began to expand his land holdings here.[1]

Whereas Keene Richards became interested in Thoroughbred Running Horses in his youth, Alexander became one of the most influential breeders of Shorthorn cattle in the United States, importing notable English stock. It was not until 1853 or 1854, about the time Richards was abroad seeking to add more Arabian horses to his stable, that Alexander began to breed horses, Thoroughbreds and Trotters. As his biographer, William

Preston Mangum II, observed, "Alexander's knowledge of all kinds of stock was clear and accurate, but the thoroughbred horse was his greatest love." Under his management, Woodburn Stud would become the greatest equine breeding operation in the nation.[2]

Keene Richards and Robert A. Alexander were the most important patrons of the renowned artist Edward Troye. In this era, photography was yet in its infancy, and the only way to capture images of outstanding livestock was to have a sketch or portrait made by a competent artist. The foremost painter of animal portraits in the country was Swiss-born Troye (1808–1874), who specialized in rendering realistic paintings of cattle and horses. America, unlike England, did not produce an important school of sporting art during the nineteenth century, but Thomas Cook, a British authority on sporting art, said that, of the Americans, "Troye was the best of them all." A prolific artist, he produced more than 350 known paintings, estimated to be less than half of his actual work. The horse, however, was always Troye's favorite subject. Keene Richards was his primary patron, having commissioned twenty-seven paintings, mainly of horses, for which he generously paid the artist enormous sums; among these were eight landscape scenes of Syria and the Holy Land, which Troye considered to be his finest work. Troye was far more than a hired artist to Richards, becoming a close personal friend. After Richards, Robert Alexander was Troye's most important client, for whom the artist created eighteen paintings, of both horses and cattle. The group pictures of Shorthorn cattle painted for Alexander in 1854 were, in the opinion of Troye's biographer, "undoubtedly the best portraits of cattle ever painted in this country."[3]

Richards's grand plan was interrupted by the Civil War. His friend Robert Alexander remained in the North and continued to prosper after the war, his lands and fortune intact. Keene Richards embraced the southern cause, serving in the Confederate army as an aide to General John C. Breckinridge, and lost nearly everything. After the war, it was only through the generosity of his friends that he was able to reclaim his position as one of Kentucky's equine aristocrats, although always in perilous financial straits, and to restore Blue Grass Park as one of the nation's premier Thoroughbred breeding establishments. His quest to improve Thoroughbred endurance had not yielded success in the few years since its inception, and indeed became irrelevant in postwar America as the style of racing evolved to favor short "dash" races instead of the grueling, long-distance competitions that had inspired his experiment.

Richards has remained of great interest to equine historians down to the present day, who have had a wealth of material to draw upon. On several occasions he published his own views on breeding, and as one of the country's most prominent turfmen, during his lifetime Richards and his Bluegrass estate were described many times in newspapers and sporting journals. Accounts of his life, however, have generally focused on his role as the primary patron of Edward Troye or on his quest to improve the Thoroughbred Running Horse with an admixture of Arabian blood. In the latter case, while expressing admiration for the boldness of his Near Eastern adventures, most historians have denounced his experiment as a folly that squandered a great fortune. None have ever attempted to draw all the threads together to provide a complete portrait of the man behind the experiment.

The most substantial biographies of Keene Richards were provided by Thornton Chard in the mid-1930s and by the noted equine historian Alexander Mackay-Smith in 1981. Chard's account appeared as a series of articles in *The Horse,* a magazine for horse fanciers and breeders, and was entirely focused on Richards's Arabian importations. His work is of particular interest because Chard developed a correspondence with Dr. George A. Feris, an elderly Texas horseman who had been one of Keene Richards's most ardent supporters when he was first beginning his experiment, and remained so thereafter, and thus Chard was able to obtain some firsthand information about the project. Penned by a meticulous scholar, Mackay-Smith's *Race Horses of America, 1832–1872: Portraits and Other Paintings by Edward Troye* was first and foremost a biography of Edward Troye, but he gave considerable space to Keene Richards. Although his coverage was limited to the span of time when Richards was Troye's patron, this still represented more than half of Richards's lifetime and was accordingly of great benefit.

The equine literature is enormous and largely hagiographic, with biographies representing a major segment. Relatively few comprehensive biographies, however, have been written about leading American breeders, and in the modern era their focus has been mainly on superstar Thoroughbred horses and the jockeys who rode them to victories. Biographies of famous horses are popular with the reading public and far too numerous to list more than a sampling. Some notable recent publications in this category include Hillenbrand's *Seabisuit* (2003), Clee's *Eclipse* (2012), Kirsan's (2019) and Wickens's (2023) accounts of the celebrated Lexington, and numerous entries in the "Thoroughbred Legends" series sponsored by Blood Horse publishing, among them featuring Man o' War (Bowen 2000), Native Dancer (Boyd 2000), and Secretariat (Capps 2003). The lives of jockeys have not drawn as much attention as their mounts, but several prominent riders have been subjects of books or have written autobiographies. From colonial times through the nineteenth century, most jockeys were Black, and a recent trend in racing historiography has been efforts to illuminate the lives of America's forgotten Black jockeys, many of whom were enslaved men prior to the Civil War. Significant examples here would include Hotaling's *Great Black Jockeys* (1999) and Mooney's *Race Horse Men* (2014), both providing good overviews of the subject and the latter's work also dealing with grooms and trainers. Biographies of specific Black jockeys include Hotaling's (2004) and Drape's (2006) accounts of Jimmy Winkfield, and McDaniels's (2013) and Mooney's (2023) examinations of Isaac Murphy, perhaps the best known of these Black athletes.[4]

Works focused on specific Thoroughbred breeders, as is the case for jockeys, are limited in number compared to those written about celebrity horses, most being brief accounts or chapters in books about racing. Examples of this approach would be Welch's *Who's Who in Thoroughbred Racing* (1947), Bowen's *Legacies of the Turf* (2005), and Johnson and Crookshanks's *Virginia Horse Racing: Triumphs of the Turf* (2008). Among the more prolific writers on this subject was Fairfax Harrison, who tended to profile breeding establishments more so than their owners, whose lives were part of the broader treatment. His works of this type feature the early eighteenth-century Belair Stud of Maryland, the mid-eighteenth-century John's Island Stud of South Carolina, and the nineteenth-century Roanoke Stud of Virginia. Similar in nature, focusing on the establishment and families involved rather than specific individuals, is Auerback's 1994 *Wild Ride*, an examination of the vicissitudes of famed Calumet Farm at Lexington, Kentucky. A number of biographies of men who were noted Thoroughbred breeders actually devoted little space to horses, because for these wealthy men breeding and racing were but one aspect of their complex lives. In this category can be found Black's biography of August Belmont (1981), Kamoie's account of the Tayloes of Virginia (2007), and Johnson's *John Randolph* (2012). Pierre Lorillard was such a man, heir to the Lorillard Tobacco Company fortune but nevertheless passionately devoted to Thoroughbred racing, and it was this aspect of his life that was singled out for examination in 1916 by Walter Vosburgh.[5]

Comprehensive biographies of turfmen whose lives primarily concerned their stock are rare indeed, and the only example I have been able to locate is the 1999 account of Robert A. Alexander of Kentucky by William Preston Mangum II. The present biography of Keene Richards, like Magnum's work, should help to provide the detail necessary to understand the lives of such men and the world of Thoroughbred breeding and racing in which they were immersed.

During the course of my research into the life of Keene Richards, I was able to make contact with several of his descendants, residents of Louisiana, who generously made many family documents available to me. One of them asked me a very important question: "Why do you want to write a book about him?" Many possible responses occurred to me: Richards was an important horse breeder whose English importations made a lasting impression on American bloodlines; Richards and his companions were the first westerners to venture directly into the desert lands to bargain directly with Bedouin tribesmen for their Arabian horses; Richards was a visionary with a grand albeit unsuccessful plan for improvement of the American Thoroughbred Running Horse. All of these things flashed through my mind, and I would so inform my inquirer directly, but my first reaction was simply to reply in complete honesty, "Richards was a fascinating man who led a remarkable life." This was the real reason I wished to tell his story.

1

REINVENTING THE AMERICAN THOROUGHBRED

The year 1857 was momentous in the life of Alexander Keene Richards of Scott County, Kentucky, one in which he came into great wealth and began to publicize his theory and breeding experiment. Thirty years old, slight in build and mild of manner, standing five feet seven inches in height with clear blue eyes and brown hair, he was one of the wealthiest men in Kentucky. In that year, he inherited vast estates in Louisiana from his grandfather, physician William B. Keene, and now was free to pursue, without limit, his recently developed passion for the breeding of racehorses. Richards was convinced that the key to improving the breed, in both speed and stamina, was to return to the same roots that had produced the superlative English Thoroughbred, believed to be largely a product of crosses between the horses of Britain and the magnificent steeds of the Near Eastern desert. Larger and faster than their Oriental ancestors, English Thoroughbreds were brought to America beginning in the mid-eighteenth century. Sponsored by his doting grandfather, Richards had already accomplished an amazing feat, traveling tens of thousands of miles across Europe and the Near East, leading two expeditions into the heart of the Syrian desert, in 1851–1853 and 1855–1856, to obtain Arabian breeding stock of the purest blood. He was the first American, indeed, the first westerner of any national origin, to venture into the desert to bargain directly with the nomadic tribesmen for their horses. His exploits would not be duplicated until the expeditions of Roger Upton and of Wilfred S. and Lady Anne Blunt in the 1870s. The horses Richards acquired were transported back to his grandfather's farm at the western edge of

Portrait of Alexander Keene Richards, oil on canvas, painted posthumously by Benjamin Franklin Reinhart, date illegible. Private collection.

the small Bluegrass community of Georgetown, which Richards transformed into a premier breeding establishment known as Blue Grass Park.[1]

Growing up in the pervasive equine culture of the Inner Bluegrass region during the antebellum period, he was among numerous Scott County gentry in having a passion for horses, for many of his neighbors were engaged in breeding and racing fast horses. Landowners such as Abraham Buford, James K. Duke, Willa Viley, and Ralph B. Tarlton were prominent turfmen of the county who befriended young Richards and served as role models while he was building his reputation as an importer and breeder of first-class racehorses. Just north of Georgetown, tucked into a curve of North Elkhorn Creek on the east side of the Cincinnati Road, was the Gano racetrack, built in 1793 by Lynn West and used during the early antebellum period as a venue for meetings of the Georgetown Jockey Club and for occasional meets through 1905. Nearby Lexington contained the track of the Kentucky Association, and many other Bluegrass communities also possessed racing venues. When, in 1857, Richards came into his inheritance, he built a private, mile-long racing oval on his Blue Grass Park estate at Georgetown.[2]

The Inner Bluegrass was admirably suited for raising running horses. The landscape here was, in all essential respects, a virtual duplicate of the Yorkshire region, where the English Thoroughbred was first developed and long the center of northern racing on the island. Possessing a generally mild climate, the gently rolling karstic terrain favored agriculture and stock breeding, with deep, fertile soils rich in calcium and phosphate derived from the underlying limestone and fostering abundant growth of nutritious bluegrass, *Poa pratensis.*[3]

The first Thoroughbreds in the American colonies were imported from England by wealthy southern planters who wished to emulate the aristocratic lifestyles of the mother country. Breeding and racing these horses became firmly rooted in colonial New York and in the southern states, particularly the Tidewater region of Virginia, Maryland, and South Carolina. During the Revolutionary War, destruction of infrastructure by the British invaders along with confiscation and deliberate slaughter of bloodstock devastated the lowland racing establishment and promoted the westward shift of breeding and racing running horses into Kentucky and Tennessee. The central areas of these states, both known collectively as "the Bluegrass region" prior to the Civil War, were the first trans-Appalachian areas to be settled, and the hardy pioneers brought livestock with them to help tame the new land. Racing horses became a common form of recreation for Bluegrass residents, usually informal matches between a pair of horses down a straight path cleared for the purpose, or through the streets of a community.[4]

The Tidewater gentry who came to the western frontier imported English Thoroughbred horses and brought order to the sport, laying out oval courses of measured length, establishing jockey clubs, and promulgating rules and regulations to govern the conduct of race meetings in the British tradition. Prior to the Civil War, however, the American Thoroughbred horse had not yet emerged as a distinct breed; instead, turfmen bred and raced the long-established domestic breed known as the American Running Horse, from which the American Thoroughbred would be developed. Racing was essentially a gentlemen's sport, indulged in by wealthy elites who had the means to acquire and maintain these expensive animals. The racing associations were exclusive clubs for the benefit of members who raced their horses against those of other members, with prizes awarded out of a racing fund raised by member subscriptions and entry fees. The first "jockey clubs" in Kentucky were established in Woodford County and at Lexington in 1797. The rules established by the Lexington club, reorganized as the Kentucky Association in 1826, served as the model by which race meetings in the commonwealth were conducted. Common folk and nonmembers were welcome as spectators and were not required to pay admission. Although gambling was prohibited on the grounds of racecourses, numerous wagers on the outcome of races, often substantial, were arranged beforehand. By 1810, nearly every significant community in the West possessed a racecourse and conducted meetings on a regular basis, usually in the spring or fall of the year. The period of the late 1820s through the 1830s witnessed an increase in Thoroughbred importations and a proliferation of racing venues that ushered in what might be considered a "golden age" for the sport during the early antebellum period. The racing of running horses was the first mass spectator sport in America.[5]

This expansion was short-lived, for a financial crisis, the Panic of 1837, resulted in a significant contraction of racing and breeding operations. Racing all but disappeared from New York and the North, where capitalists whose wealth allowed them to maintain racing stables and support expensive breeding operations were no longer able to indulge in such extravagances. Facing financial ruin, many northern breeders were forced to sell their bloodstock and farms, and without a steady supply of first-rate racehorses available for competition, the region could no longer support racing venues. During this period, the southern states experienced a consolidation of the numerous community-based racing venues into a handful of tracks operating in the larger cities. The Bluegrass region of Kentucky and Tennessee became the undisputed focus of racehorse breeding, and the racing capital of the nation shifted from New York to the new Metairie track in New Orleans, established in 1838. That same year marked thc peak for horse racing in Kentucky, with no less than fifteen tracks across the state offering race meetings. By 1855, as Keene Richards began his Anglo-Arab breeding experiment, the numerous local venues of Kentucky had all but disappeared, having been consolidated into a few better-supported facilities. In the years just prior to the Civil War, horse racing was being offered with regularity only at Lexington, Louisville, and Crab Orchard.[6]

Prior to the war, the racing style practiced in America was quite different from that experienced by race fans in the modern era. Races at the time were far more prolonged and punishing to the horses involved, being tests more of endurance—a trait known as "bottom"—than of speed. The most common form of competition during the period was heat racing. A "heat" consisted of multiple circuits of a mile or more each around the track. The same group of horses competed in several such grueling races in a day, the overall winner determined at the end of the day as the horse winning the greatest number of heats. "Our mode of running," an American turfman explained in 1857, "is to rush from the start, at the highest rate of speed that can be sustained." Individual horses might be expected to run as much as twenty miles in a day at full gallop, a practice that we would today consider abusive, and it often resulted in horses dropping dead on the track or becoming permanently lame, their racing careers terminated. Long a staple of English racing, these heroic long-distance contests had faded in popularity in Britain by the time of the American Revolution, replaced by relatively short "dash" races consisting of a single turn around the course, but heat racing continued as the prevailing form in the United States. A British observer, appalled by the continued American practice, noted that "Four mile heats are, with us, considered a barbarity, which went out of fashion at about the same time as bullbaiting and dogfighting."[7]

Long-distance heat racing being the order of the day for American tracks, Keene Richards's breeding program was primarily motivated by a desire to produce racehorses that possessed greater stamina and were capable of withstanding the rigors of such competitions. For a constant reminder of this goal, he need look no further than his own stables, which housed the former champion mare Peytona, a domestically bred true Thoroughbred who was the very first horse he purchased when he began his program. Owned by Thomas Kirkman of Alabama, Peytona's racing career ended abruptly after the six-year-old mare, undefeated at the time, was brought north in 1845 to compete in a match race, one on one, against the equally famous northern mare, Fashion, at the Union Course in New York. On race day, May 13, Peytona defeated Fashion in two consecutive four-mile heats and was declared victor, but was lamed during the event. Nevertheless, she was forced to race again on May 28. This time, she collapsed on the track, unable to finish. Her career now ended, she was retired to Kirkman's farm. When, in 1853, an opportunity presented to acquire this outstanding mare, Richards did not hesitate but immediately purchased her and brought her home to his Georgetown stable.[8]

The logic of his breeding program was also predicated on a belief Richards shared with several other breeders. During the antebellum period, Richards and many other turfmen, in both England and America, believed that racehorses had deteriorated in quality from those of the previous century, a viewpoint that was vigorously challenged by equine authorities who denied any such degradation, maintaining that contemporary racehorses were just as fast and stalwart as their forebears. There was also an aspect of patriotism in this controversy, in that most Englishmen considered the English racehorse to be superior to those of America, believing the latter to have declined in quality over time.

The presumed degeneration of American horses derived initially from the highly influential work of Georges-Louis Leclerc, Comte de Buffon (1707–1788), whose monumental *Histoire Naturelle, Générale et Particulière* was published in thirty-six volumes from 1749 to 1788. Subsequently translated into many different languages, Buffon's *Natural History* was released in English editions from 1775 to 1815. The most comprehensive encyclopedia of life on Earth ever written, his work was read by nearly every educated person on both sides of the Atlantic. Although Buffon never visited the New World, he seemed to have a particular distaste for the Americas, asserting that all life here was degenerate, from the animals to the native peoples. Based on reports by French travelers, he assumed the North

American climate was colder and more humid than that of the Old World, and that degeneration of the native life forms could thus be attributed to the unfavorable environment. Imported livestock would also be adversely affected, such that "all the animals which have been transported from Europe to America, such as horses, asses, oxen, sheep, goats, pigs, dogs, &c. all these animals, I say, have become smaller." Domestic animals that "by the gentle influences of another climate, have received their full form and their entire extension," when brought to America "shrink, shrink under this miserly sky and in this empty earth." Buffon's concept of New World degeneration was extremely popular in Europe, but, as might be expected, sparked outrage in America.[9]

Thomas Jefferson was among those who were incensed by Buffon's allegations of American inferiority. No mean naturalist himself, Jefferson set about to set the record straight. In 1787, he published an overview of his home state, *Notes on the State of Virginia,* and devoted a considerable portion of the text to refutation of Buffon's claims of American degeneracy. The idea of American degeneration would persist in European perceptions through the antebellum period, finally fading in the mid-1850s. With the passing of the main advocates of degeneracy, there was no longer a great deal of interest in the debate. By this time, transatlantic travel had become commonplace, and many European visitors wrote detailed accounts of the great diversity of American wildlife and of the nobility of the native peoples. The study of natural history had also advanced considerably since the time of Buffon, and it had become clear that there was no evidence of American degeneration.[10]

The notion of racehorse degeneration in the New World persisted, however, largely as a result of British snobbery. During the nineteenth century, the most widely read and authoritative book on equines was *The Horse,* authored by English veterinary surgeon and animal welfare writer William Youatt. First released in 1831, with a second edition in 1843, this popular book was revised and expanded by other authors after Youatt's death in 1847, so that different editions had different perspectives on the subject. The Thoroughbred horse was developed in England during the seventeenth and eighteenth centuries by breeding imported Oriental horses from the Near Eastern region with English mares. In the first edition, published in London, Youatt wrote, "improved and perfected by the influence of the climate . . . and British skill, made the thoroughbred horse what he is." An 1853 revision, also published in London, asserted that the Thoroughbred could only achieve and maintain its superior form in England, stating, "The climate of England has no doubt almost as much to do with our breed of horses as has the purity of their Arabian pedigree. When an English horse leaves his native country, he is observed to degenerate, and his progeny remarkably so."[11]

In contrast, an American edition of Youatt's book published in New York in 1843 contained a lengthy introductory essay by John Stuart Skinner, founder of the *American Turf Register* in 1829, that thoroughly debunked the idea of Thoroughbred deterioration in America, at least as far as American readers were concerned. "Climate and food have their influence on the form and character of animals," he acknowledged, but "these influences in England are less auspicious to high perfection of the Horse than the warmer and dryer climates of the United States." He cited several authorities on animal physiology to this effect, including the English writer Thomas Brown, who in 1830 observed that "the degenerating effects of a British atmosphere and pasturage, can only be successfully combated, by the occasional introduction of Asiatic blood. A permanently excellent breed can never be expected in this climate." Skinner concluded, given that American breeders had, over the last century, imported some of the finest English bloodstock, "on this continent the Horse ought to reach and retain powers at least equal to any he has ever attained in England."[12]

Those who perceived a general degeneration of Thoroughbreds as compared to forebears attributed the decline to excessive inbreeding and a tendency by breeders to favor the attribute of speed at the expense of endurance. Such incestuous breeding can concentrate and perpetuate genetic defects, and is generally disparaged for this reason by breeders. Some writers believed that the Thoroughbred was an exception to the general rule, noting that inbreeding occurred naturally among wild horses as a result of the tendency for a strong stallion to collect and protect a group of mares, which served as his harem, and would consequently breed with his daughters and granddaughters. This was how the English Thoroughbred was originally developed in its superior form, they observed, because in the early days there were only a limited number of imported stallions, necessitating inbreeding.[13]

Many breeders were nevertheless determined to develop ever faster horses by breeding only to the handful of sires and dams who had exhibited the single quality of speed and consistently proved to be winners on the turf. In 1665, the King's Plate races inaugurated by Charles II to encourage stamina and better cavalry mounts made long-distance heat racing, with horses carrying heavy weights, the prevailing mode in Britain for more than a century. Runaway victories by fleet-footed horses such as Flying Childers in 1715 and Regulus in 1739, however, convinced English breeders that the key to winning races was speed rather than stamina. This led to an increasing demand for shorter races, lower weights, and fewer heats, so that by the time of the American Revolution single-heat races were introduced at major British courses, run over distances of two miles or less.[14]

The consequences of this single-minded obsession with speed were deplored by some turf writers, who believed that the sacrifice of endurance was detrimental to the overall quality of the English Thoroughbred. "When our Racers run longer distances, and carried greater weight, their forms were more compact and muscular," wrote one observer in 1836, noting, "The single quality of speed possessed by the modern racer is a bad substitute for the fine union of speed, stoutness, and structural power possessed by the old racers." According to these critics, breeding for speed had resulted in degeneration of the racehorse, which had become "weedy" with longer legs, long backs, and weak loins, more delicate and lacking vigor of constitution. As a result of such changes, English Thoroughbreds were more prone to become lamed for life even during short races. The solution, many felt, was to return to long-distance multiple-heat racing, for which stamina was an essential quality.[15]

Many also believed that the speed of the modern horse was inferior to those of the past. Although few knowledgeable turfmen would give credence to the idea that modern horses were less swift than their forebears, the belief was apparently so widespread among the uninformed that Henry W. Herbert, author of *Frank Forester's Horse and Horsemanship of the United States,* felt compelled to devote a considerable amount of text in his book to its refutation. Writing under the pseudonym Frank Forester, Herbert was a frequent contributor to the New York sporting journal *Spirit of the Times,* and his enormously popular book, first published in 1857, provided the first comprehensive examination of horses and horse racing in the western hemisphere. Herbert addressed the general assumption that the "racehorse of the nineteenth century, whether English or American, has degenerated from the famous worthies of the eighteenth" in a well-written and persuasive essay that argued against the loss of either speed or stamina in modern running horses.[16]

Herbert attributed the assumption of degeneracy primarily to exaggerations of the speed of a few famous English horses of the previous century, notably Flying Childers and Eclipse. Cecil (Cornelius Tongue), he noted, had in 1855 referred to these stories as "wonderful tales" that, "like the snowball, have increased in their progress," ever growing with the passage of time. The horse named Childers was foaled in 1714, sired by the Darley Arabian, one of the great foundation sires of the English Thoroughbred, and became known as "Flying" Childers after he achieved fame. Although Flying Childers only ran in two races at Newmarket, being undefeated, he sired a great number of accomplished progeny, and approximately 90 percent of all Thoroughbreds today can trace their lineage to this horse. In his 1840 *History of the British Turf,* James Whyte referred to Flying Childers as "the fleetest horse that ever ran at Newmarket, or, as generally believed, that was ever bred in the world." In 1721, during a trial at the Newmarket course, which measured three miles, six furlongs, and ninety-three yards, or 3.3 miles, Flying Childers covered the distance in six minutes and forty seconds, or an average of 29.8 miles per hour. In the same year, Flying Childers ran the 4.1-mile Beacon course in a reported time that gave an average of 33 miles per hour, supposedly covering twenty-five feet with every stride. Although Flying Childers was admittedly a very fast horse, such times as these are not astonishing. On April 2, 1855, the famous American horse Lexington ran a time trial against Lecomte at the Metairie track in New Orleans. To the delight of spectators, he covered four miles in 7 minutes, 19.75 seconds, for an average speed of 32.7 miles per hour. What fired the imagination of eighteenth-century British turf enthusiasts, however, was a dubious but generally accepted report that Flying Childers had achieved a burst of speed in which he moved eighty-two and a half feet in one second, a velocity of nearly a mile a minute.[17]

Claims of mile-a-minute running are, however, absurd, for as Herbert and many others later pointed out, no horse that ever lived could achieve anything near sixty miles an hour. Such reports are most likely a result of inaccurate measurements. As "D.P." commented in the *Spirit of the Times* in 1855, "In the former period, little or no attention was given to the indications of the watches, either slow or fast, nor were the tracks measured with scientific accuracy. It was then a matter of but little importance whether a track was measured with a grapevine or the surveyor's chain; or whether the time of a race was kept by the use of a town clock, or a gentleman's watch." Herbert expressed doubt as to whether, in Childers's day, there even were watches in existence by which seconds could be stopped and counted accurately. Competitions over very long distances were more common in the 1700s than later, and formed a basis for asserting the greater endurance of the horses of the time. The horse Quibbler, for example, was reported to have run twenty-three miles at Newmarket in fifty-seven minutes and ten seconds. Examining the evidence, Herbert concluded that, even if the recorded time trials of Childers and other legendary horses were granted to be true, their performances were not beyond the reach of modern racers. In his opinion, the general run of eighteenth-century horses was inferior to the general run of later generations. As to stamina in heat racing, he wrote, "I deny utterly the superiority of the horses of the olden time." Degeneracy of either the English or American horse from its original ancestry was "an idle and absurd fallacy."[18]

Keene Richards of Georgetown, Kentucky, was among those who believed that the racehorses of his time had degenerated in quality from those of the past, but in stamina rather than speed. "We are not one of those who believe that a horse ever ran a mile in a minute," he stated, bluntly. Richards laid out his thesis in 1857, writing, "The English horse is a hothouse plant, forced in his growth. They have become more gross and leggy than their ancestors, and they may stride a little longer, but their strides are at the expense of their long legs, which not unfrequently give way." As an American turfman, where horses were expected to compete in multiple four-mile heats, strength and stamina were essential qualities for racehorses. Too many racehorses, such as his own Peytona, had been permanently lamed because breeders had become obsessed with speed over endurance. "The English horse of the present day is inferior to what he was in the days of Eclipse, no one will doubt who examines the performances of that day. The present race of horses are fleet," he wrote, "but how few remain on the turf, and one hard race of four miles would injure the best horse in England." Even American horses did not possess the desired stamina, being prone to injury during the long-distance racing that was standard fare in this country.[19]

Richards expressed his views in a pamphlet published in Lexington in 1857, intended to promote the superiority of stock resulting from his breeding program. He proposed a solution to the problem of stamina: a fresh infusion of Arabian blood was needed to strengthen this quality in the modern racehorse. Arabian horses were thought to have extraordinary powers of endurance, and two centuries before, as it was then universally believed, the Arabian had been used to develop the English Thoroughbred. Richards was already involved in breeding Arabians to American Running Horse bloodstock. His 1857 pamphlet describing his rationale and program also featured expositions on several of the Arabians he had recently secured from trips to the Near East. It was handsomely illustrated with reproductions of paintings by the renowned horse portraitist Edward Troye of three of his own Arabian stallions, Mokhladi, Massoud, and Sacklowie.[20]

Few horsemen of the nineteenth century would allow that the Arabian horse could ever outrun the modern Thoroughbred, but all acknowledged that the desert horse possessed an amazing endurance equaled by no other breed, capable of traversing long distances at full gallop under a broiling sun with little in the way of rest, food, or water. The Arabian reputation for stamina was common knowledge in the mid-seventeenth century when Oriental horses were first being imported into England, for as William Cavendish, the Duke of Newbury, had been informed, these were ridden "Fourscore miles in a day" without a bridle. Writing in 1828, John Stark, referring to the Arabian as "the noblest of the species," asserted that this horse combined "the qualities of endurance, vigor, and temper, in a higher degree than any of the other varieties." The explorer John L. Burckhardt, who spent considerable time observing the Bedouins, wrote of encounters between hostile tribes on horseback: "If the contest happen in a level country, the victorious party frequently pursue the fugitives for three, four, or five hours together at full gallop; and instances are mentioned of a close pursuit for a whole day. This would not be possible with any but the Bedouin breed of horses, and it is on this account that the Bedouin praises his mare, not so much for her swiftness as for her indefatigable strength." Another well-seasoned Near Eastern traveler of the period, Austen H. Layard, noted that "the most remarkable and valuable quality" of the Arab horse was "the power of performing long and arduous marches upon the smallest possible allowance of food and water." Eugène Daumas, an authority on the Sahara region, in 1851 observed that desert horses commonly journeyed seventy-five to ninety miles a day for five or six days, and could repeat the performance after a few days' rest.[21] In modern times, Arabian horses are the preferred mounts for long-distance endurance racing.

Although Arabian horses were thought to be the foundation of the English Thoroughbred, a number of horsemen believed the full potential of Arabian blood had never been realized because those Arabians imported into the island kingdom had been poor specimens of the breed. For example, in 1802, the Englishman John Lawrence observed that "the far greater part of those horses brought over to this country, under the general appellation of Arabians, have never seen Arabia, or have been of its inferior breed. They are usually purchased in the Levant, Barbary, or the East Indies, by persons totally unacquainted with horses . . . hence a number of inferior and half-breed Arabians have been brought over at a useless expense, to deteriorate, instead of amending, our racing breed, and to bring Arabian blood into disrepute." Layard expressed a similar sentiment, stating, "I doubt whether any Arab of the best blood has ever been brought to England. The difficulty of obtaining them is so great, that they are scarcely ever seen beyond the limits of the Desert."[22]

Most horsemen of Richards's time were adamant that further Arab-Thoroughbred crosses would result only in worthless progeny. Cecil, for example, bluntly informed readers of *The Farmer's Magazine* in 1853 that it was foolish to assume that Arab horses could improve the stamina or powers of English horses. If "resorting to the primitive stock would improve the breed of any class of our domestic animals," he wrote, "it would be an avowal that the primitive stock is superior to that which has been cultivated for ages." An American commentator observed that there was almost universal opposition to the Arab cross. "On the turf it is a failure. We do not improve the race horse of the present day with an admixture of Arab blood." Much later, in 1905, John Speed wrote: "To most horsemen in America the name of the Arab is anathema. They will have none of him." By this time, the failure of Keene Richards's breeding experiment was well known, and was considered an object lesson on the folly of attempting to reintroduce Arabian blood into the racehorse lineage. Speed, however, qualified his commentary. "Prejudice in this instance, as in most others, is the result of ignorance. The truth is that seven out of ten of the Arabian horses taken into Europe or brought to America have been inferior specimens and not of the correct breed; twenty percent at least have been mongrels and impostures, while of the remaining ten percent not more than one percent have been correct in their breeding, conformation, and capacity to do what was expected of them."[23]

Despite the opposition, a few remained confident that, given enough time, a breeding program designed to infuse Arabian blood into the modern running horse would produce beneficial results. In 1853, an English veterinarian asserted, "We derived our first blood from the Arab, and to the Arab we must return for the required reinvigoration." A breeding program to accomplish this goal would not achieve results with a single cross, nor even a second or third generation, "though ultimately there would seem every probability of our attaining so desirable an end, and thereby improving . . . our breed of racers." John Speed estimated that to obtain a collateral strain of Thoroughbred, "equal to the present," from fresh Arab and Barb blood, would require a breeding program over a period of at least fifty years.[24]

In Kentucky, Elisha I. Winter was an early supporter for reintroducing Arab blood. Having purchased the horse that became known as Winter's Arabian—despite being described as a Barb—he advertised its services at Lexington during the 1820s, encouraging prospective breeders by asserting, "an occasional resort to the original stock of Oriental horses is as necessary to preserve an imported breed as it was in the first place to obtain it." Although Keene Richards shared this belief, he was convinced that nearly all the Arabian stock imported into England or America, including Elisha Winter's prized stallion, were inferior specimens. "For years the English have tried the modern Arab cross, but with not much success," he wrote, and went on to explain that the horses imported for this purpose were not pureblooded Arabians.

> After having examined the Arabs imported into England, as well as those on the continent, the question arose in my mind—has the fail-

> ure been owing to a degeneracy of the Arab, or has it been because so few Arabs have been imported? In investigating the character of modern importations, I found that the most of them had been purchased on the coast of Syria, in Egypt, and some from India—besides few, if any, of the modern importations have been well tested, on account of the strong prejudice existing in England against the Arab. This prejudice is founded upon the fact of the failure of the Arab cross for more than fifty years; and even in the time of the three great progenitors of the English horse, hundreds of so-called Arabs were imported which were worthless.

It was so difficult to obtain the best Arabian horses, found only in the deep desert lands of Arabia and the Levant, that importers had been content to purchase whatever horses of alleged Arabian stock could be had on the Mediterranean coast and other regions frequented by European travelers. Richards then posed the question, "If the English horse is degenerating, is it too late for us to do what England did not two centuries since?" That is, to cross English horses with true Arabian bloodstock. He concluded, ". . . the modern Arab cross will be successful if proper selections are made."[25]

This was the rationale behind Keene Richards's Anglo-Arab breeding experiment, to venture into the Near Eastern desert lands of the Bedouin tribes, purchase the finest pureblooded Arabian horses, and breed these with specimens of the best English Thoroughbreds and American Running Horses the western world had produced. In 1857, when Richards laid out his reasoning, he had already made two trips to the Near East to purchase Arabian horses. During the first trip, from 1851 to 1853, the young man was pursuing his passion for horses by visiting a variety of breeding establishments across Europe. While still in France, he expressed a desire to visit Egypt to purchase an Arabian horse. With this goal now fixed in his mind, after viewing some Arabians in Spain Richards was able to persuade his companions to extend their journey to the East in order to learn more about these magnificent animals in their native environment. At this time, fresh out of college, he had not yet formulated his thesis upon the improvement of thorough-bred stamina. In the Levant, as the eastern Mediterranean region was then known, he made the same error that he later cautioned against, purchasing Arabian horses from dealers in the coastal cities of Jerusalem and Beirut rather than from Bedouin breeders. Despite this transgression, he remained convinced that he had acquired superior specimens of the breed. His second trip took place during 1855–1856. By this time, Richards had assembled a respectable personal library, studying the acknowledged authorities on Arabian and Thoroughbred horses and the lands of the Near East. This research allowed him to develop his philosophy and to begin his breeding program, first with top-notch American horses, and later with some of the best Thoroughbreds England had to offer, which he obtained on a third sojourn abroad in 1858.[26]

There was, however, a fundamental flaw in Richards's hypothesis. The Arabian ancestry of the Thoroughbred, viewed as an established fact by horsemen of his era and even by many today, was in truth no more than a cherished myth. Modern genetic studies show that English, and later American, Thoroughbred horses possess little Arabian blood. So, his plan to replenish the bloodline by a fresh infusion was an effort to replace something that was never present in the first place.

In any case, Richards's grand experiment was doomed by circumstance, for he was not allowed even a single decade in which to carry it out, let alone the fifty years John Speed later estimated was necessary to obtain a satisfactory result. He barely began trials of the first crosses between American horses and imported English Thoroughbreds and his Arabians when the project was interrupted by the convulsions of the Civil War. As a southern sympathizer, Richards was forced to flee Kentucky, first as a participant in the Confederate army, and later, seeking refuge in England until the conclusion of the conflict. Much of his breeding stock, and the Arabian crosses, were scattered across the country by war's end. Ruined financially by the Civil War, he declared bankruptcy in 1868. The plantations in the Deep South, the main source of his income, were lost. His breeding farm in Scott County, inherited from his grandfather and including the historic family home, was now in other hands. Only the kindness and support of his friends in the Bluegrass, who allowed him to take up residence once again on the family farm as proprietor, if not owner, allowed Richards to slowly rebuild the reputation of Blue Grass Park as a first-rate breeding establishment. However, there would be no more trips to exotic foreign lands in search of Arabian bloodstock.

2

INVENTING THE THOROUGHBRED

The English Thoroughbred was a product of crosses made during the seventeenth and eighteenth centuries between native English mares and stallions imported from the Near East and Mediterranean regions. This established bloodlines that have remained closed, more or less, to the present day—hence the term "thoroughbred," meaning selectively bred from superior specimens, applied to such horses. Most of the horses termed "Arabian" and imported to England during the formative years of the Thoroughbred were not, in fact, true Arabians, since this term was rather loosely applied to any horse originating from the Near East and North Africa. Such horses were also referred to as "Eastern" or "Oriental," but were in fact disparate if closely related breeds.

The term "Oriental" was long used historically to designate horses that resemble the Arabian type and was not intended as a specific geographic indicator. Previous vernacular usage was formalized in 1875 by Ludwig Franck, who also applied the term "Occidental" to horses not of an Arabian type. A similar (and equally unscientific) method for generalizing horse types is classification into hot-, cold-, or warm-blooded types, which has nothing to do with body temperature but is used rather loosely to describe either a physical type or a type by temperament. "Hot-blooded" horses are generally considered to be those of a lean and energetic nature, such as Arabians and other breeds derived from Oriental types, such as the Thoroughbred. "Cold-blooded" is applied to larger horses with a placid disposition descended from European breeds used for heavy work—draft horses. "Warm-blooded" may refer to a cross between types, but more commonly to a disposition intermediate between the two. This classification system remains in common use in modern nonacademic equine literature.[1]

Although still subject to considerable debate, domestication of wild horses appears to have taken place many times over a wide geographic area between 3000 and 2000 BCE. They were first exploited as captive sources of meat and milk, then later harnessed for labor and as a form of transport, and ultimately adapted for use in warfare. By 1500 BCE, centuries of breeding domestic equines had refined the original stock into two basic forms: the Celtic ponies of western Europe and larger Arabian-type horses of the central Asian steppes. From these latter were produced several distinctive breeds of light horse that differed in minor characteristics: the Turkoman, Barb, and the true Arabian. These breeds, still in existence today, served as foundation stock for the development of many other horse breeds.[2]

The Turkoman is among the oldest breeds of horse in the world today, developed in stages from ancestral stock in the steppe grasslands east of the Caspian Sea, a land long known as Turkmenistan. Turkoman horses are still prized and bred today in a large area of Turkmenistan and northeastern Iran, part of their ancestral homeland. The ancient blood of this breed today has been somewhat diluted through interbreeding with imported Thoroughbreds from Pakistan, although a number of breeders have endeavored to preserve the Turkoman strain. From the same ancestral stock, horses brought by migrating peoples or invading armies into Egypt and North Africa, circa 1700 BCE, spread along the Barbary Coast of Algeria, Morocco, and Tunisia, where they were refined into the Numidian and Barb breeds. Barbs taken to the Iberian Peninsula, first by the Carthaginians in preparation for the Second Punic War (218–201 BCE), and later during the eighth-century CE Muslim invasion, most likely served as foundation stock for the Andalusian horses of Spain. The Barb horse exists today in a variety of regional strains across North Africa.[3]

The origin of the Arabian horse, while almost certainly derived from the same ancestral stock as the Barb and Turkoman horse, remains obscure. Because of its perceived significance to horse breeding in England and Europe, speculation on the origins of the Arabian horse has held a special fascination for natural history writers to the present day. One of the earliest writers to comment on this was Leo Africanus, whose firsthand account *Descrittione dell'Africa* ("Description of Africa"), first published in 1550, claimed that Arabian horses were descended from wild horses indigenous to the hot desert lands of Arabia. Georges Buffon referred in passing to this desert origin theory of Arabian horses in the fourth volume of his influential *Natural History* (1753) without endorsement or providing an alternative theory.[4]

Buffon's mere mention was, however, taken as sanction by some writers on the subject, such as Thomas H. Morland, writing in 1810, who accepted the supposition without question or elaboration. In 1873, Roger D. Upton, one of the most ardent advocates of the Arabian horse as a superior breed, asserted that the Arabian is the ancestor of all modern horse breeds, with a history dating back nearly four thousand years. Basing his argument almost entirely on biblical texts, Upton concluded that the original horse taken into the ark by Noah was perfect in form—i.e., the Arabian form—and that on the grounding of the ark, the horse came to the Arabian desert and spread from there into other lands. He concluded, "Is it not more reasonable to believe that by these means the horse has been preserved very nearly in his original perfection, than that he should have been bred up from a poor miserable animal such as is seen in the highlands of Central Asia, and showing very little of the true character of the horse."[5]

The assumption that Arabia was the ancestral home of the horse was soon abandoned by most chroniclers in favor of origin theories that proposed ancient Mesopotamia or Egypt as sources for horses imported into Arabia, basing this conclusion on examination and interpretation of historical writings, including the Old Testament. Writers such as William Youatt (1831), Karl Ammon (1834), Charles H. Smith (1841), and John H. Wallace (1897) concluded that, in the words of Smith, "no proofs of an indigenous wild race of horses can be traced" in Arabia. The nearly waterless desert lands of the region, in their opinion, were entirely unsuitable habitats, incapable of supporting a natural population of wild horses.[6]

Youatt and Smith both suggested the possibility of importations from Egypt, during the first millennium BCE or even earlier, of horses that had originally come from Mesopotamia. Wilfrid S. Blunt, writing on the origins of the Arabian horse as an addendum to the account of eastern travel published in 1879 by his wife, the Lady Anne Blunt, proposed that

Arabian horses were derived from wild animals native to ancient Mesopotamia, captured and taken directly to Arabia. However, Lady Blunt's daughter, Judith Blunt-Lytton (the Lady Wentworth), a noted breeder of Arabian horses in England, returned to the theory of a desert origin for these horses; her work, although influential, was based on seriously flawed scholarship. Equally shaky scholarship also marred William Ridgeway's 1905 theory that Arabians were derived from a natural breed of Libyan horses "produced by nature before domestication by man" in North Africa "a thousand years before the Arabs ever bred a horse." Spencer Borden, who was strongly influenced by both Upton and Ridgeway, declared in 1906 that "The race of pure bred Arab horses was in existence three thousand years before Mohamet was born." As late as 1937, Thornton Chard asserted a five thousand-year history for the purebred Arabian horse.[7]

A more recent origin for Arabian horses was suggested by Ammon in 1834, who noted that the first reliable report of horses in the region dates to the second century CE, and horses described as "fast, slender" and having "enormous stamina" had become relatively numerous throughout the peninsula by the fourth century. Writing in 1897, Wallace believed the most likely source of equine stock, from which Arabians were bred by the Bedouin tribes, were those brought to Yemen in the Arabian Peninsula from Cappadocia (part of Persia in ancient times) during the fourth century CE, a gift to the king of the Himyarites by the Holy Roman Emperor Constantius II.[8]

Modern scholarship, now better informed by archaeological and genetic evidence, also inclines to a more recent origin for the Arabian breed, although there remains considerable disagreement as to the time frame, as well as to the geographic origins of the stock involved. Klynstra (1990) suggests that the Arabian horse as a distinct breed was developed during the eighth century CE, at about the time of Mohammed, from stock earlier obtained from a wide region including Mesopotamia, Syria, Egypt, and Palestine. Azzaroli (1985), in contrast, places the origin of Arabian horses in Egypt, bred there from Turkoman stock, during the fourteenth century CE. Bennett (2017) is also inclined to an origin between the eighth and fourteenth centuries, but developed in the Syrian region, "entirely the product of Bedouin taste, Bedouin needs, and Bedouin priorities, which were . . . the hard realities of guerilla warfare, gazelle hunting, and other forms of long-distance chase and racing." A 1978 text on equine genetics reasonably suggested that the Arabian is closely related to the Turkoman and Barb horses, and was first brought into Arabia during the second century CE. While agreeing with the date of introduction, Epstein and Mason (1971), however, asserted that the Barb and Arab horses had quite different origins, and this is borne out by more recent DNA analyses that show little contribution from the Barb to the Arabian breed.[9]

Taken as a whole, the historic literature on the Arabian horse constitutes a body of work that is sometimes scholarly, frequently a romantic mixture of fact and fantasy, and almost always speculative. Despite the best efforts of science and historiography, the current state of knowledge is perhaps best summarized by Bowling and Ruvinsky, who in 2000 stated flatly: "The Arabian has no origin in recorded history." What is certain, however, is that over a period of centuries the nomads of the Arabian desert lands selectively developed one of the world's finest horses, noted for its beauty and stamina, that would consistently breed true to form. During the seventeenth and eighteenth centuries, many of these Oriental horses were imported to England and used to craft one of the swiftest and most elegant of equine breeds, the English Thoroughbred. The choice of Barb, Turk, and (allegedly) Arabian horses for improvement of the English horse was not made for speed, for in racing they proved no swifter than the common stock of England, but for their relative genetic uniformity and prepotency, the ability to transmit a greater proportion of their own characteristics to offspring. This was the primary characteristic that breeders wished to cultivate.[10]

Occasional importations of stock with some proportions of Oriental blood were made during the Middle Ages and under the Tudors, primarily stallions from Spain or Italy that represented Barb or Arabian crosses. In 1616, James I purchased a horse known as the Markham Arabian, said by some to be the first true Arabian brought into the kingdom. William Cavendish, Duke of Newbury and one of the great stud owners of the period, inspected this horse and was not impressed, although he was a great champion of Oriental bloodstock and advocated breeding English mares to Barb stallions to produce the best running horses. As a result of the duke's disparagement, so-called Arabian horses were held in disdain for some time.[11]

The Hobby Horses of Ireland, derived from the small horses of north-

The Arabian horse Namaro Myyas (Hariry Al Shaqab x NN Mayasa), a seven-year-old gray gelding stabled at Belle Vista Farm, Lawrenceburg, Kentucky. Photograph by Gary A. O'Dell (2023).

ern Iberia (Spain) brought to the island by Celtic settlers from about the fifth century BCE, were much admired by English breeders and, by the sixteenth century, were quite possibly the swiftest horses in the world. The reputation of Irish Hobbys for speed was well-known in England. In 1517, the Bishop of Armagh reported to King Henry VIII that Ireland "produces absolutely nothing but oats and most excellent, victorious horses, more swift than the English horses." Both the Tudor and Stuart monarchs, as well as many nobles, were devotees of horse racing, and they supported efforts to improve the kingdom's horses. Henry, who reigned from 1509 to 1547, imported many Irish Hobbys from his stables in Ireland, and often gave them as gifts to members of the nobility. Several of the great nobles, who bred Hobbys in their own Irish stables, also brought them over to compete in English races. Imports of Celtic horses into England and bred to English common stock produced the Hobby Horse of England, similar in appearance to the Irish Hobby but greatly inferior in speed. Continued crosses with Barb and Turkoman blood developed the English Running Horse, a sprint racer that preceded the Thoroughbred. Gervase Markham, who wrote knowledgeably on horsemanship during the early seventeenth century, provided lengthy accounts of the Running Horse in several of his works. The Running Horses, he stated, "being of great courage and mettall are intended to be of greate speede and swiftnesse, for it is impossible to finde toughnesse and furie joynd together, because the one doth ever confound the other."[12]

By 1577, Richard Stanyhurst noted three types of horses in England: The Hobby "of pace easie, in running wonderful swift," horses used for military service which "amble not, but galloppe and run," and "a bastard or mongrel hobbie—strong in travelling, easie in ambling and verie swift in running." He was thus describing the Irish Hobby, the Running Horse, and the English Hobby. Importation of Irish Hobbys was continued by James I, who reigned from 1603 to 1625, and being popular for military use, these were also exported from Ireland to other European countries. By the early 1600s, native Hobbys had nearly disappeared from Ireland because of excessive exports, constant local warfare, and the British conquest of Ireland under the Tudors. Today the breed is considered extinct, but the blood of the Irish Hobby is preserved in the Irish Draught Horse and Connemara Pony. By the onset of the eighteenth century, the Running Horse of Britain also disappeared from existence, having lost favor to the new Thoroughbred horse.[13]

During the latter part of the seventeenth century, after the Restoration, increasing numbers of Oriental horses were imported into England. The crossbreeding of the three swift sprinting breeds, Irish Hobbys, English Running Horses, and select importations of Turkomans and Barbs, would in time produce the fastest of all horses, the English Thoroughbred. The span from about 1650 to 1750 is generally considered to be the period when the foundation for the modern Thoroughbred horse was laid. The first registered horse whose pedigree combined all three strains, and thus the first known Thoroughbred, was a bay known as Spanker, foaled in 1678. This horse was bred by George Villiers, the Second Duke of Buckingham; Spanker's sire was the D'Arcy Yellow Turk, from which derived the Running Horse blood. His dam was Old Peg (Old Morocco Mare), and his grandam was Old Bald Peg, a foundation mare whose bloodline included the Hobby strain. Spanker passed into the hands of Charles Pelham and stood at his Lincolnshire stud, alleged to be the best horse at Newmarket during the reign of Charles II (1660–1685).[14]

It was during this time that the "three great progenitors" referred to by Keene Richards were brought in: the Byerley Turk (1680–1696), the Darley Arabian (1700–1733), and the Godolphin Arabian (1724–1753). The origins of these horses as to breed, let alone their pedigrees, is obscure. For the Byerley Turk, brought to England in 1689, there is no indication of origin, other than the name itself, in any historical records. Charles M. Prior suggested that this horse may have had the same origin as the Lister Turk, captured from a Turkish officer at the 1687 siege of Buda (now Budapest), and most modern accounts seem to have accepted this theory. Other historians have suggested that the horse was captured during the siege of Vienna in 1683. In any case, the Byerley Turk does seem most likely to be a Turkoman horse. The Darley Arabian, which has traditionally been portrayed as Arabian or part-Arabian, was foaled at Palmyra in Syria, purchased at Aleppo, and brought to England in 1704. John Wallace, however, concluded that the Darley must be a Turk, and recent DNA research confirms that the Y haplotype of the Darley originated from the Turkoman horse. Controversy also surrounds the ancestry of the Godolphin Arabian, imported from France in 1730. The Godolphin was long thought to be an Arabian, or possibly a Barb, but painstaking research by noted equine historian Alexander Mackay-Smith has dispelled most of the romantic fables long associated with this horse and suggests that the Godolphin was more likely a Turkoman with some traces and characteristics of Arabian blood. In any case, modern research into the mitochondrial DNA of horse breeds indicates that the Arabian haplogroup is rarely found in the Thoroughbred horse, which possesses mtDNA markers that more closely resemble those of the Turkoman and Barb. One can thus conclude that not only the foundation sires, but also other Oriental horses imported to create the English Thoroughbred, were primarily of the latter breeds rather than Arabian.[15]

The modern Thoroughbred horse has long been considered to derive primarily from these three sires, and was essentially established as a separate breed by the middle of the eighteenth century. The incorporation of Oriental blood into existing stock was not made for speed, because neither the Oriental horses nor their offspring resulting from crosses with native horses were capable of outpacing the best of English horses routinely on the track, but simply to produce a horse that would breed true generation after generation. Once the Thoroughbred breed was established, speed then became the criteria of choice for selective breeding.[16]

Modern research combining analysis of pedigree records and genetics has confirmed the genetic dominance of the three noted sires, together with a rclatively limited number of dam lines. Ever since the Thoroughbred breed became established, writers have chosen sides as to both the preponderance and the virtues of Oriental blood. The extreme positions are represented by John Lawrence, who stated in 1829 that "The designation thoroughbred belongs to the racer of pure Arabian or Barb blood," and Admiral Henry Rous, who in 1850 asserted, "the English racehorse boasts of a pure descent from the Arabian," compared to John H. Wallace, who in 1897 wrote, "in all of the discussions of the past three hundred and fifty years it has never been shown in a single instance that a horse from Arabia, with an authenticated pedigree and tracing as such, has ever been of any value, either as a race horse or as a progenitor of race horses." Although Wallace was unjustly harsh in his criticism of the Arabian horse, he was more or less correct in his surmise that there was far less of the true Arabian blood involved in the development of the Thoroughbred than was commonly supposed. This is supported, as noted, by modern scholarship and genetic science.[17]

In less than a century, an entirely new breed of horse, the English Thoroughbred, was developed from English and Oriental horses based on a limited number of mares and even fewer sires. The bloodlines became even more concentrated as time passed and some lines were extinguished. Until the late eighteenth century, there was no uniform and accepted method to provide an accurate and continuous record of matings and pedigrees for these racing horses. To address this need, in 1791 James Weatherby published the first edition of the *General Stud Book,* which set down the pedigrees of mares, their offspring and sires, year by year, as far back as they could be traced. The Weatherby family has continued this process to the present day in successive editions of the *Stud Book.*[18]

The first book was only a preliminary effort and acknowledged that there were errors and duplications that would be corrected, wherever possible, in future editions. Genetic research by Hill and associates, published in 2002, confirmed the presence of errors that have persisted for more than two centuries. The modern definition of a "Thoroughbred" horse is one whose pedigree can be traced through the *General Stud Book* to a supposedly pureblooded Oriental ancestor. This definition was not officially adopted until 1970, however, so for most of its history the concept of "thoroughbred" was more of an agreed convention than a hard and fast rule.[19]

A large part of the problem was a tendency toward laxity in classifying a horse as a pureblooded Oriental, such that any horse brought in from North Africa or the Near East was automatically assumed to be a purebred type, and that the location of purchase likewise automatically determined the breed of Oriental horse, physical characteristics to the contrary. As John Lawrence noted in 1809, referring to English breeders, "among us, sometimes, all southern Horses are called Arabians." This again suggests that many of the horses registered as purebred Arabians during the founding era possibly were not even Arabian, let alone purebred. The confusion was accentuated, Peter Willett observed, by the tendency "to label horses of Eastern origin 'Arabians,' 'Turks,' and 'Barbs' indiscriminately and irrespective of their real breeding or country of origin. The possibilities of false identity were aggravated by the even looser and more reprehensible practice of describing animals, and particularly mares, as Arabians, Turks or Barbs merely because their sires were such."[20]

Entries in the *General Stud Book* indicate that English breeders of the seventeenth and eighteenth centuries were apparently attempting to establish a pure stock of Oriental horses in the kingdom, the exact source of Oriental blood seeming of little import as long as it was Arabian, Barb, or Turk. If this was in fact the design, it was thwarted by the frequency of misidentifications or misrepresentations of identity, so that the foundation stock in truth consisted not only of purebred Orientals but also many crosses with English and other horse breeds. Despite—or because of—these faults in execution, the result was a horse, the English Thoroughbred, that was both larger and swifter than the Oriental breeds, yet retaining many of their finer qualities. From this uncertain beginning, the elite horses of the *General Stud Book* served as the basis for the establishment of Thoroughbreds around the world, including the United States.

During the seventeenth century, there were several general types of horses in the American colonies. These included a stock of "common" horses of mixed blood imported from England, France, and Holland; well-bred Barb-type horses imported directly from Spain by wealthy planters; and Irish Hobbys and English Running Horses that were used as both saddle and racehorses. From this imported stock, New World breeders would, in time, develop the distinctively American racing breeds of Quarter Horse, Standardbred, and Thoroughbred. From the establishment of the first colony, Virginia, in 1609, more than a century would pass before the first English Thoroughbreds were imported into America.[21]

Notices appearing in Lexington's *Kentucky Gazette*, beginning in 1788, advertise "thoroughbred" stallions to stand for stud, the term indicating both Oriental horses and English Thoroughbreds. Bluegrass gentry with the means to bring in imported Thoroughbreds from the eastern colonies began to do so to improve the bloodlines of Kentucky horses. Since stud horses generally commanded higher fees for service in the Atlantic states, many of the stallions originally imported into Kentucky represented older horses whose value had declined with age. These horses were generally advertised as being "full bred" or "high bred," and partial pedigrees were often included that noted ties to ancestors registered in the *General Stud Book* of England. For example, the March 15, 1788, advertisement for the services of Darius noted that the stallion was "bred by Mr. Daniel Hardaway of Amelia County, Virginia, and was got by the noted imported horse Janus"; the grandsire of Janus was the famous Godolphin Arabian.[22]

After the War of 1812, racehorse breeding in America remained moribund for nearly another decade. By 1820, following the long wartime interruption, breeding and racing sport horses began to revive in America, but the geographical focus shifted from the Tidewater westward, to southwestern Virginia, Kentucky, and Tennessee. These areas became the breeding centers for the revitalized industry, and as the sport expanded throughout the antebellum South, they began importing increasing numbers of English Thoroughbreds and shipping young horses to stables and racecourses across the country. Although the South continued to dominate the turf in all its aspects, the new structure of the industry had now become national, rather than provincial, as it had been in the pre-Revolutionary era. In the final years leading up to the Civil War, Kentucky became the primary breeding terrain, and New Orleans, with three major racecourses, the capital of thorough-bred racing.[23]

American gentry were just as enthusiastic about breeding and racing fast horses as their counterparts across the Atlantic. As the Thoroughbred horse was being developed in England, American sportsmen were simultaneously creating our own distinctive domestic racehorse—the American Running Horse—through selective breeding of imported Irish and English Hobby stallions and mares. This was the original sport breed in the American colonies, closely related to the English Running Horse but developed in isolation in North America and during the early colonial period, lacking the infusion of imported Turkomen and Barb blood that took place in England. Oriental blood would enter the American Running Horse lineage both from Oriental horses imported into America and from breeding with English Thoroughbreds. From the American Running Horse and imported English Thoroughbreds would be developed the American Thoroughbred, but this was a long process, as significant numbers of English Thoroughbreds would not arrive in the American colonies until the mid-eighteenth century.[24]

Thoroughbred importations were sporadic at first. The first record of a Thoroughbred importation to America was of a horse sired by the Darley Arabian and known as Bulle Rock, brought into Virginia in 1730, but by 1750 many blooded mares and stallions were being brought into the New World. New York and the Tidewater became the earliest centers of the turf and regions where American Thoroughbred lines began initial development. Importers were primarily merchants, who largely viewed English Thoroughbreds as simply another commodity, and wealthy Tidewater planters, who had been raised in the English turf tradition. Imports were interrupted during the Revolutionary period, but many blood horses brought over by English officers were captured and subsequently became part of American pedigrees. After the Revolution, English horses were once again imported in quantity, their numbers increasing substantially during the final decade of the eighteenth century. There were regional differences as to the type of equine stock most desired. Demand in the North was mostly for saddle and harness horses, but in the southern states a greater proportion of imports were Thoroughbreds intended for racing. Importations of English horses declined abruptly after 1805, in large part a result of escalating tensions between Britain and the United States and the consequent interruption of Atlantic trade by embargoes and blockade.[25]

Breeding an imported English Thoroughbred to an American Running Horse did not produce offspring that were Thoroughbred; the progeny were still of the Running Horse type. Development of the American Thoroughbred would require many generations of crosses that gradually increased the proportion of English Thoroughbred blood. Early American stud books, such as Edgar's *American Race-Turf Register* (1833) were in fact registers for American Running Horses. As equine authority Kathleen Kirsan points out, the term "thoroughbred" was used by eighteenth-century breeders to describe various types of livestock, such as cattle, sheep, goats, and horses, to indicate stock that was scientifically bred from superior specimens. Until after the American Civil War, "thoroughbred" when applied to horses was an adjective indicating a perceived standard of breeding, rather than a noun, Thoroughbred, designating a particular breed. This can also be seen in stud horse advertisements, which apply the term "thoroughbred" indiscriminately to imported English Thoroughbreds and to American-bred Running Horses that may or may not be part Thoroughbred. The problem of identity was exacerbated by a tendency in the early stud books to engage in "considerable fudging of lineages" by inventing English Thoroughbred bloodlines for some entries while omitting Running Horse ancestry. "This stupid practice has taken centuries to clean up," Kirsan observed, "and the mess it created hid our true equine heritage from us."[26]

With increasing infusion of English Thoroughbred bloodlines into those of the American Running Horse, by the mid-1800s the breed had been improved to the point where it might reasonably be referred to as the Thoroughbred Running Horse, but this was still not the American Thoroughbred in the modern sense. Kirsan makes a compelling case for establishment of the American Thoroughbred as a distinct breed by 1868. Since the seventeenth century, our Running Horses competed in both long distance and sprint racing. Long distance heat racing, as previously noted, was out of fashion in England by the time of the American Revolution, being replaced by a single turn around a course. Heat racing, however, persisted in America during the antebellum period, but also began to lose favor shortly before the Civil War and was gradually phased out of American racing afterward. American horsemen, observing this trend, began breeding our Thoroughbred Running Horses to excel at sprint or "dash racing," a new performance measure that was characteristic of the English Thoroughbred. As Kirsan observed, "The setting of performance standards for a breeding population of sport horses usually identifies the emergence of the new breed," and it was the setting of the new standard, bred for sprint racing, that signaled the birth of the American Thoroughbred.[27]

In conjunction with this, publication of new stud books by John H. Wallace and Sanders D. Bruce just after the war clearly delineated the American Thoroughbred as a distinct breed. For all its prestige, Bruce's 1868 *American Stud Book* stud book was largely a work of fiction. The English definition of a Thoroughbred horse required pedigrees that demonstrated a lineage of five uncontaminated generations of English Thoroughbreds, without a cross of any other horse type (such as Running Horse) during that period. In order to meet these requirements, American breeders falsified pedigrees or omitted non-Thoroughbred ancestors, all of which was uncritically accepted by Bruce. In contrast, John H. Wallace investigated pedigrees more carefully for his 1867 *Wallace's American Stud Book,* and in the process acknowledged that a great many American horses thought to be Thoroughbred would not qualify as such. His stud book contained an appendix of nearly four thousand racehorses that did not meet the pedigree requirements. Curiously, Bruce's largely bogus registry was accepted by the Jockey Club of England rather than Wallace's. Kirsan speculates that this may have been because the English did not want Americans to establish a competing running horse breed of their own, or wished to be able to incorporate the stamina of American bloodlines into their own.[28]

Although many modern-day breeders and equine experts might consider her chronology of the American Thoroughbred heretical, Kirsan's work, published and unpublished, is based on a thorough review of primary sources and supported by the latest DNA research; it is both groundbreaking and convincing. Accordingly, in the text that follows, I have chosen to refer to American racehorses as "thorough-bred" or "Thoroughbred Running Horses" prior to 1868, rather than as Thoroughbreds, unless directly quoting from a source.

3

BLUE GRASS PARK AND TRANSYLVANIA PLANTATION

On the eve of the Civil War, one of the most lavish thoroughbred breeding operations in Kentucky was Blue Grass Park, the Scott County estate of Keene Richards. The three hundred-acre farm was considered by many visitors to be one of the finest estates in Kentucky. One visitor, who stated that he had through the years observed most of the breeding farms in America, lavished praise on Richards's establishment:

> There is a line of beauty in every swell of the meadows, and then the woodlands are absolutely perfect. The acres run up into the hundreds, and yet so few are the weeds on the domain that you can count them. The trees are magnificent specimens of the oak, the ash, the locust and the hickory, and nearly every one is as straight as an arrow, while all reveal a great length of trunk before putting forth a branch. Look in almost any direction, and you mark the horizon through long vista shadows. Pass into the open and the grass under your feet contrasts delicately with the blue sky over your head.[1]

Richards lived in the house built as a residence by Elijah Craig, founder of Georgetown. His home was a substantial two-story mansion of brick and stone sixty feet across the front and twenty feet deep, located on rising ground overlooking the famed Royal Spring, the largest spring in the region. The house was surrounded by a well-kept lawn and gardens that extended down to the spring, and the acreage of the farm was divided into neatly fenced five-acre paddocks. All this extravagance was made possible by the generosity of his grandparents, Dr. William Billingsley Keene (1775–1857) and Hannah Bodien Keene (1786–1851). Dr. Keene could easily afford to indulge his favorite grandson. Born into a wealthy Maryland family on the eastern shore of Chesapeake Bay, Keene received a medical degree from the University of Pennsylvania, where he studied under Benjamin Rush. Keene first established his practice at Greensboro, Maryland, and later moved to Baltimore. In 1799, he was one of the founders of the Medical and Chirurgical Faculty of the State of Maryland, a body established to license physicians and promote medical knowledge in the state. Prior to 1800, at about the time William was finishing his education and setting up his practice, six of his uncles and his father, Thomas B. Keene (1737–1804), removed to Scott County, Kentucky. Dr. Keene remained in Maryland for some time after the departure of most of his family, elected in 1809 by the medical society as Orator for the Eastern Shore for their annual meeting, but by early 1812 he followed his father to Scott County, establishing his practice in Georgetown.[2]

On June 18 of the next year, 1813, Dr. Keene attended a sheriff's sale at Georgetown and purchased 129 acres of gently rolling Bluegrass farmland immediately west of Royal Spring for a little over $5,000. Here he resided for nearly a half-century, moving into the stately old Craig mansion with his wife and two young children: his eleven-year-old son Alexander by his first wife, Elizabeth Clayland (1780–1805), and his four-year-old daughter, Eleonora. Two years later, another son, John Wallis Keene, would be born in Scott County.[3]

During 1821–1822, Alexander C. Keene attended the Medical Department of Transylvania University in Lexington. Although there is no record of him having received a degree from the institution, he subsequently practiced at Georgetown. Dr. William B. Keene acted as medical preceptor for both his son and his future son-in-law, William L. Richards, who attended Transylvania at the same time as Alexander and received a medical degree in 1823. Since Richards married Alexander's sister, Eleonora, in 1826, for a time medical care in Georgetown was almost a family affair. William and Eleonora's only child, Alexander Keene Richards, born October 14, 1827, was orphaned as a toddler; his mother died in 1830 and his father was carried away in the 1833 cholera epidemic at Georgetown. Dr. Richards spent most of the year, the cooler seasons, in Louisiana,

KEENE FAMILY TREE
(PARTIAL)

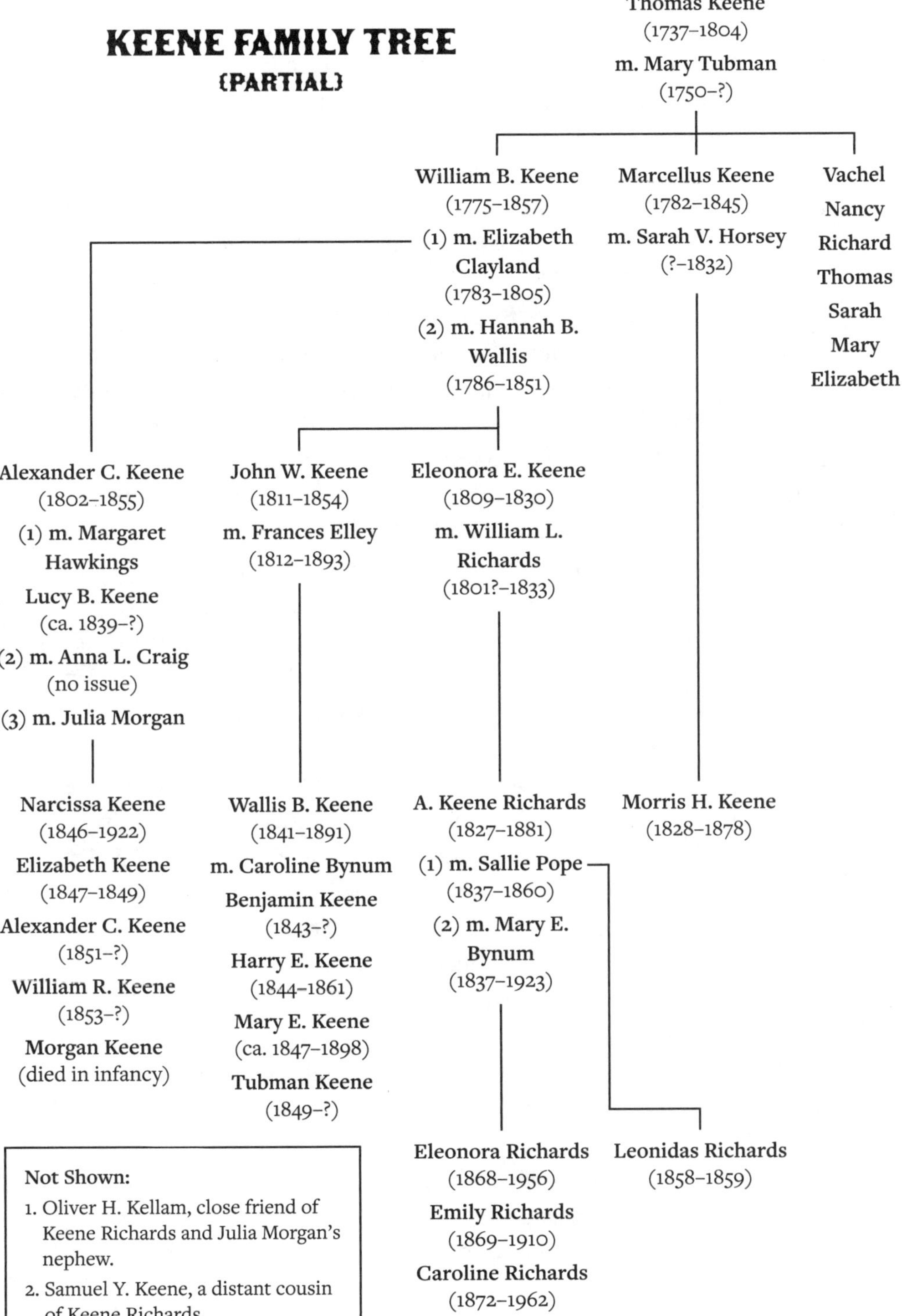

Not Shown:

1. Oliver H. Kellam, close friend of Keene Richards and Julia Morgan's nephew.
2. Samuel Y. Keene, a distant cousin of Keene Richards.

and during the autumn of 1832 he witnessed the effects of cholera in the South. When the dreaded disease appeared in Georgetown during the summer of 1833, "the people sought to avail themselves of the advantages of his experience. Charging nothing for his services, the poor flocked to him for advice, and thus oppressed with business, he sunk under the Epidemic, in the midst of its reign." Six-year-old Keene Richards was taken in and raised by his doting grandparents, William and Hannah, who lavished attention on their grandchild.[4]

Some years earlier, in 1828, grandfather Keene set off for the southlands, and in the northeastern corner of Louisiana he purchased a block of about 170 acres of surveyed land in the fertile floodplain next to the Mississippi River, in what was then Ouachita Parish and is today known as East Carroll Parish. This trip was motivated by the opportunity provided by the Federal Land Act of 1820, intended to promote growth and westward expansion by making it easier for potential settlers to purchase land. The Act eliminated sales of federal land on a credit basis but reduced the minimum tract size from 160 acres to only eighty acres and lowered the price from $1.65 to $1.25 per acre. While this allowed a settler with only $100 in cash, equivalent to about $2,700 today, to purchase a farm of respectable size, it was an even greater boon to wealthy investors who had the money to purchase cheap land in quantity. Government surveys of the lands along the Mississippi were completed by about 1825, and the Ouachita Land Office opened for the first time during the following year. At first, only a handful of persons took advantage of the new land policy to purchase land in this region, but by the end of the 1830s there was a veritable flood of thousands of land purchases here.[5]

Members of the Keene family were among the earliest large investors purchasing land in northeastern Louisiana. In 1829, William L. Richards followed the example of his father-in-law and purchased 327 acres adjacent to the Mississippi and named it Transylvania, honoring the school from which he had received his medical degree. Dr. Keene bought another tract of land next to Transylvania in 1830, and purchased Transylvania itself from Richards in 1831. Between March 1828 and December 1830, William B. Keene purchased twelve tracts totaling nearly twenty-nine hundred acres for just under $3,600, far less than he had paid for a few

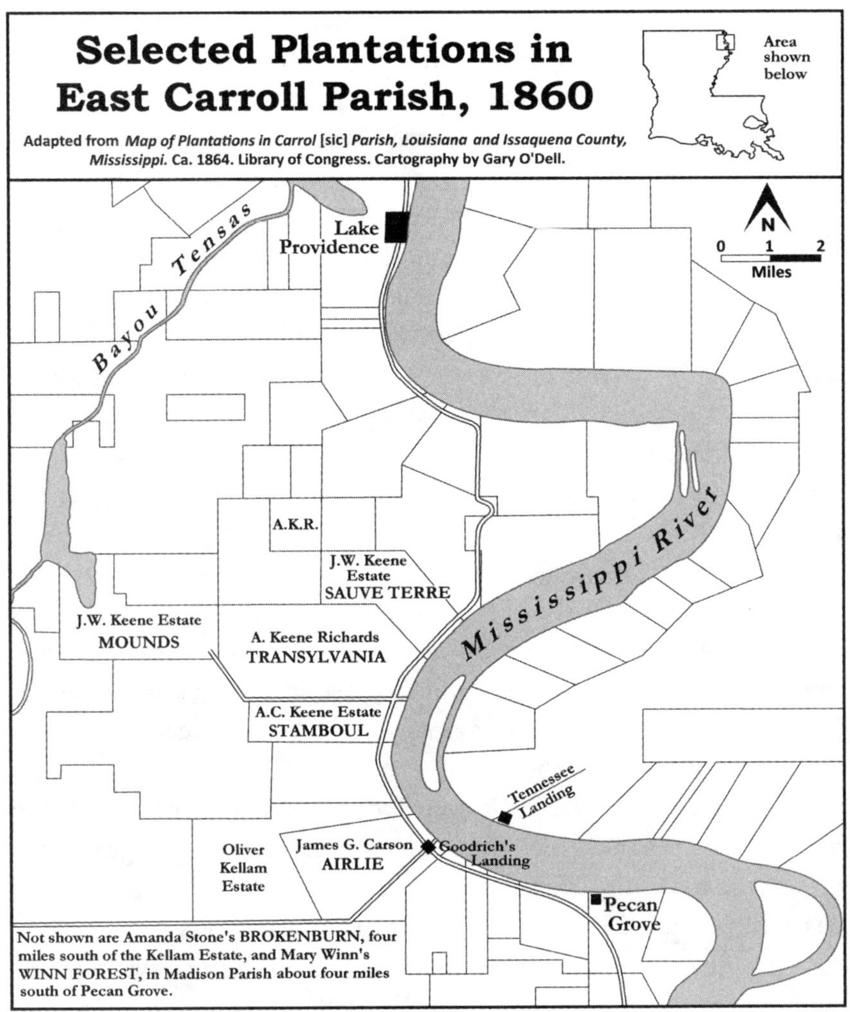

Plantations of northeastern Louisiana. Map by Gary A. O'Dell.

hundred acres in Scott County, Kentucky. Keene continued to purchase federal land during the 1830s, and acquired another two thousand acres in the same vicinity. In addition, he bought and sold and traded land with other purchasers as each sought to consolidate their holdings. Over time, Keene put together three large and separate plantations in the vicinity known respectively as Transylvania, the Mounds (named for the presence of Native American burial mounds), and Suave Terre. In the meantime, Dr. Keene's son Alexander also invested in land during 1830–1836, purchasing several blocks just to the south of Transylvania totaling 1,350 acres, which he named Stamboul Plantation.[6]

The acquisition of these vast acreages was driven by the desire to take advantage of the cotton boom then sweeping the country. Following the invention of the cotton gin in 1793, cotton production came to dominate the national economy, becoming America's most important export commodity. Originally confined to the Atlantic seaboard, production moved westward to the Gulf region as soil fertility was depleted in the Carolinas and Georgia, so that by 1830 great swaths of land were being cleared for cotton cultivation in Mississippi and Louisiana. The national cotton boom was furthermore responsible for a resurgence of the domestic slave trade, as the new agricultural land required slave labor to bring the land into production.[7]

In the early 1830s, when Transylvania and other great plantations of northeastern Louisiana were being assembled, the deep and fertile alluvial soils of the Mississippi floodplain were still cloaked by a dense hardwood forest of oak, hickory, sweetgum, and cypress. Clearing this for agriculture was a long and arduous process, and probably proceeded in much the same manner as on the plantations of the Atlantic states, where, as yields declined, new land was stripped of trees and brought into production. To accomplish this, William B. Keene, like the other large planters of the region, began acquiring enslaved workers. By 1850, a total of 204 enslaved people were in residence on two of the doctor's plantations; in addition, his elder son, Alexander, claimed ninety-seven slaves at Stamboul, and his younger son, John Wallis Keene, had 126 slaves on his Sauve Terre Plantation. Most of these enslaved people were probably brought in from Kentucky, which became a major supplier of slaves to the lower South. In addition to opening land for cultivation, enslaved workers built grandiose homes for the planters as well as slave quarters and necessary outbuildings.[8]

Behind the main house on a typical Carroll Parish plantation were quarters for the enslaved persons who directly served the white residents, along with various outbuildings, such as barns, stables, and cotton gins. Quarters, for the most part identical cabins, for the enslaved persons who worked in the cotton fields were set along both sides of a long lane.

Each plantation had a family cemetery. The main houses on some parish plantations were two-story structures of brick, formed and baked on-site by enslaved workers. More often they were "wide, rambling, frame buildings, following a prescribed fashion; two large front rooms, separated by a spacious hall, with two smaller rooms and a lesser hall at the rear." Some houses had an added ell, which contained the kitchen, but usually the kitchen was placed at some distance across the yard. "Always there was a gallery, as it was called in the South, which extended across the front, usually around the side, and not infrequently completely encircling the house." These galleries, or porches, were supported by heavy columns. Rooms had high ceilings, many doors and windows, and were heated by large, open fireplaces.[9]

A contemporary description of Transylvania Plantation and its operations is provided by the journal entries of Thomas Butler Gunn (1826–1904), an English journalist then serving as a salaried correspondent for the *New York Times,* who was invited by Keene Richards to an extended visit in late October through early November 1853. The plantation house was set back nearly a mile from the river, reached by a broad, straight road from the riverside landing with two gates, the last set just before the house. The residence was a large but simple ten-room, tree-shaded structure. The "neatly built, plain edifice of wood, had no upper story. It was two spacious rooms wide, some five in length, most rooms having a door leading to the covered way in front. The garden was neatly laid out with flowers, shrubs and bushes, tall china trees with their small, fine leaves, and large yellow berries in front. The spiky 'Spanish dagger,' red roses and evergreens and variously tinted flowers were all round." The house was decorated with a collection of curiosities and mementos from Richards's travels abroad, including antique armor and weapons, bits of marble and architectural items salvaged from classical buildings and ruins in Europe and Africa, Arab costumes, Turkish pipes, paintings, and much more.[10]

More detail as to its construction can be surmised from the mansion house at Stamboul Plantation, which was built by William B. Keene for his son Alexander and was likely very similar to the Transylvania residence. At Stamboul, the house followed the usual plan of large rooms separated by halls and surrounded by deep galleries. The one-story wooden structure was framed with hand-hewn cypress timbers, mortised and pegged together without the use of iron nails. The sills were from twelve to fourteen inches square, and the floor and ceiling joists five inches by twelve or fourteen inches, all hand-planed. As was true for most houses of that period and region, Stamboul was built entirely of wood from local trees.[11]

After dinner, Gunn rode out with Keene Richards to view the surroundings, including the estates of his uncles Alexander and Wallis Keene, "through the vast cotton fields, all covered with the full, white, bursting bolls, tall bare tree trunks rising up out of them." There was no sugar cane grown in this part of Louisiana; cotton was the primary commercial crop. The Mississippi floodplain landscape was nearly dead level, except for "a sort of little embankment about a bayou" and some prehistoric Native American ceremonial mounds, one of which was surmounted by the overseer's home, overlooking the slave cabins below. Soon they came to "a miniature jungle, and rode through it for half an hour, thick vegetation, everything grown wild in Tropic-like fertility. The Canebrake, which, tying our horses to the fence we enter. The Cane might have grown twenty and thirty feet in height, close together, so as to be inaccessible in some parts. Fine domain for the bear and panther."

A few days later, Gunn "rambled about," observing the enslaved workers in the fields and ginhouse. "Saw the whole cotton process," he noted on November 2. Harvesting was "done very rapidly, the boll being plucked off the cotton which is put in large bags, one or two of which is attached to each person & they pass up the long rows with them. At nightfall each persons work is weighed, a record kept by the overseer. There's a stated quantity for each slave, but its often exceeded." He visited a new gin on Wallis Keene's place, "a spacious, steam worked building, always at work (save on Sundays). At the top of these buildings is an extensive place for drying the cotton, then in the gin it is all torn into shreds, the seed extracted, passed into a room where it's curious to peep into, and notice the feathery flakes; thence to be packed and pressed below. Thence the bales are taken to the landing by the river side, to be transported to New Orleans."[12]

In Gunn's opinion, the labor required of the enslaved workers was not difficult, although they toiled long hours. "They rise early, by daybreak, or before, to the sound of a bell, take their dinner, perhaps other meals, in the fields, and work on to 8 or 9," he wrote. "The younger or weaker have tasks apportioned to their strength. They have two suits of clothes a year,

Thomas Butler Gunn, an English journalist reporting for the *New York Times,* met Keene Richards and Oliver Kellam at Mammoth Cave in autumn 1853, shortly after the two southerners returned from their eastern travels. The men became friends, and Richards invited Gunn to accompany them to visit Transylvania Plantation, where the writer observed life and slavery on a Deep South plantation. The sketch is a self-portrait made by Gunn shortly before meeting Richards and Kellam, courtesy of the Missouri History Museum Library and Research Center.

stout durable ones. Tobacco is given them, no spirits." One Sunday evening, Keene Richards handed out new clothing to a large crowd of workers assembled outside the house for the purpose. The clothing had been made in Kentucky, the shoes made to order in the Eastern states and shipped to Transylvania in large cases. Yusef Badra (a Syrian guide and translator Richards brought back from the Near East to work for him) read out the names in a loud voice, while Richards's cousin Morris Keene recorded the names of those receiving garments. "I never heard any harsh word addressed to a slave during the whole time I stayed here," Gunn reported.[13]

As an Englishman who had lived and traveled only in the North since arriving in America in 1849, Gunn had never been exposed to the mass subjection of Blacks characteristic of the plantation system in the Deep South. Although it is apparent throughout his numerous journals that he believed in the inherent superiority of the white race, he was deeply disturbed by what he saw of slavery at Transylvania and on other plantations of the region. Gunn's entries during his stay in Carroll Parish, where he was routinely subjected to justifications of slavery by men he considered friends, supremely confident in the moral correctness of their position, reveal a certain ambivalence on the issue. He was firmly abolitionist in sentiment, but unsure how such a deeply rooted institution could be eradicated without devastating consequences. "Sudden Abolition is the idea of a lunatic, amiable insanity it may be, but still insanity," he wrote on November 2 as part of a long and thoughtful essay. "It would turn all the South into a Wilderness, and the Negroes into their native Savage African life again." For Gunn, "One hope remains—Liberia." Liberia declared its independence in 1847, and Gunn believed the country would "spread and prosper, and educated African nature [would] have a field to develop itself. Meantime there are frightful Evils in Slavery, the worse that they are untouchable."[14]

After being confined to bed with a fever for a week's time, digesting all that he had seen of plantation life, Gunn finally departed up the Mississippi River by steamboat on November 12. In the years ahead, his personal views on slavery, as expressed in a multitude of diary entries, hardened into revulsion against the institution.[15]

Dr. Keene maintained a dual residence in both Kentucky and Louisiana, and made an annual journey to his southern plantations to tend to business affairs there, probably in the fall of the year. This was a time when the ripe cotton bolls were being picked, ginned, and baled for shipment downriver to New Orleans. Young Keene Richards, who often attended his grandfather on such visits, learned plantation management firsthand, and probably accompanied him downriver to New Orleans to deal with the factors, or agents, who sold the cotton crop.[16]

Before and after the Civil War, Carroll Parish, in which Keene's properties were located, and a handful of neighboring Mississippi River counties were among the leading cotton-producing regions in the South. In 1859, there were ninety-one plantations in Carroll Parish, each holding at least fifty enslaved persons. Transylvania Plantation, then recently inherited by Keene Richards, fell almost exactly in the average among these in terms of acreage and slave population. However, it had a higher cotton production than most, which suggests better management. The plantation encompassed 1,830 acres, of which 950 acres were considered improved land. Twenty-two dwellings had been erected, most being habitations for the plantation's 104 enslaved persons. The "farm" was valued at $93,500. From Transylvania's rich alluvial soils, 960 bales of ginned cotton, weighing 400 pounds per bale, were produced that year. With cotton then bringing about 12 cents per pound, or $48 per bale, the value of Transylvania's cotton crop was $46,080. Adjusted for inflation, this sum was approximately equivalent to $1.7 million in year 2024 dollars. This, then, was the basis of the fortune that allowed Dr. Keene to indulge his grandson's growing fascination with horse breeding, and which passed, in large part, to Keene Richards on his death: land, slaves, and cotton.[17]

4
THE HORSE WHISPERER

In the nineteenth-century world in which Keene Richards grew up, horses were, of course, the dominant means of transportation. For a teenaged boy of his era, working with horses would be an obvious attraction, just as modern generations of American youth often honed their skills as shade tree automobile mechanics under the tutelage of an older, more experienced relative or friend. Richards was fortunate that in his very own hometown lived one of the most remarkable horse trainers of the century, a man who broke with long-established methods to help forge a new style—one based on persuasion rather than domination—to bring horses under human control. Denton Offutt of Scott County, Kentucky, is perhaps best known to history as the man who, in 1831, gave young Abraham Lincoln his first real job in his store at New Salem, Illinois, but he was later renowned as one of the first "horse whisperers." Offutt advocated kindness and a sympathetic touch in training and handling, a style that he preferred to call "gentling" rather than the customary "breaking" of a horse. Richards later described Offutt as "a queer genius . . . an uneducated man but full of originality," and noted that "Some of my earliest recollections are of him. I was one of his pupils."[1]

There is now no way to know if Keene Richards came to Denton Offutt because of a prior interest in horses, or whether this was an activity, perhaps arranged by his grandfather, that planted a seed that subsequently blossomed into a lifelong fascination. The time Richards spent with Offutt, receiving practical instruction in the care and training of horses at the hands of a master, must have been a significant formative period in the young man's life. More than fifteen years after taking lessons, Richards still carried Offutt's book of instructions and training philosophy with him when he traveled abroad.

Much of Denton Offutt's early life is shrouded in mystery; he is not recorded in any U.S. census, and even the year of his birth is unknown. Family records tentatively place his birth between 1803—1807, and so Denton was born in Kentucky shortly after his family emigrated from Maryland. Denton himself stated, "I was born on the waters of Hickman Creek, eight or nine miles south of Lexington, and raised to farming." He grew up in a comfortable two-story house on the Jessamine County farm of his father, Samuel Offutt, a livestock breeder who raised not only fine horses but also mules, sheep, cattle, and hogs, which were shipped down the Ohio and Mississippi rivers to southern markets. His older brother, Tilghman, also became a successful horse breeder in Logan County, and Denton often assisted him in driving large herds of stock to Tennessee.[2]

In 1831, Denton Offutt established a store at New Salem, Illinois, and employed young Abraham Lincoln to operate it for him. The location was poorly chosen, however, and in spring 1832 a penniless Denton Offutt left New Salem and his friend Lincoln to return to his family in Kentucky. He spent the next ten years training horses and driving them to out-of-state markets for his brothers Otha and Sam Offutt, each of whom owned a farm in the Bluegrass region. In 1840, by his own recollection, Denton embarked on a career as a professional horse trainer and soon became well known through the region. Offutt was willing to work with horses of any sort: draft horses, carriage horses, saddle horses, stock horses, and hunters, as well as racehorses. His distinct specialty was to tame "unbroken" horses so that they could be safely handled and ridden. These included young horses yet to be saddled and older horses who, from ill treatment or disposition, were vicious or otherwise unmanageable. In the autumn of 1841, Offutt submitted a short exposition of his philosophy and methods as a letter to the *Spirit of the Times,* the leading sporting magazine of the day. In this essay he revealed the basic methods that, in later years, he endeavored to guard as trade secrets. "My secret for Taming Vicious Horses is gentleness and patience," he began, "which removes fear and gives the animal confidence in man."[3]

Offutt's methods recognized that horses were not mere dumb brutes but sensitive and intelligent creatures, possessed of needs, desires, dislikes, and fears. Horses are genetically programmed to flee from danger when possible, and to fight when they cannot run. For a horse, the human world is filled with unfamiliar sights, sounds, and smells, and that which is unfamiliar is best treated as potentially dangerous. Through an approach that combines a soothing voice and gentle handling, Offutt believed, the horse can be conditioned to trust the trainer. "Rubbing a horse in the face will cause him to present his head to you, and talking kindly to him will attract his attention," he wrote. "I suppose in some horses it is important to whisper to them. You may use any word you please, but be constant in your tone of voice." Through gradual introduction and repetition, accompanied by gentle handling and reassurance, a horse can be brought to calmly accept that which once was strange or even frightening, such as blankets, saddles, or even gunfire. Horses have long memories, he noted, and it was best, before attempting to train them, to take them away from any place where they had been ill-used.[4]

The methods described in his letter to the *Spirit* were set out more fully in a pamphlet published during the following year, titled *Denton Offutt's Method of Gentling Horses, and Curing Their Diseases.* This pamphlet was not copyrighted until 1846, but was advertised throughout the United States by a handbill printed in Washington, D.C., in 1843 that contained endorsements from numerous horsemen in Kentucky and elsewhere in the country. In 1848, his pamphlet was enlarged to a full-scale volume, *A New and Complete System of Teaching the Horse on Phrenological Principles.* In a handbill printed in Lexington in April 1853, Offutt solicited subscriptions for a greatly expanded treatment of his methods, noting, "The work will be published as soon as a sufficient number of subscribers have been obtained to justify it, and on a large clear print, and well bound in cloth . . . offered to subscribers at the moderate price of $5." The volume was published in March of the following year under the rather intriguing title *The Educated Horse.* Offutt was himself barely literate, shown by his letters to Abraham Lincoln and a letter published verbatim in the *Spirit of the Times* in 1859. They lacked punctuation and were filled with bizarre spelling and grammatical errors. He obviously must have had considerable assistance in the preparation of these manuscripts, although the identity of the editor is unknown.[5]

Advertisements such as the handbills were not intended to sell his book to the general public, but to promote the man himself, to gain publicity, pupils, and patrons. Offutt had come to realize that his methods were a marketable product, and that it might be of greater financial benefit to impart his secrets for a fee to a select group of students than to give them away freely. Accordingly, his books were made available only to his pupils and others he trusted. Recipients of *The Educated Horse* were required to sign a lengthy pledge of confidentiality, and to post a financial bond to keep his secrets. Offutt retained a copy of the pledge with the signatures of all his students recorded thereon: "We, the undersigned, have each of us purchased of Mr. Denton Offutt a copy of his book in relation to educated horses, laws of mind and physiology and diseases of animals, which he has disposed of to us on the express condition that all its contents are to be kept secret from all other persons, with certain exceptions hereinafter mentioned, and under a specified penalty." The exceptions were limited to "a son or daughter of the paternal family" and to servants caring for horses, who might be provided with simple instructions but not the book itself.[6]

Offutt did not limit his services as a horse trainer to just the Bluegrass region but took engagements in other regions of the South, including Virginia, Tennessee, Mississippi, and Texas, where he demonstrated his ability to tame even the most cantankerous horses. Grateful clients provided him with testimonials and accolades, which he made up into advertisements such as the handbills of 1843 and 1853, and another printed in February 1859. The latter included a reference given Offutt a decade before from the noted statesman Henry Clay of Kentucky, who recommended Offutt as "a person of uncommon skill in the treatment of horses and domestic animals, especially in training, breaking, and curing them of diseases," who could, "in a very short time, render the wildest animal gentle and docile, insomuch that he will subject it to his easy control and direction. Mr. Offutt has been many years engaged in the study and practice of his remarkable method of dealing with the horse, and has given many satisfactory evidences of his great success."[7]

Offutt began taking on pupils as early as 1840. "The perfect art of training horses," he wrote in his execrable prose to the *Spirit of the Times* in 1859, "sens 1840 which I commens teaching it ther has now som Ten or more Teachers of Art At that time 42 to 1848 in Cincinnatti Ohio." His handbill of 1843 stated, "Other persons can be taught the same Management, as many of his pupils are equally as successful as himself." When Hamilton Busbey, editor of the New York-based sporting journal *Turf, Field and Farm,* visited Blue Grass Park in October 1877, Keene Richards showed him a copy of *The Educated Horse,* published in 1854. In conversation with Busbey, Richards recalled his acquaintance with Offutt as among his "earliest memories." This suggests that he learned the "gentle" methods of horse training and management as an adolescent. Richards would have been fourteen years old in the summer of 1842, and very likely began his training with Offutt at about this time. A list of Offutt's pupils would include not just young boys and horse breeders but successful men in a variety of professions. Among those who completed a course of instruction and received copies of his book, who signed the pledge of confidentiality and posted bond never to reveal Offutt's secrets, were Henry Clay, who served as both U.S. representative and senator from Kentucky; Sam Houston, U.S. senator from Texas (1846–1859) and later governor of the state (1859–1861); Thomas J. Rusk, also a senator from Texas (1846–1857); John Minor Botts, three-term U.S. representative from Virginia (1839–1843, 1847–1849) and owner of the famous racehorse Revenue; and John S. Rarey, who at the time of his first acquaintance with Offutt was a little-known horse trainer from Ohio.[8]

Born December 6, 1827, to a prosperous farm family in Franklin County, Ohio, John Rarey demonstrated a remarkable affinity for horses as he grew up, and while yet a teenager he developed a local reputation as an accomplished horse trainer. As Keene Richards later recalled, Rarey came to Georgetown in 1850 with a traveling circus, with which he probably was employed as a horse handler. When the circus moved on, Rarey remained in Georgetown to study with Offutt, and in due time he "graduated" and received his copy of Offutt's book. He then returned to Ohio, where his reputation continued to grow as he took on many more clients and began to instruct others in his methods. In 1855, Rarey traveled to Texas and spent several months there helping to capture and tame the wild mustangs of the prairie, and thereafter embarked on a career imitating Offutt but with far greater success.[9]

Alexander Keene Richards as a teenager. It was at about this time that he was instructed in training horses by Denton Offutt. Photograph courtesy of Palmer Ragsdale.

In 1856, Rarey published a book, *The Modern Art of Taming Wild Horses*, and took on pupils, whom he also bound to a pledge of confidentiality. Rarey's book described essentially the same principles and methods that he had learned from Offutt, but it gave no credit to his teacher. Like Offutt, he referred to his methods as "gentling" of horses, working in harmony with the horse's natural instincts and using gradual familiarization to promote acceptance of objects and situations. Rarey was a more aggressive promoter than Offutt; his book was first published in Columbus, Ohio, and during the next three years was reprinted in several editions across the country. Later, after he had achieved considerable fame in England during his visit there from 1857 to 1860, Rarey's book was published in London, and, in translation, in Paris and Copenhagen. Rarey released his students from their secrecy pledge after his book was published in England.[10]

Rarey decided to pursue fame and fortune by taking his methods abroad. He arrived at Liverpool on November 29, 1857, and was able to gain an invitation from Queen Victoria to demonstrate his skills. He quite enthralled the royal family and the court in attendance. On March 2, the *London Morning Post* issued a challenge for Rarey to attempt to tame Cruiser, the most vicious horse known in the kingdom. Rarey transformed the homicidal beast into a horse as gentle as a kitten. After subsequently taming a zebra at the London Zoo, there no longer remained any doubt as to his abilities. An account at Tattersall's of London was opened, and Rarey received more than two thousand subscriptions, at ten guineas each (equal to about $2,000 today), to learn his system. He was feasted and feted in the courts of Europe and became a wealthy man before his return to the United States in the autumn of 1860.[11]

Fame and fortune eluded Offutt, despite his own efforts at promotion. He made several determined attempts to promote his unique methods and obtain sponsorship from government at both state and federal levels, but given the fantastic and unsubstantiated nature of his claims, apparently no action was taken in any case. By autumn of 1858, Offutt had been hearing of Rarey's English celebrity with increasing anger, no doubt fueled by reports of the enormous sums garnered by his former pupil. He had never released Rarey from his pledge and bond of secrecy, and so he considered Rarey's public performances to be a serious breach of confidence. Finally, he had had enough, and in mid-April 1859 he boarded a ship for England, armed with a bundle of endorsements, intending to denounce Rarey as a fraud and villain. The *Spirit of the Times* took note of his departure, referring to him as "the original horse-tamer of the United States," whose purpose in traveling abroad was to "teach his art of taming vicious animals to the nobility and gentry of Albion, and he claims that he can do all that was ever accomplished by Rarey, and something more."[12]

Unfortunately for Offutt's ambitions, the British public took little note of his presence, viewing him as just one more of the many imitators who sprouted there in the wake of Rarey's celebrity. Perhaps the only man in England who recognized his true worth was Keene Richards, then in the country to purchase Thoroughbred horses for his stable in Georgetown. Having arrived when the Rarey mania was at its height, Richards may have attended one of Rarey's performances out of curiosity. He acknowledged that Rarey's system was of value, but made an effort to set the record straight where his former teacher was concerned. If Offutt and Richards were able renew their acquaintance while in England, the reunion was brief since Richards departed not long after Offutt's arrival. Offutt became increasingly embittered by the indifference of his reception, even as John Rarey continued to be lionized in the British press and was invited to visit the estates of the nobility.[13]

Offutt returned to the United States on August 13, 1859, aboard the steamer *Liverpool.* Rarey, accompanied by Cruiser, returned to a hero's welcome in New York in December 1860 and began a series of lectures and demonstrations before overflow crowds. Denton Offutt was still hopping mad over the whole Rarey situation, and now that his nemesis was back in America, he filed suit in the New York Supreme Court against his former pupil for breach of contract. Offutt's suit worked slowly through the court system; then, two years after the action was filed, the complaint was dismissed on April 18, 1863. Other than indirectly, through the existence of the New York legal action, Denton Offutt disappears from the historical record after the spring of 1861. The simplest explanation is that Offutt may have died during 1862, and this may in fact be the primary reason for the termination of the suit. Lincoln biographer William Townsend notes that Offutt was "old, broken financially, and in the late stages of consumption [pulmonary tuberculosis]" in February 1861 when he penned his last letter to Abraham Lincoln. Townsend did not provide a citation for this information, and confirmation could not be found through other sources. Hamilton Busbey, editor of *Turf, Field and Farm,* wrote in 1878 that "Denton Offutt has been in his grave a good many years," suggesting a date of death at least a decade prior to his observation. John Rarey died from a stroke on October 5, 1866.[14]

When Hamilton Busbey visited Keene Richards at Blue Grass Park in October 1877, dinner table conversation turned to the subject of horse taming and he became "deeply interested" in what he was told about Denton Offutt. Richards, one of the most influential horsemen in Kentucky, claimed Offutt was "the founder of the horse-taming school." Richards agreed to loan his copy of *The Educated Horse* to Busbey if it would be used "in doing justice to a former citizen of Georgetown." Busbey took it with him back to New York and was so impressed by its contents that he mentioned the book to Robert Bonner, editor of the *New York Ledger* and one of the richest men in America. Bonner was an expert horseman with a sizable stable of trotting horses, and he had taken lessons from John S. Rarey. Bonner took the book with him when he left the offices of the *Spirit of the Times,* and on the next day Busbey received a note that read, "There are some very interesting things in Offutt's book—some things that are entirely new to me and well worth copying. The 'Dialogue between Man and Horse' contains the substance of all that Rarey ever taught. He evidently based his system on that." According to Busbey, Bonner kept the book for ten days, rereading it numerous times.[15]

Hamilton Busbey took Robert Bonner at his word, also believing that Offutt's book was "worth copying." On January 4, 1878, he announced the forthcoming serialization of *The Educated Horse* in the pages of *Turf, Field and Farm,* noting that whereas Offutt's students had been bound by a pledge of confidentiality, "The time has come for the veil of secrecy to be torn aside. The claims of Denton Offutt to the foundership of the horse-taming school can be established in no other way." The first installment appeared in the *Spirit's* January 11, 1878, issue, and the byline was attributed to Denton Offutt of Georgetown, Kentucky, "the preceptor of Rarey." Offutt, who had been unable to establish his claim during his lifetime, was at last vindicated.[16]

Teenaged Keene Richards received a true horseman's education during the time he spent with Denton Offutt at Georgetown. He learned many practical aspects of horse handling, from teaching a horse to stand while being mounted to dealing with a horse that kicks, from preventing a horse from scaring at a bridge crossing to preparing one to withstand an ocean crossing aboard a steamship. Offutt gave this advice for racehorses: "Most racehorses are whipped too much. . . . Many need only the encouragement of the voice, and if trained to it, it answers all purposes." As set out in *The Educated Horse,* all of these practical instructions were indelibly embedded within a philosophy of patience, kindness, and sensitivity to a horse's fears.[17]

Historians have not always been kind in their descriptions of Offutt, particularly in reference to his time at New Salem. He has sometimes been referred to as a "frontier hustler," a "hard drinker," and a "speculator and mountebank," all of which contain some truth. But whatever else may be said about Denton Offutt, clearly he had an important and positive role in shaping the destiny of three young men: Abraham Lincoln, John S. Rarey, and Keene Richards.

5
THE GRAND TOUR

In 1846, when Richards was eighteen years old, grandfather Keene sent him off to Virginia (now West Virginia) to attend Bethany College. The selection of this particular institution for his grandson's education was a consequence of the Keene family's involvement in the Disciples of Christ and a personal friendship with Alexander Campbell, a pillar of the Christian Church and founder, in 1840, of Bethany College. Campbell, writing in 1860, referred to Keene Richards as "descended from a family who, from my earliest acquaintance in Ky., have honored me with their friendship, and aided me in all my labors."[1]

The community of Georgetown played a significant role during the formative years of the church. The Christian Church in Georgetown was chartered in 1829 and led by pastor Barton W. Stone, an evangelist who gained a considerable following in the region subsequent to the Great Revival of 1801 in Bourbon County. Campbell spent three months touring Kentucky in 1824, and meeting Stone for the first time in Georgetown, he found much common ground in their beliefs. This shared vision led to a union in 1832 between the followers of Stone and those of Campbell, which took place initially in Lexington, Paris, and Georgetown, and subsequently spread through the state. The first educational institution associated with the Disciples was Bacon College, established in Georgetown in 1836 and moved to Harrodsburg in 1839 because of Baptist hostility and competition with Georgetown College. Doubtless because of his friendship with Alexander Campbell, in 1846 Dr. Keene chose to send Keene Richards to Bethany rather than Bacon College.[2]

The curriculum at Bethany emphasized the formation of moral character and the study of the physical sciences. In the mornings, Alexander

(*Above*) Alexander Campbell, charismatic leader of the early Christian Church. Chromo oil portrait published by R. W. Carroll and Co. of Cincinnati, Ohio. Lithographed by Colton Zahm and Roberts, New York. Library of Congress. (*Below*) Bethany College, West Virginia, operated by the Christian Church and attended by Alexander Keene Richards from 1846 to 1850. Strobridge Lithographic. Library of Congress.

Campbell, when not absent on a lecture tour or fundraising, conducted Bible studies for the entire college. The influence of Campbell and Bethany College on Keene Richards was profound; for the rest of his life he was known as a man of strong moral character, who seldom drank and never swore or gambled, not even to place a wager on his own horses. For the modern reader, this viewpoint must be balanced against the fact that Keene Richards and his extended family held hundreds of enslaved people in Kentucky and Louisiana.

Richards grew to maturity in Scott County, Kentucky, at a time and in a place where slavery was not only generally accepted by most of the population, but perceived as desirable and necessary. In 1850, Scott County had one of the highest proportions of enslaved Blacks to free persons in the state. Slaves in the county numbered 14,946 persons out of a total population of 24,056, with only 219 free persons of color. In that year, nine enslaved persons, four male and five female, were in residence at the Keene farm and home at Georgetown. Though most enslavers in Kentucky, where farms were generally small, possessed five or fewer slaves, many of the more successful horse breeders in the Bluegrass region held a substantial number of enslaved persons. In Scott County, James K. Duke and Willa Viley, men whom Keene Richards admired and respected, were among the largest slaveholders; forty-nine slaves inhabited the Duke farm and twenty-four on the Viley property.[3]

The only possible counters to this pervasive and relentless acculturation of Richards's youth could be his affiliation with an abolitionist church or his education at an institution distant from the slave culture, where abolitionist sentiment dominated rhetoric and discourse in the classroom and in campus life. Yet, the message Keene Richards received from both church and school was ambiguous at best. Membership in the Christian Church was centered in the Midwest and the border states of Kentucky and Missouri; in 1851, Campbellites held more than one hundred thousand persons in slavery. Earlier in the century, like many other churches, the Disciples of Christ had been enthusiastic for the abolition of slavery, but as the antislavery debate grew more heated in the 1830s and 1840s, Campbellites withdrew to a more moderate position. Under the leadership of Alexander Campbell, at Bethany College only a watered-down abolitionist message provided guidance to students.[4]

Described by a modern biographer as having assumed a "full embrace of American white supremacist ideology and conviction that whites and blacks could never live together as equals," Campbell was opposed to slavery on moral and economic grounds and consistently and openly criticized the institution, but argued that slavery was biblically permissible. He came into possession of several enslaved persons upon his marriage to Margaret Brown in 1811, whom he subsequently emancipated, and he emancipated several others whom he had purchased, stating, "I have set free from slavery every human being that came in any way under my influence or was my property." Campbell was, however, opposed to immediate emancipation of slaves and favored a gradual approach, advocating for the constitutional enactment of a colonization scheme "until the land would not be trod by the foot of one slave, nor enriched by a drop of his sweat or blood." Enslavers, Campbell argued, were obliged to treat their servants in a Christian manner, to look after their welfare, treat them kindly, and provide for their education and religious instruction, and these would have been the lessons absorbed by Richards during his time at Bethany.[5]

Richards never expressed his personal views on slavery in any of his published letters or works, which were almost exclusively devoted to equine matters. Some insight can be provided from the journal of Thomas Gunn, who visited Richards at Transylvania Plantation in 1853 and occasionally engaged his host in conversations upon the subject. On one occasion, Richards mentioned an old man who was one of his grandfather's favored slaves at the farm in Georgetown, Kentucky. This was almost certainly Pompey, the house slave for whom Richards, circa 1860, built a new house next to his own home after the elderly slave was afflicted with dementia. Pompey "managed the farm, and kept the house in order during the absence of the family; had control of money matters, and might be trusted with every thing." He was a deeply religious man who attended his church and read his Bible. Pompey, according to Richards, did not desire freedom, "believing that the Bible justified Slavery to his race as descendants of Ham," parroting a widespread belief among southern enslavers. One summer, Richards took Pompey and his sons to Transylvania Plantation for a visit, where one of the sons happened to displease the overseer. The boy was ordered to strip and receive a whipping. "He had been a sort of favorite with the family, and demurred. Whereupon his father, then present, went up to him, and bade him strip immediately, or he would himself take his coat from him, ordering always to obey when a White Man bade him, whatever might be his opinion of the justice of it." Pompey, of course, had little recourse but to support his enslaver regardless of his personal feelings.[6]

Upon hearing this story, Gunn inquired, "Is not that anecdote a terrible protest against slavery? Here's a good, brave, honest human creature who really believes that God wills he shall be flogged, justly or unjustly as another human creature in a white skin wills it?" Richards reflected upon this, and then responded, "It is so, but it has to be, we can't get along without it!" Richards argued that the Bible justified slavery; since it "was nowhere explicitly condemned by Our Savior, he approved of it." Such was the position of Alexander Campbell. Gunn was appalled by the twisted logic he observed in Richards and among other enslavers. "I do not think he saw the horror of investing that most Divine, Sad, Suffering, All-Wise, loving nature with such a sentiment. He saw not that Christ's teaching dwelt not in details, varying ever with age and time, but laid down broad, universal principles, catholic, immutable and eternal as God himself." From this account, and the observations of other visitors to his Georgetown home, Richards adhered to Campbell's philosophy. He looked after the welfare of his enslaved people and allowed them to attend church and, some at least, to receive some education, but it is also clear that he was firmly committed to the institution of slavery.[7]

In 1848, Keene Richards studied ancient languages, botany, chemistry, and natural philosophy and was recognized as an outstanding student. The student body of 129 students in that year represented fifteen states and included three from Britain. Among his classmates were Joseph Desha Pickett (1822–1900), a native of Washington County, Kentucky, and Oliver H. Kellam (1832–1854), of Carroll Parish, Louisiana. Pickett was five years older than Richards and, having already obtained a degree from Princeton, was in the unusual circumstance of being both a student and a member of the Bethany faculty. Kellam's family was linked to the Keenes through marriage (his mother was a sister of Keene Richards's Aunt Julia, Alexander's wife). The three young men became close friends, such that when, in 1851, Dr. Keene sent his grandson on a Grand Tour of Europe to celebrate the completion of his education, Pickett and Kellam were his companions.[8]

Joseph D. Pickett followed a career dedicated to higher education. After graduating from Princeton in 1841 (and according to some sources, further education in France), Pickett was appointed to the Bethany faculty in 1847, a post he held until embarking on the European tour with Richards and Kellam, and was awarded a B.A. with honors from Bethany in 1849. In 1858 he returned to Bethany as a professor of modern languages and served in this position until the outbreak of the Civil War. During the war he served as a chaplain in the Confederate army. Afterward, Pickett was a member of the faculty at both the Agricultural and Mechanical College (later, the University of Kentucky) and Transylvania University in Lexington, and was briefly president of the former institution during 1868–1869. In 1879 he was elected state superintendent of public instruction, and reelected for a second term in 1883. Kellam's presence as companion to Richards and Pickett is known from Richards's 1851 passport application, which contains an attestation of citizenship for Pickett, Richards, and Kellam by Pickett's father, James C. Pickett, and from Richards's correspondence during the trip. There is also an indirect reference in the *Millennial Harbinger* for June 1853 that refers to Pickett's return from "a tour of two years in Europe and the East" on which he was accompanied by "two other young gentlemen, formerly students of Bethany."[9]

Oliver Kellam was a Bethany graduate (1848) and heir to Pecan Grove Plantation in Carroll Parish, Louisiana, not far from Transylvania. He was the son of John H. Kellam and Ann M. Kellam, both of whom passed away when Oliver was still very young. In September 1853, Thomas Gunn visited Mammoth Cave in Kentucky and there met Keene Richards and Oliver Kellam, recently returned from their rather lengthy Grand Tour and spending time at this famous tourist attraction while en route to Louisiana. Gunn quickly developed an affinity for Kellam, whom he described as "a goodlooking manly fellow, who might sit for a portrait of Tom Jones. He has brown hair, grey eyes, white teeth (which a hearty laugh shows pleasantly) a hasty disposition, and curses very energetically when in a passion. Withal he's a very frank generous impulsive sort of fellow, who may in life do so much good, or ill. A Louisianan born, he is ward to a grandfather, and will be in part, his heir, to plantation and negroes. He played the devil at college, then travelled three years in Europe, the East, and Africa." Gunn also provided a description of Keene Richards, who was "rather slender in shape, with a keen face, and full large eyes; I at first scarcely noticed his worth, and good claims to respect and liking. A just, self respecting fellow, who never swears, drinks naught but temperance liquors, and controls his temper admirably. He's a lover of horses."[10]

Richards and Kellam were distantly related through intermarriage between their two families, both of whom owned plantations in Carroll Parish. Richards's uncle, Alexander Keene, married Julia Morgan, whose sister Ann (Morgan) Kellam was Oliver's mother. The Pecan Grove Plantation was one of several owned by Oliver James Kellam, a very wealthy man, whose sole heirs were Julia Keene and Oliver H. Kellam. Keene Richards's friend Oliver married Melinda T. Mason in April 1854, and the union produced a child, Oliver H. Kellam Jr. Tragically, twenty-two-year-old Oliver H. Kellam died from yellow fever after a few days' illness in the autumn of 1854, before his son was born, and his grandfather's estate was later subject to considerable litigation.[11]

The Grand Tour of the Continent was a European custom, originated by the British, and intended as an educational rite of passage for the sons of wealthy families. On completing their university education, many young men of means embarked on an extended tour of the great European cities, such as Paris, Rome, and Venice, often accompanied by a knowledgeable guide or tutor. Such a journey to the primary centers of western civilization might last for months or even years, providing a young man with both necessary cultural polish and connections to aristocratic and fashionable society. During the nineteenth century, even as the custom began to decline among Europeans, the Grand Tour was enthusiastically adopted by the rapidly growing wealthy classes in America. Perceiving themselves as heirs to a great western tradition, Americans extended the customary tour of the Continent to include not only their historic roots in England, but also the ancient and classical sites of the Mediterranean.[12]

On their excursion, Pickett, who had visited Europe before coming to Bethany, was intended to serve as the customary guide and informal tutor to the younger Richards and Kellam. Dr. Keene provided sufficient funds, in the form of letters of credit, to cover traveling expenses for Richards and his companions and to allow his grandson to indulge himself during the tour of Europe. Arrangements for this were made through Green and Company, an American banking firm in Paris that provided such services for American visitors to the Continent. The bank also handled correspondence between the young travelers and their friends and family across the Atlantic. Whatever the original plans may have been for the excursion, Richards, however, had his own agenda above and beyond cultural enrichment. Richards's personal goal for the grand tour was to make "a specialty of studying the different breeds of horses of every continent." Such was his determination that he was able to persuade his companions to forego the traditional circuit of European capitals to follow him on an equine odyssey as far as the wilderness of the Arabian desert.[13]

The three young men, Richards, Pickett, and Kellam, obtained their passports in the early spring of 1851, and they reached England in time to attend the seventy-second running of the Derby at Epsom Downs in Surrey, during the first weekend in June. One of the most prestigious Thoroughbred races in the world, the Epsom Derby is the second leg of the English Triple Crown. They also visited the Great Exhibition, the very first world's fair, that was held at the Crystal Palace in London. Although further details of their stay in England are unknown, doubtless Richards remained in the island kingdom for a few weeks beyond the Derby, taking the opportunity to make the acquaintance of some of the Thoroughbred breeders and perhaps visit their establishments.[14]

From England, Richards and his companions crossed the Channel into Normandy, one of the primary horse breeding regions of France. After spending some time examining the local stock, they traveled south and spent several weeks exploring the Pyrenees mountains, a lofty and rugged chain that straddles the border between France and Spain. Bayonne, a coastal city on the Bay of Biscay, was their headquarters for these adventures. At their lodgings on November 6, Richards sat down and penned a letter by candlelight to his uncle in Louisiana, John Wallis Keene. In this letter, Richards indicated that he had already developed an interest in Arabian horses and intended to extend their tour to the Near East. "If I can get an Arabian Horse cheap and have the means I think it would do very well to bring me home as it would be a benefit to us all. What think you? I could purchase one at Cairo and ride him across the Desert and then ship him from Constantinople to Liverpool and Alexander [probably a shipping agent in Liverpool] says he can send Horses to New Orleans without any trouble." Richards informed his uncle that he had written to his grandfather Keene and expected to find a letter of credit awaiting him at Constantinople that would finance their return to America. This indicates that he had already persuaded his companions to travel east to the desert lands.[15]

From Bayonne, the American travelers went directly to Madrid, where Richards had the opportunity to inspect the elegant Andalusian horses for which Spain has long been famous, and to view several Arabians recently imported from Bagdad by Queen Isabella. The sight of these magnificent animals reinforced Richards's impulsive fixation on their Oriental homeland as the ultimate goal of his tour. His ambitions in this direction were most likely twofold: to inspect the Arabian horse in its native setting and purchase some of the finest specimens, and to visit the Holy Land for religious reasons. This latter rationale was probably the means by which he convinced his companions to extend their journey so far afield. Several years later, writing to his old Bethany mentor, Professor William K. Pendleton, he noted that the morning lectures of Reverend Campbell, describing the landscapes of the Holy Land, "created in me an intense desire to witness these sacred scenes. It has been my good fortune to realize *this day dream of my college life.*"[16]

The subsequent journeys of these three young travelers were nothing short of remarkable. A few writers claimed that Richards was a delicate child, or an invalid almost from infancy, and that his grandfather had sent him to Europe in 1851 to improve his health. Given the circumstances of Richards's adventures in North Africa and the Near East, if ever he had been in ill health, he made an amazing and immediate return to vitality on this journey.

Reconstructing the travels of these young men must remain in part speculative. From a number of sources, we know the route that they followed, the cities that they visited, and certain of their activities. The chronology, however, is problematic. When they arrived at a particular locale, or how long they lingered, is unclear for most of the journey. Three chronological markers are known with certainty: the presence of Richards's party at Epsom Downs, England, in June 1851; their being at Bayonne, France, on November 6; and his purchases of Arabian horses in the Levant in February and March 1852. Between and beyond these markers, no definite dates can be established, only estimates based on logic and the experiences of other contemporary travelers.

Europe and the Mediterranean in 1853. Map by Gary A. O'Dell. Numbers designate waypoints on Keene Richards's first journey that were associated with breeding and racing horses. Visits to locations 1–8 are documented; locations 9–11 are speculative but very likely on his itinerary. (1) Thoroughbred breeding and racing region of Britain. (2) Normandy breeding region. (3) Queen Isabella's Arabian horses at Madrid. (4) Barb horses at Tangier. (5) Algerian breeding region. (6) Purchase of Arabian at Jerusalem. (7) Purchase of Badra's Arabian at Beirut. (8) Damascus, launch point for desert travel and purchase of Bedouin Arabians. (9) Lipizza stables at Trieste. (10) Spanish Riding School at Vienna. (11) Neustadt stud near Berlin. (12) Royal stud at Trakehnen.

Based on this hypothetical chronology, Keene and his companions probably spent about four months in their journey through France and Spain to inspect the various breeding establishments and in other adventures, covering over a thousand miles to arrive at Gibraltar in mid-November of 1851. From Spain, the travelers crossed the Strait of Gibraltar to Morocco, most likely landing at Tangier. Sometime prior to this point, Richards would have converted a significant portion of his letters of credit into gold coin, knowing this would be necessary as they traveled beyond Europe. Richards wished to examine the Barb horses for which this land was famous, and here, in this ancient city, he probably outfitted himself and his companions with these very steeds for the next leg of the journey. The coastal region of northwest Africa was rugged, and wild in parts, but the land was green and fertile, separated by the Atlas Mountains from the forbidding expanse of the great Sahara Desert to the south.[17]

After a journey of more than two hundred miles on horseback, they reached the Algerian border, and here the party visited several breeding establishments. French passports obtained earlier gave them access to the large equine facilities operated by the French territorial government, but Richards also made time to seek out and inspect the horses of several tribal leaders, many of whom had until recently been engaged in a long guerrilla war with France. From Algeria, the companions crossed into Tunisia, where Richards searched for traces of the ancient Numidian horses, long since vanished, that had served Hannibal so well as light cavalry. When the young men arrived at Tunis, they were now nearly a thousand miles from Tangier. Given that an average horse can travel twenty-five to thirty miles in a day, they most likely entered the city in late December. Here they embarked onto a sailing ship bound for the British island of Malta.[18]

From Malta, the Richards party caught a steamer to Alexandria, Egypt, nominally ruled by Pasha Abbas I but a de facto British colony. At Alexandria, the travelers would have boarded a Nile boat known as a canja, about a hundred feet in length with an enclosed cabin and two masts with lanteen-rigged sails. The canja was towed down the length of the Mahmudiyya Canal, a distance of about forty-five miles, to its junction with the Rosetta branch of the Nile River at the village of Atfeh. From this point, travelers might board a steamer or continue up the river under sail to Cairo. A German visitor described the canal trip as experienced in 1842: "An Arab steersman, and two rowers of the same nation, aided by four horses, set the gondola in motion, and a man stationed in the forepart spoke through a most discordant trumpet, at the approach of any boat. This always created a commotion; before they could resolve to which side they should respectively keep, both parties cried, shouted, and heartily abused each other; sometimes they got so entangled that our rowers were compelled to swim to the bank and take the towing line from the horses." The canal was hurriedly built by order of provincial governor Mehemet Ali Pasha between 1817 and 1819 using the forced labor of hundreds of thousands of Egyptian peasants. The canal trip from Alexandria became the usual route of access for European travelers seeking to visit both Egypt and the Holy Land. Having reached Cairo, the Richards party may have journeyed just a little farther to view the Pyramids, located a short distance south of the city. Once their curiosity was sated, they began to prepare for their journey into the desert of Arabia Petraea and to the Holy Land.[19]

Arabia Petraea was the designation given by the Romans to one of their three Arabian frontier provinces, a region that included parts of modern Jordan, Syria, northwestern Saudi Arabia, and the Sinai Peninsula and was populated by nomadic tribes. The ancient name persisted through the centuries and continued to be used by classically educated Europeans of Richards's time. At Cairo, the Bethany travelers fell in with a group of European tourists and their guides in a camel caravan intended to pioneer a new route (for Europeans) directly across the Sinai Peninsula to visit the ruins of Petra, an ancient fortress city that was once an important center for caravan trade. Unknown to the western world prior to 1812, when the extensive ruins were located by Swiss explorer Johann Ludwig (John Lewis) Burckhardt, Petra thereafter became a popular tourist destination. The direct route across the Sinai that Richards apparently helped establish became the customary passage from Egypt to Petra, a journey that typically required twenty-four days by camel from Cairo. The caravan that Richards and his companions joined probably departed Egypt sometime in early January 1852, since knowledgeable travelers to the East generally tried to follow a schedule that would avoid the scorching heat of midsummer in the desert lands.[20]

On the nearly five hundred-mile journey through barren desert, Keene Richards amused himself by learning to break dromedaries (the single-humped camel of the region) for riding. One must wonder if he attempted to apply Offutt's methods to "gentle" these beasts, which have an ill-deserved reputation as bad-tempered but in reality are amiable and patient. As a skilled horseman, Richards quickly mastered camel riding and often participated in impromptu races mounted on one of the small, swift

Arab mounted on a deloul, or single-humped swift camel used for courier service and in racing. During his journey across the Sinai Peninsula in a caravan during autumn 1851, Keene Richards competed in impromptu camel races on one of these mounts. Image from *Frank Leslie's New Family Magazine* 3 (July 1858), 21.

camels, trained for the saddle, known as "deloul" and used for courier service and in warfare among the Bedouin tribes.[21]

As they approached Petra, the travelers crossed an invisible line in the desert sands, leaving the domain of the Egyptian Pashalik to enter lands ruled directly by the Ottoman Sultan Abdülmecid. This boundary was located at approximately the southern border of modern Israel. Deriving wealth and power from its strategic location astride the trade routes of three continents, the Ottoman empire at its peak controlled much of southeastern Europe, the Near East, and North Africa. By the time of Richards's visit, the empire had entered a long period of stagnation and decay, such that in 1853 Tsar Nicholas of Russia, discussing his plans for a partition of Turkish lands with the British ambassador to St. Petersburg, referred to the empire as "the Sick Man of Europe." During the past half-century, the Ottomans had lost territory on all fronts, much of the Balkans ceded to Austria, and Algeria and Egypt nominally independent but controlled by France and Great Britain. Even the lands of the eastern Mediterranean, known as the Levant and including Syria, Lebanon, and Palestine, were recently lost by the empire to Egyptian conquest and regained only through intervention by the so-called Great Powers of Europe—Britain, France, Austria, Prussia, and Russia.[22]

After admiring the ruins of Petra, Richards and his companions followed the caravan road north, skirting the southern edge of the Dead Sea and traveling on to Hebron and Jerusalem. The young men spent two weeks in the holy city of Jerusalem and visited many of the sacred sites in the vicinity so vividly described to them by Alexander Campbell in the morning Bible classes at Bethany. In an 1860 letter to his former professor William K. Pendleton, Richards recalled having bathed in the Dead Sea, and then at the ford of the Jericho River having "washed away with its pure water, the stinging effects of the Sea of Death." He and his companions thereafter "visited the shores of the Sea of Galilee—drank of its pure water—feasted upon fish drawn from its sacred depths, and ate of loaves made of grain grown upon its consecrated mountain sides." Before departing from Jerusalem, Richards purchased Mokhladi, a gray Arabian stallion fourteen hands and one inch in height, foaled in 1844. Horses are traditionally measured by units known as "hands," equivalent to four inches, from the ground to the highest point of the withers, the top of the shoulders between the neck and the back. Mokhladi, at fourteen hands and one inch, was thus fifty-seven inches at the shoulder. Arabian horses were generally smaller than Thoroughbreds or part-Thoroughbreds; the famous Lexington, foaled in 1850, stood sixty-three inches at the shoulder, and more recently Man o' War and Secretariat both measured about sixty-five inches. Mokhladi had been bred by the Tarabin tribe in the Sinai, and was a horse considered to be "the finest animal in the city . . . with the exception of a magnificent mare owned by the French Consul." The young men then traveled on to Beirut in the Ottoman province of Lebanon, part of the region known as Greater Syria, probably arriving in late February or early March.[23]

6
THE LAND OF ARABIAN HORSES

Beirut was the main point of entry for European visitors to the Holy Land, and although not a large city, it carried on a lively commerce as it served as port for the much larger city of Damascus, two days' travel to the east. In the decades after Keene Richards's visit, Beirut would experience rapid growth and increased significance in the region. John P. Durbin, an American visitor in 1843, noted that the streets of the town were narrow, crooked, and badly paved, crowded with windowless buildings of heavy masonry whose upper stories extended out over the street, giving the impression of passing through a tunnel. About twelve thousand people then resided within the walls of Beirut, and about five thousand inhabited the gardens and orchards surrounding the city. "Escaping from within the walls," Durbin wrote, "you emerge suddenly from gloom and darkness into the bright light of day, and find yourself in the midst of mulberry groves, of orchards laden with figs, peaches, lemons, oranges, and apricots, and of gardens rich in every variety of fragrant and beautiful flowers. Scattered among these gardens are private dwellings, whose porticoes and lofty rooms are filled with the rarest plants. It is, indeed, almost a fairy land." Many of these well-appointed homes on the outskirts of Beirut were occupied by "Franks" or Europeans: consuls, mercantile agents, and missionaries.[1]

Richards and his companions needed to locate an experienced local guide who could speak English, deal with the Ottoman authorities, and care for the horses they acquired. Inquiries in Beirut led him to Yusef Badra. Badra was a Syrian (Lebanese) Christian, a member of the indigenous Maronite sect associated with the Roman Catholic Church. He held the title of "dragoman," an official position in the Ottoman empire that

Alexander Keene Richards in 1853, photographed at the C. W. May studio in London, England, while returning from his first trip to the Middle East. Courtesy of Lowry Schneider.

required fluency in Arabic, Turkish, and European languages. For a fee, dragomen served as interpreters and guides for foreign visitors and assisted with arrangements for transportation and provisions.[2]

From late November 1851 to early January 1852, just before Richards's party arrived at Beirut, Badra served as dragoman for John Ross Browne (1821–1875), a widely read travel writer, also from Kentucky, who was then in the Holy Land gathering material for another book. Browne described the Syrian as having a "face open and intelligent, eyes round and full of fire, mustache fierce, temperament nervous-sanguine, costume rich, careless, and dashing; figure well-knit and of medium height; manner frank, self-relying, and chivalrous; whole tone of character imposing, captivating, and Oriental." On introducing himself to Browne and his companions at their hotel room in Beirut, Badra produced a small, black book from his sash and, while they inspected it, made the following speech: "Gentlemen, I am Yusef Simon Badra, the dragoman for Syria. This is my book of recommendations. I have taken a thousand American gentlemen through Syria. Yes, sir; the Americans like me; I like the Americans! I hate Englishmen; I won't take an Englishman; they don't suit me; can't get along together; I know too much for 'em. But the Americans suit me; always ready; up to everything—fun, fight, or frolic."[3]

Browne developed such an attachment to the Syrian that his subsequent travel book, published in New York shortly before Richards re-

Yusef Badra in 1851. Keene Richards considered his Syrian guide and interpreter to know more about horses than any other person he had met in the East, and brought him back to the United States to care for his newly acquired Arabian horses. Sketch by John Ross Browne, in Browne, *Yusef*, 178.

turned to America and titled *Yusef*, was as much about the adventures and philosophy of his Syrian guide as it was about the landscape and culture of the region. Browne's travel writing was marked by a cutting wit and keen observation, a style that later inspired two important writers of the nineteenth century, Herman Melville and Mark Twain. Twain visited the Holy Land in 1867, and his subsequent book *The Innocents Abroad* appears to have been influenced by Browne's *Yusef*, although the experiences of the two men were quite different. Browne and Twain had very similar writing styles, marked by humor and exaggeration and the use of storytelling.

Another name that would certainly be in Badra's book of recommendations, a name with which Richards and the other Bethany students would have been quite familiar, was that of James Turner Barclay. Dr. Barclay, a trained physician, was a follower of Alexander Campbell and was the first appointee of the new American Christian Missionary Society of the Disciples of Christ, who spent 1851–1854 on a mission to convert the Jews of Jerusalem. While staying in the holy city, Barclay carried out research on the sacred and historic sites of the locale, and his subsequent book *The City of the Great King* remains a primary source of information about Jerusalem during the nineteenth century. He later held an appointment as professor of natural sciences at Bethany College from 1866 to 1868. Barclay, along with his wife, Julia, and three children, arrived at Beirut on January 24, 1851. After contacting the other missionaries in the city for assistance in making arrangements to travel on to Jerusalem, a dragoman was hired, who proved to be none other than the indomitable Yusef Badra. Barclay's fourteen-year-old daughter Sarah, who was an excellent artist and provided most of the illustrations for her father's book, kept a journal of their stay in the Holy Land, and in her own account, published in 1858, writes of their first encounter with Badra:

> A glance at his bristling girdle suffices to elicit from us a favorable answer. It is overflowingly supplied with dirks, sabres, and pistols; accoutrements to which no one, in anticipation of a passage through a wild region of country, alleges the slightest objection. Thus equipped, and mounted on his fiery Arabian steed, we deem him a match for half a dozen Bedawin: a most consoling thought, in view of the double capacity in which he is about to act, as guard and dragoman to

> Jerusalem. He wears the usual gay costume of the Greek Arabs. A tarbouch of bright crimson, a jacket of purple, richly embroidered with gold, a vest of delicate green embroidered with silks, a white plaited skirt, twenty yards wide, and boots of bright yellow morocco, complete his attire.

The Barclay party, escorted by Badra, arrived at Jerusalem on February 9. One year later, after serving in the employ of John Ross Brown, Badra was recommended to Richards as the best guide in the region.[4]

The flamboyant Yusef Badra must have delighted Richards and his companions, and impressed them with his qualifications, since Richards hired Badra to care for the horses in Syria and to look after them during the ocean voyage back to the United States while the Bethany graduates continued their tour. This, despite the fact that in the first week of January 1852, when Browne set sail for his return to the States, Badra was at that moment languishing in the Beirut jail. He had been sentenced to a term of six months by the Turkish authorities for assaulting a Turkish man on the road to Beirut, notwithstanding vigorous efforts by Browne and the American consul to have him set free.[5]

Badra only remained jailed for a few days. He petitioned the Ottoman governor of Beirut for an audience, which was soon granted. The pasha unrolled a large paper that contained thirty-two complaints against Badra, some dating back more than a decade. Badra pointed out that most of the complainants were dead, and there was no proof to any of the charges. The pasha dismissed him, and then sent again for Badra in an hour's time. He then inquired as to whether Badra would convert to Islam and serve in the sultan's army, whereupon Badra replied, "I was born a Christian and I hoped to die a Christian." The pasha then set the dragoman free, saying, "Go back to your prison but feel yourself my guest tonight and tomorrow go wash off these complaints in the Bath and be free." No doubt the pasha also included a few words of warning for Yusef to behave himself in the future. Quite possibly Badra, recently released from jail, conveniently neglected to mention his incarceration when presenting himself to Richards and his companions a few weeks later, sometime in February 1852.[6]

One of Richards's primary objectives during their time in the East was to journey into the desert and bargain directly with the Bedouins for

Arabian horses, which he felt was certain to obtain the purest blood. The gateway to the desert was the ancient city of Damascus, sixty miles east from Beirut, separated from it by the ranges of Lebanon and situated in a fertile plain. Home to more than 180,000 people in 1850, fabled Damascus was the most important trade center of the Levant, the destination of caravans from India bearing such exotic items as pepper, cinnamon, nutmeg, musk, camphor, indigo, porcelain, silks, and finely worked gold and silver. Heavily laden caravans of a thousand or more camels arrived in Damascus twice each year from Bagdad. Trade with western nations was, however, transforming the nature of the markets. In 1843, John P. Durbin was sorely disappointed to find the bazaars filled with European goods, particularly textiles from British looms, a development also observed by Frederick Walpole in 1850, who stated, "English goods are much superseding the native manufactures."[7]

Richards made inquiries at Beirut and Damascus among the American and British missionaries and consular agents for a knowledgeable guide who could lead him east through the desert to seek out Arabian horses among the Bedouin tribes. He was warned that such a journey would be extremely dangerous, but Richards was determined, and finally found the right man in Abdul Medjuel el Mezrab.[8]

Almost the same age as Richards, Medjuel was the younger brother of the sheikh of the Mezrab section of the Sba'a, a subtribe of the Anizah Bedouins of Syria, and a sheikh in his own right who would one day lead the tribe. Lady Isabel Burton, wife of the famous explorer Sir Richard Francis Burton, described Medjuel as a "very intelligent and charming man." Short in stature at five feet, six inches but of average height for a Bedouin Arab, Medjuel was softspoken, slim, and graceful. For a Bedouin, he was relatively well educated, at the insistence of his father, able to read and write Arabic and to speak several languages, including Turkish and some Italian. Providing guide service across the desert to the historic ruins at Palmyra for the slowly increasing number of western visitors was a major source of income for the tribe, although Medjuel was selective as to whom he would escort.[9]

American travelers to the Near East, such as Richards and his companions, carried with them a mythic perception of Palestine as analogous to the western frontier region of North America. As Jacob R. Berman

Sheikh Abdul Medjuel el Mezrab, painted by Carl Haag in 1859. The sheikh was hired by Keene Richards in 1852 to lead him into the desert to seek horses among the Bedouin tribes. Courtesy of Tareq Rajab Museum, Jabriya, Kuwait.

observed, "In the mid-nineteenth century, the genre of the Near Eastern travel narrative came into market prominence at the exact same time that the US government was dramatically expanding its continental territory. In these narratives, the American frontier is mirrored in the Arabian desert." The Bedouins of the desert, modeling a traditional culture and natural freedom, living in harmony with nature and associated into often-warring tribal groups, were a visual analogy for Native Americans in the American West. For American travelers who eagerly sought out the places in the Holy Land associated with the life of Jesus, viewing Bedouins in their traditional garb provided living visual analogues for biblical patriarchs such as Abraham. They could imagine themselves transported back in time or understanding the Near East to exist as a "timeless realm unaffected by history."[10]

Medjuel agreed to take Richards east into the desert on a horse-buying expedition to the Anizah tribes. He may have already been favorably disposed toward foreigners, or perhaps Richards made a good impression on him during their time together, for in August of the following year, 1853, Medjuel agreed to escort Englishwoman Lady Jane Digby across the desert to the ruins of Palmyra. On this journey, as Lady Burton relates, "the young Shaykh fell in love with this beautiful woman, and she fell in love with him," and in March 1855 they were married under Islamic law. Jane adopted Islamic culture, and the couple spent half of each year living as nomads in a desert tent, and half in a house in Damascus, where the Burtons were among their neighbors. Medjuel was twenty years younger than his English bride, and, in becoming her fourth husband, added to the cloud of scandal that had surrounded her for most of her life; nevertheless, they remained happily married for twenty-six years until Jane's death at Damascus in 1881.[11]

The dangers of such an excursion were quite real, for European travelers had occasionally been murdered for their possessions. Given the unrelenting state of internecine warfare that had long existed among the nomadic tribes of northern Arabia, even inhabitants of the region were not exempt from ambush. The Anizah, of which Medjuel was a minor sheikh, and the Shammar were the most numerous of the regional tribes, but these consisted of loose amalgamations of smaller tribes who were as inclined to make war on one another as on their hereditary enemies. At the time of Richards's visit, the Anizah tribes occupied the area of northwestern Arabia adjacent to the settled communities of the Mediterranean coast, whereas the Shammar region was farther to the east toward the Euphrates River. The Anizah and Shammar were traditional rivals and enemies, and the government of the Ottoman Turks, who nominally ruled this region, encouraged feuds among the tribes to focus their attention away from the settled areas. While most such conflicts were relatively bloodless, the object of raids being mainly to gain horses or camels, Richards's planned expedition would take them very close to the Shammar lands and there was a real risk of a fatal encounter.[12]

Medjuel led the three young American men and Yusef Badra northeast across the desert for nearly 150 miles to the ruins of the ancient caravan city of Palmyra, and returned safely with them to Damascus. What the consummately dignified Sheikh Medjuel thought of the garrulous dragoman, who boastfully styled himself as "the Destroyer of Robbers," is nowhere recorded, although Yusef probably acted as translator. Despite having a guide, Medjuel, who was well-known and respected among the Anizah, Richards was apparently unsuccessful in obtaining any Arabian horses from the Bedouins at this time.[13]

Instead, Badra persuaded the Americans to buy his own horse, a chestnut Arabian stallion known as Syed Sulemin. Oliver Kellam made the initial purchase, according to a later (1878) traveler in the same region, Kentuckian Henry R. Coleman, and this horse was subsequently acquired by Keene Richards from his friend and renamed Massoud. This was the very same horse ridden by Badra during his journey with John Ross Browne, to whom Yusef had bragged, with typical exaggeration, "a horse that must be known even in America, for Syed had leaped a wall twenty feet high, and was trained to walk a hundred and fifty miles a day, and kill the most desperate robbers by catching them up in his teeth and tossing them over his head." Browne humorously described the relationship between Badra and his beloved Syed:

> Every morning, regularly, before mounting, Yusef greeted Syed Sulemin in the most brotherly manner. He asked him how he felt; how he had slept; what was the general state of his health; had any body stolen his oats; and upon being answered, as Syed Sulemin was in the habit of answering, by a peculiar working of the ears, a neighing and nickering, and other well-understood signs, Yusef could never restrain his affection, but invariably hugged him round the neck, exchanged kisses with him, and shook hands with his forefoot to show him that they were still devoted friends, and never could be separated by any adversity of fortune.

Badra was a man of his word, for when the newly christened Massoud departed aboard ship for America, his devoted companion accompanied him to the New World to care for him. Richards later wrote of Badra, "this man knew more about horses than any one I had met in the East."[14]

Yusef Badra with Massoud. Painted in 1854 by Edward Troye at Georgetown, Kentucky. Private collection.

Back in Damascus, Sheikh Medjuel and the Americans parted company. Richards now had two fine Arabian stallions, and he and his friends were ready to continue their Grand Tour northward from the Levant into eastern Europe. Just as they were about to depart from Beirut, a splendid gray Arabian mare caught Richards's eye and he purchased her on the spot. Like Massoud, the mare Sadah had been bred by the Anizah Bedouins. Having gone to so much trouble to acquire these valuable horses, Richards would not care to risk their health or losing them to thieves on such a long and arduous trip. He was doubtless anxious to have them shipped back to Kentucky as quickly as possible, and Yusef Badra was an obvious choice for this important task.[15]

Export of Arabian horses from the Ottoman empire required a special dispensation from the sultan, Abdülmecid, and this had been arranged for Richards through a personal request from U.S. President Franklin Pierce to the Turkish authorities. Export restrictions on Arabian horses from the Ottoman empire had always existed, Lady Anne Blunt informed Homer Davenport in 1906, but had become more strictly applied in recent years. Exportation of Arabian mares was particularly forbidden. Richards was thus indeed fortunate in being able to obtain mares on both his first and second expeditions. The export prohibitions were evidently applied with considerable irregularity, and the various sultans had long made a custom of presenting visiting foreign dignitaries with matching pairs of Arabian stallions. Fortunately for Richards, the sultan, a progressive reformer, was at this time actively seeking to build alliances with western nations to help improve the security of his ailing empire. Although the United States was neither an important trade partner for the empire nor a significant player in regional politics, the Ottoman monarch was thus predisposed to promote favorable relations with representatives of any western power.[16]

Like Richards before him, Davenport used political influence to secure permission from the Turks to purchase and export Arabian horses. Having contacted President Theodore Roosevelt on this matter, Davenport received a letter in 1906 from U.S. Secretary of State Elihu Root that he successfully used to secure an Iradé, or decree of the sultan, allowing him to visit Arabia to purchase and export "six to eight mares" and as many stallions as he thought appropriate.[17]

Having obtained permission to export his three Arabians, Richards left Badra in charge of the two stallions and the mare, then departed Beirut with Kellam and Pickett bound for Smyrna and Constantinople. Richards had been considerably impressed by Badra's recommendations and such measure of the man's character as he had been able to gain during their time together; this responsibility represented an extraordinary level of trust. Possibly Richards, at this time, already had in mind further trips to the East to secure additional stock, and offered Badra the opportunity for return passage in the future should he not find America to his liking. The voyage of the Arabian horses to America was related by Badra in a letter to his friend and former employer, John Ross Browne, dated January 16, 1854, at Transylvania Plantation, Louisiana:

> I remained [in Beirut] several months waiting for a steamer. I at last started on board of a screw steamer for Liverpool after we had been out about two days we had a storm which broke the engine and so we had to put into the port of Alexandria. I was compelled to take all the Horses ashore and perform quarantine. Before the steamer got ready to start I was severely wounded in my side by a dagger in the hands

> of a Turk who was once I thought my best friend. My wound was so severe that my friends thought for several weeks I would surely die; but God was with me. I remained in Egypt 92 days and then I started again for Liverpool, from Liverpool I shipped for New Orleans where I arrived safe on the last day of last June [1853] from there I took a steamboat [up the Mississippi] for this place, where I arrived on the 4th of July and here I have been ever since.[18]

There can be no doubt that Yusef Badra was a highly intelligent and resourceful man, having shepherded his charges safely from the Near East to America, a distance by sea of more than eight thousand miles, all the while dealing with novelty and strangeness.

From the time that Richards last viewed his horses, in early spring 1852, to their arrival in New Orleans, the journey of the Arabians, including the initial delay in Beirut and layovers in Alexandria and Liverpool, took more than a year. Although most maritime commerce during the 1850s was still carried under sail, faster, steam-powered ships were becoming more common. The voyage from Liverpool to New Orleans by sailing ship might take ten weeks or longer, but only three to five weeks by steamship, a duration soon greatly reduced by improvements in steam power technology. As it was, shortly after departure from Liverpool the mare Sadah gave birth to a foal on board the steam vessel *Warbler.* Yusef Badra later wrote, "I saved its life . . . I call him Sinn Boherr (Ocean) because he was born on the Ocean and he is always moving like the waves." The gray colt was sired by the stallion Mokhladi; this may have been arranged by Keene Richards before departing the Levant, or may have been a simple accident.[19]

When Yusef Badra stepped off the ship in New Orleans on June 30, 1853, he was greeted at the wharf by Morris Keene, a cousin of Keene Richards who was then serving as overseer and general manager for Transylvania Plantation. Keene later wrote, regarding the arrival at dockside of the two stallions and the mare, with a colt at her side, that after their long voyage "They were so low in flesh that they appeared to great disadvantage, and excited but little admiration." Two days later, Badra, Keene, and the three Arabian horses boarded a paddlewheel steamer for the brief trip up the Mississippi River to Transylvania Plantation.[20]

"This is a fine country for horses," Badra wrote to Browne, having been on the plantation for six months. "I can ride all day without striking a stone or sinking in the sand." His true love, Syed (or Massoud), like the other horses, had recovered from the rigors of the long voyage. All were thriving in the Louisiana climate. "I do not think you would know Massoud now he is looking so much better than he did when you saw him in Syria. . . . I like you very much Gen Brown, but I believe I like Massoud better than anybody else." Badra was unabashedly enthusiastic about America, and he had every intention of remaining.

> Oh! General I tell you the truth I like this country better than Syria. I have signed my intention to become an American. . . . I don't have to carry any arms here to defend myself, there are no Bedouins to watch for at night. I clean my arms and hang them up in my room to look at. I keep on my coat, smoke my pipe and take it easy for this side of Jordan there is no hard roads to travle [*sic*]. There is plenty of game here in the brake cover. The bears in Syria are brown but here they grow black—the gazelle horns don't grow straight but they branch out like the cedars on Mount Lebanon. I have killed one large bear but bear-hunting in a brake cover is very hard work. I had rather run down a gazelle in the desert.

Badra concluded with an invitation to Browne, who was then in New Orleans, to visit him at Transylvania.[21]

The publication of *Yusef* catapulted Browne to national recognition, marking the point at which his writing career really took off, and also endowed Badra with the status of a minor celebrity. In New Orleans on January 12, 1854, Browne wrote to his wife, Lucy, "I have met with hundreds of friends old and new everywhere, from Georgia to New Orleans, and have the fortune to ride gloriously on the shoulders of my worthy dragoman Yusef. In the South he is a household word, and my unworthy self comes in for a goodly share of the favor with which his exploits are regarded. Although I only stopped one night in Mobile, the papers of that City chronicled the event as something notable in history. [Here also] the newspapers all out in glorious style announcing the arrival of Yusef's biographer." Browne left the city within days for Galveston and the West, in

John Russ Browne hired Yusef Badra as a guide immediately prior to Keene Richards, and wrote a popular book about the colorful dragoman. In America, Browne visited his Syrian friend at Transylvania and became acquainted with the Keene family. *Harper's Weekly* 12 (February 22, 1868), 125.

pursuance of his duties as a recently appointed federal custom house inspector, but he was back at the St. Charles hotel in New Orleans in March, where Yusef's letter caught up with him. Subsequent events indicate that Browne acted upon his former dragoman's invitation and made a visit to the plantation, and there became acquainted with Morris Keene as well.[22]

In the spring of 1854, Badra and the Arabians traveled to Georgetown, Kentucky, and here Yusef, in his colorful Syrian attire, accentuated the exotic, Eastern flavor of Blue Grass Park that Richards sought to cultivate. When attired in his finest garb, Badra made a lasting impression on visitors: "His turban," wrote John Ross Browne in 1852, "was of the richest texture and most flashing colors; his vest actually glittered with gilded embroidery and silver buttons; his sash was of flaming vermillion; his sword and atagar of Damascus, dazzled the eye as they swung by his side in the morning sunbeams; his legs were swathed in crimson velvet;

and his feet seemed to spurn the earth in the glory of yellow embroidered slippers, the richest productions of Aleppo." During the summer of 1854, working at Blue Grass Park, the celebrated equine portrait painter Edward Troye created one of his finest works for his friend and patron, Keene Richards. Yusef Badra is shown posed with his cherished Massoud in an outfit nearly as grand as that described by Browne, holding a blunderbuss in his hands and with what appears to be a saddle beside him. In the left foreground is the corner of an Arab tent; a kilij, or curved Turkish sword, lies at his feet.[23]

When Keene Richards and his companions bade farewell to Yusef Badra in the early spring of 1852, they were next bound for Smyrna (today Izmir, Turkey), a port city on the western coast of Anatolia. Smyrna was, after Constantinople, the most important commercial and shipping center of the Ottoman empire. Most likely they chose to travel by sea. The distance from Beirut to Smyrna was about the same by land or by water, approximately eight hundred miles, but the land route to Smyrna, up the coast of the Mediterranean and across the length of Turkey, would have taken longer and been far more risky.[24]

A steamer route had been established between Beirut and Smyrna more than a decade before, so that passage could be made in only five days, with brief stops at the islands of Cyprus and Rhodes. John P. Durbin described the scene in April 1842 as the steamer prepared to depart from the Beirut dockside:

> [I] leaped into the boat which was to take us to the steamer, and in a few minutes we were on deck. But such a deck! It was literally covered from stem to stern by two hundred and eighty hadjis, or pilgrims, returning from the holy cities. They were divided into small squads, each surrounded by its furniture. Some lay on mats, some on carpets, others on rich cushions, and not a few upon the hard boards. The women were hid behind piles of provision sacks, waterpots, saddlebags, and what not, or were half suffocated under quilts hung over them for concealment.

As seen from anchorage, the city of Smyrna, he wrote, "is exceedingly beautiful. It sweeps like a crescent for two miles around the eastern end of the bay, and swells away up the side of Mount Pagus until it blends with the dense cypress groves which shade its vast cemeteries, and beyond these the massive remains of the ancient Acropolis crown the summit of the mountain." The ancient Greek city had been located on the hilltop northeast of the Gulf of Smyrna; sacked in the sixth century BCE, Smyrna was rebuilt three centuries later on the low ground and hill slopes to the southeast. At the time of Richards's visit, the city contained a population of 145,000, primarily Turks and Greeks.[25]

The exact details of Richards's subsequent itinerary are unknown, although their journey included stops in Austria, Prussia, and Russia. Constantinople, the greatest city in the Ottoman empire, was less than a day's travel from Smyrna by steamer. The Bethany graduates may have taken the opportunity to visit this historic city before continuing their travels into eastern Europe. Since Richards's stated objective during this Grand Tour was to visit the various equine breeding establishments in the nations through which they traveled, the most likely next move would have been to board a steamer at either Smyrna or Constantinople bound for Trieste, a port city on the Adriatic coast in the Austrian empire. A short distance inland from the city were the royal stables of Lipizza, a popular tourist stop for visitors to the region.

Founded by Archduke Charles of Austria in 1580, these were the stables where the famous Lipizzaner performing horses were bred from Spanish and Arabian bloodstock. Isabel Burton described the establishment as it appeared to a visitor in the 1870s, although her use of the term "thoroughbred" was in the sense of "pure bred": "It is about two hours from Trieste. You come to a kind of farm, where you may get something to eat. You are then taken to the stables, where the Emperor keeps about nine thoroughbred Arab stallions, and afterwards you are taken through the park, where are herds of thoroughbred mares, chiefly Hungarians and Croats, most of them with foals, perhaps two hundred including foals." As they traveled through the Austrian empire, Richards and his friends likely paused for a time to savor the attractions of Vienna. Given the equine focus of the tour, perhaps they visited the Spanish Riding School in that city, the oldest riding academy in the world, where the very best of the Lipizzaner horses performed for the Habsburg emperor and elite guests.[26]

From Vienna, the Richards party would have traveled to Berlin in the kingdom of Prussia. The stud at Neustadt, established in 1788 by Friedrich Wilhelm II, was located only about fifty miles northwest from the city. Since this operation was developing a Thoroughbred-type horse using Thoroughbred and Anglo-Arab mares bred to Arabian and Turkoman stallions, this would have been of considerable interest to Richards. The next likely destination would have been in far eastern Prussia. The royal stud at Trakehnen was located about eighty miles east of Königsberg, today Kaliningrad, a Russian exclave located on the Baltic between Poland and Lithuania. Here the elegant Trakehner horse was developed during the early eighteenth century by Frederick Wilhelm I, breeding the native Lithuanian horses with a mixture of Arab, Turkoman, and English Thoroughbred blood. Keene Richards's final declared goal was to investigate the Orlov trotting horses of Russia, but a journey to the Khrenov stud near Voronej in central Russia, three hundred miles south of Moscow, would have been too long and arduous. Instead, he was probably required to satisfy his curiosity by examination of whatever specimens were closest at hand in Königsberg (now Kaliningrad) or nearby Russian communities. Richards may have taken a ship to St. Petersburg, a distance of about 450 nautical miles, where, as elsewhere in the country, "Orloff Trotters" were commonly used as carriage horses.[27]

Having been absent from the United States for more than two years, Keene Richards and his companions, Joseph D. Pickett and Oliver Kellam, were ready to go home. Since leaving England, these young men had traveled nearly ten thousand miles by land and sea, by horseback and camelback, sailing ship and steamer. To bring their grand circuit of three continents to a close, returning to London would require a journey of a thousand miles or more from eastern Prussia. Most likely they embarked by ship from the port of Königsberg, across the Baltic and the North Sea to the Thames estuary, or may instead have traveled a longer route by rail across Europe to the Flemish coast. During the last two decades, Prussia and the various German republics had engaged in constructing a railway network that was then the most extensive in Europe, linking with that of Belgium. Whatever the route taken, Richards was by now eager to return to America and commence his program to breed improved Thoroughbreds. Early in 1853, he was back in the States.[28]

It was not an entirely happy homecoming for Keene Richards. During his absence, on December 20, 1851, Grandmother Hannah Keene had passed away at the age of sixty-five. For Dr. Keene, with his favorite grandson on the other side of the world, the big brick house on the hill at Georgetown must have seemed very empty for the next two years.

7
SETTING UP THE EXPERIMENT

Keene Richards and his little band of adventurers, now seasoned world travelers, arrived in New Orleans on March 12, 1853, having first debarked briefly at New York and taken the mail steamer *Crescent City* bound first for Havana and then Louisiana. On this voyage Richards made the acquaintance of fellow passenger Richard Ten Broeck, who, as manager of the Metairie racetrack in New Orleans, would prove quite significant to his developing career as a horse breeder. Richards would be quite eager to check on the welfare of his Arabians, now recuperating at Transylvania from their long ocean voyage. Grandfather Keene may have been in residence on the plantation that fall, even more likely to be spending the winter season of 1853–1854 in the southland since he was now quite elderly at seventy-eight years of age. From New Orleans, Richards and his companions traveled up the Mississippi River to Kentucky, stopping briefly at Transylvania. After spending the summer months in the Bluegrass, Richards set off again for Transylvania, accompanied by Morris Keene and Oliver Kellam. Rather than using waterborne passage for the return trip, Richards elected to follow a more leisurely route through the southland, heading first for southwestern Kentucky, where he and his friends checked into the Mammoth Cave hotel and spent some time investigating the great cave. At the hotel he made a new friend, Thomas Gunn, whose journal subsequently records how Richards acquired his first Thoroughbred horse, a very famous mare.[1]

Richards desired brood mares of proven quality to mate with his Arabian stallions. His first acquisition toward this end was the chestnut mare Peytona, purchased from Thomas Kirkman of Florence, Alabama. This was a real coup, since Peytona was one of the outstanding racing mares of the era and celebrated throughout the southland for her 1845 defeat of the famous northern mare Fashion. Her career earnings on the turf amounted to $62,400, a record that would not be surpassed by any American horse for fifteen years. Peytona's pedigree was flawless, descended from the best true Thoroughbred aristocracy on both sides of the Atlantic, and so she was exactly the sort of American horse Richards needed to launch his experimental breeding program.[2]

Peytona's racing career began even before she was born. On May 19, 1838, an advertisement appeared in the *Spirit of the Times* proposing a "produce stake" race (a type designated as a "futurity" today) to be held at the Nashville course in the autumn of 1843 for four-year-old colts and fillies foaled in the spring of 1839. The challenge was issued by well-known Tennessee horseman and politician Bailie Peyton (1803–1878), and was allegedly born out of a card game in which the respective merits of two eminent stud horses were debated: Luzborough, owned by Peyton, and Glencoe, owned by James Jackson (1782–1840) of Alabama. During this game (at which neither Peyton nor Jackson were present), the participants proposed to settle the matter by a wager of $5,000 on a race between any of Luzborough's progeny against any one of Glencoe's. Jackson, on hearing of this, suggested that the match should instead be a national event, open to all. Jackson's entries would be offspring of Glencoe, an English Thoroughbred stallion he imported in 1836.[3]

The subscription fee was set at $5,000 per entry, equivalent to more than $200,000 today. Over the succeeding months thirty subscriptions were obtained, making the race stakes, at $150,000, the largest in the history of racing on either side of the Atlantic. The forthcoming race became a highly publicized international sensation, known as the "Peyton Stakes" and eagerly awaited. By post time on race day, October 10, 1843, the field of contestants was reduced to only four entries, two colts and two fillies. These last were a filly owned by Bailie Peyton, sired by Luzborough, and a filly from the Jackson stables sired by Glencoe. The stakes had accordingly been reduced to $35,000, but this still represented the wealthiest race ever held.[4]

James Jackson did not survive to witness the great event he had helped to promote. He passed away on August 17, 1840, and his great plantation, Forks of Cypress, along with his equine stock, were inherited by Thomas

Kirkman, his nephew and partner in the business. Peytona, a Glencoe filly, was foaled on February 28, 1839, at the Forks plantation, near Florence in northern Alabama. Her dam was Giantess, sired by Jackson's imported Leviathan. Like her mother, she was an exceptionally large mare, more than sixteen hands high, and to mark this she was given the rather unlovely name of Glumdalclitch, after the giantess in Swift's *Gulliver's Travels*. With her great height came a lengthy stride, said by some to be more than twenty-seven feet.[5]

The race on the Nashville track would be four miles in length, and the event would be run as four successive heats over that distance, the contestants allowed a brief period in which to recover between each heat. In the first two heats, the Glencoe filly finished near the end. In the opinion of those present, however, she had been handled with skill. With the third heat coming up, she seemed scarcely to have exerted herself. "She had cooled off beautifully," wrote the correspondent for the *Spirit of the Times*, "and was considered by some to be the only really dangerous nag in the race." The last two heats of the day were each won decisively by the Glencoe filly, who in each case came from behind in the home stretch, the jockey urging her to a "burst of speed which . . . defies description, and is almost beyond belief." The event went indisputably to Kirkman's entry, who thereafter would no longer be known as "the Glencoe filly" or even as Glumdalclitch, but instead was given the name Peytona to commemorate her victory at the Peyton Stakes.[6]

The Nashville race catapulted Peytona to national recognition, but true fame awaited her in 1845, when she was pitted, one on one, against Fashion, possibly the finest racing mare of the nineteenth century. This event, which took place at the Union Course in Queens, New York, was the culmination of a series of elite North-South competitions between the best horses of each region, the first of which was held in 1822. These intersectional matches were a natural development of interregional and interstate contests in which breeders challenged others from outside their own geographical area to determine who had the fastest horses.[7]

The North-South races were quite different from any type of sporting event held before, and they represented a significant transformation in American sport. They were true media events, highly publicized in advance, attended by crowds numbering in the tens of thousands, and on which wagers were placed in unprecedented sums. These were the first mass spectator sports in America, and for viewers the competing horses had been "elevated to the same acclaimed status later generations would reserve for football and baseball stars." Initially conducted in an atmosphere of friendly rivalry, as the century matured intersectional races became increasingly politicized and partisan, reflecting the sectional antagonism dividing the country over the issue of slavery. These contests between horses representing North and South "served as substitutes for real war, with rivals battling symbolically rather than with weapons and blood, [pitting] one American region against another, one way of life against another. Slave holders against slave opponents. Planters against industrialists. Each saw its side as superior and saw the race as a chance to emphasize that superiority." By the time of the last of the "great" North-South matches, that of Peytona versus Fashion in 1845, sectionalism, national economic instability, and a general decline in public support combined to bring this era of racing to an end.[8]

On race day at the Union Course, May 13, 1845, there was little indication that the era of major North-South racing events was drawing to a close. This was the fifth of the series of major intersectional matches, each of which had been run at Union Course, and the score between northern and southern horses was now tied at two apiece; this would be the tiebreaker. Attendance was estimated at between seventy thousand and one hundred thousand, a larger crowd than had ever before assembled for any occasion in the United States. Fashion, the northern representative in the race, was an eight-year-old satin-coated chestnut, bred by William Gibbons of New Jersey, and would be ridden by her usual jockey, Joseph Laird, the son of her trainer, Samuel Laird. Prior to her meeting with Peytona, she had won twenty-three out of twenty-four races, claiming a total winnings of $35,600. Peytona, two years younger, had run only four races since her victory in the Peyton Stakes at Nashville, but she was undefeated. To attend the race, Peytona traveled on foot from Mobile to Charleston, accompanied by four other potential contenders, and thence to New York, cheered by thousands along the route. The two mares would vie for a purse of $20,000.[9]

The day was fair, the track deep in dust. Commenting on the mood of the crowd, a correspondent for the *Charleston (S.C.) Courier* newspaper reported, “the feeling of the South against the North was aggravated to almost fury.” When Fashion was led out, she was made nervous by the tremendous noise and commotion, so that she “trembled . . . from head to foot,” whereas Peytona appeared unmoved by the din. Like the Peyton Stakes, this would consist of successive heats over a mile course, each heat being four laps around the track, for a total of four miles per heat. The winner would be the first horse to win two heats, with a third heat to be run if necessary. For the first race, Peytona promptly claimed a slight lead but was then edged by Fashion, the two horses running almost nose to nose until Peytona pulled away in the final stretch to win in the clear by a full length. After a cooling-off period of twenty minutes, the horses were led with difficulty through the dense crowds back to the starting position. The second heat began much as the first, Peytona taking the early lead with Fashion close beside her, but by the quarter-mile Fashion had pulled ahead. Well into the third mile, Fashion maintained her lead, and

Peytona and Fashion, pitted against each other in a match race at the Union Course in New York, May 13, 1845, and won by Peytona. Keene Richards acquired Peytona in 1853 to begin his breeding project. Lithograph published by N. Currier, New York, between 1835 and 1856. Library of Congress.

then was edged by Peytona once more. Head-to-head the mares ran the last mile, the lead shifting back and forth by mere degrees, until at last Peytona crossed the finish line just ahead of the northern mare, to claim victory amid the jubilant roar of her supporters.[10]

This contest ensured Peytona eternal fame in the annals of American racing, but, lamed in the event, her racing career was all but over. Peytona was pitted against Fashion again four days later at the Camden course in New Jersey, but she was unable to start and remained in the stable, allowing an easy win against Kirkman's substitute by Fashion, who merely trotted around the track over the last mile. Ten days later, on May 28, the two mares again contested at Camden, and in the first heat, after leading Fashion in three fast miles, Peytona collapsed during the final mile and was unable to finish the race. During the second heat of the match, Peytona proved unable to provide any real competition, so that Fashion's jockey, Laird, held her back so as not to unduly embarrass Palmer and the southern mare. Although Fashion and Peytona never again met on the track, Fashion continued her racing career until 1848. In her eleven years of competition, she won thirty-two of her thirty-six races and never finished less than second place. Peytona was retired from the track to Kirkman's Alabama plantation, producing a foal in 1850 after being bred to the imported stallion Ruby.[11]

Keene Richards's purchase of Peytona, like many of his equine acquisitions, was made on an impulse, a matter of being in the right place at the right time. He knew there could be no better mare to breed to his imported Arabians than this celebrated champion. She had the speed, no doubt about that; Arabian sires, he believed, would convey to her progeny the long-distance endurance that she lacked. In mid-October 1853, Richards was traveling by horseback through northwest Alabama on his way to Transylvania Plantation, in company with Oliver Kellam, Morris Keene, and the English journalist Thomas Gunn, whom he had invited to accompany them on their journey. On the morning of the 14th, the four men reached Florence, where they learned from the "town idlers" that Peytona was presently being exhibited in the community. Kirkman's three thousand-acre plantation, Forks of Cypress, was located just west of town. They set off to see the famous horse, who was being both "admired and criticized" by onlookers. After spending a little time examining Peytona, they pressed on, crossing a toll bridge over the Tennessee River and into Tuscumbria by four in the afternoon, where they checked into a rather miserable excuse for a hotel. On the following day, Saturday, Gunn recorded in his journal that "Keene Richards having conceived a desire to possess Peytona, resolved on riding back to treat with her owner about it. He was willing to pay $1500 for her." While his companions continued on, southwestward toward the Mississippi border, Richards rode back to Florence to make a deal for Peytona, promising to catch up with them later.[12]

Richards was able to negotiate terms of purchase for the mare with the owner's representative, agreeing to pay $2,000, but Kirkman was then in New Orleans and would have to be contacted to finalize the arrangement. Unfortunately, the Florence telegraph was out of order, and so, anxious and frustrated, Richards took to the road again and caught up with his friends before breakfast on Monday. (They had taken overnight lodgings at a roadside tavern in the swampland of eastern Mississippi.) Resuming their journey, the travelers reached Pontotoc, Mississippi, on Tuesday afternoon, October 18, and put up at another dirty, ramshackle hotel. On the following morning, while Gunn and Keene rode ahead, Richards was finally able to telegraph Kirkman and ratify the agreement. Eminently satisfied with his acquisition of such a first-rate mare, Richards's party continued, reaching Transylvania Plantation on October 28.[13]

Peytona's purchase was funded through the generosity of his grandfather, who continued to support his grandson's equine enterprise. Richards soon acquired five additional thoroughbred mares for his breeding program: Blonde, Sallie Hardin, Chloette, Dido, and a mare known only as the "Woodpecker mare." Frequently, when a mare was not raced but used only for breeding, the owner would not bother to bestow a name. Blonde, like Peytona a Glencoe filly, was perhaps the most notable of the group, a large chestnut mare foaled in 1850. Bred by James K. Duke of Scott County, Richards described her as "one of the best race nags of her day. She won a three-mile heat race at New Orleans in 1854, faster than it had ever been run before." The bay Sallie Hardin was an older mare, foaled in 1838, bred by Colonel William S. Buford of Woodford County, Kentucky, and sired by Bertrand. Two of the new mares, Chloette and Dido, were both sired by Grey Eagle during the 1840s.[14]

These new acquisitions were a clear indication of Richards's determination to select only superior blood, whether Arabian or Thoroughbred Running Horse, for his breeding program at Blue Grass Park. Each of the bloodlines—Glencoe, Grey Eagle, and Woodpecker—was through a leading sire; Grey Eagle was perhaps the most famous of the group. A striking silvery-gray stallion foaled in 1835, Grey Eagle was bred by Henry T. Duncan of Lexington and purchased as a yearling by Miles W. Dickey of Georgetown. He set a record for a two-mile heat at Louisville that spring, and a half-interest was subsequently acquired by Yelverton N. Oliver, owner of the Oakland course where this record was set. Later that year, Oliver arranged and promoted a match between Grey Eagle and Wagner, another champion horse, that proved to be one of the most exciting events of the racing season. In the autumn of 1836, Grey Eagle severely and permanently injured one of his feet in the fall races at Louisville, and was afterward retired to stud at Edward M. Blackburn's farm in Woodford County. "The feeling throughout Kentucky," equine historian Hervey wrote, "was that Grey Eagle was far and away the best thing ever seen there." Woodpecker, Grey Eagle's sire, was foaled in 1828 and owned and raced by Ralph B. Tarlton of Scott County, becoming, like his son, one of the most popular and successful studs in the Bluegrass.[15]

Richards did not possess any English Thoroughbred stallions until 1857 and 1858. His purchase of the elderly imported Glencoe in the summer of 1857 represented a prize of even greater potential than his acquisition of Glencoe's famous daughter Peytona, since Glencoe was one of the most successful sires of winning horses in America. Unfortunately, Glencoe, twenty-six years old and in poor health, died only three weeks after his purchase, bred only to a few of Richards's mares.[16]

In late summer of 1855, shortly before Richards's departure on his second horse-buying expedition to the Near East, the equine stock acquired for his breeding experiment consisted of the two Arabian stallions, Massoud and Mokhladi; the Arabian mare Sadah; Sadah's two-year-old colt Boherr (by Mokhladi), foaled at sea in 1853, and her filly Zahah (by Mokhladi), foaled in 1854; and the seven American thoroughbred mares. Thus far, from this stock, four living hybrid foals had been produced, all in 1855. Some writers, notably John H. Wallace, a leading American equine authority and a personal acquaintance of Richards, have claimed that the failure of his Anglo-Arab crosses to compete successfully prompted Rich-

(*Above*) Reel, a foundation mare owned by Louisiana turfman Thomas Jefferson Wells of Rapides Parish, was the dam of Lecomte and War Dance, the latter becoming an outstanding stud horse at Blue Grass Park after the war. Painted by Edward Troye in 1859. Photograph courtesy of Sotheby's, 2024.
(*Below*) Glencoe, one of the champion sires of the nineteenth century, acquired by Keene Richards in 1857. Painted by Edward Troye in 1861, a duplicate of the Glencoe portrait made at Georgetown in 1857. Courtesy of the Georgetown/Scott County Museum.

ards to return to the Near East to seek out better Arabian horses. Writing in 1897, Wallace, who apparently despised Arabian horses root and branch, asserted that when Richards's "half-breeds" were put to trial, they were soundly defeated by the American horses against which they were pitted: "Under these humiliating defeats a careful man would have hesitated before he went further, but he at once jumped to the conclusion that his defeat was not in the fact that Arab blood could not run fast enough to win, but in the fact, as he supposed, that the rascally Arabs had sold him blood that was not Arab blood. In a short time he was off for Arabia again."[17]

Wallace's chronology is grievously in error. At the time Richards set off again in 1855 to purchase more Arabians, he did not possess any Anglo-Arab crosses that were old enough to compete in any racing event. Both Boherr and Zahah were pureblooded Arabian, and even Richards acknowledged that pure Arabians were not competitive against Thoroughbred Running Horses. Although he purchased Peytona in autumn 1853 and subsequently bred her to Massoud, this likely would not have occurred before spring 1854, since the traditional season for breeding horses was from March to June. Mares, having an eleven-month average gestation period, were typically bred at this time so as not to deliver a foal during either the chill of winter or the heat of summer. The result of the Massoud-Peytona match, a filly named Transylvania, was foaled early in 1855. Not even a yearling, she would not have been eligible for racing. According to Richards's obituary in the *Kentucky Live Stock Record,* "it was not until 1856 that his colors, silver gray and white stripes, were seen on the turf."[18]

Keene Richards's published statements clearly indicate that he was planning a second trip back to the Near East immediately on return from his first expedition: "I commenced preparing to make another trip to the East, determined to spare no trouble or expense in procuring the best blood, as well as the finest formed horses in the Desert. For two years I made this subject my study, consulting the best authors as to where the purest blood was to be found, and comparing their views with my own experience. . . . After two years spent in close investigation as to the best means of obtaining the purest blood of the Desert, I matured my plans and started again for the East."[19]

Richards received further encouragement for a return trip abroad when he was invited by members of the Metairie Association of New Orleans to meet with the Texas horseman George A. Feris during race week in April 1855. Established in 1838, the Metairie course was the oldest and most fashionable track in the city. Under the management of Richard Ten Broeck, it had become the leading track in the nation. In 1851, Ten Broeck formed the Metairie Association, a joint stock company, and purchased the old track. He set about to turn Metairie into an operation of the first class, making extensive improvements to the course and greatly increasing the size of the purses offered, which encouraged many reputable horsemen from the upper South to bring their horses to compete. As a result, in short order New Orleans dominated the American racing scene, a situation that prevailed until the Civil War. As John Hervey observed, "The most important racing took place almost invariably at Metairie, [just as] the most important breeding had come to focus in the Bluegrass." In the future, Keene Richards would be a frequent visitor and competitor at Metairie.[20]

Hosting the meeting were some of the leading Thoroughbred Running Horse breeders of the South, most of whom were also shareholders in the Association: Abraham "Abe" Buford II and Willa Viley of Kentucky; Adam Bingaman and William J. "Jack" Minor of Mississippi; and Auguste Lecomte, Duncan F. Kenner, and Thomas J. Wells of Louisiana. In this distinguished company, twenty-eight-year-old Richards was clearly the novice horseman. He had not yet entered a horse in a race at any track in the nation. Richards's acquisition of the famous mare Peytona would be well known, and the arrival of his imported Arabians at the docks of New Orleans certainly would not have escaped the attention of these gentlemen. His grandfather, William B. Keene, was a respected businessman and a member of the Louisiana gentry, but whether his grandson was something more than a dilettante in the world of horse breeding and racing had yet to be proven.[21]

Conspicuous by his absence from this meeting was the Association's majority shareholder, Richard Ten Broeck. Relations between Ten Broeck and most of the other members had deteriorated into bitter hostility. The leader of the opposition was Thomas J. Wells, commonly known as "General" Wells, whose Dentley Plantation in Rapides Parish, near Alexandria, Louisiana, was the largest Thoroughbred Running Horse stud operation in the Deep South.

The antagonism between Ten Broeck and Wells appears to have been a product of both personality conflicts and a deep-seated resentment on the part of Wells. Richard Ten Broeck (1811–1892) was a northerner, the scion of a prosperous Dutch family from Albany, New York, who turned professional sportsman and gambler, spending the early part of his adult life on riverboats cruising the Mississippi. Ten Broeck has been described as "a man of medium height, with a slimly elegant figure always fastidiously garbed but without a trace of flash or swagger. In deportment he was cool, quiet, self-contained and bore himself like what in reality he was—a man of high breeding." He developed an interest in horse racing, and rose rapidly to prominence, during the winter of 1847–1848, taking over the management of both the Bingaman track in New Orleans and the Bascombe track in Mobile, where he became treasurer of the jockey club. At about the same time Ten Broeck acquired an interest in the Metairie operation, taking complete control a few years later to become virtually "the dictator of racing in New Orleans."[22]

This was an intolerable development for Wells, who, prior to the rise of Ten Broeck, was considered the premier magnate of the Louisiana turf. The loss of this leadership position was a considerable blow to his aristocratic pride, especially since, in his view, Richard Ten Broeck was "a mere adventurer, a northern interloper, and professional sporting man." By 1855, the group of influential horsemen who formed the Metairie Association to control racing in New Orleans had split into two hostile factions, the majority allied with General Wells against Ten Broeck; only Adam Bingaman remained on friendly terms. The bitter conflict between the two men was reflected and magnified by the competition on the Metairie track between two extraordinary horses: Wells's Lecomte and Ten Broeck's Lexington.[23]

These two horses were half-brothers, both sired by the champion horse Boston ("Old White Nose" to thousands of race fans), who won forty out of forty-five starts in his career and, at stud, produced many outstanding progeny in addition to Lecomte and Lexington. In 1847, aged fourteen, Boston was retired from the turf and sent by his owner, James Long of Virginia, to stand at the farm of Edward M. Blackburn in Woodford County, Kentucky, until his death on January 31, 1851.[24]

The Wells family, originally from New England, had been settled in central Louisiana for several generations and had accumulated great wealth and social prestige. Thomas J. Wells (1803–1863), one of three brothers, owned Dentley Plantation, located in the gently rolling hill country south of Alexandria in Rapides Parish. The primary business at Dentley was the training of Thoroughbred Running Horses, most of which Wells had purchased in Tennessee and Kentucky. Wells had attended Transylvania University in Lexington, Kentucky, and had many connections among the horse breeders in that state. Most of his brood mares were boarded on Kentucky farms belonging to his friends and associates and bred there, the foals sent down to Dentley after they had been weaned. On his Louisiana plantation, Wells constructed a mile-long oval track, used both for training his stock and as the scene of annual race meetings.[25]

The mare Reel was one of Wells's prized possessions, a Glencoe filly whose racing career, like her half-sister Peytona, was never marked by defeat until her last race, when she went lame. Wells purchased Reel, a rich chestnut mare, from her breeder, James Jackson of Alabama. After a string of victories, he sent her to Kentucky about 1845 to serve as a brood mare. She was bred to Boston in 1849 and produced an outstanding colt during the following year that Wells named Lecomte to honor his friend and fellow Louisiana turfman Auguste Lecomte. The colt was brought back to Louisiana to be trained at Dentley Plantation.[26]

Richard Ten Broeck was in Lexington, Kentucky, on May 27, 1853, attending a racing event called the Citizens' Stakes. Among the entries, which also included James K. Duke's Blonde, later purchased by Keene Richards, was a bay colt named Darley, owned by Dr. Elisha Warfield of Lexington. Warfield gave him this name in commemoration of the great English Thoroughbred progenitor, the Darley Arabian, whom he somewhat resembled although not descended through that line. Ten Broeck was apparently in Lexington looking to purchase a suitable horse to run in the forthcoming Great State Post Stake at Metairie next April, and was so impressed by the appearance of the colt Darley that with great difficulty he persuaded the doctor to sell him the colt for $2,500, on the condition that the two-year-old would be advertised as representing Kentucky in the field. Darley was a posthumous son of Boston, out of Warfield's mare Alice Carneal; Boston died in January 1851, and Darley was foaled less than two months later, on March 17. Ten Broeck immediately changed the name of the colt to Lexington, because "I desired him to be a distinctly American horse." The purchase of Lexington was made by a coalition of Ten Broeck with three prominent Bluegrass horsemen, Abe Buford, Willa Viley, and Junius R. Ward. Lexington was subsequently shipped south to Natchez to be trained on the farm of Adam Bingaman.[27]

The Great State Post Stake race, the winner taking two of three four-mile heats, was held at Metairie on April 1, 1854, on a muddy track. Horses from four states were entered, three of which were sired by Boston. Thomas J. Wells's Lecomte represented Louisiana, and for Kentucky, Ten Broeck's Lexington. Lexington won the first heat easily by three lengths, and the second by four, giving him the stakes victory. Although defeated, Lecomte had shown up well in the contest, and a rematch was scheduled to take place at Metairie on the next Saturday, the eighth of April. Willa Viley, one of Ten Broeck's Kentucky partners, was opposed to this, wanting to retire Lexington for the season; the two men argued violently about it, and in the end Ten Broeck bought out the interests of his partners to obtain sole ownership and control of Lexington. The result of the altercation was, of course, that another prominent horseman shifted to align with Thomas J. Wells against Ten Broeck.[28]

The day was fair and the track dry on April 8, and an entirely different course of events took place. In the first heat, Lecomte took the lead immediately, with Lexington trailing closely in a desperate struggle to close the gap. In the final mile, Lecomte pulled away to win easily by six lengths. The scene was reversed in the second heat, Lexington taking the lead for the first two miles, until, in the third mile, Lecomte caught and passed Lexington, the two battling around the course until at last Lecomte sped ahead to claim victory by four lengths. Keene Richards, recently returned to Louisiana from the East, may have been among those in attendance for the first two contests between Lexington and Lecomte.[29]

Each horse having claimed a victory, Ten Broeck immediately issued a challenge to Wells for a final and decisive match. Wells initially refused the rematch, but after months of antagonistic negotiations, the contest, in which Lexington and Lecomte were to be the only entries, was scheduled to be held at Metairie on April 14, 1855. At the start, "a spectacle never seen before was witnessed. The two contenders immediately began an attempt to run each other down at topmost speed—something unprecedented in a four-mile heat." Lexington took the lead from the first and sailed to victory, leaving Lecomte farther and farther behind, the Louisiana horse finishing in a state near to collapse. General Wells withdrew his horse from further participation, leaving the field to Ten Broeck and Lexington. This was the final race of Lexington's career, his only defeat being to Lecomte during the preceding spring.[30]

Richards was almost certainly in New Orleans this week to observe the highly publicized race, one of the great historic events of the American turf. While socializing with the other horsemen in attendance, he probably ran into Willa Viley, who, like Richards, was a resident of Scott County, Kentucky, and thus personally acquainted. Viley was probably responsible for arranging the meeting with Feris and members of the Metairie Association. The meeting must have been prior to the April 14 race between Lexington and Lecomte, because Wells was devasted by the loss and likely would not have been inclined to attend afterward. Even so, with the epic denouement about to take place, the General and his allies must have been under a state of extreme tension.[31]

George A. Feris was an old friend of the Keene family before he met Richards in New Orleans. A native Kentuckian, born in Lexington in 1813, he attended Georgetown College and subsequently earned a medical degree from Transylvania Medical College. Afterward, he practiced with his father, Maise A. Feris, at Georgetown until 1836, when he obtained a position as general surgeon in the U.S. Army. As physicians, both father and son would have been well known by William B. Keene. Although Richards had been a child when Feris left Georgetown, most likely Feris sought him out at Metairie because of the family connection.[32]

Feris requested this meeting because, like Richards, he strongly believed that America would benefit from the importation of Arabian horses to breed with native thoroughbreds. During the Mexican War, Feris was mounted on a stalwart Anglo-Arab steed, lost in February 1847 to a thrust of a lance during the battle of Buena Vista. "I knew how to appreciate the value of my lost comrade," the crusty Texas pioneer wrote many years later, "and conceived the idea of supplying my country with the same noble race." The two Arabian horse partisans, Richards and Feris, labored vainly to persuade the others of the great potential benefits to be gained. "All present except Richards and myself vigorously opposed the fresh importation of Arabians and cited English writers to prove the failure of oriental lines since the Godolphin and Darley era," Feris recalled. "We met this by showing that all importations of modern date (English) were mere commercial speculations and managed by unscrupulous men who knew [little] about horses." Although the immediate outcome of the meeting was unsatisfactory, both men now knew that, in the other, he had a friend and supporter who shared his views on Arabians. In later years, Feris kept a stable of Anglo-Arab horses on his ranch near Richmond, Texas, who were descendants of horses imported from the East by Keene Richards. One measure of the esteem that the Texan held for Richards was that in 1859 Feris named his newborn son Keene Richards Feris.[33]

Richards and Feris were certainly opposing conventional wisdom. John Lawrence and Admiral Henry J. Rous may have been among the English authorities cited by the Metairie Association members at this meeting, who asserted that, regardless of the role of Arabian blood in originally developing the English Thoroughbred horse, efforts to breed Arabians with Thoroughbreds in the present were doomed to produce second-rate animals. Lawrence stated, "The inferiority of the new blood, intending that of horses imported since the Godolphin Arabian, was becoming gradually more and more apparent. . . . in latter days it has become almost literally useless, since scarcely any breeder will send his mares to an Arabian." According to Rous, "The clearest proof of the improvement that has taken place in the English racehorse is the fact that no first or second cross from the imported Arab . . . is good enough to win a £50 plate in the present day."[34]

Richards came away from this meeting unshaken in his belief that reintroduction of Arabian blood into the lines of American thoroughbreds was both desirable and necessary to increase the stamina of racing animals, a perception that was doubtless heightened by the distress and near-collapse of Lecomte during the race. Despite their opposition to his Arabian importations, the Association members must have been quite impressed by the young man's knowledge of horseflesh, so that the meeting also served to cultivate his social connections among some of the most important turfmen in the South. Thomas J. Wells, recovering from his postrace depression, would become one of Richards's closest friends and a significant contact in the racing world. Likewise, Richard Ten Broeck, although absent from this meeting, would also become a close friend. Both men would, in the future, be of great service to Keene Richards.

The hostility between Ten Broeck and Wells and the other Association members only intensified in the aftermath of the great race, so that Ten Broeck's position as leader of the Metairie Association became increasingly untenable. On April 14, 1856, one year to the day after the final Lexington-Lecomte match, Ten Broeck sold his interest in the Metairie track to the other members. The Association was subsequently reorganized with General Wells at the head. Inexplicably, at about the same time, Wells sold Lecomte to Ten Broeck, along with another outstanding foal out of Reel, the filly Prioress. Shortly afterward, Ten Broeck departed the southland forever, taking most of his stable to race in England.[35]

By this time, Keene Richards had already made and returned from a second expedition to the East to purchase Arabian horses. On this occasion he was accompanied by his cousin Morris Keene, Yusef Badra, and a new friend—Edward Troye, the acclaimed painter of equine portraits.

8

RETURN TO THE EAST

Edward Troye (1808–1874) was one of the most talented animal painters of the nineteenth century. His specialty was horse portraits, and his services as an artist were in great demand by the horsemen of his day, so that Troye was able to capture the qualities of many of America's most celebrated racehorses, including American Eclipse, Boston, Henry, Grey Eagle, Lexington, Wagner, and Kentucky, among others. William T. Porter, who reproduced many of Troye's paintings between 1839 and 1843 as engravings in the pages of his two sporting magazines, *American Turf Register* and *Spirit of the Times,* wrote, "He is the only animal painter in this country who is thoroughly master of his art; and the felicity with which he hits off the precise color of the animal, is one of his most striking characteristics." Troye's biographer, Alexander Mackay-Smith, lauded the artist's talent, observing that he painted portraits "for which accuracy of color and conformation have never been surpassed, and whose lovely backgrounds entitle him high rank among landscape painters in general and among sporting painters in particular."[1]

Troye's artistic skills made him an ideal choice as a traveling companion on Keene Richards's second expedition to the Near East. Because of his substantial knowledge of equine anatomy, he was an authoritative judge of the horse, and so his advice would be invaluable when it came to selecting the best Arabian specimens. Since, in this early era, photography was a difficult undertaking, Troye's ability to execute accurate and detailed sketches on the spot, which could later be transformed into paintings, would be a useful skill. Although such practical considerations originally determined Troye's inclusion in the party, during the expedition Richards and Troye would become close friends.

Edward Troye, the accomplished animal portrait painter. Keene Richards was his principal patron, and Troye accompanied him to the Middle East in 1855. Photographed by William R. Phipps in Lexington, Kentucky, 1872. Courtesy of the National Sporting Library and Museum, Harry Worcester Smith Archive.

Edward Troye was born on July 12, 1808, near Lausanne, Switzerland. After the death of his mother, when Edward was but an infant, his father moved the family to London, England. As Troye grew up, he showed a considerable aptitude for drawing animals, and was an accomplished artist by the age of fifteen. At about the age of twenty, he determined to seek his fortune in the New World, and sailed for the West Indies, where he managed a sugar plantation on the island of Jamaica. Troye came to America in 1831, arriving at Philadelphia on October 5, where he took up residence for several years.[2]

His skills as a painter of animal portraits rapidly gained him considerable employment among the affluent horsemen of the east, and he traveled widely from one commission to the next. Since the focus of horse breeding and racing was moving westward, Troye began to travel farther afield—into the South and West—in search of patrons. He made a brief visit to the Bluegrass region of Kentucky during the fall of 1834, painting equine portraits for both Willa Viley and Ralph B. Tarlton of Scott County. Both men owned farms near Georgetown, where seven-year-old Keene Richards, recently orphaned, was growing up in the household of his grandparents, William and Hannah Keene.[3]

Troye returned to the Bluegrass during the summer of 1837, attending a meeting on August 3 at the Phoenix Hotel in Lexington. The purpose of the meeting was to engage Troye to produce a series of portraits of some of the outstanding horses and cattle of the region, to be published in a subscribed volume entitled *The Kentucky Stock Book.* Troye appears to have spent much of his time in Kentucky from 1837 to 1839 working on these portraits. Thirty-two lithographs are known to have been made from his paintings, mainly of cattle, but in consequence of a depressed national economy the book was never published.[4]

The time spent by Troye in the Bluegrass had some significant personal consequences. On July 16, 1839, Edward Troye married Cornelia Ann Vandegraff of Georgetown. The couple, both Presbyterians, apparently first met at the Bethel Presbyterian Church, since the Vandegraffs had no association with pedigreed livestock that might have led to contact through his artistic services. At the time, both of Cornelia's parents were deceased, and she lived in the old family home in southern Scott County near the Fayette line with her sister and brother-in-law. The ceremony was performed in the Vandegraff home, where afterward the new couple set up housekeeping. Troye made some effort to farm the relatively small acreage inherited by his wife from her father, but continued to travel about the Southeast, painting racehorses for wealthy patrons.[5]

In 1845, the Troyes sold their Scott County farm and moved to McCracken County in far western Kentucky, purchasing a large tract of land there. Troye, for the time being, gave up his artistic career and devoted his efforts to becoming a full-time farmer. No known portraits were produced by Troye during the years 1846 through 1849. He did not long persist as a farmer, selling the property in the late summer of 1847. His movements during the next two years are uncertain, but in September 1849 Troye accepted a position at Spring Hill College near Mobile, Alabama, where he taught drawing and French. He remained at Spring Hill for the next six years, resigning his appointment in 1855 when persuaded by Keene Richards to accompany him on a journey to the Near East.[6]

Richards first became acquainted with Troye in 1854, meeting him while the artist "was painting some portraits at Lexington." Certainly Troye, as a foreigner and celebrity artist, must have been well known by the Georgetown community, since the Vandegraff farm where he and his wife lived from 1839 to 1845 was little more than a mile from town. The Keene family would have known of Troye even if they never actually met the man. As Richards grew into maturity and developed an interest in racehorses, and certainly on his return from the East and increasing socialization with other horsemen such as Willa Viley, he could not but have been aware of the reputation of the artist as an accomplished painter of equine portraits.[7]

On June 15, 1854, at the end of the school term at Spring Hill, Troye left Mobile and traveled north to Kentucky to spend the summer, probably accompanied by his wife, who would be looking forward to visiting her sister in Scott County. It was during these summer months that Troye became acquainted with Richards, who became not only a friend but his most important patron, and acquired another long-term patron, Robert Alexander of Woodford County, Kentucky. Alexander had not yet begun to assemble the premium equine bloodstock for which he became well known in racing circles, but he commissioned Troye to produce a series of portraits of his pedigreed Shorthorn cattle. Later, when Alexander was a noted horse breeder, he and Keene Richards would become intimate friends, "ever ready to assist one another," and both would provide considerable support for Edward Troye.[8]

Richards, having returned from his Eastern expedition with two elegant Arabian stallions, was eager to have their qualities captured on canvas. Troye's 1854 oil on canvas portraits of Massoud and Mokhladi must be considered among his finest work. The portrait of Massoud, or as he was once known to Yusef Badra, Syed Sulimen, shows the colorfully dressed Yusef standing beside his beloved charge. The details of this painting have

Alexander Keene Richards in Arab garb with his imported Arabian stallion Mokhladi. Painted in 1854 by Edward Troye at Georgetown, Kentucky. Private collection.

been previously described. The second portrait was of the gray stallion Mokhladi, accompanied by Keene Richards dressed in a complete Arab costume, holding the bridle in his right hand and a spear, butt on the ground, in his left. Although painted at Blue Grass Park in Kentucky, the background is a desert landscape; in the far distance, Troye placed a dimly seen walled fort or city and some palm trees. Troye appears also to have made a portrait of Peytona at this time, whom he had previously painted in 1844, although the present whereabouts of the painting are unknown.[9]

Having completed these Kentucky paintings, Troye returned to Spring Hill College in Mobile for the beginning of the fall term. By the following spring, 1855, Richards, "having matured my plans," was ready once again to depart for the East on a horse-buying expedition. This was to be no Grand Tour, but primarily a business trip. During the previous two years, in preparation for this trip, Richards read extensively about Arabian horses. He found that "most authors who have written on the subject differ materially as to facts, and that those who have seen the Arab on his native soil, knew more about the idle legends of the country than about the fine points of a horse."[10]

In Richards's opinion, the only English writer with reliable knowledge of Arabian horses was archaeologist Austen H. Layard. Layard spent 1845–1847 excavating the Assyrian ruins of Nimrud on the Tigris River, and returned to the East in 1849 to carry out excavations of Babylon and the mounds of southern Mesopotamia, being thus engaged at the time of Richards's first visit to the region. A keen observer and entertaining travel writer, he praised the beauty and endurance of the Arabian horses he had seen, noting that "the most esteemed breeds" were to be found away from the coastal regions, among the Mesopotamian tribes and the great plains watered by the Tigris and Euphrates, and hence not available to western buyers. This was also the conclusion drawn by Keene Richards from his research. Explaining the rationale behind his Arabian importations in an 1857 pamphlet, Richards proposed that Anglo-Arab crosses made since the days of the Godolphin and Darley Arabian had failed simply because so few true Arabian horses had been imported to England. He concluded that most of the so-called Arabians had been purchased "on the coast of Syria, in Egypt, and some from India." Richards must have winced inwardly as he penned these words, for on his first trip to the East, in his naiveté and enthusiasm, he had made just this same error. His trip among the Anizah tribes had been a failure, since he had been unable to purchase a horse directly from the Bedouins of the desert. Instead, he had acquired Mokhladi in Jerusalem; purchased Massoud from his guide, Yusef; and obtained Sadah in Beirut. Magnificent animals all, to be sure, but he had no proof other than the word of their sellers that they were truly purebred specimens. Richards was determined that, this time, he would acquire horses of the purest Arabian pedigree from among the Bedouins.[11]

Yusef would accompany him as guide and interpreter, for the Syrian had proved both reliable and a good comrade. His cousin Morris Keene was an agreeable fellow and knowledgeable horseman, close to the same age as Richards, and would doubtless make a good travel companion. For the fourth member of the party, none other would do but Edward Troye, whose expert knowledge of horses would complement his own. Troye's participation may have been arranged well in advance; Richards could have approached him on the subject during the summer of 1854 while Troye was at Blue Grass Park, producing the portraits of Massoud and Mokhladi. Alternatively, Richards may have visited Troye at Mobile in late March or early April 1855 when he traveled to New Orleans for the Lexington-Lecomte match. More than likely, Troye was himself present at Metairie for this race, since no one with any interest in fast horses would have missed it for anything, particularly when living so close as Mobile.

Even though he would have to give up his position at Spring Hill, Troye required little persuasion by Richards as he, too, was devoutly religious. An opportunity to visit some of the sacred biblical scenes of the Holy Land with Richards as his sponsor was not to be passed up. What a grand adventure this would be, to journey to the exotic lands of the East, to venture into the desert wilds where few westerners had ever been! Troye would have the chance to paint some of the most beautiful horses in the world, in their native settings, and perhaps to enhance his reputation as an artist by portraying biblical scenery.

Troye's modern biographer, Alexander Mackay-Smith, assumed that Troye departed Mobile on June 15, 1855, at the end of the college term, and traveled to Kentucky, where he painted a portrait of Lexington, a commission he had obtained from Richard Ten Broeck after the great race at Metairie in April. Lexington was then standing at stud in Kentucky on the farm of William F. "Frank" Harper, in Midway, sent there immediately after the race with Lecomte. After executing this portrait, according to Mackay-Smith, Troye then left for England. This chronology is highly unlikely, since Troye's passport application is stamped, dated, and notarized June 26, 1855, placing him, "duly sworn," in the notary's office at City Hall in New York on that date. If Troye had left Spring Hill College on June 15, he would barely have had sufficient time to reach New York by this date, let alone make a side trip to Kentucky to paint a portrait of Lexington.[12]

There are more plausible interpretations of the events involved in Troye's departure for the East. Either Troye left Spring Hill prior to the end of the college term, or the portrait of Lexington was not made on site in Kentucky. The latter seems more likely. Troye had the portrait of Lexington with him when he arrived in London, in July, from which a limited-edition hand-colored aquatint rendition was engraved and published in December 1855 by Lloyd Brothers. Troye typically rendered a preliminary sketch of his subject before he began painting, and so may have made some drawings of Lexington during April while the horse was still at New Orleans. He could then have worked on the portrait in Mobile, or taken the Lexington painting, still in an unfinished condition, to England to be completed there. Richard Ten Broeck was still in the United States when Troye left the country; if the Lexington portrait had been completed, most likely Troye would have delivered the painting to him. Whatever the actual chronology, Troye could not have left Mobile on June 15, gone to Kentucky and there painted Lexington, and then traveled to New York, all in the space of ten or eleven days.

Troye resigned from Spring Hill and traveled to New York, probably by steamship, and from there sailed to England, reaching London sometime in mid-July. There he joined Keene Richards, Morris Keene, and Yusef Badra, who voyaged together across the Atlantic on an earlier ship. Keene's passport application is dated at Washington on April 24, 1855, two months earlier than Troye, and was witnessed by John Ross Browne, the very same man who employed Badra in 1851 as a guide in the Holy Land. In 1853, soon after returning from the East, Browne was appointed by the U.S. Treasury Department as a custom house inspector. Browne remained in contact with Badra, and, having completed his tour of custom houses, returned to Washington, D.C., to spend some time with his family before moving to California and his next assignment as inspector to the Indian Agencies of the Pacific coast. Browne was thus on hand to vouch for Morris Keene and to wish a safe voyage to Badra, his old friend and former guide. Little did either suspect that they would never meet again.[13]

Once the Americans rendezvoused with Troye in England, Richards's initial European itinerary did not differ greatly from that followed in 1851, save that his attention was now more focused on Arabian horses imported to the Continent. "We traveled through England and France expressly to examine and compare the horses of those two countries," his cousin Morris Keene recalled. "We saw no Arabs in England that we considered Thoroughbred," meaning pureblooded, "and but two in France. These belonged to the Emperor [Napoleon III]." They viewed many horses alleged to be Arabian, but closer investigation revealed these to be mixtures of the various Oriental types. Because the goal of this expedition was to purchase horses from the desert Arabs, Richards would have brought ample gold coin for this purpose.[14]

Troye kept a detailed journal of his experiences on the expedition, and while direct references to his companions are infrequent, the record indicates that the activities of Richards's party in Europe involved far more than just equine inspections. In September 1855, they arrived in Paris, which at the time was hosting the Exposition Universelle, the second international world's fair. Just days previously, Queen Victoria had returned home from a nine-day state visit to the emperor, and the streets of the capital city were still decorated with the colors and symbols of the two nations hung together. Troye, who visited "most of the public exhibitions," was, of course, particularly interested in art and architecture, and in his opinion the fine arts exhibition was "truly beautiful, containing the works of many artists of every school." The travelers also made time to visit some of the magnificent cathedrals for which Europe is noted; those at Rouen, north of Paris, Troye found particularly impressive. From Paris, they journeyed south to Lyon, and then to Marseilles, where on September 2 they boarded a steamer bound for Constantinople.[15]

Troye noted that at Paris and Lyon they encountered many wounded soldiers from the Crimea, and that the eastbound steamer was, "like all steamers to that point, crowded to overflowing with soldiers, and their officers" headed for the war zone. The officers, he wrote, were generally well behaved and well informed on the political and military situation then prevailing. Most of the soldiers, in contrast, "were beardless men some not above eighteen," who had been drafted. In early 1853, when Keene Richards and his companions were returning home from his first trip to the East, the opening moves of the Crimean War had already begun. One of the bloodiest wars of the nineteenth century, the inaptly named Crimean War (1853–1856), which neither began nor ended in the Crimea, would reshape the balance of power in Europe. During this war, Britain and France were allied with the Ottoman empire against Russia. From the carnage, France would emerge as the strongest military force in Europe, while Britain maintained its rule of the world's oceans. The Ottoman empire achieved a long-sought goal, being recognized as a member of equal standing with the other European states, its territorial integrity guaranteed by the Great Powers. For Russia, the outcome was less advantageous; greatly weakened, the empire of the tsars was forced to retreat from Central Europe for nearly a century afterward.[16]

The root of the conflict lay in what was termed the "Eastern Question," the longstanding international problems resulting from the decline of the Ottoman empire and its perceived imminent collapse. As the Turkish empire's weakness became apparent through a series of wars with Russia during the eighteenth century, the Great Powers of Europe engaged in a struggle to protect their various commercial, military, and strategic interests in the Ottoman domains. Britain, Austria, and France sought to preserve the integrity of the Ottoman empire and hence the existing, if fragile, balance of power. Expansionist Russia, however, stood to benefit from the empire's collapse, being primarily concerned with control of the Black Sea and access to the Mediterranean through the Turkish-held Bosphorus and Dardanelles straits. Early in July 1853, Russian troops invaded Ottoman territory, crossing the Prut River into the Danubian Principalities of Moldavia and Wallachia (present-day Romania in the Balkans). On March 28, 1854, after Russia ignored a joint ultimatum to withdraw from Ottoman territory, Britain and France, allied with Turkey, formally declared war. In September 1854, Allied troops landed on the Crimean Peninsula and, after a series of savage land battles, at Alma, Inkerman, and Balaklava, began to lay siege to the city of Sevastopol, home to Russia's Black Sea Fleet and the potential launch point for operations into the Mediterranean.[17]

The Russians scuttled their fleet in the harbor to block access and added the naval guns to the city defenses. The siege, consisting primarily of murderous exchanges of artillery fire, would last for a year, interrupted only by the harsh conditions of the winter of 1854–1855. The most severe bombardment of the campaign commenced on September 5; more than three hundred Allied cannon fired 150,000 shells, resulting in nearly two thousand Russian casualties daily. Three days later, as Keene Richards and his companions were steaming through the Mediterranean on their way to Constantinople, the Allies launched an all-out assault involving sixty thousand troops against the Russian defenses. By the morning of September 9, Russian forces had moved across the harbor and abandoned the southern side of the city, destroying the defensive works in their retreat. The victorious Allied troops moved in and occupied the city.[18]

The ship carrying Keene Richards and his three companions took eight days to make the voyage from Marseilles to Constantinople, steaming along the coasts of Corsica, Sardinia, and Italy and into the Ionian Sea. Despite the crowding, as passengers of some importance they had a relatively pleasant voyage, taking their meals with the French officers in the dining cabin. Yusef Badra, having the status of a servant, most likely would not have been welcomed at the table. The meals were served "table d'hôte" (literally, "host's table"), passengers ordering a complete meal for a specific price, which was served to them by a ship's steward. At the beginning of the voyage, the two young Americans' unfamiliarity with the dining customs offended the French officers' rather strict sense of etiquette.[19]

Rather than wait for service, one of the Americans (probably Morris Keene) began to help himself to the food he saw on the table. The officer seated directly across the table made some rather pointed and insulting observations about this breach of manners in his native language. Neither Richards nor Keene was conversant in French, but the disdainful tone of the comments clearly transcended all language barriers. Greatly annoyed, the American, who was then holding a loaf of bread in his hand, vigorously whacked the contemptuous Frenchman across the face with the loaf. The outraged officer returned the favor, and for a moment considerable confusion reigned as a food fight began, "much to the astonishment of some, and the merriment of others." Troye, sitting next to the American combatant and across from the French officer and thus in the line of fire, was thankful that "the missals of warfare was not of a more dangerous character such as knives, forks plates bottles etc." When order was restored, the offended parties agreed to settle the affair after dinner. The French officers were incensed, believing that any insult offered to one of their own was an insult to all. Fortunately, Troye, fluent in French, acted as peacemaker and managed to reconcile the two sides.[20]

Passing between the Peloponnesian Peninsula and the island of Crete, the steamer anchored just offshore from Athens. Using a telescope, Troye and his friends spent several pleasant hours viewing the historic coastline. On the next day, the steamer continued northeast through the Aegean Sea and in the late afternoon entered the Dardanelles, the long strait that, together with the Bosphorus, separates Europe from Asia and connects the Black Sea to the Mediterranean. The steamer anchored at Gallipoli, a small city of about thirty thousand inhabitants that was busy with ships arriving from and departing for the war zone. Here the party disembarked for a few hours to stretch their legs and observe the hustle and bustle, becoming so absorbed in the sights that they had to hurry back to board their ship before it departed. Their steamer continued through the Sea of Marmara to the Bosphorus and at last, on Monday, September 10, came to fabled Constantinople, passing into the bay known as the Golden Horn that divides the city to dock at the custom house wharf at Galata on the north side.[21]

As soon as they set foot on the wharf, they were beset by a noisy group of porters who clamored for the privilege of carrying their luggage up the hill to their hotel, arguing among themselves almost to the point of combat. One man seized two heavy trunks belonging to Troye which, the porter declared, he would not give up his right to even at the expense of his own blood. Fortunately, Yusef Badra, who spoke Turkish, was on hand to sort out the unruly porters and deal with the Turkish customs officers. Soon the heavily loaded porters, bent almost double by the luggage on their backs, followed by Richards and his companions, began a procession through the crowded cobblestone streets of Galata and up the hill to the Hotel d'Angleterre, about three-quarters of a mile from the landing.[22]

It was September 10, and Sevastopol had fallen to Allied forces the day before their arrival. The city had been celebrating ever since the arrival of the news. Lady Emilia B. Hornby, who arrived at Constantinople by steamer on September 8, described the "gay and beautiful spectacle" as viewed from the roof of her hotel on that Monday: "All the ships-of-war and crowds of merchant vessels of all nations were decked with flags, and many large and splendid ones floated from the principal balconies. The roar of guns from the different vessels was tremendous." Not all the citizens of Constantinople were delighted by the news. Tsar Nicholas was the titular head of the Orthodox church, and so the Greeks of the city had hoped for Russian success; "hating their masters the Turks, would have loved to see them, and their friends the Allies, humiliated." Since Lady Hornby was staying at the Hotel d'Angleterre at the same time as Richards, it is possible that he or one of his party made her acquaintance.[23]

Established in 1841, the Hotel d'Angleterre was located on rising ground on the Grand Rue de Pera, the central avenue, sixty feet wide and more than a mile long, through the European enclave of Pera. This was a region where, since the Byzantine era, peoples from many nations mingled. The most westernized section of Constantinople, its appearance was quite different from the old city on the south side of the Golden Horn, where the skyline is shaped by the minarets of many mosques. Upper Pera, on the hill, contained European embassies, hotels, and the residences of mission officials, bankers, merchants, shopkeepers and their families, a total population of about thirty thousand persons. During the Crimean War, the district also housed a substantial population of British and French officers and their families. The back of the Hotel d'Angleterre was across from the British embassy, and nearby were the embassies of Russia, Austria, Prussia, France, and Sweden. Galata, the lower and older section of Pera, was the business district, which contained most of the European shops, cafes, restaurants, and places of entertainment.[24]

The hotel was filled to capacity during Richards's stay, mainly with military personnel. In a letter written to her husband shortly after arriving at the hotel, Lady Hornby described the conditions at d'Angleterre on September 10: "The hotel is crowded—not even a sofa to be got; the large hall is almost filled with the baggage of officers coming and going, and constantly resounds with the clinking of spurs and the clank of swords upon the stone pavement." Keene Richards, while not averse to "roughing it," had substantial financial resources and was probably able to obtain a comfortable set of rooms for himself and his companions. Walter Thornbury, a guest at the d'Angleterre in 1859, rather spitefully described his accommodations: "It was a gaunt, bareboned-looking room, its floor a skeleton of bare planks, unclothed with carpet, for the sake of coolness; it contains a wiry-looking bed, looking like the first sketch of a gigantic birdcage. . . . For furniture, a bad sofa that resembled a sarcophagus, a rickety washstand, and a chest of drawers that served for toilet-table." Thornbury despised the Ottoman empire in general, and the hotel and its proprietor specifically.[25]

Richards and his companions remained in Constantinople for ten days, combining business and pleasure. Like many visitors, Troye was interested in both Islamic culture and the magnificent architecture of the city, and so paid a visit to the Achmed Mosque, considered by many visitors to be the most beautiful mosque in Constantinople. For those not of the faith, a *firman,* or permit issued by the sultan, was required to enter any of the mosques of the city. These were not particularly difficult to obtain by the mid-nineteenth century, although earlier in the century visitors were discouraged. Generally, the Porte, or civil government of Constantinople, was issued a number of blank *firmans,* which were then distributed to the foreign embassies. Upon application to the consular staff and payment of a modest fee, these were provided to visitors who wished to visit the mosques.[26]

The dragomen of the Pera district usually also had a supply on hand, which they would sell to tourists at an inflated price. The 1859 English guest Walter Thornbury complained of the unscrupulous practices involved in the selling of these permits: "At Misseri's [d'Angleterre] the firman is the perpetual subject of intrigue, mystery, and cheating, among the motley polyglotic tribe of couriers, interpreters, guides, and waiters. . . . They beleaguer the new arrivals with stories of the enormous trouble and expense requisite to obtain firmans." Thornbury noted that dragomen might charge a large group as much as a guinea apiece, whereas an Englishman could obtain a *firman* easily from his own consul for a few shillings. There was no limit to the number of people who could be listed on a single *firman,* and once issued, the permit was valid for an indefinite period and would admit the bearers to any mosque in Constantinople. For this reason, tourists tended to visit the attractions in groups consisting of those who had purchased a particular *firman.*[27]

Troye was accompanied on some of his perambulations around the city by a new friend, a French lawyer he met on the steamer from Marseilles who had attached himself to the Richards party for the length of their stay in Constantinople. "We found him a valuable acquisition," Troye wrote, "as he afforded a store of fun." The other members of the American coterie took some time to play tourist, but Keene Richards, true to his nature, bought a horse while in the city—an Arabian, of course.[28]

He must have been struck by the irony of the situation as he paid the owner, since he had come to the East this time determined to buy horses only from the desert Bedouins, to ensure acquiring pureblooded Arabians. This lovely white mare, however, was one he could not resist despite his resolve to avoid purchasing horses in the coastal cities. At least he had some confidence as to the Arabian pedigree of the mare, being provided with a certificate in which the purity of her blood had been attested to by the American vice consul at Aleppo. When Henry Wood, the American consul at Beirut, saw this mare a few weeks later, he, too, was captivated by her beauty: "When I cast my eyes upon this child of the Desert, her thin mane lying upon her neck like ringlets of silk, her clean limbs made up of nothing but bone and sinew, her wide nostrils indicating the fires which slept within, while her soft, clear, and benignant eyes beamed with an intelligence and gentleness, almost human, I could not fail to unite in my friend's admiration. The gazelle itself seemed hardly lighter or swifter." The former owner had spent $1,000 to acquire this mare. Keene Richards was so determined to have her, "so struck . . . with the animal's graceful form and marks of fleetness," that without hesitation he offered him a great deal more. Her name was Lulie.[29]

Lovely Lulie was doubtless left in the care of Yusef Badra when Richards and the others, accompanied by Troye's new friend, the French lawyer, boarded a steamer at Constantinople on September 19 bound for the battlefields of Sevastopol. Ten days beforehand, as the besieged city fell to the Allied troops after some of the fiercest fighting of the war, Russian forces retreated over floating bridges across the harbor to occupy the heights and fortifications north of the city. Neither side, however, was eager to resume combat. From time to time the Russians lobbed a few artillery shells at the city to keep the new occupants from becoming too comfortable.[30]

The Americans' voyage into the war zone was far less comfortable than their previous cruise from Marseilles to Constantinople. The steamer was smaller and crowded with French and Turkish soldiers en route to the Crimea. Shortly after the ship left the Bosphorus and entered the Black Sea, the weather became very rough, and most of the passengers, including Troye, were miserably seasick. Troye wrote: "The cabin we occupied was crowded in the same way as the decks everything had to be closed in order to exclude the sea which made it so unsufferable even to suffocation. I endeavored to go out to breathe some fresh air, but as soon as I put my head out I was met with a heavy sea and saw the deplorable condition of those on deck. I was forced to the alternative of returning to the suffocating as well as sickening smell of the cabin." The travelers arrived at Balaklava, about six miles south of Sevastopol, after suffering from nearly continuous seasickness for the day and a half required to transit the three hundred miles from Constantinople. Balaklava, which had a small but adequate harbor, served as staging point and supply depot for siege operations. The harbor at Sevastopol was filled with sunken hulks of the Russian fleet, scuttled at the beginning of the siege to deny access to the Allies. Richards and his friends had only a short time to visit the battlegrounds and satisfy their curiosity, since their ship was scheduled to depart again for Constantinople on the third day.[31]

The city of Sevastopol lay in ruins. Thousands of explosive shells had rained down on the city during the bombardments of the last year. As the Russians began to evacuate on September 9, they set charges to destroy the forts and magazines in the city. Allied observers watched from the hills and redoubts as fire spread throughout the city until all within the walls was ablaze. Although the fires did not deter hordes of looters, Allied troops were prevented from occupying the city in force until September 11, after torrential rains had extinguished the raging flames.[32]

The land before the city walls was a complex maze of trenches, in zigzags and parallels, though which the besiegers had dug their way ever closer. As the victorious Allies entered the city, they came across scenes of horror: bodies piled in the trenches and behind the walls in heaps. William H. Russell, a correspondent for the *Times* during the final days of the siege and subsequent occupation of Sevastopol, was with the troops entering the city, and his dispatches provided graphic detail for London readers. On September 12, he wrote: "Inside the sight is too terrible to dwell upon. The French are carrying away their own and the Russian wounded, and there are four distinct piles of dead formed to clear the way. The ground is marked by pools of blood, and the smell is already noisome; swarms of flies settle on dead and dying; broken muskets, torn clothes, caps, shakos, swords, bayonets, bags of bread, canteens, and haversacks, are lying in indescribable confusion all over the place, mingled with heaps of shot, of grape, bits of shell, cartridges, case and canister, loose powder, official papers, and cooking tins." During the remainder of September, the Allied occupiers prepared to settle into winter camps outside the city, clearing debris and building roads, and emplacing mortars and artillery capable of threatening the Russian positions north of the harbor. The capable Royal Engineers of the British army methodically began demolishing the infrastructure of Sevastopol, blowing up anything that could be of future military value to the Russians that had not already been destroyed during the siege.[33]

When Richards, Keene, and Troye arrived at the Sevastopol battleground on September 21, there was little activity save for an occasional exchange of shells between Russian and Allied forces. There was no imminent threat of attack from the Russians across the harbor, nor were the Allies preparing for a major offensive against their positions. Although much of the mess had been cleaned up by the time Richards and his friends visited Sevastopol, sufficient remained to provide a grim picture of the savage conflict that had taken place. Troye, whose journal entries tended to be rambling at best, was evidently so upset by what he saw as to be even less coherent than usual. Making a few attempts to describe the disaster, he gave up, saying, "I shall leave this part of the picture for the imagination to fill up." Before leaving Sevastopol, the Richards party received a pointed reminder that battlefields could be hazardous for the tourist. The sporadic bombardment of the city by the Russians might appear casual, but it was aimed, and harm was intended. "Visitors to the exterior works continue to be occasionally pretty numerous," *Times* correspondent Russell wrote a few weeks after Richards's visit. "Fewer persons go into the town, the fire, which sometimes is really heavy, rendering a visit unpleasant." One of the three men in the Richards's party, not named, had "a hairbreadth escape from a cannon ball, which came whizzing by his head as he was imprudently gratifying his curiosity in seeing the operations of the siege."[34]

Sobered by their experiences, the three Americans left the Crimea on September 24 to return to Constantinople and a world where the very air did not reek of death. For months afterward, the de facto armistice at Sevastopol continued, the Russians and the Allies staring across the harbor at one another as peace discussions were initiated in Paris. The Treaty of Paris, signed on March 30, 1856, put an end to the Crimean War. By its terms, the borders and security of the Ottoman empire were guaranteed against Russian expansionism, and the Black Sea was open to all nations for trade.

Keene Richards and his companions rejoined Badra and the Arabian mare left in his care at Constantinople and almost immediately took a ship for Beirut, arriving there on October 1. Richards scarcely had time to begin renewing his contacts in the city when tragedy struck their little company. Yusef Badra, that colorful and garrulous Destroyer of Robbers, was dead. Upon their arrival in the city, as Badra's presence became known, his friends and relatives were jubilant at his return and began to make immediate preparations for a great feast in his honor on that very night. The occasion, attended by his American friends, was a great success, and Badra went to his bed that night fully expecting to begin in the morning making the necessary arrangements for an expedition into the desert lands. This was not to be, for he was stricken by an attack of colic during the night and did not live to see the sun rise. The loss was a severe blow to Richards. From all evidence, Yusef was more than just an employee; he was a trusted companion. Richards made certain that his friend received a proper funeral, for which he paid all expenses, and erected a "handsome and expensive monument over his remains" in the Maronite Christian cemetery in Beirut, located in the Sodeco section near the center of the city and known as the Cimetière Maronite de Ras el-Nabeh.[35]

The death of Badra forced Richards to revise his plans for the expedition. He had counted on Badra to provide the same valuable services as in 1852, that of guide, expediter, and interpreter. Furthermore, he had trusted Badra, as the man who "knew more about horses than any one I had met in the East," to care for the stock he purchased. In consequence, Morris Keene was given the challenging task of learning the Arabic language, "as we could find no one to trust in interpreting, to carry out our plans among the Bedouins." Funeral arrangements completed, Richards traveled to Baalbek, a town about forty miles northeast known for its monumental and well-preserved Roman temple ruins, where he had heard of "a horse of admirable beauty, owned by the sheikh, or governor of the village." Troye, temporarily left behind in Beirut, occupied himself in creating a portrait of Lulie, painted at night "in two sittings of two hours each, partly by candlelight" on October 13. This portrait was stolen in 1976 from the Richards's descendants while on public exhibition. Lulie's ears were depicted as laid back, indicating that she was probably irritated at being awakened in the night to pose for the artist.[36]

Richards's trip to Baalbek was in vain. The American consul, Henry Wood, who later wrote a long letter to the *New York Journal of Commerce* describing the adventures of Richards's party during 1855–1856, reported on the outcome: "So suspicious was the Sheikh, and so resolved on keeping for his own uses only the noble animal on which he so much prided himself, and which brought him so much renown, that he ordered him to be shut up in his stable, not allowing the American to see him or even approach him. Whenever the horse was mentioned, the Sheikh at once turned aside the conversation, inquiring for the news, or else talking politics." Learning that the horse belonged to the former sheikh of the village, deposed and now residing in Damascus, the frustrated Richards, who was determined to possess the horse, returned to Beirut. With Troye and Keene, he traveled on to Damascus. He obtained an interview with the sheikh, but during preliminary courtesies he gained the impression that his proposal had no chance, and so he never raised the question.[37]

The Americans soon relocated to a comfortable house in Damascus in late October that could be used as a headquarters for expeditions into the desert and which Troye could occupy as a studio for his painting. Shortly after arriving in Damascus, Richards learned that Sheikh Medjuel, the Mezrab Bedouin who had, in 1852, provided him and Yusef Badra with an escort to Palmyra in search of horses to purchase, was now living in the city with his new wife, Jane Digby, who now called herself Jane Digby el Mezrab. Married on March 27, 1855, the couple resided in a large, new house, whose design and construction was overseen by Jane. Pleased to renew this acquaintance, Richards and Troye paid a call on the newlywed couple in late October. On the 24th, Jane noted this visit in her diary: "Two other American gentlemen called. One the artist Edward Troyes. I felt pleased at being able to speak of subjects that interest me, and still more at the manner of one of them [Richards] to the Sheikh, and his praise of him which was so well deserved." Construction of Jane's house was nearly complete at this time. It was in a garden outside the city wall, built on three sides around a large central court. Their residence came to be considered one of the most remarkable houses in Damascus.[38]

At about this time, Troye began work on the first of his five so-called "Oriental" oil paintings, a depiction of one of the bazaars in the city located at the entrance to the Great Mosque. The *Bazaar in Damascus* depicts the mare Lulie in the center, ridden by an Albanian officer. All his onsite work in the Near East would, later in his brother's Belgian studio, be rendered much larger in their final versions. Along the sides of the bazaar are the shopkeepers and a throng of Damascenes shopping for bargains, their heads covered with turbans and dressed "in all the fashions and col-

Jane Digby, the former Lady Ellenborough, was an English aristocrat who led a scandalous life and, at the age of forty-eight, married Sheikh Abdul Medjuel el Mezrab in March 1855. Keene Richards and Edward Troye met Jane at Damascus in October of that year when paying their respects to the sheikh. This miniature painted by William Charles Ross shows Jane as a young woman. Public domain.

ors of oriental life." Troye procured a "sitter" for each of the dozens of persons in the scene; each was a likeness of a living character. Jane Digby soon paid a return call on the Americans at their residence and viewed the work in progress. Henry Wood, who before his appointment as American consul in Beirut had been a pastor in New Hampshire, mentioned the "Lady Ellenborough" with considerable disapproval for her marriage to "an ignorant, barefooted, Moslem Bedouin, whom she picked up in the Desert and with whom she now lives in Damascus in splendor upon her ample revenue." He rather grudgingly noted that Troye considered her to be a rather skilled artist, "excelling . . . in the use of the pencil."[39]

Troye's work on the bazaar canvas attracted other visitors, who were fascinated by the creative process. Two pashas of the city, military officials of high rank, frequently called on the artist in his studio, expressing their pleasure and admiration as the scene unfolded. They invited Troye to go out riding with them in the region about Damascus, and he often did so; this was, as Consul Wood observed, an honor that had never been offered to any American visitor. One of the pashas became so interested in America, from his conversations with Troye, that "he actually proposed emigrating to the United States, provided he could be appointed an officer in the army—a hope which Mr. Troye did not encourage." The dis-

Bazaar in Damascus, painted in 1856 by Edward Troye. The white horse in the center is the Arabian mare Lulie, purchased by Keene Richards at Constantinople in September 1855 and used as a model for this painting. Courtesy of Bethany College, T. W. Phillips Memorial Library, Archives and Special Collections, Bethany, West Virginia.

appointed official decided, instead, to lead a caravan of Muslim pilgrims down to Mecca.[40]

Having failed in his efforts to purchase the celebrated horse at Baalbek, but unwilling to abandon this ambition, Richards directed his companions to spend the winter in Damascus negotiating with the owner. Meanwhile, he returned to Beirut, where he boarded a steamer bound for the United States. He was eager to return to Blue Grass Park to oversee his breeding program, and was confident that Edward Troye and his cousin Morris Keene would, during the spring, be able to secure a number of superior Arabian horses for him. Busy studying the Arabic language, Troye and Keene settled into their new quarters at Damascus.[41]

Troye continued to work on his painting of the Damascus bazaar until, in the first week of February 1856, he put his paints and brushes away and, with Morris Keene, prepared to set out on a major excursion through Palestine. This was intended as a pleasure trip, not a horse-buying expedition during which they would act as agents for Keene Richards. Their excursion would take them to many of the sacred and historic sites of the Holy Land. Troye packed his painting supplies and during this leisurely journey would take time to sketch and paint scenes that appealed to his artistic fancy. On Monday, February 11, they set out from Damascus on horseback, having purchased three sturdy and surefooted mounts. The guidebooks warned them that many of the routes through the mountains were very rough and often precipitous. Troye and Keene may have relied on Conder's *The Modern Traveller: Palestine or the Holy Land,* first published in 1824, to plan their route to Jerusalem and beyond. They were accompanied by a Syrian guide and a hired muleteer and his assistants, who would look after the four mules carrying their baggage. This included a large tent made of goat's hair that was so bulky that it required two of the mules to carry it.[42]

Keene recalled that they were "well armed with Colt's revolvers and Minié rifles." In his journal, Troye recorded that "Mr. K." had a pair of Colts and a "Remic" rifle, and "I had a brace of pistols myself." The revolvers were probably either the .44 caliber Colt Model 1848 Percussion Army Revolver, known as the Colt Dragoon, or the .36 caliber Colt Model 1851 Navy Revolver. Both were single-action six-cylinder revolvers and became extremely popular for civilian use, famed in the settlement of the

American western frontier. These were percussion weapons, meaning that they were loaded from the front of the cylinder with loose powder and ball and then primed at the back with a percussion cap. Metallic cartridges were not invented until the late 1850s.[43]

The Minié rifle was a very recent invention at the time of the Richards expedition, a muzzleloader with a rifled barrel that employed percussion caps to ignite the charge and propel a conical bullet, known as the Minié ball, to ranges far greater than smoothbore muskets. Minié rifles were adopted by the British army in 1851, and the .58 caliber 1861 Springfield Minié-type rifle was widely used during the American Civil War, but the latter were not available at the time of Richards's second trip. The rifles carried by Troye and Keene were probably English .702 caliber 1851 models, popularly known as the "Minié rifle," obtained during their stay in Britain.[44]

As the two men set out on their extended journey among the Bedouin tribes, bristling with weapons and leading horses and mules loaded with supplies, they doubtless imagined themselves as assuming roles much like the pioneers of the American western frontier, so similar were the circumstances. The closest archetype for their undertaking would be the traders who ventured into the wilderness beyond the Mississippi to barter with Native Americans for furs. Their role was akin to the itinerant western traders who lived peacefully among the Indians in their villages and made no claim to their lands, seeking only to encourage the production of furs, yet by their very presence accelerating the process of cultural change. For many of the Americans who traveled through the Near Eastern desert lands, the arduous and challenging journey allowed them to establish a claim to a primitive masculinity. This was certainly the case for Troye and Keene in 1856, as it had been for Richards and his Grand Tour companions in 1851, when they traveled by horseback across North Africa, engaged in camel racing, and pioneered a new route across the Sinai.[45]

Having made arrangements for the care of Lulie in their absence, the little expedition left Damascus on Monday, February 11, following the traces of the old Roman road that once connected the city with Tyre, Jerusalem, and Egypt. They traveled at a leisurely pace, often rising late and following the road for a few hours before once again setting up camp, and frequently they made short side trips to visit some historic or sacred locale described in the guidebook. At last, on February 15, they came to

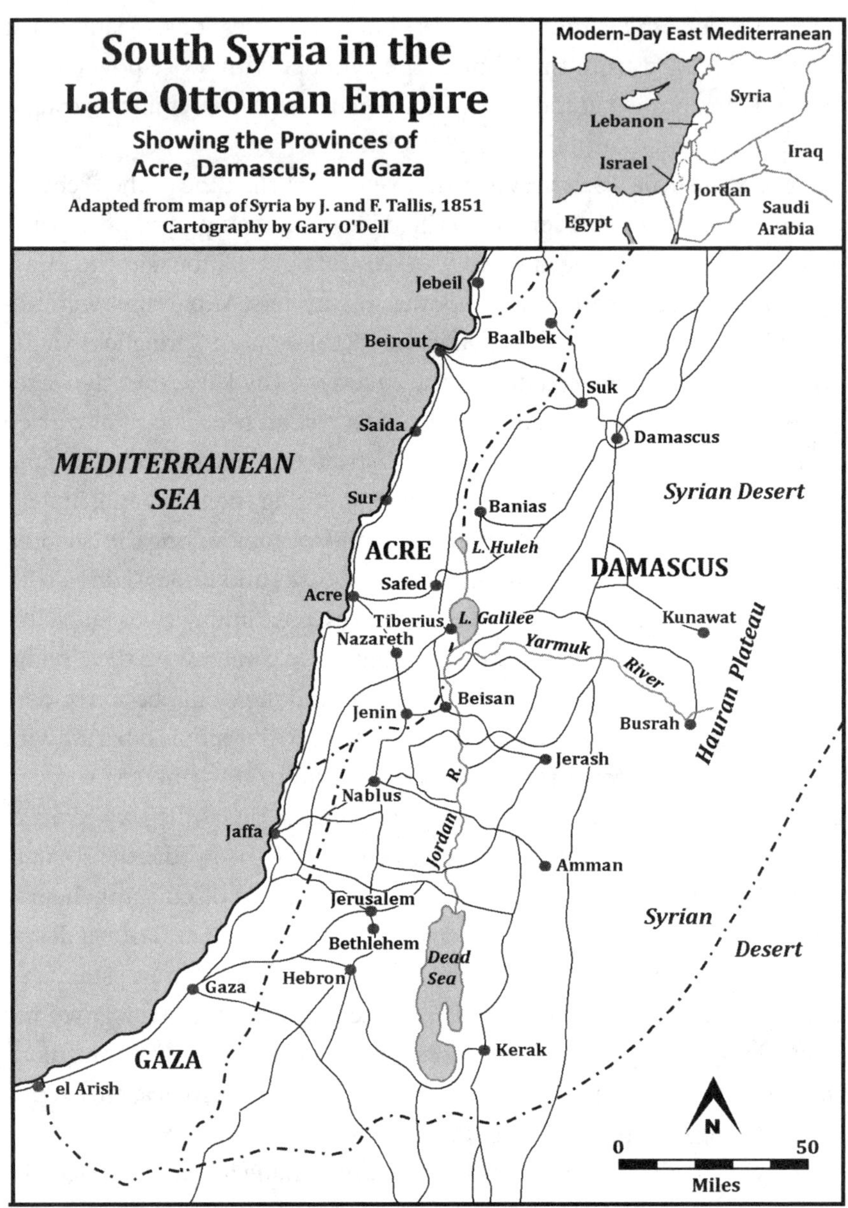

the Sea of Galilee, where Troye was inspired to unpack his paints and brushes to capture the scene in the second of his large Oriental paintings, completing it in just two days. Resuming their journey, they arrived at the holy city of Jerusalem on Friday, February 21.[46]

Troye and Keene remained in Jerusalem for two weeks, taking lodgings, as most European travelers and pilgrims did, at the Latin Convent of Saint Salvator in the Christian quarter in the northwest section of the city. "As every stranger does," Troye wrote, "I visited every place of interest in the city and out of it," focusing first on the scenes associated with the trial and crucifixion of Jesus. Before departing Jerusalem, the two Americans made a short side trip to Bethlehem to visit the Church of the Nativity, erected over a cave that tradition has long held to be the birthplace of Jesus and one of the oldest religious structures in the world. On Tuesday, the fourth of March, they bade farewell to the monks of the Latin Convent and set off for the Dead Sea, twenty miles east of the city.[47]

The terrain was mountainous, and it took the travelers two days to reach the northwestern shore of the Dead Sea, although they might have made the trip in a single day had they started early and pressed on. They turned northward and followed the course of the Jordan River to the first (or lower) ford, about four miles from the lake, which tradition held as the place where Jesus encountered John the Baptist and was baptized. After contemplating the sacred locale for a time, they followed the road west through the ruins of Jericho and, a little farther on, made camp for the night. On the following day, March 6, Troye and Keene returned to the Dead Sea, where they set up a base camp beside the saline waters of the lake. "We pitched our tent on the 6th and I commenced painting on the 7th and continued painting until the 19th," Troye recorded in his journal. "During this time the weather proved very agreeable." Troye divided his time between the two sites. The ford of the Jordan was but an hour and a half by horseback from their camp at the Dead Sea, and he created large paintings of both locations over the next two weeks, which he titled *River Jordan—Bethabara* and *The Dead Sea.* On the morning of March 20, "before sun up after eating our breakfast we raised our tent" and headed back to Jerusalem, returning by the Jericho road. They did not linger long in the holy city but soon departed for Damascus. Their pilgrimage was over; they were no longer tourists. It was time to get down to the serious business of horse-trading.[48]

9
BARGAINING WITH BEDOUINS

The surviving journal of Edward Troye ends with their return to Jerusalem from the Dead Sea, and so details of Troye and Keene's further experiences in the East must be obtained from other sources. Fortunately for the historical record, Henry Wood, the American consul to Beirut, provided a summary of their adventures in his lengthy letter to the *New York Journal of Commerce*, published in August 1856 shortly after their departure from the region. Although the day-to-day detail of Troye's journal is lacking, this letter, when combined with other sources, allows partial reconstruction of the two Americans' efforts to purchase Arabian horses after their return to Damascus in early April.

Henry Wood befriended the members of the Richards party on their arrival in Beirut in October 1855 and formed a particular attachment to Edward Troye. While he found no fault in Keene Richards and Morris Keene, describing them as "courteous, intelligent, and moral," he discovered a kindred spirit in Troye, with whom he became "intimately acquainted." Wood was deeply moved, he wrote, when, "entering his room one day, I saw the Bible lying upon his table, with indications it had just been consulted. This gave a turn to our future conversation, from which I learned he was a Christian as well as a man of taste and genius and with equal modesty and meekness speaking of himself in both relations. One of the most eloquent sermons I ever heard, was from that silent Bible, and one of the most impressive sights I ever gazed upon, was its neat leaves and lids as it lay on the table of my artist countryman." After Keene and Troye fulfilled their mission to purchase Arabian horses in the desert country, they visited Henry Wood on several occasions and entertained him with tales of their adventures before departing the East.[1]

In early April, shortly after returning to Damascus from their pilgrimage, Keene and Troye made the necessary preparations and once again set out for an extended journey. Although both men had by now an acquaintance with the Arabic language, they were accompanied by a dragoman to assist with translation. Their goal was to purchase Arabian horses from among the Anizah Bedouin. Morris Keene later wrote, "we launched out into those wild tribes East and South of Damascus, dressed as Bedouin Sheiks, and well armed." Their travels during the next two months would take them into lands east of the Jordan River seldom seen by westerners, an undertaking far more hazardous than their journey to the Dead Sea. In 1865, fully a decade after Keene and Troye's expedition, Josias Porter wrote that "the travellers who have hitherto succeeded in exploring [the Transjordan region] scarcely amount to a half-a-dozen; and the state of the country is so unsettled, and many of the people who inhabit it are so hostile to Europeans, and, in fact, to strangers in general."[2]

To ensure their safe conduct through the region, and to aid in negotiating with the Bedouins, they placed themselves under the protection of one of the Anizah sheikhs. The identity of the sheikh was not recorded, but presumably this was arranged at or near Damascus before their departure. The sheikh probably did not accompany them, but (for a fee) provided an armed escort for protection and to assist in transporting supplies and handling any horses purchased.[3]

Their travels would first take them into the region western visitors often referred to as the land of Bashan, a biblical allusion. According to the Old Testament, Bashan was the northernmost of the Transjordan highland regions settled by the Israelite tribes following their journey from the Sinai wilderness. A relatively flat basaltic tableland, the Bashan was bounded on the west by the Jordan River, on the north by the southern slopes of Mount Hermon, and to the south by the Yarmuk River, which flows westward out of the Bashan plain and empties into the Jordan just below the Sea of Galilee. To the east, the region extended some sixty or seventy miles to the Hauran Plateau, which marks its approximate southeastern boundary at the edge of the Syrian desert. South of Bashan was the higher and more rugged mountain region of Gilead, extending as far as the Dead Sea, where it became the region known as Moab. To many western visitors, whose explorations of the landscape of Palestine were largely motivated by desires to connect with and validate the roots of Christianity, such ancient biblical designations were more meaningful than contemporary Arabic place names.[4]

According to various references in the Bible, Bashan and Gilead were acclaimed for their rich soils, lush pastures, and the dense oak forests that covered the hills and mountain slopes. This description remains true today, although forested areas have been reduced to mere remnants. The western edge of the Transjordan region, like the adjacent Jordan valley, has a relatively humid climate, rainfall being carried inland from the Mediterranean. The land becomes drier and drier eastward, transitioning from subtropical greenery to semiarid steppe grasslands to barren stony desert. The lush steppe vegetation was noted by nearly all travelers to the region. Josias Porter, who visited the land of Bashan in the middle of the nineteenth century during his ten-year stint as a missionary, noted: "the oak forests still cover its mountainsides; its pastures are still celebrated for their richness, and its soil is proverbial for its fertility." Fifty years later, in 1905, William Libbey described the steppe as "the richest grazing country in all Syria. The spring pasturage reaches the height of a man." From the rich volcanic soils, he wrote, spring "succulent grasses affording the richest fodder to the Bedawin flocks."[5]

Keene and Troye, on their return, told Henry Wood that the plains of Bashan reminded them of the pastures of Kentucky, "the whole country at the season they visited it [April–May] was one great field covered by a kind of grass resembling oats, and fully a knee high, which cattle, sheep, goats, mules, dromedaries and camels, were cropping." Wood noted that, lacking rainfall to sustain their growth, the luxuriant grasses "dry up and disappear" during the summer season. The two men also were struck by the ruins of cities and towns "in every part of the country," which in ancient times "must have been large and opulent, as the remains of walls, pillars, monuments and works of various kinds, clearly indicate." Other travelers were also impressed by the abundant ruins present throughout Bashan (as elsewhere in Palestine), and attributed this as evidence of a Divine historical plan, the fulfillment of prophecy.[6]

Old Testament prophets predicted that the Holy Land would be laid waste for the sins of its inhabitants and left in desolation until the end of days. The prophet Isaiah warned that the Lord's anger would continue

"Until the cities be wasted without inhabitant, and the houses without man, and the land be utterly desolate" (Isaiah 6:11 KJV), and Jeremiah prophesied, "I beheld, and, lo, the fruitful place was a wilderness, and all the cities thereof were broken down at the presence of the LORD, and by his fierce anger" (Jeremiah 4:26 KJV). To western visitors the land appeared to be filled with the ruins of an ancient splendor, and Jerusalem, Bethlehem, Nazareth, and other famous cities of the Bible appeared to be mere impoverished villages. The desolation of the country seemed to be an apparent fulfillment of prophecy.[7]

Josias Porter, riding through Bashan, wrote, "The country is filled with ruins. In every direction to which the eye turns, in every spot on which it rests, ruins are visible—so truly, so wonderfully have the prophecies been fulfilled." The rise of Islam and the conquest of much of the Near East led Europeans to identify Arabs or "Saracens" as "God's chosen agents of desolation, who destroyed the fertility and prosperity of the Holy Land as punishment for Christian corruption and sin." Jeremiah 4:7 (KJV) proclaims, "the destroyer of the Gentiles is on his way; he is gone forth from his place to make thy land desolate; and thy cities shall be laid waste, without an inhabitant." In nineteenth-century Christian ideology, as expressed by western writers such as Porter, the "destroyer" was held to be the desert Arab.[8]

Leaving Damascus, Keene and Troye again followed the old Roman road west from the city to Banias, at the foot of Mount Hermon, and the headwaters of the Jordan River. This time, however, instead of crossing the river to the west, they remained on the eastern side and traveled southward through the district then known as the Jaulân, along the western boundary of Bashan. This region, a basaltic plateau studded with old volcanic mountains, steps upward in terraces from the Jordan River valley. According to Deuteronomy 4:43, the city called Golan was under the jurisdiction of the Manesseh tribe of the Israelites; after the conquest of the region by Alexander the Great in the fourth century BCE, the name Golan (Gaulanitis in Greek) came to be applied to the entire district. The locale today is known as the Golan Heights and is the subject of continuing dispute between Israel and Syria, from which the region was captured during the Six-Day War in June 1967.[9]

The two men followed the valley of the Jordan River through the Jaulân as far as the ancient ruins of the city of Gadara, located on the heights overlooking the Yarmuk River and the Sea of Galilee. Troye and Keene considered the ruins of this city to be the most impressive of all they saw during their journeys in April and May. Gadara was one of a loose confederation of at least ten cities occupied by the Macedonian Greeks after the death of Alexander and known collectively as the Decapolis during the Selucid period, which ended with the imposition of indirect Roman rule over the borderland region during the first century CE. All these cities, with the exception of Scythopolis, were located east of the Jordan River in the area that is today Syria and Jordan. Gadara, situated at the junction of several important trade routes, was one of the leading cities of the region during the Roman era, declining after a destructive earthquake in the eighth century. In the modern era, the site of Gadara is occupied by an Arab village known as Umm Qais.[10]

"From the region of Bashan our adventurous countrymen struck into the Desert," wrote Henry Wood, waxing poetic. "The country is nearly all one great plain, as far as they traveled, in which the eye seeks relief in vain by forests, trees, mountains, hills, and streams. And yet there is a certain wild beauty about it, from the patches of coarse grass which appear here and there, the thorny bushes and thistles which the camels love to crop . . . and from the black tents scattered here and there, with innumerable flocks of sheep, goats, dromedaries and camels, giving picturesqueness and life to desolation." On their return, one of the two men told Wood, "If he had seen one camel in the Desert, he had seen a hundred thousand!"[11]

According to Wood, and from statements made at various times by Morris Keene and Keene Richards, the Americans went "into the Desert" to negotiate the purchase of Arabian horses with the Bedouins. Wood's observation that they struck out "from the region of Bashan" and Keene's "East and South of Damascus" are the only direct geographic indicators as to where they traveled in the vast expanse of arid lands in pursuit of this goal. The horses they ultimately acquired were, however, all purchased from tribes or allies of the Anizah Bedouin, and this information helps to focus the known limits to their wanderings. Although the desert Arabs engaged in seasonal migrations in search of pasturage for their livestock, each tribe tended to occupy a particular zone and did not often encroach on the lands of other tribes, except for raids or in time of war. Keene and Troye were provided with safe conduct by a specific sheikh, and so this guarantee would have been valid only for the tribal group of which the sheikh was a member. Since they made their purchases from the Anizah Bedouin, the two men would have confined their journey to the lands of the Anizah, between the Jordan River and the Euphrates, and would not have ventured into Mesopotamia, where the Shammar Bedouin were dominant. The two Americans apparently traveled widely within the Anizah tribal lands, since horses were purchased from bands of both northern and southern Anizah.[12]

John L. Burckhardt, who traveled through the region in 1810, noted that during the winter months the Anizah Bedouins of Syria resided in the Hammad desert, which was without flowing water but contained seasonal pools "in deep grounds" and provided rough forage for their livestock. The al-Hamad desert is the southwestern half of the Syrian desert. Largely a gravelly plain with occasional swatches of sand, it gradually transitions southward into the Nefud, the northern part of the Arabian desert. In the spring, Burckhardt wrote, the Anizah "approach the frontiers of Syria, and form a line of encampment extending from near Aleppo to eight days' journey to the south of Damascus. Their principal residence, however, during that time is the Hauran and its neighbourhood, where they encamp near and among the villages. In these parts they spend the whole summer seeking pasture and water, purchase in autumn their winter provision of wheat and barley, and return after the first rains into the interior of the desert." The Hauran region, one of the most fertile areas of Syria, is centered around a low volcanic plateau, triangular in shape, about thirty miles south of Damascus and forty miles east of the Sea of Galilee. During the summer months, the Anizah remained camped near springs and seeps of the Hauran for three to four days at a time, until their livestock cropped the grass short, and then moved to another location.[13]

The Syrian climate is of the Mediterranean type, with hot summers and mild winters. Most of the rainfall occurs in the winter season, beginning about October. With the onset of the rainy season, the steppe and Syrian desert are briefly lush with grass, which begins to wither with drier weather in May. Staged to take advantage of seasonal changes in pasturage, the annual pattern of Anizah migration noted by Burckhardt was confirmed by later observers, such as Charles Addison (1838), Lady Anne Blunt (1879), and Gottlieb Schumacher (1886).[14]

The account of the first Arabian horse purchased by Keene and Troye gives an indication of where their travels first led. This was "a horse of superior form and blood," purchased from one of the sheikhs of the "Beni-Zahr" [Beni Sakhr]. The Beni Sakhr was an independent and relatively settled tribe that occupied the region east of the Jordan below the Sea of Galilee, or the lands known in biblical times as Gilead and Moab. The territory of the Beni Sakhr would have been the first tribal area entered by Keene and Troye as they turned their path eastward toward the desert, and so the first opportunity for purchasing Arabian horses. Although generally hostile toward the Anizah, the Beni Sakhr were accustomed to foreign visitors.[15]

Negotiating a transaction with the Bedouins—for horses or any other objective—could be a time-consuming affair. Selah Merrill, who visited the region during 1874–1877 as an archaeologist for the American Palestine Exploration Society, described the drawn-out process:

> [Their] business is accomplished sometimes in half a day, and sometimes it requires two whole days. For with the Arab the process of coming to the point is a long one. He begins as remotely as possible from the business in hand, and works up to it little by little. For instance, if a man wanted to buy your horse, he would come to your tent and talk about everything he could think of except the horse itself, and quite likely, for a whole day, he would not even mention the animal. Were he to approach the matter at once and abruptly, he would expect that the price would be three or four times the real value of the horse. In making purchases of the Arabs, or bargains of any kind, it will not do to appear too anxious. It is not their nature to come to an agreement directly; besides time is of no consideration to them, while to the Yankee it is everything.

Captain John W. Thompson, dispatched to Syria in spring 1854 to obtain Arabian horses for the British army in the Crimea, found the whole process infuriating, noting that the Anizah were the most difficult of all Arabs with whom to deal. As he described it, horse-trading with the Bedouins was a series of negotiating rounds, at the conclusion of each the owner of the horse, feigning grave insult, was liable to ride away in an apparent

Depiction of a Bedouin with Arabian horse. Lithograph by Victor Adam, "Cheval Arabe" (1835). Public domain.

fury, returning in a matter of hours or days for another bout. Thompson observed sourly, "As a general rule, it may be said that those who have the best horses are the touchiest to deal with."[16]

Even protracted negotiations sometimes failed to achieve the desired result. During their expedition, Keene and Troye learned that the Bedouins were often reluctant to part with their prized Arabian horses, no matter what financial inducements were offered. Morris Keene related the story of one occasion when he attempted and failed to purchase a mare "of the most symmetrical form and the purest blood. A Bedouin never fixes a price, but leaves you to bid until he is satisfied with the offer. I commenced bidding, and at last went to what I considered a very extravagant price; but still [the owner] merely shook his head and showed his teeth. Then I asked him if he wouldn't sell her if I doubled my offer. He threw out his arm, and pointing toward her, asked me if I could load her with gold. I told him that was beyond my means. 'Well,' said he, 'if you could the gold would still be yours, the mare mine.'" Keene concluded, "Such is the Bedouin's appreciation of his horse. And yet that same mare stood chained in front of the tent, exposed to cold nights and rains, or ready at any time for a run of twenty miles over the burning sands of the desert."[17]

The two men made every effort to gain the friendship and trust of the Bedouin tribes. "In order to get 'inside the ring,'" Keene Richards later told equine authority John Wallace, his friends Morris Keene and Edward Troye "spent several months among the different tribes . . . they ate with the Arabs, slept with the Arabs, and worshiped with the Arabs." Their tent, which they had previously used on their pilgrimage, was the same type used by the Bedouins among whom they stayed, made of black goat's hair and barely affording clearance for a man standing upright. Nearly all of the milk provided by the Bedouins' goats and cattle was converted into butter; camel's milk was used exclusively in cooking and as a beverage. The two Americans found camel's milk to be "very sweet and nutritious." The most common daily fare was a dish known as ayesh, flour and sour camel's milk made into a paste and boiled. The Bedouins eat a great deal of rice (obtained through trade) with their mutton, Keene and Troye told Henry Wood. For a feast, a sheep or lamb is killed, and "Having baked it in the ground or boiled it in a great kettle, it is set on a table raised six or eight inches from the ground, around which the family sit on their haunches, each one reaching his hand toward the immense platter, and in the absence of knife or fork, tearing the meat in pieces with his fingers. He then rolls a piece of meat and a quantity of rice into a solid ball, and squeezing it into his mouth, gulps the whole without mastication." Burckhardt observed that "the Arabs eat heartily, and with much eagerness. The boiled dish set before them being always very hot, it requires some practice to avoid burning one's fingers, and yet to keep pace with the voracious company." Women were excluded from these communal meals, eating the leftovers later and separately from the men. During the month of Ramadan, which in 1856 commenced on May 5, the two Americans were forced to keep "an unwilling fast," as their hosts would give them nothing to eat until sunset; for Muslims, this time of religious observance is marked by fasting from sunrise to sundown as an exercise in self-restraint, along with prayer and contemplation.[18]

Keene and Troye intended to obtain only superior Arabians from the Bedouins, horses of the first class, rather than *kadish*, as horses of mixed breed were known. At the time of their visit to the region, there was little direct knowledge of Arabian horse breeding, existing accounts being mainly a mixture of legend and secondhand reports, and much of it incorrect. One of the primary misconceptions in this regard was that there were distinct and separate breeds of Arabian horse, of which the so-called Nejd breed was the best. Although this supposition was later corrected by better-informed observers, such as Roger D. Upton, who in 1873 flatly stated, "there is really but one breed of Arabian horses, although many families," the concept of separate breeds was widely believed at midcentury.[19]

The Arabian horse is the product of centuries of selective breeding by the Bedouin Arabs of the Near East, resulting in a distinct breed of domestic animals visibly similar in most characteristics. The Arabian differs from other horse breeds in the same way that, for canines, golden retrievers differ from Labrador retrievers; each will consistently breed true to form with minor variations resulting largely from environmental differences. Although the Arabian constitutes but a single breed of horse, during its long history there has been a modest differentiation into what are recognized as separate strains or family lines. Long before the nineteenth century, five distinguished family lines were developed, known collectively as the Khamsa. Arab breeders trace the lineage of a horse through the female line, and, according to tradition, these five strains allegedly trace back to five foundation mares belonging to either King Solomon or to Mohammed. Even modern equine authorities, however, disagree on which family lines constitute the Khamsa, let alone how many different strains of Arabian horse may exist.[20]

The family lines known as Keheilan, Seglawi, Abeyan, Hamdani, and Hadban are generally considered to represent the purebred Khamsa lines. Each of these lines had a reputation for certain traits or characteristics that distinguished it from the others; for example, as noted by Morris Keene, the "Coheylan" for its "bottom," or endurance, and the "Sacklowee" for its speed. The so-called Nejd horse, supposed to be the best of all, did not exist as a bloodline, but simply referred to any horse, of whatever bloodline, that had been bred in the Nejd region of central Arabia.

Pure blood and association with one of the Khamsa lines did not necessarily guarantee that the animal was of the first class. Burckhardt observed, "It would be erroneous to suppose, that the horses of the khomse, or the noble breed, are all of the most perfect or distinguished quality and beauty. Among those fine horses, there can be found only a few worthy of being entitled 'first rate,' in respect to size, bone, beauty, and action; perhaps not above five or six among a whole tribe. Accordingly, the reputation of a bloodline alone was insufficient to assure a superior horse; the potential buyer must also be a good judge of horseflesh."[21]

The Anizah Bedouins had a reputation for possessing the best horses. Burckhardt observed that the finest Arabians were to be found in the Hauran district of Syria, and in 1876 Roger Upton declared that Arabian horses were to be found "in the highest perfection among the Anizah tribes, and that certain tribes of this people are possessed of better horses and are more particular in breeding than others." Keene and Troye were launched on a venture among "those wild tribes" of the desert, in the vicinity of the Hauran, no doubt with a copy of Burckhardt's *Notes on the Bedouins* (considered an important reference by Keene Richards, and thus most likely by Morris Keene as well) packed in their baggage, and with the benefit of Richards's earlier experiences among the Arab tribes. They had previously "travelled through every part of Palestine and Western Syria without meeting a single horse that would do to import." During April and May, they would visit many encampments of the Anizah and view many horses.[22]

"Mr. Troye was very hard to please," Morris Keene recalled. "We would sometimes see an animal that looked perfect, but something would be wrong about the pedigree, and however given a Bedouin might be to lying, he will always speak the truth about his horse." The Bedouins kept no written records of these pedigrees, relying on an oral tradition in which the men of a tribe knew the lineages of all their horses as well as they knew their own genealogies. "An oath, too, is always required by the buyer from the owner, and from the Sheik of the tribe," Keene noted. "Thus we would find about six out of ten whose pedigree could not be established." According to Burckhardt, the only time a Bedouin possessed a written pedigree was on those occasions when horses were taken to market at any town, such as Damascus or Bagdad. When Keene Richards, during his previous visit to the East, purchased Massoud and several other Arabian horses, no mention of their family line was ever made in any subsequent record, only of the Bedouin tribe from which they were obtained. Evidently Richards was, at that time, unaware of the importance attached to bloodlines of the Khamsa, a deficiency corrected by his studies in preparation for the second expedition. Keene and Troye determined to obtain only pedigreed Arabians, and their purchases included horses of two of the purebred strains: Seglawi and Keheilan.[23]

With their first Arabian purchase in tow, Keene and Troye left the lands of the Beni Sakhr and continued their travels into the summer abode of the Anizah Bedouin. Since they would, in the weeks ahead, purchase horses from both the southern and northern bands of the Anizah, it seems reasonable to assume that their travels took them southward first, so that they finished their expedition back in the northern area near Damascus, from where they had first embarked. How far south or how far east they traveled is unknown, as are the names and locations of most of the specific Anizah subtribes with whom they had dealings. In the camp of one of the southern tribes, however, they found a stallion of the first class whose owner was willing to sell, for sufficient gold.

According to their Bedouin host, the horse Fysaul, a four-year-old Keheilan-Seglawi mix bred in the Nejd, was the best young horse of the Anizah. He was chestnut in color, with a small star on the forehead and one white hind foot, having a "beautifully indented and tapered head" and a slim neck. When first viewed by Keene and Troye, the stallion had just been put up for stud, and as Keene recalled, "about thirty mares were picketed around him, whose owners vehemently opposed his sale . . . when informed of the proposition to purchase him." On purchasing this horse, Keene asked for a written pedigree; he was told, with some amusement, that everyone in the tribe knew the horse and his pedigree. Persisting in this request, at last "the usual form of pedigree was written out by one of the sheik's scribes, and certified to by the old men who knew well the horse's family and history." Of all those purchased on the expedition, Fysaul was Morris Keene's favorite, and later Keene Richards formed the same opinion.[24]

Fysaul's written pedigree has not survived the years since his purchase, but the historical bloodline of a subsequent acquisition has been preserved, published in its entirety by Keene Richards as an example of an Arabian pedigree. The horse was a yearling gray colt of Keheilan stock, again asserted to be "the finest that could be found in the tribe." The stock from which he came, Richards wrote, "had been in the family of the Sheik, from whom he was purchased, for more than three hundred years." The gray was given the name Hamdan, which seems a puzzling choice, since his bloodline was Keheilan, not Hamdani, but Hamdan is a common proper name in the region. Morris Keene also tried, without success, to purchase the dam of this colt, which he regarded as superior. The pedigree was translated and the copy witnessed by Henry Wood in Beirut after their return from the desert.

Ramadon 21st, 1272 [May 26, 1856]

This is to certify, That at the date of this document, Messrs. Keene & Troye, bought from Sheik Hammed, Esq., Sohiman, the son of Shalan, the grey horse, even the horse of Hammed, the son of Sohiman who is the son of Shalan, even the Sheik of the Arabs of Aneyza. The said horse is Koheylan, the son of an old Koheylan father, and of an old Koheylan mother; we declare this by fortune, to which God, and Mohamed, the Apostle of God, are witnesses. There is no better horse, being from the side of both father and mother a blood horse. He is a Koheylan, the son of a Koheylan, and his mother is a Koheylan purer than milk. He was born and brought up in the land of Nejd.

This is the genealogy of the said horse. God is omnipotent.

The sale was made in the land of Sophira.

[SEAL]

HAMMED ES. SOHIMAN
The son of Shalan

WITNESSES:

The writer of this document who stands in need of God

ABDALLAH, the son of Nowphal, the lecturer.

MOHAMMAD. the son of Mashial.

AKHLIEF, the son of Mashaul.

ISHSHERATAH, agent of Fysal-Ish-Shalan.

UNITED STATES CONSULATE

Beyrout, June 12th, 1856

This is to Certify, That the above is a correct and true translation of the original document attached to it.

[SEAL] HENRY WOOD, Consul[25]

The tribe can be identified from the certificate as the Rwala of the Anizah Bedouin, whose leader at the time of these desert expeditions was the Sheikh Faisal ibn Sha'alan. The Rwala, in Burckhardt's time and today, was the most numerous tribe of the Anizah and the largest to acknowledge a single ruler. Seasonal migrations of the Rwala were similar to those of other Anizah tribes, camping in the region of the southern desert, al-Hamad, and the Nefud during the winter and early spring, and moving gradually northward to the vicinity of Jaulân in midsummer. Sheikh Hammed's summer encampment was probably among the northern Anizah, not far from Damascus, since Keene and Troye were in Beirut with their Arabians less than three weeks after the sale date. At about the same time as the purchase of Hamdan, they were able to secure another fine stallion from among the northern tribes, which they named Sacklowie.[26]

The horse Sacklowie was descended from a subclass of the Seglawi known as Jedran. Long ago, according to Arabic folklore, a man named Jedran owned three Seglawi mares (four, in some accounts), all being sisters having the same sire and dam. One of these mares he kept for himself, and all of the Jedran line are descended from this mare. Another mare he gave to his brother Obeir, which founded the line of that name, and the third was given or bequest to a servant or slave, from which descended the line known as Seglawi al Abd, or the "Seglawi of the Slave." The Seglawi were held in high esteem, and the Jedran was considered the best of all the bloodlines. Abbas Pasha, who governed Egypt from 1848 until his death in 1854, had a passion for Arabians and put together a stud comprising more than a thousand horses. His agents, among whom was Faisal ibn Sha'alan, combed the desert lands for the finest specimens, often paying outrageous prices, so that by the time of Richards's second expedition to the East the prized Seglawi Jedran were quite rare throughout the region even among the Anizah, and virtually extinct among the Shammar Bedouins.[27]

When Morris Keene first laid eyes on Sacklowie, he realized that this was one of the finest horses they had come across in their travels among the Bedouin. Without hesitation, he struck a bargain for this horse, trading the stallion obtained earlier from the Beni Sakhr tribe and giving an additional $500. Although Keene still thought Fysaul to be the best of their selections, Troye was quite taken with the latest addition and considered Sacklowie to be his favorite of all their acquisitions—indeed, the best horse they had seen. Sacklowie was a four-year-old "mahogany bay" with a star on his forehead and a white stripe on his nose, and four white feet. Keene described him as "a beautiful, strong, active, and bloodlike horse, and certain to secure admirers."[28]

According to Burckhardt, the northern tribes, from whom Keene and Troye obtained Sacklowie, "encamp during the whole year among the villages of Eastern Syria, partly in the once cultivated desert from Hauran towards Palmyra." The Seglawi Jedran were a particular favorite of the Sba'a, the tribe of which Medjuel was a minor sheikh, and so this may provide a clue as to where in their journeying Keene and Troye came across the horse Sacklowie. The Sba'a were described by Anne Blunt as "Wealthy in camels and mares, of which last they possess by far the best in Arabia. They are a well-bred, courteous people; hospitable and honest. They fight only in self-defense." Blunt also noted that the summer pastures of the tribe were eastward from Hóms and Háma, towns about one hundred miles north of Damascus. This was possibly where Keene and Troye purchased Sacklowie, and the northern limit to their travels.[29]

Their expedition having come to a successful conclusion, Keene and Troye returned to Damascus with their entourage, which now included three Arabian stallions and two thoroughbred dromedaries. The camels were purchased, Keene wrote, for the "milk of the female to be supplied to the foals of the Arabian mares, as is done in 'Araby the blest.'" He probably witnessed this practice often during their sojourn among the desert tribes, and likely had received instructions to purchase camels for this purpose by Keene Richards, who would have read about the diet of Arabian foals in his copy of Burckhardt's *Notes on the Bedouins.* Foals were allowed to nurse from their mothers for thirty days, Burckhardt observed, and then weaned, being fed nothing but camel's milk for a period of one hundred days thereafter. At the end of this period, a daily ration of wheat flour mixed with water was introduced into the foal's diet, the milk of the camel continuing, however, as its primary food. By the end of a second hundred days, the young horse would be starting to browse on grass and other forage. The Blunts also observed this practice during their travels in the region in 1878.[30]

From Damascus, the two men soon traveled on to Beirut, arriving there sometime before June 12. Arranging for the temporary stabling and care of their charges, they paid a call on the American consulate. Henry Wood made the necessary arrangements to have the pedigree certificates translated from Arabic to English, and they regaled him with tales of their adventures since they had departed Beirut the previous February. Both Keene and Troye had greatly enjoyed their travels in the Holy Land and among the Bedouin tribes. Keene told the consul that he would very much like to return to the region next year and journey into southern Arabia. During the recent expedition, one of the sheikhs of the Anizah had offered to "travel with him and be his protector . . . inviting him to 'make his house his home' as long as he pleased to stay in the desert." Troye, as well, was enchanted by the romance of the country; for the rest of his life he longed to return to the Holy Land and once again "bathe his feet in the river Jordan." Neither Keene nor Troye were able to realize these dreams. In his declining years, whenever Troye began to ruminate about his travels and declared himself ready once more to set out for the Orient, his family and friends, who considered him to be too old for any more such adventures, gently persuaded him to put it off yet a little longer, until at last he ran out of time.[31]

Both men returned to Damascus, although Morris Keene stayed only a short while since he needed to make shipping arrangements for the bloodstock left behind in Beirut. Troye was not quite ready to leave the East, however; instead, traveling four miles to the east of Damascus, he set up his workspace at the edge of a field and began the fifth and last of his large Oriental paintings, executed with his usual attention to detail, down to the least blade of grass. Titled *The Syrian Ploughman,* Troye described it as "painted on the spot, and there is nothing imaginary introduced, from the smallest thistle to the soft shadows falling upon Hermon's loft peak."

The perspective, just east of the city, shows a field being tilled by a Syrian farmer in traditional garb, in the act of turning two heifers attached to a plow, guiding them by lines attached to their ears and by use of a goad.[32]

On the right of the picture, a boy is leading a goat to a little stream of water, while two more goats and a sheep, each tethered by one leg, await their turn. On the left is a structure Troye identified as "a small mosque or tomb of a SHEIK or Chief." Near the tomb is a man seated on a camel, which, as Morris Keene commented, "appears to be taking the world easy (a luxury seldom allowed to a camel in the East)." Behind the plowman can be seen fields of barley, oats, and other grains, some freshly cut and others ripening. Beyond the fields lies the city of Damascus, and looming in the distance are the snow-covered peaks of Jebel es-Sheikh, Mount Hermon. Troye had not quite finished the picture when Keene left again for Beirut, but "it was far enough advanced to give an idea what it would be after leaving his hands."[33]

In Beirut, Keene needed to arrange shipment to the United States for the three stallions purchased from the desert Bedouins, along with the mare Lulie, the two dromedaries, and a female Arabian greyhound he had picked up on a whim. The animals were shipped together from Beirut to Liverpool aboard "an English screw steamer," probably in late June, since, in a letter from Liverpool dated July 31, Keene wrote that he was staying there for several weeks to rest the animals before sending them on to New Orleans. Wood's letter to the *Journal of Commerce* dated July 21 indicated that the American travelers had left sometime previously. According to Wood, shipping costs for the horses and dromedaries to Liverpool alone, including feed, amounted to $200 per animal, or a total of $1,400, and the cost for the second leg of the voyage to the United States was likely to be equal or greater in amount.[34]

The livestock was to be shipped from Liverpool to New Orleans on August 10 aboard the steamer *Sultan*. Wood states that this voyage would be made in two stages, first to New York, and then from New York to New Orleans. To the cargo manifest, Keene (who was apparently fond of dogs) added two English foxhounds acquired in Liverpool, the whole now comprising a considerable menagerie. From New Orleans, writing to the *Spirit of the Times* on November 3, Morris Keene stated, "You will be pleased to learn that Mr. A.K. Richards' second importation of Arabian horses arrived safely at Mobile, after a voyage of seventy one days from Liverpool." The animals and Keene were accompanied by a Dongolese groom, who cared for the livestock during the voyage and would become a fixture at Blue Grass Park, much in the same manner as the late Yusef Badra. Like Sadah, who in the previous importation delivered a foal at sea during the voyage, the mare Lulie arrived in America "heavy with foal," having been bred to "Ahzees Pasha's Arab Bagdad"; the foal, a colt, was lost early in 1857. Keene noted that a great many people visited Garnett's stables in New Orleans, where the animals were being kept for the time being, but he knew not whether they were attracted by "the beauty of the horses, the ugliness of the dromedaries, or the swarthy groom (who looks like a mustached mulatto) in his foreign costume."[35]

In the meantime, Troye completed his painting of the Syrian ploughman and, packing up, bade farewell to his new friend, Henry Wood. His creative efforts during his stay in the East had produced five major canvases, the Oriental paintings (in order of execution): *Bazaar in Damascus, Sea of Tiberias or Galilee, River Jordan—Bethabara, The Dead Sea,* and *The Syrian Ploughman,* plus several smaller works. These latter included the portrait of Lulie; *Bashan Cattle,* depicting a bull, a cow with calf, and a yearling heifer, probably painted in April 1856 while Troye and Keene traveled southward through the Jaulân region; and an unfinished portrait, *Syrian Mother and Child,* the latter probably painted in Damascus during the winter of 1855–1856.[36]

Troye left the East and traveled to Antwerp, Belgium, to the studio of his brother, Charles de Troy, a noted artist in his own right. Here Edward made full-size copies of his Oriental paintings. Keene Richards purchased both the originals and the copies for a substantial sum, although it is unlikely that the $9,000 reported by *Turf, Field and Farm* as given by Richards for a single painting, *The Syrian Ploughman,* is correct. This would be equivalent to nearly $325,000 in adjusted dollars today, and while Keene Richards was a generous patron, it stretches credulity to the point of absurdity to imagine that his largess extended to this magnitude. Most likely the amount reported by *Turf, Field and Farm* had either a zero inadvertently added to the sum, or the amount was for the entire group of paintings. Even in the latter case, this would be an astronomical amount. Richards subsequently donated the copies of the Oriental paintings to his alma mater, Bethany College, which were delivered personally by Troye in July 1860. The originals became part of the decorative furnishings for Richards's house at Blue Grass Park.[37]

Leaving Europe, Edward Troye arrived at New York on January 17, 1857, "bringing with him some of the finest stock brought to this port," Porter's "new" *Spirit of the Times* reported on the 24th, including "a magnificent Arabian mare." The competing "old" *Spirit of the Times* also reported on Troye's arrival and provided more detail of the mare, who had "suffered a good deal on her passage here." The horse was purchased by Troye for Keene Richards, and on the voyage it gave Troye considerable "trouble and anxiety."

> Had she not been held by [Troye] as beyond price, he would have ordered her overboard. As it was, he had encountered and overcome so many difficulties that he was encouraged to persevere, and thus brought her safe to land. She was immediately sent to the stables of Dr. Gracie, Veterinary Surgeon, 53 White St. under whose skillful care and treatment she is now sufficiently recovered from the effects of the voyage to be able to have visitors. . . . The mare is grey in color, 15 hands 1 inch in height and 7 years old, her external configuration is very symmetrical, possessing great elasticity, with the progressive powers well developed for speed.

Mackay-Smith, Troye's biographer, was puzzled by this account. The identity of this horse "remains a mystery," he wrote, and speculated that the mare had been bought for delivery to another breeder.[38]

There is no real mystery here. This animal could only be the mare Zariphe, listed in Richards's 1857 stock catalog and described in the *American Stud Book* as "ZAREEFA, imported gray Barb mare from the desert of Zaharah [Sahara], imported in 1856 by A. Keene Richards." It is clear that Zariphe was not purchased before Morris Keene's departure from the Levant. In his account of the expedition, written in Liverpool, he stated, referring to the desert journey, "We at last selected two stallions and a yearling colt." Later, in New Orleans, he listed and described the horses he had brought to the United States: "a brown horse" [Sacklowie]; "a chestnut horse" [Fysaul]; "a grey colt" [Hamdan]; and "a white mare, heavy with foal" [Lulie]. There was no other horse mentioned, neither a gray mare nor a Barb. Troye, no question as to his expertise, had likely been authorized by Richards to make independent purchases. As a Barb horse, Zariphe obviously had not been bred by the Bedouins of the local region and so probably had been spotted by Troye at Beirut as a mare of superior form, one worth purchasing. The so-called Arabian mare was not the only animal brought back by Troye. The *Spirit* article referred to his stock in the plural, but it provided no information as to whether these were horses or some other species. A visitor to Blue Grass Park in 1860 reported seeing some Arabian cattle, including a bull, so these may have been some of the animals imported by Troye for Richards.[39]

From New York, Troye traveled to Mobile to rejoin his family, the livestock having been shipped to Kentucky. Richards had given permission for Troye to exhibit the Oriental paintings before taking possession, and so, beginning at New Orleans in April, and at New York and other locations in the northeast in 1858, Troye arranged public exhibitions of his work. His Oriental paintings were received with public and critical acclaim. On the inside cover of a pamphlet printed for the New York display, containing the text of Troye's lectures accompanying the exhibition, was the following dedication:

> To KEENE RICHARDS, ESQ.,
>
> Whose pilgrimage to the Eastern lands has afforded him a well improved opportunity of visiting the scenes, which are the subject of these strictures, and of whose generous worth the friend and artist cherish a living recollection; these speculations as a token of gratitude, and in the hope that their crudeness will not detract from the sincerity of the tribute, are inscribed,
>
> With affectionate respect,
> E. TROYE[40]

10
BECOMING A HORSEMAN

During the winter of 1855–1856, while Morris Keene studied the Arabic language and Edward Troye was happily engaged on his painting of the Damascus bazaar, Keene Richards came home. Although the exact timing of his return to the United States is unknown, certainly he was back in Kentucky before the commencement of the breeding season in March 1856, and possibly earlier to be on hand for the delivery of foals conceived during the previous season. At this time, given the limited stock then available to Richards, his Arabian breeding program had produced only six surviving foals, four fillies and two colts, of which two were pure-blooded Arabian and the others Anglo-Arab crosses. In 1853, at sea during the crossing from Liverpool to New Orleans, Sadah had foaled Boherr, a gray dappled filly sired by Mokhladi at Beirut. Sadah was bred again to Mokhladi, and produced the gray filly Zahah in 1854, and in 1856 foaled the gray colt Abdel-Kadir, again by Mokhladi. The champion mare Peytona produced Transylvania, a chestnut filly sired by Massoud, in 1855, but in the spring of 1856 lost a colt sired by Mokhladi. The mare Sallie Hardin was bred to Mokhladi in 1854 but miscarried and lost twin foals. Chloette, Dido, and the Woodpecker mare all produced live foals sired by Mokhladi.[1]

The mare Transylvania, only a yearling in the spring of 1856, would prove to be one of the crown jewels in Richards's program. She was raced by Richards as a yearling, and again as a three-year-old. Injured both times, she was retired to serve as a brood mare. Year after year, from 1860 through 1878, she produced live foals as regular as clockwork, nineteen in all with never a miss. Her most significant offspring was the chestnut colt Limestone, foaled in 1870, who had a very successful racing career during

1874–1875. Limestone was sired by the Thoroughbred Running Horse War Dance, whom Richards acquired during the war years.[2]

Richards did not forget the personal debt he owed to George Feris, of Texas, for supporting him at Metairie in April 1855 in his proposal to make further importations of Arabian horses, against the opposition of some of the most prominent horsemen of the South. Early in 1859, Richards allowed Feris to purchase some of his prized Arabian bloodstock, Boherr and Abdel-Kadir, both the produce of Sadah, along with Hamdan. This Arabian mare belonging to Richards was, as Feris noted, "my favorite of the entire importation." Feris took them to his ranch near Richmond in the Fort Bend country of Texas, and considered these horses to be the most valuable assets in his stud. Abdel-Kadir, Feris wrote, "was my choice of all the stallions . . . known as the 'Feris Arabian' [he] is the horse who made his mark in Texas by his produce. He was 'par excellence' the grand gentleman of his race. The colts of this horse were sold at enormous prices to Mexican stockmen." Hamdan, however, did not long survive his move to Texas, for he died in December of the same year, possibly in the same fire that destroyed a painting made of him. Feris wrote, "I regard his death as a public calamity." Later, at the onset of the Civil War, Feris also acquired the bay colt Bazar, sired by Fysaul out of the Barb mare Zariphe.[3]

Now, in the spring of 1856, Richards continued his breeding program with his ever-growing stable. Sadah, who was proving to be a very reliable brood mare, was bred again to Massoud after having produced three foals for Mokhladi in 1853, 1854, and 1856. The result was a chestnut colt foaled in 1857 whom Richards named Yusef, in memory of the Syrian groom who had so loved Massoud, his Syed Sulimen. Peytona was also bred to Massoud, but missed. Later in the year, once the new importation shepherded by Morris Keene arrived, Fysaul was bred to a mare belonging to Richard Ten Broeck, known only as "Sister to Pryor #1." This took place at Transylvania Plantation, where Fysaul was taken and remained for the next few seasons, as Richards wrote in 1857, "now being used for my own stock in Louisiana." Sister to Pryor #1 was a Glencoe mare, a full sister to Ten Broeck's Pryor who raced against Lecomte at Natchez on March 15, 1856, and won. Not long afterward, this mare was acquired by Richards for his Georgetown stable.[4]

Because the goal of Richards's program was not merely to breed superior thorough-breds but to produce winning racehorses, his racing stable needed a top-notch trainer. In Kentucky and the southern states, breeding and racing Thoroughbred Running Horses had been wholly dependent on Black labor ever since the colonial period. As Katherine Mooney observed, "the racetrack was not just a stage on which white men acted out the world they wanted to make. It was a place run on the labor and skill of black men." The enslaved were customarily occupied in caring for their enslaver's bloodstock, the majority of them being stable boys or grooms in charge of the horses' daily needs. The highest ranking slaves were jockeys and trainers, viewed as valuable assets and often granted extraordinary privileges and authority not allowed to other slaves. A trainer usually began his career as a groom or rider, and was in charge of daily oversight of the stable. "When Thoroughbreds were shipped to the track to race and the enslaved stable force went with them, the trainer supervised both horses and men. He worked the horses, had the last word on their welfare, made sure the grooms did their jobs properly, gave instructions to the jockeys, took the brunt of the owner's wrath, and walked the tightrope of his trust. Enslaved trainers were highly valued and carried commensurately high price tags. Opportunities to acquire such expertise were to be seized . . . on those skills white men's whole racing world depended." Their expertise and judgement were acknowledged and trusted; they were given authority over other slaves and unusual mobility, traveling with a string of horses to race events across the region, delivering horses to buyers, examining animals for sale, and carrying messages to other turfmen. Skilled horse trainers were in great demand in the antebellum South, more likely to be widely known than even the best jockeys, and most of them were Black men.[5]

As in everything else concerned with his equine stock, Richards sought out the best available trainer of the day. He found the right man in Ansel, who had trained Brown Dick—a very fast horse with a winning record owned by Thomas B. Goldsby of Alabama. Ansel, born into slavery in Virginia about the year 1806, first began training horses during the 1850s for Goldsby, who was a major slaveholder on his plantations near Selma. Ansel and Brown Dick made national headlines in 1855 when the horse won seventeen out of twenty-five starts, including a phenomenally fast time on the Metairie course in his defeat of Arrow on April 14. Richards must have witnessed this great race, since he was at the track during this week to meet with Feris and the Metairie stockholders' association, and probably took the opportunity to meet Brown Dick's owner and trainer. Richards purchased Ansel from Goldsby sometime prior to Morris Keene's return from the East in late October 1856 with the newly acquired Arabians, as Keene reported that Ansel was then present at New Orleans and considered Sacklowie to be the best of the imported horses.[6]

Richards had a great deal of respect for Ansel, as well he should, for the Black trainer was one of the most knowledgeable and successful horsemen in the business. He may even have thought of him as a friend, within the social constraints of the institution of slavery. Mooney observed, "White turfmen were often strikingly sincere in the ties they pro-

Ansel Williamson, enslaved horse trainer for Keene Richards and later for Robert A. Alexander. Detail from *Undefeated Asteroid*, painted in 1864 by Edward Troye. Courtesy of the Virginia Fine Art Museum.

fessed with black horsemen, with these particular privileged slaves. But as clear as their sincerity is their complete inability to see black horsemen as full human beings. They recognized these black men as competent professionals and often as congenial companions. But they only saw black horsemen in relation to themselves; they could hardly imagine them with lives and feelings in which white interests played no part." As two men who shared a common interest in horses, they would often speak face to face on topics of mutual interest, and shared jokes and a certain amount of comradery, part of a system "that assured white Southern turfmen that slave society could flourish in harmonious unity." Ordinary slaves routinely faced threats and actual violence, and jockeys were often subjected to routines intended to maintain small size and weight that essentially amounted to torture, such as being buried up to their necks in manure to sweat off pounds, but the best-known horsemen, such as trainers, were less subject to the constant threat of violence. Despite the privileges and often celebrity accorded to trainers such as Ansel, at the end of the day they were still slaves.[7]

When the new Arabian imports arrived at New Orleans, after having been rested for a while, they were taken on to their new homes. Fysaul was temporarily retained at Transylvania Plantation, but the others were sent on to Blue Grass Park in Kentucky. During the following months, Richards continued to select and purchase additional Running Horse mares to serve as breeding stock for his Arabian stallions. Richards was also determined to convince his peers, the other breeders of the region, of the great potential benefit of Anglo-Arab crosses. Beginning in March 1857, he frequently placed notices in sporting magazines such as the *Spirit of the Times* announcing that "at the solicitation of some of the breeders" the services of his imported Arabian horses Mokhladi, Massoud, and Sacklowie would be made available to the public at Georgetown, Kentucky. The stud fee was $100 per season for these stallions, payable twelve months after the date of breeding; any mare that failed to obtain a foal would be provided with a second season free of charge. Richards offered a silver plate, worth $100, to the best weanling sired by these horses from a thoroughbred mare. Further, he would provide a silver pitcher valued at $50 to be awarded to the best weanling, regardless of pedigree, exhibited at the fair at Lexington in the fall of 1858. As a final inducement, Richards stated his intention to sponsor a forthcoming race of two-mile heats at either the Lexington or Louisville courses specifically for three-year-old foals produced by his stallions. He would not enter any of his own stock in competition for the prizes, which would be $500 for the winner of the race and a silver plate worth $500 to the finest colt or filly.[8]

In late summer 1857, Richards took his Arabians to the fifth annual U.S. Agricultural Exhibition at Louisville, which opened on August 31. Although not as well attended as the previous years' fair in Philadelphia, the five-day Louisville exhibition attracted daily crowds estimated at twenty-five to thirty thousand persons, including media representatives from across the nation. The Arabian horses excited considerable interest. On Friday, the final day of the fair, "Immediately after dinner the vast amphitheater was crowded to repletion with persons eager to see these 'children of the desert.' Seven of Mr. Keene Richards' stud were introduced into the arena and commanded the utmost admiration. They are perfect beauties in form, grace, and every other imaginable quality." Apparently only five of these horses were Arabians. The correspondent for the *New York Times* referred to five Arabian horses belonging to Richards, although he confused the names with those of some of the Thoroughbred Running Horses shown at the fair. The *Spirit of the Times* correspondent identified the stallions Mokhladi, Massoud, and Sacklowie by name and referred to two gray Arabian mares, almost certainly Sadah and Lulie. "I visited them again and again," he wrote, "I look forward to great results following their introduction."[9]

In the following season, 1858, Richards advertised the services of Massoud and Fysaul alone at Georgetown, indicating that Fysaul had by this time been brought up from Louisiana to Kentucky. He repeated his prize offers, although now the prize for the best three-year-old at a race sponsored by Richards was to be "a handsome gold vase," again worth $500. At Georgetown, the advertisement noted, farm manager Frank Sherritt would receive the mares at the stables on the Ross Place, the southernmost section of Blue Grass Park. The public was also informed that Sacklowie would spend the 1858 season at Thomas Barry's establishment, "Barrymore," at Gallatin, Tennessee, and Mokhladi would be at Transylvania, Louisiana.[10]

On the first of July 1857, Richards published a pamphlet, "The Arab

Horses Massoud, Mokhladi, and Sacklowie," that contained an explanation of the potential value of Arabian blood for regenerating Thoroughbred Running Horse lines, and a list of some of his stock in residence at Blue Grass Park. This stock included five Arabian stallions, two Arabian mares, one Barb mare, five thorough-bred mares listed by name (Peytona, Blonde, Sallie Hardin, Eagletta, and Sister to Pryor #1), and the Anglo-Arab cross Transylvania, plus an additional six thorough-bred mares and one yearling colt, whose names were not provided. The *Stud Book* and other records allow identification of the mares as Chloette, Dido, the Woodpecker mare, Blanche, Glycera, and a "Zenith mare"; the colt was later named Colossus. Like Chloette and Dido, Eagletta was a Grey Eagle mare, foaled in 1841. Blanche, a half-sister to Blonde, and obviously the unnamed Zenith mare were both sired by Zenith. Glycera and Colossus were both progeny of imported Sovereign, both bred by Richards out of his own Glencoe mare, Sister to Pryor #1. Richards noted that he also possessed "a number of other well bred mares for the harness and the saddle, besides a lot of two year olds, yearlings and weanlings, half Arabs."[11]

Zenith was another horse well-known in Kentucky, sired by the great American Eclipse. He had an outstanding racing career before retiring to stud in 1842. Unlike the other sires, who were all native-bred, Sovereign, imported by Wade Hampton II of Virginia in 1837, was an English Thoroughbred, bred at the Royal Stables for King William IV, and purchased in 1857 by Abe Buford II of Woodford County, Kentucky. Because of a training injury, Sovereign was never raced, but nevertheless he became one of the nation's leading sires in the number of races won by his progeny. What should have been Richards's greatest triumph, the addition of the legendary imported Thoroughbred Glencoe to his stable in 1857, was frustrated by the death of the elderly horse within weeks of his purchase, before there was much opportunity to put him to stud.[12]

Glencoe was one of the premier horses of the nineteenth century, second only to Lexington in the number of his progeny and in their performance as racehorses. During his quarter-century lifespan, Glencoe sired more than five hundred foals. Age was no deterrent to his performance; fifteen of these foals were engendered by the chestnut stallion in 1856, his twenty-fifth year. At stud, he developed a reputation as a "filly-getter," since two-thirds of his offspring were female. These fillies constituted some of the outstanding racers in the country, including the celebrated Reel and Peytona. The track record of Glencoe's colts was less illustrious, as few were worthy of note. Because of his prodigious sire record, and the reputation of his numerous female progeny, there are few Thoroughbred horses in America today whose pedigree cannot be traced back through Glencoe.[13]

Foaled in England in 1831, bred and owned by Lord Jersey, Glencoe proved himself a superior racehorse in short order, his numerous victories including the prestigious Goodwood Cup in 1834. He was imported in 1836 by James Jackson, who established major breeding operations in Tennessee and Alabama. Jackson was determined to buy one of the three best horses in England for his stud, who at the time were held to be Priam, Plenipotentiary, and Glencoe. Neither of the first two could be obtained at any price, but his agent managed to purchase Glencoe from Lord Jersey for 2,000 guineas, or about $10,000. Glencoe was brought over to the United States in August or September 1836 and taken to Jackson's Forks of Cypress plantation in northern Alabama. Here Glencoe remained for seven years, commanding a stud fee of $100. In 1844, he was taken to the Jackson stud near Nashville, and then, in 1848, sold by the Jackson estate for $3,000 to William F. Harper, whose farm was near Midway in Woodford County, Kentucky.[14]

Richards purchased Glencoe from Harper sometime in early to mid-June 1857. A letter written on June 21 by horseman Abe Buford II to the *Spirit of the Times* informed readers that "Old Glencoe was sold a few days since to Mr. Keene Richards for $3,000. If he lives three years longer Richards is to pay an additional thousand dollars." In his pamphlet, Richards noted this acquisition: "Glencoe has recently been added to my Stud for the purpose of breeding to mares of my own selection, knowing his stock to be the best suited for crossing with the Arab, on account of his being more heavily muscled than any other. He is in vigorous health, and his colts this spring give proof that he is still able to compete with the best stallions in this country as well as England." Richards also indicated that the services of his Arabian stallions were available to breeders commencing in March 1858, for a fee of $100 for the season for each stallion. Fysaul was not included in this offer, and was presumably still located at Transylvania Plantation in Louisiana.[15]

Richards almost immediately commissioned Edward Troye to create a portrait of Glencoe, in all his faded glory. Troye had just returned to the Bluegrass region, after exhibiting his Oriental paintings at New Orleans during April 1857. His position at Spring Hill in Mobile having been given up, Troye now moved to Central Kentucky. He took up residence with his family, which now included a daughter, at the home of his wife's niece, "Sunnyslope," located in the countryside adjacent to Robert A. Alexander's Woodburn Farm in Woodford County. At about the same time, Troye established a studio in Midway, a small community conveniently located halfway between Lexington and Frankfort, and only a few miles from Georgetown. Troye also received a commission from Alexander, the first of many to follow, to paint another portrait of the great racehorse Lexington, now belonging to Alexander and residing at Woodburn Farm. For many years thereafter, Richards and Alexander would be Troyes's most important patrons, supporting the artist with numerous commissions.[16]

Troye's portrait of Glencoe, then twenty-six years old, is true to the artist's dedication to render his subjects in faithful detail, "true to nature," instead of in idealized form. It shows "his badly swayed back, a goiter in his throat, with all the marks of age inevitable in a successful racehorse with a long and honorable stud career." According to Glencoe's death notice sent to the *Spirit of the Times* by Richards, Troye rendered this portrait in early August 1857. On the 25th of August, Glencoe was dead from a "violent attack of lung fever." Only two weeks after having his portrait made, Glencoe, who from every appearance was in perfect health up to that time, was seized by "a spasmodic colic, caused by a sudden change in the weather. . . . He remained on his feet for three days. Several hours before he died, blood commenced flowing profusely from his nose. . . . He fell from the exhaustion, and died in less than an hour." This was a tragic loss for Keene Richards, who had great plans for the famous horse: "I have to regret that he could not live to serve the mares selected for him next season." One account states that Glencoe was buried "in a field across the pike, which was formerly used by Mr. Richards as a training track." Most accounts, however, place the horse cemetery in the gardens near the residence, one stating that the great stallion was laid to rest "under a giant oak." The location was marked by a simple stone, and in 1864 his daughter Peytona was laid to rest at his side. The marker has since vanished, and the area developed as residential housing, so no one now knows the grave sites of these great racehorses.[17]

Richards was now the master of Blue Grass Park and Transylvania Plantation. His grandfather, Dr. William B. Keene, passed away at Transylvania on April 9, 1857, and, by the terms of his will, Keene Richards now had access to much of his grandfather's wealth and could at last pursue his ambitions as a horse breeder without limitation, transforming the Georgetown farm into a first-class breeding establishment. Dr. Keene's will was a lengthy document, as might be expected for a wealthy man with extensive land holdings in several states. Not including real property, Keene's estate was valued at nearly $340,000 in stocks and promissory notes, equivalent to about $12 million today. Most of the will consisted of bequests of slaves, money, and bank stocks to his grandchildren in Louisiana, who, with Keene Richards, were his only living descendants. At the time Dr. Keene made out his will, September 27, 1856, he no longer had any living children. His daughter, Eleonora, Keene Richards's mother, died in Kentucky 1830; his son John Wallis Keene died in Louisiana on February 20, 1854; and his last remaining son, Alexander C. Keene, died in Louisiana on August 3, 1855. Both Alexander and Wallis Keene had become wealthy, owning large plantations in Carroll Parish near Transylvania, and so Dr. Keene made no specific provisions for their widows.[18]

Dr. Keene had ten grandchildren in Louisiana, five each by his sons, Alexander and Wallis. At the time of his death, his holdings in Louisiana included two plantations in Carroll Parish: Transylvania Plantation and, a few miles directly west, the property known as Mounds Plantation, so named for the presence of numerous prehistoric burial mounds. This was a huge property consisting of four full sections of land, or more than twenty-five hundred acres. Keene devised Mounds Plantation to the five children of John Wallis Keene, to be leased out by his executors until his grandson, Wallis B. Keene, then fifteen years old, reached the age of twenty-one and would assume charge of the property. There were many enslaved persons on Mounds Plantation, more than 150, since Keene's bequests of slaves from this property totaled 149 and his will directed that "all the old negroes" and any others not specifically mentioned were to remain on the "Mound place" and "be supported comfortably during their lifetime." Nine of his grandchildren were allotted an average of sixteen slaves each from the Mounds property, and the tenth, Lucy B. Keene, received fifteen from the holdings at Transylvania Plantation. In these slave bequests, Dr. Keene was careful to maintain family units intact, specifying each family by name along with their children. Horace B. Tebbetts was named as one of Keene's executors in Louisiana, and 1860 census slave schedules list Tebbetts as the "admin" of 125 slaves for five minor children.[19]

The balance, and the greater part, of William B. Keene's estate went to his favorite grandchild, Keene Richards. There was a very close relationship between Richards and his grandparents. Orphaned at the age of five, he had been taken into their home and raised as their own child, growing up in the spacious brick house at Georgetown. William Keene catered to his grandson's desire to become a horse breeder, supporting him financially without hesitation in his trips abroad in search of Arabian stock, and in purchases of expensive Thoroughbred horses such as Peytona. With his backing, Richards began to transform his grandfather's farm into a premier breeding establishment, and so it was only natural that Dr. Keene would pass the Scott County homeplace acreage on to him. So that his grandson would have the necessary income to realize his dream, Keene also devised Transylvania Plantation to Richards in its entirety: land, livestock, farm implements, and human chattel, save for the fifteen enslaved persons bequeathed to Lucy B. Keene. Keene also gave his grandson an additional square-mile section of land located north of Transylvania, separated from it by a section belonging to the estate of Wallis Keene. The cotton crop from these Deep South plantations, produced by slave labor, comprised the basis of Richards's considerable wealth and allowed him to pursue the gracious lifestyle of a Kentucky gentleman and horse breeder in the antebellum period.[20]

Now a wealthy and established member of the Bluegrass gentry, Richards was ready to take a major step in his personal life. On October 15, 1857, thirty-year-old Keene Richards was wed at Georgetown to twenty-year-old Sallie Pope (1837–1860), daughter of Edmund Pendleton Pope and Nancy Johnson Pope of Louisville. Pendleton Pope (1809–1857), born in Scott County, was a practicing attorney and served as clerk of the Jefferson County Court for thirty-six years. His wife, Nancy Johnson Pope (1815–1849), was descended through an important Scott County pioneer family, her father being Colonel James Johnson of Great Crossing, a member of the U.S. Congress from 1825–1826, and her uncle, Richard M. Johnson, being vice president of the United States under Martin Van Buren. Keene Richards's connections with the prominent Johnson family doubtless led him to become acquainted with Sallie Pope.[21]

The home to which Richards brought his new wife reflected well on his position as a man of wealth and status at Georgetown. The substantial two-story brick house built in 1808 by Elijah Craig, in which Richards was born and had been raised by his loving grandparents, was sixty feet across the front and twenty feet deep, located about two hundred yards from the Frankfort Road on rising ground above and fifty yards west of Royal Spring. The interior was elegantly trimmed in locust and black walnut and outfitted with "substantial, but at the same time, rich and beautiful furniture." The parlors on the first floor were built with large folding doors opening into the hallway, which ran between them, so that they could be thrown open and the entire space used for religious services on Sundays. Richards officiated at these services for family and visitors, drawing on his training under Alexander Campbell at Bethany College and providing a unique, firsthand perspective to biblical accounts by virtue of his travels in the Holy Land.[22]

Within were to be found Richards's extensive personal library and his collection of "rare and valuable curiosities [and] ancient relics," acquired on expeditions to the Near East. "It would require days to critically examine his collection," Hamilton Busbey wrote after a visit in 1872. "There are trophies from the Alhambra, vases from old Rome, pipes and fabrics and precious stones from the Orient, and fresco specimens from churches built more than five centuries ago." According to Sanders Bruce, one of his prize possessions was the mummy of an Egyptian princess. The house was filled with works of art, many with religious themes, including copies of Rubens's *Crucifixion* and *Descent from the Cross.* The work of Edward Troye could be seen throughout the house, for Richards not only gave the artist many commissions but became a significant collector of his work. Pride of place in the dining room was reserved for the equine portraits of Richards's imported Arabian stallions, Mokhladi, Massoud, and Sacklowie.[23]

As part of his efforts to transform his estate into one of the premier breeding establishments of Kentucky, Richards carried out an ambitious building program between 1857 and 1860. Soon after receiving his inheritance, he more than tripled the size of the Georgetown estate by purchasing some adjoining farms, beginning in autumn 1857 with the 106-acre Webb Ross tract to the south. Ross had decided to retire from farming and move to Lexington, and was in the process of selling off his land holdings in Scott County. Richards purchased the Ross homeplace in September 1857 for $12,200. The acquisition of this land must have been particularly satisfying to Richards, since it had once belonged to his uncle, Alexander C. Keene, but was sold to Ross in 1845 when Alexander moved to Louisiana. Two years later, Richards bought the Lewis L. Herndon property of 135 acres that adjoined the Ross tract to the southwest. The combined purchases brought Richards's holdings to 325 acres. This would provide sufficient space to accommodate all the operations of the first-class breeding establishment he intended to create.[24]

As one of the foremost breeders in the nation, Richards often received visitors, who wrote glowing accounts for sporting journals of the magnificence of the Georgetown estate. Blue Grass Park, as it was known, was considered one of the finest holdings in the commonwealth; one 1860 visitor called it "the garden spot of Kentucky," observing that "There is no building upon the estate which has not a stamp of refined and cultivated taste about it." He reported, "The pastures are rich, fertile, and clean, and in them are running large numbers of brood mares and foals, and yearlings, and two-year-olds. The yearlings by Mr. Richards' Arabians are very fine, and larger and better formed than others of the same age, and their foals are very promising."[25]

Although there are no existing maps or plans of Blue Grass Park, nor have any photographs of the property been found that indicate the location and layout of various structures, some clues can be gleaned from period documents. The house was surrounded by a well-kept lawn and gardens that extended down to the spring, and the acreage of the farm was divided into neatly fenced five-acre paddocks. Immediately to the right of the Craig house was the home of the elderly house slave Pompey, who had been allowed to retire as a result of his advanced age and declining mental capability. The new house was built specifically as a reward for Pompey's years of service. On the other side of the main house was the house stable, a substantial stone structure, home to three matched sets of

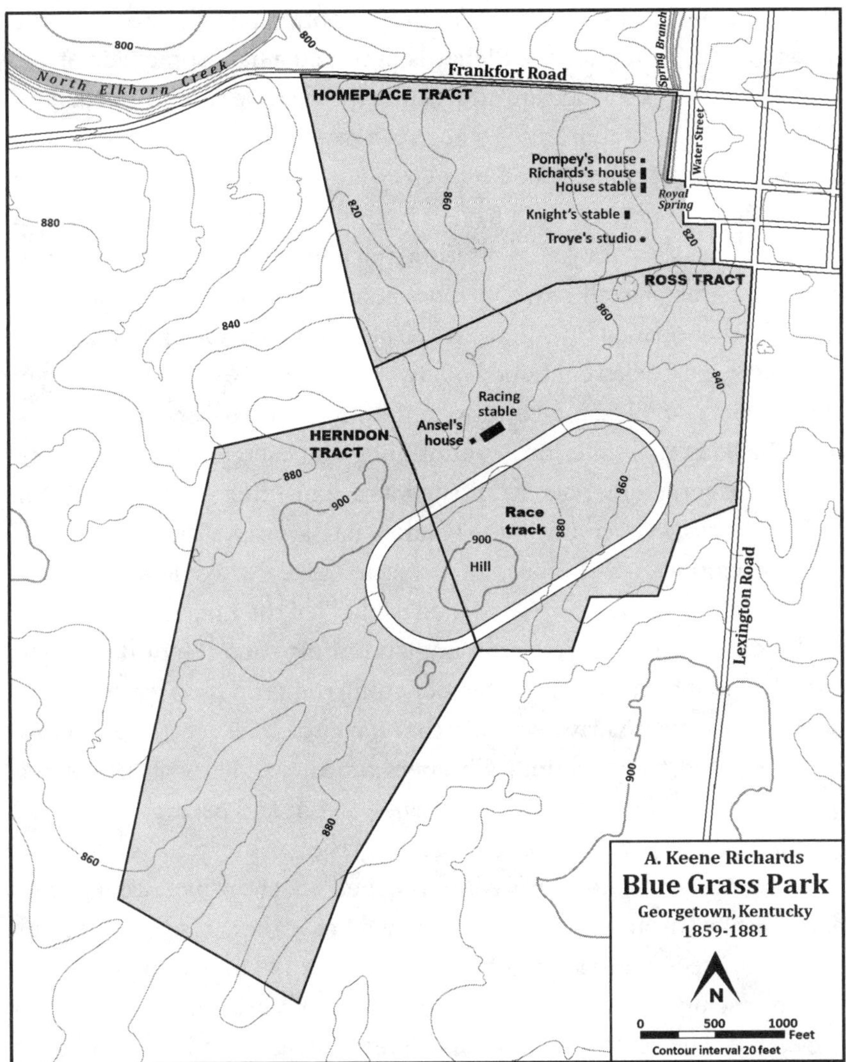

Blue Grass Park, the estate of Alexander Keene Richards in Georgetown, Kentucky. Map by Gary A. O'Dell, based on Scott County deeds and descriptions in various sporting journals. Only selected buildings shown. Locations of the Knight's stable, Troye's studio, and Ansel's house are approximate.

horses trained for comfortable transport. "Mr. R's buggy team" was a pair of "fast, handsome bay mares" capable of making twelve miles in forty minutes. Two bay geldings, both the offspring of Glencoe, pulled Richards's carriage, described as a "low coach-body, two seats facing, box for driver in front, and a standing-place for a footman behind, worth sometimes $1,600." For his wife, Richards provided a handsome pair of gray Anglo-Arab mares, "which are attached to the carriage when Mrs. Richards drives out." These mares were both offspring of Mokhladi, one out of Eagletta and the other foaled by a Grey Eagle II mare. In his 1866 catalogue, Richards noted that "I have driven them for seven years." In addition to horses used for transportation, the house stable was also home to his prized Arabian stallions, kept close at hand. A road from the house led to a gate that opened on Water Street, next to Royal Spring.[26]

The property also contained many other structures, including elegant and spacious stables, a racetrack, and homes for workers. On the Ross tract, he laid out a mile-long oval training and exercise track, where his farm manager, Frank Sherritt, hosted a race meeting in May 1862 while Richards was away serving in the Confederate army. A visitor to the farm, heading southward from the main house to the track, would first encounter the stable, "built of brick with odd gables," of the Knight of St. George, a Thoroughbred imported from England in 1859 and the pride of Richards's breeding stock. A little farther along the farm road was the short path that led to the private studio that Richards built for Edward Troye, his dear friend. Troye periodically spent time in residence at the Georgetown home of his friend and generous patron, and here, in this small, circular building, with its pastoral setting, the artist created some of his most famous works. Richards commissioned no fewer than twenty-seven paintings by the artist, mostly of his own horses, and was given or purchased eighteen more from other horsemen to add to his collection.[27]

The racing stables, located behind the racetrack, were the largest on the estate. The stables contained "sixteen boxes, each large enough to contain four horses, stalled as is done North, with large water tanks, a wide passage between the two divisions, a loft above for hay, straw and corn, and a walk around the entire building wide enough to drive a buggy round, except at the corners, all of which is under the same roof. All the stables are built somewhat on the Gothic or Moorish style of architecture." The racing stables measured 147 feet long by 56 feet wide, and the interior from floor to roof was about 30 feet.[28]

The stables were supervised by Ansel, widely acknowledged as one of the best horse trainers in the business, and his residence was located nearby. Ansel's home was described as having "as neat and pretty an exterior as many of our businessmen's cottages"—a pleasant domicile, befitting the importance of his position. Ansel was assisted in caring for the stock by four grooms and a corps of stable boys, the latter residing in the stables. In the stable hallway, at the head of each stall, was "a comfortable berth for stable boys—sixteen in all—each having a closet for clothes &c, and a window or board shutter, opening at the foot of each berth, so as to enable the boys to have easy access to their horses at all times." Also at ground level were several storage rooms and a reception room for trainers and grooms.[29]

An 1859 visitor reported that the stables were provided with "clean and wholesome rainwater" from cisterns, which Richards preferred to spring water, to avoid potential deleterious effects of a change of water when the horses were moved to tracks elsewhere, which generally were supplied with rain water. This policy was not always followed, since another visitor that year observed that several stallions, after being briefly exercised, were brought down to a spring, where they were allowed to "drink a certain number of swallows, walked awhile, finish drinking, come into the stable, receive a little bundle of nice clean hay and bucket of chop feed, after they are rubbed off." There was another spring in addition to Royal Spring on the Richards property, since the racing stable was situated on a "very beautiful rise, just above a nice spring of clear water, which courses its purling way through five or six lots of beautiful pasture land." This was evidently the spring at which horses were sometimes watered, not Royal Spring.[30]

The mile-long racing oval, unlike most tracks in America, was "over the sod, similar to English courses." American tracks were usually "skinned," consisting of bare dirt from which the sod had been removed, an American innovation believed to allow faster running as opposed to the custom in England, where horses ran on the turf of racecourses. This was probably attributable to the time Richards spent in England and his admiration of English racing customs. Beginning at about the half-mile post, a prominent hill of the infield obscured the back third of the course from the view of spectators. Observers were thrilled as the leading horses disappeared from sight, forcing them to speculate as to what they would see when the competitors rounded the hill and came back into view. One visitor to the May 1862 races at Georgetown wrote, "Bettie West jumped off with a commanding lead, which she held until they left our sight . . . on appearing again, Bettie West still leading. . . . This is the best mile race ever!"[31]

Keene Richards's passion for the Near East was apparent throughout the landscape of Blue Grass Park, since he had imported more than just Arabian horses and Egyptian antiques. One visitor noted that the estate, prior to the war, "had an oriental look. Camels and Damascus cattle grazed on the lawn, and real Arabs in native costume led Arab horses out for service." At his annual sales, in addition to young horses Richards also offered calves "sired by [his] Arabian bull." For a few years, before his untimely death in 1855, Yusef Badra was a fixture at Blue Grass Park and delighted Georgetown residents with his colorful ways. One citizen recalled, "He was quite a gentleman in manners, cultivation, and clothes, as we found from a personal acquaintance during his recent residence in this country."[32]

In addition to expanding the acreage of Blue Grass Park, in 1859 and 1860 Keene Richards made substantial land purchases in Phillips County, Arkansas, in association with his cousin Morris Keene. Phillips County is in the Delta region of Arkansas, adjacent to the Mississippi River, and the rich alluvial soils are prime land for cotton cultivation. Arkansas entered the Union in 1836 as a slave state under the Missouri Compromise, providing the necessary labor force for a plantation economy. Cotton production in Arkansas increased dramatically between 1840 and 1850, reaching 26 million pounds by the end of the decade. Richards apparently sought to emulate his grandfather, William B. Keene, whose land acquisitions in Louisiana served as the basis for his great wealth.[33]

Arkansas, like Louisiana, was a public domain land state, in which all the land originally belonged to the federal government. Earlier in the century, members of Richards's wife's family, the Johnsons, took advantage of federal sales of inexpensive Arkansas land to patent extensive tracts of fertile cotton lands. Between 1838 and 1849, Sallie's great-uncle Richard M. Johnson accumulated nearly five thousand acres of Delta land, most of which lay in Phillips, Chicot, and Desha counties of southeast Arkansas. Her mother, Nancy Johnson, was a co-patentee on many of these land warrants. Lesser, but still considerable, acreage was obtained by Leonidas L. Johnson (1818–circa 1888), who with his wife, Irene, took his adolescent niece into their home near Georgetown after the death of Sallie's mother, Nancy, in 1849. Keene Richards became a very close friend of Leonidas Johnson following his marriage to Sallie. Yet another, if less significant, connection to Arkansas existed for Keene Richards through the Pope family lineage, Edmund Pendleton Pope being a distant cousin of John Pope, a former Lexington resident who was the third territorial governor of Arkansas from 1831 until statehood.[34]

Most of the best federal land in Arkansas along the Mississippi had already been taken up by the time Keene Richards was able to buy land in this region, so his purchases were instead from private individuals rather than the government. His first acquisition was a gift from his friends Leonidas and Irene Johnson, a township section of 640 acres conveyed to him on September 28, 1859, by reason of their "love and affection" and the payment of 1 cent. This initial gift may well have stimulated Richards to obtain additional acreage in the vicinity. One and three-quarters sections were thereafter purchased from Francis Suggett in July 1860, who had bought the land from the government in 1842, bringing the total acreage held jointly in Phillips County by Richards and Morris Keene to 1,760 acres. Later documents describe the land as being adjacent to the property of Leonidas Johnson and "about nine miles from Helena and lies partly on Beaver Bayou." The Phillips County lands were located on the Mississippi between Richards's Kentucky home and his plantation in northeastern Louisiana, allowing convenient visits when in transit from one location to the other. Richards may have brought Morris Keene into the arrangement as a way of rewarding his friend for his past loyalty and service, giving him an equal share in a large cotton plantation. Keene evidently found the region to his liking; after the Civil War he moved to Arkansas and settled there.[35]

Richards made his racing debut on the Metairie track in New Orleans on January 8, 1857, entering the horse Viley, on loan from his Scott County neighbor, Webb Ross. At this time Ross was still resident on the property south of Blue Grass Park and was a horseman on a small scale; at Metairie and Lexington during the previous two years, this colt was Ross's only race entry. Since he was getting out of the horse business, Ross probably loaned his seasoned race mare to Richards in exchange for a share of any prize money. Viley, now a three-year-old colt, was sired by Grey Eagle in

1854 out of a twenty-year-old mare once known as Mary Porter during her racing days, purchased and renamed Blinkey by Ross in 1851. During the spring meeting at Metairie in April 1857, Viley was entered again under Richards's name in three races. This suggests that Richards spent the winter season in Louisiana rather than returning to Kentucky. Viley's performance was modest at best, never finishing better than second in a field of three to four horses running one- and two-mile heats. This was the only horse raced by Richards in 1857, although at Lexington in the autumn an unspecified Glencoe colt was entered by Morris H. Keene in a race for two-year-olds but failed to start.[36]

During the following year, 1858, Richards, now with more experience and having increased his racing stable, greatly expanded the scope of his participation, although still limiting his attendance to only two tracks, Metairie and the Kentucky Association course in Lexington. In New Orleans for the winter and spring meets, he entered Viley again in several events, but once again the Ross horse failed to perform well and, after this season, Richards never raced him again. The first horse from his own stable was Miss Duke, a sister to Blonde, who raced at Metairie in April. His favored entry seems to have been the bay mare Glycera, a two-year-old bred by Richard Ten Broeck, sired by Sovereign out of Sister to Pryor #1. Richards entered Glycera in six races at Lexington in May, September, and October, and three races during the following year. Another horse from his stables raced by Richards in 1858 was the recently purchased filly Wax Wing, sired by the notable stallion Wagner, one of the few horses to beat Grey Eagle. Transylvania, by Massoud out of Peytona, was the first of his Anglo-Arab crosses to be entered at a course. She was scratched from a race at Metairie in April, but ran at Lexington on May 28 and again on September 14 and 16, never finishing better than second place. During the last of these events, Transylvania was severely injured and thereafter was retired to a very successful career as a brood mare.[37]

Keene Richards must have been disappointed by the lackluster performance of his initial racing stable. The entire purpose of his breeding program was not just to make more horses, but to produce superior horses capable of winning races. The horses he now possessed were clearly not capable of competing effectively. There was no point in trying to race his pureblood imported Arabians; they had not been trained as racers and their strength was in their endurance, not speed. This was, after all, the characteristic he sought to impart to Anglo-Arab crosses in his breeding program, but the fruition of this program lay in the future, perhaps several generations removed.

To enter the ranks of America's leading horsemen, Richards needed to possess exceptional horses that consistently won races. Certainly, native-bred animals such as Sir Archy, American Eclipse, Boston, Lexington, and Fashion were undisputed champions of the turf, and had produced many distinguished progeny, but American horsemen frequently resorted to importation of English bloodstock to improve their racing stables and breeding programs. Richards's ill-fated 1857 purchase of imported Glencoe was just such an effort to infuse the bloodline of an English Thoroughbred of proven ability. With the loss of Glencoe, and indifferent racing performances by his current stock, Richards felt a need to emulate his peers by acquiring some of the best blood horses of England for his own stable.

A visit to England for this purpose would have to be of relatively short duration, perhaps no more than a few months, for he was no longer a young man without care and able to spend a year or more on leisurely tours. He had family responsibilities and a business to run. Even though Morris Keene was well capable of supervising agricultural operations at Transylvania, and he had a knowledgeable horseman, Frank Sherritt, as farm manager at Blue Grass Park, he could not afford to be away for long. Fortunately, Keene Richards had a friend in England who was familiar with the racing scene and the available bloodstock and could advise him in his selections: Richard Ten Broeck.

11

THE "AMERICAN INVASION" OF ENGLAND

For several decades American horsemen had discussed the possibility of taking American horses to England and pitting them against their English counterparts, convinced that American running horses were superior to those in England. There would be significant expense and risk attached to transporting horses across the Atlantic, since highbred horses seldom traveled well by ship and would have to acclimatize on their arrival. In 1856, Richard Ten Broeck was the first American horseman to take a racing stable to England, although his horses would not compete until the following year. They performed poorly at first, but ultimately, to the astonishment of English observers who were convinced that American horses could not possibly compete successfully against English Thoroughbreds, Ten Broeck's horses were able to capture several of the most prestigious English races. Much of Ten Broeck's success can be attributed to the unwavering support of Keene Richards, who selected and shipped a number of outstanding racehorses to his friend in England.

Ten Broeck's longstanding ambition to bring American horses to compete in classic English races probably solidified after April 1856, when he was forced to withdraw from association with the Metairie course of New Orleans. Ten Broeck's own pockets were not quite deep enough to finance a venture to England, but he found willing sponsors in Keene Richards and millionaire Francis Morris (1810–1886) of Westchester County, New York, president of the Central American Transit Line and the American Telegraph Company. Morris was interested in becoming involved in the racing industry, and beginning in 1860 he established a Thoroughbred breeding

Richard Ten Broeck, onetime owner of the Metairie course in New Orleans and a close personal friend of Keene Richards. From *Baily's Magazine of Sports and Pastimes* 9 (April 1864), following page 54.

operation on his land at Throggs Neck on the East River that became among the largest in the North. The farm was initially stocked with English horses shipped to America by Richard Ten Broeck. Morris's son, John A. Morris, traveled to England to learn about racing at the feet of the master, so to speak, and presumably to keep track of his father's investment.[1]

Ten Broeck's champion Lexington, by this time nearly blind, had to be left behind in Kentucky, standing stud at Harper's farm in Woodford County. Ten Broeck, however, owned other outstanding racehorses. After Lexington, his three best Thoroughbred Running Horses were Lecomte, Pryor, and Prioress, and these were the horses he took with him in autumn 1856 to England in what was known in the sporting press as the "American invasion." Prioress was bred and owned by Ten Broeck, sired by imported Sovereign out of Thomas J. Wells's mare Reel and foaled in 1853, and thus a half-sister to Lecomte, who was a Boston colt out of Reel.

Prioress made a spectacular debut as a two-year-old at Metairie in 1855, then racing under the name "Poison." Pryor, foaled in 1852 out of Gipsey by Glencoe, made his first appearance at Metairie on April 5, 1855, just a few days before the final match between Ten Broeck's Lexington and Wells's Lecomte. Pitted against Lecomte a year later, March 15, 1856, at the Pharsalia course in Natchez, the little-known Pryor won an upset victory. The race results listed Ten Broeck as Pryor's owner, indicating that the four-year-old had been purchased previous to that date. Lecomte, now six years old, was purchased from Wells a few weeks later. Ten Broeck paid $10,000 for Lecomte and $2,500 for Pryor. These sales astonished the racing world, since Wells and Ten Broeck were bitter enemies, but Wells, depressed by Lexington's victory over his prized Lecomte, had decided to retire from active participation in horse racing.[2]

On July 12, 1856, the three horses embarked from New York aboard the Inman Line's steamship *Edinburgh* for Glasgow, accompanied by trainer David P. Palmer, two jockeys (Charles E. Littlefield and Gilbert W. Patrick, known as "Gilpatrick"), and a full complement of grooms and stable boys. Ten Broeck had departed for Britain three days earlier. After a voyage of twelve days, the *Edinburgh* arrived at the Clyde, but was unable to proceed up the river to Glasgow for three days because of low water. Arriving in good health after their crossing, the horses were kept at Glasgow for about a month and provided with exercise and light feed. From Glasgow, they were shipped by railroad to Newmarket, which had become the most important racing center in England. Newmarket featured two racecourses and the largest cluster of Thoroughbred training yards in the country. The horses remained at Newmarket for nearly a year, given walking exercise and light galloping through the winter. During this time, Richard Ten Broeck made social contacts and increased his familiarity with the nuances of the English turf. He also purchased an English horse, Belle, by Slane out of Miss Fairfield, to add to his racing stable.[3]

Thoroughbred racing in England differed in several details from American practice, but it was similar enough that visitors from one country could easily understand racing in the other. The most important differences were the absence of heat races and the shape and nature of the track. The configuration of American courses was a derivative of the frontier mentality. During the settlement of the new land, tracks were often literally carved out of the wilderness, and so the ideal form for a racetrack became a flat oval. The establishment of a track represented a victory over nature rather than an accommodation with natural topography. In contrast, the landscape in England was "tame," the product of centuries of civilization. English courses were laid out to follow the existing contours of the landscape, and so varied widely from place to place rather than conforming to a standard pattern. On English courses, horses ran on grass; some of the first American tracks had attempted to follow this tradition, but maintaining a grass track proved to be too expensive. Although racing continued to be referred to here as the sport of the "turf," American horses ran on dirt tracks rather than grass. The dirt tracks often lacked adequate drainage and tended to become rather muddy after a rainfall. In a self-serving rationalization, American sportsmen came to believe that horses were able to run faster on dirt than on grass, at least in good weather.[4]

To most English sportsmen, horses racing around an oval track such as those in America was just a bore. Ten Broeck once invited Admiral Henry J. Rous, a leading figure of the English turf, to see his horse Satellite run for the Chester Cup. The Chester racecourse, tucked into a bend of the River Dee, was the oldest and smallest course of significance in England, just over a mile in length and roughly circular in shape with few straight stretches. The admiral declined the invitation, saying, "I would rather see horses run round a tub." Because English courses were laid out to wind around natural and manmade features, rising and falling with the topography, much of the race action was not visible to spectators. Horse racing in America had always been a spectator sport, supported by the oval shape of courses, which allowed large crowds of onlookers from all social classes an unrestricted view of the race from beginning to end. English racing was essentially a sport for the elite classes.[5]

The English regarded horse racing as a competition among horses rather than a race against the clock. The courses varied so widely in length and configuration, and conditions differed from day to day even at the same course, so what did it matter, then, how long it took to complete the race? Handicappers in England, therefore, were concerned primarily with the amount of saddle weight carried by a horse, the idea being to adjust these weights by individual horse to give each, in theory, an equal chance of winning. Each horse was assigned a weight according to past performance, age, and gender, the better horses being required to carry more weight. Americans, on the other hand, became increasingly obsessed with time as the standard for measuring performance, and handicappers on this side of the Atlantic made this a major factor in their calculations. Ten Broeck noted, "In comparison with its importance in America, I was surprised to find how little attention was paid to time in handicapping."[6]

Richard Ten Broeck had always made most of his living by his skill and luck as a gambler. To be successful in England, he had to win races—a great many races—but above all, his driving ambition (and that of his supporters in the United States) was to score victories in one or more of the five great classics of English Thoroughbred racing. Each of these classics, held once each year and restricted to three-year-olds, is a "flat" race, run over a course without jumps. The Two Thousand Guineas and the One Thousand Guineas stakes are run at Newmarket in Suffolk (about seventy-five miles north of London) in late April or early May. The Epsom Oaks and the Epsom Derby run at Epsom Downs in Surrey, about twelve miles south of the capital. The Oaks is held in early June, and the Derby, today held on the first Saturday in June, in the mid-nineteenth century was run in late May. The last of the classics, the St. Leger Stakes, was held in September at the Doncaster course in south Yorkshire, in the north of England. The One Thousand Guineas and the Oaks are restricted to fillies, but the others are open to both fillies and colts. In Ten Broeck's day, each of these races was relatively short by American standards. At a mile and six furlongs (just under two miles), the St. Leger was the longest, and the two Guineas races were the shortest, each being exactly one mile. The Two Thousand Guineas, the Epsom Derby (most prestigious of all Thoroughbred races), and the St. Leger together constitute the English Triple Crown, first inaugurated in 1853 when West Australian swept all three.

Ten Broeck came to England armed with a letter of introduction to Lord Fitzwilliam, who received him hospitably and introduced him to the leading figures of the English turf, who were fascinated by this brash American gambler. "Except that he was a Southerner," the Earl of Suffolk later recalled, "nobody knew anything about him or his antecedents, though there were plenty of wonderous tales in circulation. He had been a hell-keeper, a slave-dealer, a 'sportsman' which in the American language is not a complimentary term, etc., etc. Everybody was sure for many years, at least, that he was the sharpest of the sharp on the turf; at the card table also." Nicknamed "Tenny" by his new English friends, Ten Broeck received many invitations to parties and receptions on the estates of the aristocracy. His first taste of English life among the nobility was during the Bath races (possibly in September 1856), where a large party of horsemen were entertained at Badminton, the estate of the Duke of Beaufort. At the time, the duke served as Master of the Horse to Queen Victoria. Admiral Rous, without question the most important man in the world of English racing, was among the first to welcome him to Newmarket, and the two soon became intimate friends. Rous proposed Ten Broeck for membership in the exclusive "Coffee-Room" at the track, and advised him on matters of the English turf and in the management of his racing stable. Ten Broeck later recalled, "The Admiral and I often attended the races together, canvassing in company the horses expected to run."[7]

If the English gentry were predisposed to amicably receive Richard Ten Broeck, there were Americans then in the country who bore him nothing but malice. These were friends of Thomas Jefferson Wells, whose animosity for his former partner at the Metairie track was carried across the Atlantic. "Having failed to ruin him at home, they determined to accomplish it abroad. Atrocious stories were set afoot . . . and a studied propaganda carried on against him," wrote equine historian John Hervey. While much of this smear campaign consisted of innuendos concerning Ten Broeck's character, more serious charges were made that he misrepresented the ages of his horses in order to obtain their eligibility for certain events. In face of these charges, Ten Broeck maintained his composure, while his friends rallied to his support; in the end, his steadfast aplomb "silenced his enemies" and earned him "the respect and friendship of the leaders of the British turf."[8]

Robert A. Alexander, a friend of Keene Richards, visiting England in the autumn of 1856 to acquire English Thoroughbreds for Woodburn, his Woodford County stud, was no part of Wells's conspiracy, and he cordially conducted some business with Ten Broeck. Alexander provided a much-needed injection of cash by purchasing the famous Lexington, then standing at Harper's not far from Alexander's place, for the sum of $15,000. The largest price ever paid up to that time for an American-bred horse, it was made in two installments of $7,500 each, the first paid immediately and the second to be paid on Ten Broeck's return to America. Since Lexington survived for nearly twenty more years, succumbing at Woodburn in 1875, Ten Broeck likely received the full amount.[9]

Although David Palmer brought Ten Broeck's first shipment of American Thoroughbred Running Horses across the Atlantic and served as his first trainer, he did not long remain in this position. Ten Broeck tended to change his trainers with nearly the same frequency as he discarded his worn suits. Another American trainer, William Brown, protégé of J. B. "Ben" Pryor, came over in June 1857 to replace Palmer and began the training of Ten Broeck's horses at Newmarket at that time. Brown was described as "reserved in his habits" and constantly smoking a pipe, "which was never suffered to go out." He remained in England for several years after leaving Ten Broeck's employ; on December 9, 1864, Ten Broeck, who owed him $6,000 for his services, handed him $500 on account and said, "If you keep still about it I will some day pay you the balance." The next day Brown departed England and took employment with Francis Morris until 1875, and afterward with Pierre Lorillard. Posterity records that Ten Broeck did pay his debt to Brown.[10]

Brown was soon followed by Andrew J. Minor, who trained racehorses for Judge John S. Hunter at Hunter's plantation in Dallas County, Alabama, near Selma, before the war. Hunter had often raced at Metairie while Ten Broeck was manager there, so Ten Broeck would have been well acquainted with his trainer. Keene Richards would also know Minor, since he had purchased the mare Blonde from him for his own stable. Blonde had first raced under Judge Hunter's colors at New Orleans in 1854 and then been sold to Minor. Dismissed by Ten Broeck in 1860, Minor returned to the United States, where, by coincidence, he trained horses for an entirely different John Hunter, unrelated to Judge Hunter of Alabama. At his new employer's establishment, Annieswood Stud in Westchester County, New York, not far from Francis Morris's place, Minor conditioned the famous racehorse Kentucky, bred by John M. Clay and sired by Lexington out of Magnolia, a Glencoe mare. When the notorious pugilist and gambler John Morrissey founded the Saratoga Racecourse in 1863, John Hunter of New York along with William R. Travers and George Osgood became associates; Hunter was also the second president of the American Jockey Club.[11]

As Minor's replacement, Ten Broeck brought over Ben Pryor, who, while employed by Adam Bingaman at Natchez, had trained Lexington for Ten Broeck in 1853 for his match against Wells's Lecomte. Ten Broeck wanted the very best man available to prepare his horse Umpire for a forthcoming race in the English Derby at Epsom Downs in May 1860. Although Umpire failed to place in this most prestigious of Thoroughbred races, Pryor continued to train for Ten Broeck until 1863, when he went to France and trained for the Baron Schickler, later returning to the United States. Afterward, Ten Broeck presumably used English trainers, as he was adapting more and more to the English style of training.[12]

American training methods were considered rather harsh by English standards. One English observer recalled that the "American style," as practiced by A. J. Minor, was "very long, slow work," with a great deal of sweating. Another remarked that American training was similar to that employed by contemporary English trainer John Scott, known as the "Emperor of Trainers" and the "Wizard of the North." Scott's methods were "gradual and thorough," consisting of "long slow gallops, at short intervals, sweats, under two suits of heavy clothing," and "periodically, after one of these sweats, the pupil would be 'tapped' of what was then considered to be superfluous vital fluid. A vein in the region of the throat would be opened, and a pint or more of blood 'let' into a tin pannikin held by an attendant." Minor's system was considered even more drastic than Scott's. Although the Americans did not practice bloodletting, Ten Broeck's trainers would often "sweat" a horse immediately before bringing them to the post, or "harden their muscles" by first taking them on a good run. Minor, it was reported, possessed an open mind, and in time both he and Ten Broeck embraced less rigorous methods in the English manner.[13]

While spending the winter of 1856–1857 at Newmarket, Pryor and Prioress were in fine health and acclimatizing well, but Lecomte was in poor condition and, having an injured ankle, was unable to participate in anything more than light exercise. He also suffered from attacks of colic, both in New York before departure and while in Glasgow. Lecomte's colics were a portent of worse to come. On the first of April 1857, Ten Broeck took his stable to new training quarters at Stockbridge. The region was enduring a severe drought, and both Lecomte and Pryor received leg injuries from training on hard ground. Pryor also developed a respiratory infection that continued off and on for several months, sometimes improving for a while and then worsening. Ten Broeck's horses were entered in several races during the summer, his jockeys highly visible in red, white, and blue "Stars and Stripes" racing colors, but in most cases both Lecomte and Prior had to be scratched and a forfeit paid. Even Prioress did not fare well in the matches. American turf enthusiasts, eagerly expecting the cream of American-bred horses to soundly trounce their English competition, were sorely disappointed, and interest in Ten Broeck's enterprise began to decline in the States. In the autumn, Lecomte was again stricken with colic, and died on October 7, followed on the 22nd by Pryor, whose condition had worsened into pneumonia.[14]

During that autumn of 1857, Ten Broeck became so depressed by the poor performance of his horses that, nearly broke, he was about to give up and return to the United States. The turning point came a few days after Lecomte's death, when he took Prioress to race at Newmarket in the Cesarewitch Handicap on October 13. As Ten Broeck later recalled, "After calculating, I found that I had but £10 remaining after settling all my bills. Going to the course on horseback without the least intention of betting, I rode to the ring before the start for the Cesarewitch, and, from curiousity, inquired how much Prioress? An amateur bookmaker, Major Brabazon, said: 'I will bet you 100 to 1, Mr. Ten Broeck.' I answered, '1000 to 10. Done.' Immediately several bookmakers said, 'I will bet you the same, Mr. Ten Broeck.' Having no more money, I rode off in disgust." Before the race, as a storm appeared likely, Ten Broeck put lard on his mare's feet to help keep dirt from sticking, and wrapped her up in blankets to protect her from the weather.[15]

Prioress's usual rider was Gilbert Patrick. Ten Broeck had become so displeased with Patrick's performance that he sent him back home after the running of the Goodwood Cup on July 30, 1857, in which Patrick finished fifth. His place was taken by a new jockey, William Tankerley, brought over from the United States. Now, during the Cesarewitch, Tankerley, unfamiliar with the course, allowed Prioress to become blocked by the front rank, and as John Morris shouted directions at him from the sideline, the race ended in a dead heat between three horses including Prioress. Horses in England did not run multiple heats, as was the practice in America, but in the case of a tie, custom dictated either a runoff or a division of the prize money. Since a three-way split would have provided little reward, a runoff was called. A terrible downpour occurred before the deciding race, during which Prioress was carefully blanketed and rubbed down, while the English horses stood shivering in the rain. Annoyed by Tankerley's poor handling of Prioress during the race, Ten Broeck replaced him with English jockey George Fordham. Fordham rode the mare to victory by a length and a half in the runoff to take the prestigious Cesarewitch, the winnings giving Ten Broeck a much-needed infusion of cash. This was the first English race ever won by an American horse, and Ten Broeck thereafter kept Fordham as his principal jockey.[16]

With the loss of Lecomte and Pryor, Ten Broeck would have been down to a single horse had not his American backers shipped some additional horses across the Atlantic to replenish his stable. Many later accounts of the "American invasion" credit Francis Morris as the man who provided Ten Broeck with additional American-bred horses. Thomas B. Merry, for example, without question an authority on the history of the American turf, wrote in 1918 that "In the year following the memorable Cesarewitch, Mr. Morris sent over a half-dozen horses, among them being Babylon by Imp. Belshazzar; Woodburn by Imp. Glencoe; Satellite by Imp. Albion, and Sunnyside [*sic;* Summerside], Olive Branch and Optimist by Lexington. He also sent over Starke." A look at the *American Stud Book* and other contemporary documents demonstrates that, contrary to this statement, most of the horses shipped to Ten Broeck in England were in fact formerly owned by Keene Richards or came from Richards's friends and neighbors. While Morris was certainly one of Ten Broeck's backers, it was Richards and not Morris who played the most critical role in shipping some of the best American horses to England. Richards and Morris may have worked in concert, with Richards selecting and purchasing horses and sending them to Morris in New York, who then shipped them to Ten Broeck.[17] Although details of the financial arrangements between Ten Broeck and his sponsors are not available, it appears that he purchased these horses, as he subsequently sold some of them in England.

The *Spirit of the Times* for August 15, 1857, notes that "Mr. Brown"—certainly a reference to the arrival of Ten Broeck's new trainer—brought two "very fine yearlings" to England, the colt Woodburn and the filly Bonita. Woodburn was bred and owned by Robert A. Alexander, and Bonita was bred by Abe Buford, both located in Woodford County and both close friends of Keene Richards. Since he owned her dam, Sarah Washington, Bonita was already Ten Broeck's property. Babylon, a chestnut colt sired by Belshazzar out of a Trustee mare and foaled in 1854, was sent over at about the same time, if not in the same shipment. Race results reported by the *American Turf Register* in a separate section titled "American Horses in England" show Babylon running in several English races beginning on August 28, 1857. Babylon was bred in the Deep South, his sire Belshazzar leased by William J. Minor of Mississippi from his importer, Thomas Flintoff of Nashville, Tennessee. While Francis Morris of New York would have been unlikely to have much contact with a Mississippi breeder, Keene Richards was well known to horsemen of the region, and so was far more likely to have acquired Babylon for Ten Broeck.[18]

There can be no question of provenance for Optimist and Summerside; both were bred and owned by Keene Richards prior to being shipped to England. The colt Optimist and the filly Summerside were the produce of two unnamed Glencoe mares Richards had purchased from Ten Broeck and bred to Alexander's Lexington at Woodburn. The first mare foaled Optimist in 1857 and an unnamed bay colt in 1858; the second mare, known as Sister to Pryor #2, foaled the colt Reformer in 1859 and Summerside in 1860. All four, the offspring of Lexington, were sent to Ten Broeck in England, where, in 1866, Optimist was sold to Weatherby, publisher of the English *Stud Book*. The four foals may have been part of the purchase agreement for the two mares (plus another Glencoe mare obtained at the same time) made between Richards and Ten Broeck. The filly Olive Branch, sired by Lexington and foaled in 1859, like her half-sister Bonita, also belonged to Ten Broeck in the first place.[19]

According to Sanders Bruce, Richards purchased a three-year-old colt named Starke from Thomas J. Wells and shipped him to Ten Broeck in England. Starke was a half-brother to Lecomte and Prioress, sired by Wagner out of the matchless Reel. Starke performed indifferently at Metairie in April 1858 and was observed there by Richards, whose own horse Miss Duke had finished second to Starke's third place. A few days later, in two races at a meet held by Wells at Dentley Plantation near Alexandria, the colt defeated all challengers, but Richards was not present at this event. Starke again appeared at Metairie in the first week of January 1859, but by this time Richards had departed the United States for England on a trip to purchase English Thoroughbreds for his own stud. T. J. Wells would have been more likely to close a deal with his close friend Richards or his agent (possibly Morris Keene) than with an unknown Yankee like Francis Morris.[20]

Starke arrived in England during February 1859, so he must have been shipped from New Orleans almost immediately following the January races at Metairie. The first appearance of Starke in an English race was at Newmarket in April 1859, in which he did not place. The same shipment that brought Starke across the Atlantic may also have included Ten Broeck's chestnut colt Umpire, foaled in 1857 out of Alice Carneal, the dam of Lexington whom Ten Broeck leased from Elisha Warfield the previous year. Umpire was sired by Lecomte during the stallion's brief stay in Kentucky before being sent to England, and his first appearance on the English turf was with Starke at Newmarket in April 1858, where he also failed to place.[21]

The three-year-old chestnut horse Satellite (formerly called Sherritt, after Frank Sherritt) was shipped out from New York on September 11, 1859. Sherritt was bred by Bailie Peyton in Tennessee, sired by imported Albion out of a Leviathan mare. The sale of this horse, one of the best in Richards's stable, to Ten Broeck is a measure of the high regard in which he held the man he considered a mentor. In the opinion of Richards's trainer Ansel, Satellite was "as good as Brown Dick." Ansel should know, for he had trained both horses, and Goldsby's Brown Dick, with numerous victories on the track, was indisputably top-class. John M. Clay (the youngest son of Kentucky statesman Henry Clay), whose horse Daniel Boone was beaten by Sherritt at Lexington in May 1858, had afterward said, "Satellite could stop and take a bite of grass, and then beat them."[22]

Keene Richards's crucial role in providing Richard Ten Broeck with American horses is thus quite evident, although often overlooked today because of errors of attribution made by later turf historians. Ten Broeck himself took an active role in rebuilding his stable, purchasing several top-class English Thoroughbreds in 1858, the most notable being Eclipse, Barbarity, and Phaeton. By 1863 his racing string would be made up entirely of English horses.

Prioress's victory in the Cesarewitch was the first in a series of victories that marked a dramatic turnaround in the fortunes of American horses in England. With a renewed stable comprised of outstanding racers, Ten Broeck was thereafter able to score a series of wins in stakes and matches over many of the classic English racecourses. Many of his horses, including Satellite, won races, but the real American-bred stars of his stable were Prioress, Umpire, and above all Starke. Although never again a victor in a major contest such as the Cesarewitch, Prioress consistently secured wins in minor stakes races until, lamed in the spring meet at Newmarket in 1861, she was sold as a brood mare to Sir Lydston Johnson for $3,000. Umpire, who never raced in the United States, won thirteen stakes events and three matches in England, and was sold in 1864 to the Earl of Coventry and retired to a very successful stud career at the age of seven.[23]

In Starke, however, Richard Ten Broeck was able to realize his ambitions on the English turf, for the chestnut colt was a winning racer almost from the start. His performance during the spring meetings of 1859 was nothing remarkable, but during the summer Starke demonstrated that American horses were a challenge to be taken seriously by gathering in three of the most prestigious trophies of the English turf. At the Goodwood Course in West Sussex on July 27, a two-and-one-half-mile race against a field of seventeen, Starke captured the Goodwood Stakes, and during the same meeting two days later the Bentinck Memorial. On September 7, at Warwick, Starke took home the Warwick Cup. His crowning achievement came on August 2, 1861, when, with Fordham in the saddle, he battled with the favorite, an English Thoroughbred called The Wizard, down the home stretch to take the Goodwood Cup by a head. Ten Broeck's Optimist finished in third place. Richard Ten Broeck later recalled, "Thus did I finally accomplish the object for which I had left America." Two months later, Starke was sold to a Prussian aristocrat for $7,000 and retired to stud in that country.[24]

After the end of the racing season of 1867, Ten Broeck left England and returned to the United States in company with his American wife, the former Pattie D. Anderson of Kentucky, whom he had married in England in 1857. The "American invasion" had not quite shaped up to the vision held by many American horsemen as a spectacular rout of the English competition, but Richard Ten Broeck left England a wealthy man. During his ten years abroad, he had earned nearly $200,000 in stakes and trophies alone, and probably gained considerably more through side bets. He was a gambler, first and foremost; this was how he made his living. Unlike Richards, he had no fixed assets to provide him with an income, only his horses and his wits. One observer estimated that, in 1872, Ten Broeck was worth more than a million dollars.[25]

Despite all the public enthusiasm attending his great "American invasion" of England, the riverboat gambler and dapper racing entrepreneur did a great disservice to the Thoroughbred interests of the United States by his removal of some of the best racehorses ever bred in this country, who were never returned and thus made little or no contribution to American Thoroughbred bloodlines. In the long term, however, this may well be balanced by some of the first-class English Thoroughbreds he shipped to America, including Phaeton, Barbarity, Eclipse, and the colt—Australian—he helped Keene Richards select. Eclipse and Australian, in particular, represent two of the most significant contributors to bloodlines of modern American Thoroughbreds.[26]

Eclipse, a handsome horse foaled in 1855, was one of the fastest colts in England and, after a modestly successful career running under the colors of Henry Padwick, was purchased by Ten Broeck in 1858 for his racing stable. Apparently he did not do well in training for Ten Broeck, and ran only once or twice more before being shipped, along with Barbarity, for the United States on August 18, 1859. Arriving at New York, Eclipse began a stud career, first at the Fashion Racecourse on Long Island. Then he was sent to Kentucky in 1861, where he was under the management of Barak G. Thomas of Lexington, a close friend of Keene Richards. He was generally known as "Ten Broeck's Eclipse" to distinguish him from the famous Eclipse of England in the previous century and from the equally renown American Eclipse. Ten Broeck's Eclipse returned to the East Coast in 1864, and in 1866 he was turned over, along with the mare Barbarity, to Francis Morris of Throggs Neck as partial repayment for his financial support of Ten Broeck's English venture.[27]

These two horses were the foundation of Morris's stud farm, which subsequently became one of the major Thoroughbred establishments of the North. Eclipse remained at the Morris stud until his death in 1878. Barbarity was quite successful as a brood mare for Morris; her produce included five full sisters sired by Eclipse known as the "Barbarous Battalion": Ruthless, Relentless, Regardless, Remorseless, and Merciless, all good racers. The first Belmont Stakes, held in 1867 at the recently opened Jerome Park track in Westchester County, was won by Ruthless. Morris's son, John A. Morris, who accompanied Ten Broeck to England and learned a great deal about racing, subsequently made quite a name for himself in the Thoroughbred industry. John gained control of the Louisiana state lottery after the Civil War and made an enormous fortune in the process. His father had purchased a huge tract of land in the Hill Country of central Texas some years before his death in 1886, more than 21,000 acres, which he directed in his will should be developed for the breeding of racehorses. John A. Morris purchased the property from the executors. Under his direction and later that of his sons, the Morris Ranch became one of the largest Thoroughbred establishments in the nation, with hundreds of horses. In 1889, Morris built the lavish Morris Park Racecourse in Westchester County, New York, only a few miles from Jerome Park, which quickly replaced the latter as the region's most popular racing venue.[28]

On January 17, 1868, Richard and Pattie Ten Broeck purchased a substantial farm on the outskirts of Louisville, Kentucky, then known as "Lynnford." Ten Broeck renamed the property "Hurstbourne" to honor one of his friends in England, the Duke of Portland, whose estate carried that name. After the death of his wife in 1873, Ten Broeck became a racing advisor to millionaire horseman James R. Keene, and often returned to England for the races. Ten Broeck sold Hurstbourne Stud in 1878, and ten years later retired to California, where he bought a five-acre lot in San Mateo and built a small cottage for his residence. The last years of his life were spent alone. His fortune gone, he was reduced to living off of the sales of his racing trophies and mementoes. He became increasingly reclusive and erratic. Richard Ten Broeck died peacefully in his own bed on August 1, 1892.[29]

12
SOME NEW BLOOD

When Keene Richards arrived in England during the late summer or early autumn of 1858, one of his first actions would have been to seek out the company of his friend Richard Ten Broeck. American horsemen had been following the progress of the "American invasion" with considerable interest, and, of course, Richards was one of Ten Broeck's financial backers. As a friend of Ten Broeck and as a knowledgeable and wealthy member of America's equine gentry, Richards would have been readily admitted into the same social circles. As his express purpose for being in England was to acquire some first-class Thoroughbred horses for breeding and racing, there was no better way to evaluate the stock of the country than by attending race meetings and socializing with the leading horsemen. Richards thus probably spent much of his time in company with Ten Broeck, Admiral Rous, and other notables of the English turf discussing the merits of various horses at the races and visiting the studs and training yards of the breeders. In selecting horses to purchase and export, he depended most of all on the advice of his fellow countryman, Richard Ten Broeck.

At the time of Richards's visit to England, another American was creating quite a sensation throughout the country. John S. Rarey, the man who appropriated the training methods of Denton Offutt and claimed them as his own invention, had come to England the previous autumn and soon generated a flurry of publicity. At the height of the excitement about Rarey, Ten Broeck came to visit Richards in his rooms in London and asked what he thought about the idea of taking lessons from the celebrated horse trainer. As Richards later recalled, "I frankly told him that I thought the system which Rarey taught would prove of great assistance to him in the management of his stable, but added that it was not necessary for him to go to Rarey for instruction. I then explained to him what I knew of Rarey and Offutt, and wound up by placing Offutt's book in his hands. He took it home with him, and he afterwards informed me that he sat up all night reading it. He also pronounced it a wonderful book." Here is evidence that Offutt and the lessons he gave in Georgetown made such an impression on young Richards that, more than a decade later, he considered Offutt's book an essential part of his luggage on a voyage across the ocean. From this, it is not hard to surmise that one or another edition of Offutt's book had also twice journeyed with him to the Near East.[1]

During that autumn of 1858, Richards, with Ten Broeck to advise him, purchased seven English Thoroughbreds for shipment back to Kentucky: four mares, three with foals at their sides and two of them pregnant at the time of their Atlantic crossing, certain indicators of fertility and outstanding examples of value added. The mares included one simply known as "the Lanercost mare," with her colt, Hillsborough; Spiletta; Melrose and her filly, Target; and Emilia, with her young colt, Millington. Richards was determined to have only the best, for each of these mares was the progeny of an outstanding English racehorse. The Lanercost mare, foaled in 1844, was the daughter of Lanercost, who ran third in the 1839 St. Leger and afterward won twenty-eight races out of fifty-four starts, including five in a period of only twelve days. Along with her came her bay colt Hillsborough, sired by Stockwell, and soon after arriving in America she was delivered of a bay colt by Flying Dutchman, who unfortunately died. Stockwell was one of the leading sires in England, heading the list seven times, and his offspring were among the most successful racers of their time, producing six St. Leger winners and three Derby winners. Richards's imported mare Spiletta, foaled in 1856, was a half-sister to Hillsborough, also sired by Stockwell. The dead colt, had he lived, would have had great potential, for his sire, Flying Dutchman, won both the St. Leger and the Derby and was afterward a leading Thoroughbred sire.[2]

The mare Melrose was accompanied by her chestnut filly, Target, sired by Rifleman and foaled in 1858. Rifleman won the Great Yorkshire Stakes of 1855, and at St. Leger the same year he ran second because of bad handling and a delay at the post, although considered the best horse in the race. Melrose was foaled in 1845; her sire, Melbourne, was a direct descendant through the male line of the Godolphin and, while not as eminent as a racehorse or in the stud as Stockwell or Flying Dutchman, enjoyed modest success in both endeavors. Melbourne was described as "a great, homely horse . . . no very great performer but good enough to beat Lanercost" for the Palantine Plate at Chester. Melbourne's most famous son was West Australian, first winner of the English Triple Crown in 1853, who just happened to be sire of the little colt Millington, trotting alongside his dam, Emilia.[3]

Emilia was sired by Young Emilius, winner of the 1823 Epson Derby. Still nursing Millington at the time she was loaded aboard ship for the United States, she carried within her a foal sired by another outstanding racehorse, Fazzoletto, winner of both the Two Thousand Guineas and the Great Yorkshire Stakes in 1856. The bay colt later foaled in the United States would be named Young Fazzoletto by Keene Richards.[4]

With Ten Broeck as advisor, Richards obviously exerted careful consideration in the selection of English mares for breeding at Blue Grass Park. Each of his choices was the offspring of a horse who had won one or more of the classic Thoroughbred races, and so carried the potential for greatness within her genetic makeup. As is so often the case, time would prove that an outstanding parent did not guarantee an outstanding son or daughter. Hillsborough, for example, never amounted to much; in 1905, Thomas B. Merry dismissed nearly every one of the sons of Stockwell imported to the United States, including Hillsborough by name, as "about as trashy a lot as could well be imagined."[5]

In Millington, however, Richards "builded wiser than he knew." His importation of this colt was perhaps the most significant contribution he made to the development of the modern American Thoroughbred. Richards scarcely had time to evaluate the abilities of Millington before the Civil War disrupted all his careful planning. He sold the colt to his friend Robert A. Alexander in the winter of 1861. Renamed Australian, the bay colt became a good performer on the turf and a true star at Alexander's Woodburn Stud, where he was retired after the racing season of 1862. Australian won three of nine races as a three-year-old, and although he never led the sire list, he stood second only to the prolific Lexington. Among his numerous progeny was the famous Spendthrift, foaled in 1876, undefeated as a two-year-old and winner of the 1879 Belmont Stakes classic in New York. To Merry, Australian was anything but a "trashy" horse: "If I were a resident of Georgetown, Ky.," he proclaimed, "I would cheerfully subscribe $100 towards a monument to be erected to the memory of Mr. Keene Richards, who imported Australian from England."[6]

Richards's selection of mares was made in a relatively short time, since they were all sent off to the United States in late 1858, no more than a few months after his arrival. He still needed to obtain a top-notch Thoroughbred stallion, and in this he proceeded more slowly, remaining in England through late spring 1859 before making his final choice. His delay, of course, may have been simply to spend more time enjoying the society of his countryman Ten Broeck and the aristocrats of the English turf, or, as likely, he wished to remain long enough to witness the running of the Two Thousand and One Thousand Guineas races at the beginning of the racing season. Late in April, he made his pick, a dark bay with a small star on the forehead, known as the Knight of St. George. Bred and trained in Ireland by William Disney, the Knight was sired by Irish Birdcatcher (a highly successful racer) out of the mare Maltese and foaled in 1851. As a two-year-old in 1853, the Knight placed second in two stakes races at the Curragh course at Kildare, Ireland, and when brought to England for the 1854 season he won the Members Plate at Newcastle-Upon-Tyne and the Worcester Stakes, placed second for the Chesterfield Cup at Goodwood, and claimed the prestigious St. Leger at Doncaster in September, there racing against a field of seventeen. He finished his racing career with a win at Newcastle in October 1854, where he received an injury that resulted in his retirement from the track to stud, first for Lord Exeter and then, in 1859, at the Rawcliffe Stud Company near York, one of the largest breeding establishments in the world. Richards purchased the Knight of St. George on the first day of May from Rawcliffe, and shipped him out by steamer from Liverpool on the fourth. The Knight arrived safely at Blue Grass Park on June 10 and was immediately put to the service of several mares. Within two years, the stallion had earned Richards more than $12,000 in stud fees.[7]

Richards apparently returned to the United States aboard the same ship as the Knight, and on his arrival at Georgetown he commissioned Edward Troye to create a portrait of his prize stallion. The *Kentucky Statesman,* a Lexington paper, noted on June 14 that Troye was to be paid $7,000 for the completed painting. As in the case of *The Syrian Ploughman,* this

The Knight of St. George, an English Thoroughbred imported by Richards in 1859. Painted in 1866 by Edward Troye. Private collection.

fee seems excessive and was likely exaggerated by the *Statesman,* given that Richards's income from his Louisiana cotton plantation was less than $50,000 that year. Troye's finished painting depicted a horse rather gaunt in appearance, apparently having lost weight during his Atlantic crossing. He soon recovered, since a visitor to the farm during the following summer described the Knight of St. George as "the most perfectly formed stallion we have ever seen. Hours might be profitably devoted to studying his fine proportions—and yet we doubt if any one could point out a defect."[8]

Having seen the Knight settled in at Blue Grass Park, Richards almost immediately departed once again for England. This second trip is indicated by a new passport application dated July 15, 1859, in New York. There would not appear to be any business justification for Richards to go back to England so soon, since he had just purchased several Thoroughbreds for Blue Grass Park. This appears to have been simply a pleasure trip in which, Richards, now the seasoned world traveler, acted as tour guide for friends and family. Richards's passport application was cosigned by Leonidas Johnson, his wife's uncle, who also witnessed for Lewis L.

Herndon of Great Crossing in Scott County, who was issued a passport on the same date. Herndon was a prosperous farmer who raised a few Thoroughbred Running Horses, although never a serious horseman. Like Richards, he was a member of the Christian Church. Johnson family tradition holds that Leonidas accompanied Richards to Europe on "one of his horse-buying trips" and, while there, purchased several paintings for his Scott County home, "Clifton." Similarly, a biographical note concerning Herndon states that, in company with Richards and Johnson, he made a tour of continental Europe in 1859 "for pleasure, and the profits to be gained by observation."[9]

The three men very nearly did not make it back to the United States. Along with 229 other passengers, they boarded the Royal Mail paddlewheel steamer *Persia* and embarked from Liverpool in fair weather on Saturday afternoon, September 3, 1859. The ship carried a full cargo and was so heavily loaded that many passengers commented on the deep draft of the ship. Taking the southern channel, the steamer skirted the coast of Ireland and headed into the open Atlantic. On Monday evening the weather turned foul, the winds increasing to gale force and the seas heavy. At 10 p.m., the ship suddenly lurched and rolled heavily to one side, throwing several passengers out of their berths and creating considerable alarm. The ship's officers announced that a pin in the machinery had broken and would be soon repaired, but the damage proved to be far more serious. The port crankshaft pin, fourteen inches in diameter and nearly a ton in weight, had sheared off near its junction with the crank, which rendered it nearly impossible to extract and replace. The port paddlewheel was disabled, and because of the brisk headwinds, the sails could not be used to steady the ship. The pin was replaced with considerable difficulty during the storm, the ship rolling heavily, and at last the *Persia* was able to resume course for New York.[10]

The weather remained bad, but at last, at two o'clock early Monday morning, September 19, the *Persia* reached the safety of New York harbor. On the Saturday before making port, the passengers held a meeting in the ship's saloon and prepared a set of resolutions expressing their gratitude to the captain and crew for their diligence and skill in bringing them safely through the crisis. A collection was taken up, amounting to $600, to be spent on testimonials and to provide a bonus to the crew in appreciation.

Leonidas Johnson was appointed a member of the committee charged with disbursal of the fund.[11]

Back at Blue Grass Park, a magnificent stable was erected during Richards's absence solely to house his prize stallion, the Knight of St. George. A substantial and attractive stone structure, the stable, like the other buildings on the farm, was designed by Richards and built by his slave workers "somewhat on the Gothic or Moorish style" of architecture. Particular attention had been given to ventilation, so that air could circulate freely without permitting drafts to reach the occupant. No illustration of the Knight's stable survives today, but the style was probably similar to that of the Blue Grass Park racing stable, depicted in the background of Troye's 1857 Glencoe portrait.[12]

The arrival of the Knight of St. George at Blue Grass Park in early June 1859 effectively marks the point in time when Keene Richards, for a variety of reasons, began to alter the strategy of his Arabian experiment and to focus more on conventional thorough-bred breeding. Time had taken a considerable toll on his imported Arabian stock, losses following in rapid succession soon after Richards's return to the United States aboard the *Persia*. Of all the Arabian stallions imported by Richards, by the summer of 1860 only Mokhladi and Fysaul were still alive, and only Fysaul was still in condition to breed. The colt Hamdan had been sold to George Feris in Texas and died there in December 1859. Massoud, fifteen years old, died at Blue Grass Park on September 25, 1859, shortly before Richards's arrival back in Kentucky. One observer, visiting Blue Grass Park a few months later during the Christmas season, attributed his death to premature aging because of hard use by the Bedouins and by "improper (but kind) treatment" since that time. Mokhladi, in his opinion, once a "beautiful and good horse," had declined for the same reasons: "He runs out blanketed a part of the day when the weather is moderate, in Knight of St. George's lot; and I hope when Spring comes he will come up to something like his usual form, but he looks now as if he would ere long be added to the list of victims 'killed with kindness.' Too little exercise in the open air has ripened the seeds sown by hard and long rides over their native sands, until I doubt, if exposed for sale in your village, Mochladi [*sic*] would bring $20." Sacklowie, he noted, was spending the winter at Lexington being treated for some ailment. This illness, probably a respiratory infection, proved fatal, as the eight-year-old Sacklowie died during January 1860. Strangely enough, for a horse that both Edward Troye and Ansel considered the best of Richards's imports, Sacklowie apparently sired no more than a handful of offspring according to the *American Stud Book*, although he was advertised at stud both in Georgetown and at Thomas Barry's in Tennessee. No date of death is known for Mokhladi, but it appears that he did not survive much past 1860 since his last known foal was delivered in 1861.[13]

Fysaul, the youngest of the imported Arabian stallions, was in much better condition. A visitor to Blue Grass Park in July 1860 (possibly Sanders D. Bruce, a resident of Lexington who moved to New York after the Civil War and founded *Turf, Field and Farm*) noted that "Fysaul is the only remaining imported Arabian stallion fit for active service. Except in size, Fysaul looks scarcely inferior to the Knight." This stallion, he wrote, "has a splendid trotting action, and may astonish the world in getting trotting stock, for he has had some very good Morgan mares bred to him, and has colts from all sorts of mares." Fysaul's name, in fact, appears as a sire in the earliest editions of the *American Trotting Register.* Although retired from active service in Richards's breeding program, siring only five foals after 1861, Fysaul was a long-lived horse and survived to reach his twenty-fifth year, passing away at Blue Grass Park in 1877.[14]

With only one Arabian stallion fit to stand service from 1859 onward, Richards's Anglo-Arabian breeding program was necessarily altered from breeding Arabian stallions to American thorough-bred mares, to breeding American and English stallions to Arabian and part-Arabian mares. The Knight of St. George represented a real prize, through his bloodlines and proven racing ability potentially another Glencoe. The stables at Blue Grass Park now contained far more American thorough-bred and English Thoroughbred mares than Arabian, and so most foals in the future would be Thoroughbred Running Horses rather than Anglo-Arab crosses. During the summer of 1859, nearly every available mare on the farm was brought to the Knight for impregnation, sixteen in all: Blonde, Dido, Eagletta, Emilia, an unnamed mare by Hooten, the Lanercost mare, Lulie, Mary Cass, Melrose, Peytona, Sadah, Sallie Hardin, Sister to Pryor #1, Transylvania, Zahah, and Zariphe. Ten live foals delivered in 1860 were the result, and a visitor to Blue Grass Park in July of that year noted that their appearance attested to the breeding qualities of the Knight. Another visitor that summer observed the effect of the usurper on one of the former lords of the paddock: "When the Knight of St. George came out of his stable, old Mokhladi, who was running out in his paddock, set up a note of defiance, and but for his fence, the fine old fellow, true game, notwithstanding his old age and hard work, would have rushed upon the invader of his harem." Only a handful of Richards's brood mares were excluded from the Knight on his arrival in 1859; two of these, a mare by Hardened Sinner and Mary Christmas, were already in foal to Mokhladi. The following year, 1860, would be Mokhladi's last season at stud, and he was then bred only once, again to the Hardened Sinner mare.[15]

Richards's horses, mainly Wax Wing and Glycera, continued to appear at race meetings during his absences in England and Europe, running at New Orleans, Louisville, Lexington, and the Spring Hill track in Crab Orchard, Kentucky. These entries were probably handled for him by Frank Sherritt, the manager at Blue Grass Park, possibly with the assistance of Morris Keene, who was now living in Richards's household in Kentucky. The performance of Blue Grass Park horses remained dismal, with only two first place finishes for the entire season. The first of these victories was scored by the colt Sherritt (Satellite) at the Association track in Lexington in May 1859, while Richards was returning to Kentucky from England with his newly acquired champion Knight. Sherritt, recorded in the race results only as "ch.c. by Imp. Albion" won both successive heats of a two-mile race.[16]

At Lexington in September, another new acquisition, Bettie Ward, finished first in a single-heat race over a mile distance. The two-year-old Lexington filly had just been purchased from her breeder, Samuel Viley of Scott County, Kentucky. Like so many of Lexington's female progeny, Bettie Ward proved to be a stellar performer on the track. Although she made but the single appearance in 1859, during the 1860 season Richards entered her in more races—thirteen—than any of his other horses, where she scored a series of first and second place finishes at New Orleans, Louisville, Lexington, Memphis, and Natchez.[17]

These wins, coming after such a long period of poor performances, no doubt helped to boost Richards's spirits following the deaths not only of his prize Arabian stallions, Massoud and Sacklowie, during the previous winter, but also the loss of his new bride, Sallie Pope Richards, and his

Sallie Pope Richards, first wife of Alexander Keene Richards, who died in 1860 at the age of twenty-three. Painted posthumously at New Orleans in 1861 by Benjamin F. Reinhart, which probably accounts for the somber depiction. Private collection.

infant son, Leonidas "Lonnie" Johnson Richards, within the same period. Lonnie, born at Georgetown in August 1858, was little more than a year old when he died from an unknown cause in December 1859. Only a month later, he was followed into the grave by his mother, only twenty-three years old, who passed away at Transylvania Plantation on February 2, 1860. Young Sallie Richards may have succumbed to complications from a second pregnancy or childbirth, certainly a common cause of female mortality during the era, or possibly from inconsolable grief over her lost son.[18]

During the entire period from the establishment of his breeding operations in 1853 through the summer of 1861, Richards focused almost exclusively on racing Thoroughbred Running Horses rather than any of the produce of his Anglo-Arab hybridization experiment. In all this time, only two Anglo-Arab crosses appeared on the track under his colors: the three-year-old filly Transylvania, sired by Massoud out of Peytona, who took second place in two heats over a mile at Lexington in 1858, and the four-year-old horse Bermuda, sired by Mokhladi out of the Woodpecker mare, who finished third at Robert A. Alexander's Woodburn track on June 18, 1860, in two heats over a two-mile course. Richards must have been disappointed by the performance of his Anglo-Arab crosses, but probably not too disappointed, since he understood the payoff for his experimental breeding program would not likely be realized in a single generation.

The imported colt Millington, by West Australian, excited considerable admiration from visitors to Blue Grass Park. He was described by one visitor as "a noble looking colt, by West Australian," chestnut in color without a spot of white, and the largest yearling he had ever seen. Another visitor, writing in December 1859, exclaimed, "Among the colts, one by West Australian, imported with his dam from England, stands A No. 1, having taken the blue ribbon at the State Fair last fall." While Richards was crossing the Atlantic in the *Persia,* Frank Sherritt, perhaps acting on his own initiative, took Millington, the Knight of St. George, and perhaps a few other horses to the fourth annual fair of the Kentucky State Agricultural Society. The fair was held September 13–17, 1859, on the Maxwell Springs property near Lexington, today part of the University of Kentucky campus. The acreage was first leased in 1853 by the Kentucky Agricultural and Mechanical Association for meetings and exhibitions, and many improvements were made for the purpose. The property was landscaped with trees and shrubs, and numerous buildings were erected, including "A large and handsome amphitheater, 810 feet in circumference, with a shingle roof over the seats and offices, a beautiful gothic cottage for the accommodation of the ladies, one hundred and fifty stables belonging to the Association, besides many others which have been built by individuals, and also several houses for the accommodation of grooms." Very soon, however, the relative merits of horses at exhibitions and on the track would be of little concern, swept away by the convulsions of a nation at war.[19]

13
CHOOSING SIDES

The presidential election of 1860 shattered the unity of the nation, already fragile because of longstanding sectional divisions over the issue of slavery. The Democratic party split over the slavery issue at the April convention in Charleston, South Carolina, and the division ultimately resulted in the nomination of two candidates, Stephen Douglas, who favored a popular sovereignty solution to the expansion of slavery, and Vice President John Cabell Breckinridge of Kentucky on a slave-code platform. A new Constitutional Unionist party avoided the slavery issue and selected conservative John Bell of Tennessee as their candidate. The Republicans met in Chicago in May and, rather than supporting one of the party's more extreme antislavery spokesmen, nominated a moderate and pragmatic candidate, Abraham Lincoln of Illinois. The split in the Democratic party all but guaranteed the election of a Republican president.[1]

Although Lincoln repeatedly stated that he would not interfere with slavery in the states where it was presently legal, he was opposed on moral grounds to any further spread of the institution and believed that, if confined, it would eventually, in "God's good time," become extinct. Encouraged by inflammatory articles in the southern press, a sort of mass hysteria seized the South on the selection of Lincoln as the Republican candidate. He was denounced as an abolitionist in disguise who would bring social and economic ruin to the South, and incensed southern patriots warned that Lincoln's election would result in disunion. In nine southern states, Lincoln's name was deliberately omitted from the ballots. Republicans failed to take these secession threats seriously, believing them to be simply more of the same scare tactics that had been used in the 1856 election campaigns. The southerners meant what they said, but, as one historian observed, "It is hard to see what Republicans could have done to allay southern anxieties short of dissolving their party and proclaiming slavery a positive good."[2]

The election of 1860 accordingly developed into two separate regional contests, Lincoln versus Douglas in the northern states, and Breckinridge versus Bell in the southland. In this politically charged atmosphere, Keene Richards, as was his custom, set out from Kentucky in autumn 1860 to spend the winter in Louisiana, looking after his business interests at Transylvania Plantation and in New Orleans. His departure from Kentucky probably took place sometime after the first week of October, since he held a sale of mares, fillies, and colts at Blue Grass Park on September 24 and was at the Woodlawn course in Louisville for the fall races, which ended on Saturday, October 6. Richards took a string of horses from his racing stable, including Bettie Ward, Magenta, Hillsborough, and Millington, to match at the courses along his route southward. He was accompanied, as usual, by his trainer Ansel, and probably his cousin Morris Keene. Richards was in Memphis during the last week of October, where Bettie Ward and Hillsborough each placed second in two separate races. Following the Memphis meeting, he traveled south to spend a few weeks at Transylvania, checking on the progress of the cotton crop and resting his horses before their next race meet.[3]

The sixth of November was election day, and since Richards maintained a dual residency in both Kentucky and Louisiana, he likely cast his vote in Carroll Parish. There can be little doubt as to which candidate he favored; not only was most of his income dependent on the slave-based southern cotton economy, John C. Breckinridge, a resident of Lexington, was a friend. On the following day, the results of the election were telegraphed across the nation. Breckinridge carried all the southern states except for Kentucky, Tennessee, and Virginia, which went to Bell. New Jersey provided the only electoral victory for Stephen Douglas. Although Lincoln garnered only 40 percent of the popular vote, his 180 electoral votes gave him a landslide victory; the "Black Republican," hated and feared throughout the South, was the president-elect. The election of Abraham Lincoln, thundered the *New Orleans Crescent,* was "a deliberate, coldblooded insult and outrage" to the people of the slaveholding states. To many southerners, the nation would soon be in the hands of a man and a party dedicated to the destruction of the South, forcing them to resort to the "desperate alternative" of secession as the only perceived means for self-preservation.[4]

After the election, Richards took his horses from Transylvania Plantation down the Mississippi to Natchez, a little over one hundred river miles. At Natchez in late November, Bettie Ward placed first in a one-mile race, and Magenta and Hillsborough each placed second in races on the first day of December. Millington was scheduled to debut at Mobile during the very next week, but all of Richards's entries here were scratched, so apparently he took them on to New Orleans rather than compete at the Magnolia course that season. Richards may have bypassed Mobile in order to hasten on to New Orleans, the largest city and de facto capital of the southland, so that he could stay apprised of the rapidly developing political situation. The atmosphere throughout the region was charged with anticipation. Racing records show that he was in New Orleans for the Metairie races during the first week of January 1861.[5]

The southern states moved swiftly to separate themselves from the Union, adopting a strategy of secession on a state-by-state basis rather than a collective action that might be stalled by months of debate. South Carolina convened a secession convention in mid-December 1860, and on the 20th unanimously passed an ordinance dissolving the union between South Carolina and the other states. Although only in the Palmetto State was the vote unanimous, the secession move of South Carolina triggered a chain reaction in other states of the lower South. Mississippi passed a similar secession ordinance on January 9, followed by Florida and Alabama during each of the next two days, and Georgia on January 19.[6]

Popular sentiment in Louisiana was less supportive of secession, primarily for economic reasons. As gateway to the Mississippi and interior navigation of the continent, Louisiana was strongly linked to the commerce of the northern and midwestern regions. The legislature and the governor were, however, both militant; during his inaugural address in January 1860, Governor Thomas Overton Moore noted that sentiments had been awakened "favorable to a separation of the states." Moore called an extraordinary session of the legislature in Baton Rouge on December 10 to request a secession convention and to make military preparations to defend the state if necessary. The parish representatives were in the mood to give the governor everything he requested, and they scheduled a convention on January 26 to determine the future course of the state. The legislature approved the establishment of a state military board and appropriated $500,000 for military requirements, officially authorizing the parishes to raise companies with financial support from the state. Scarcely had the legislative session concluded when, on the twenty-first, word arrived of South Carolina's separation from the Union. Citizens in New Orleans celebrated the news with jubilation, taking to the streets in ebullient displays of southern patriotism. Fanned by the press, the secession movement gained momentum during the weeks ahead, and at the January convention the state declared its secession from the Union.[7]

Early in February, representatives from Louisiana and six other slave states met in Montgomery, Alabama, and began the process of forming an independent southern nation, the Confederate States of America. Jefferson Davis, a former U.S. senator from Mississippi who had attended Transylvania at Lexington and graduated from West Point, was chosen as president of the Confederacy. The bombardment of Fort Sumter in Charleston harbor during April 12–13, 1861, and its capture and occupation by South Carolina troops put an end to any possibility of compromise and precipitated a state of war between the Union and the Confederate states. Immediately after the surrender of Fort Sumter, Lincoln issued a proclamation calling for the states to supply troops to preserve the Union and ordered a blockade of southern ports. Lincoln's proclamation prompted four states of the upper South—Virginia, Tennessee, North Carolina, and Arkansas—to join with the Confederacy rather than fight against them. As one historian observed, "Their ties of blood and culture with the South proved stronger than their political ties with the Union." Although many persons in border states such as Kentucky and Missouri held similar sentiments, and the governors of these states refused to send troops in answer to Lincoln's call, the legislatures refused to authorize secession conventions.[8]

Jefferson Davis responded to Lincoln's proclamation by issuing a request for the southern states to furnish troops for immediate use by the Confederacy. In Louisiana, ever since Lincoln's election, New Orleans had served as one of the primary centers for organizing military companies. After the fall of Sumter, recruitment greatly accelerated and those companies already formed began to drill and train in earnest as they waited to be mustered into the Confederate army. With the rapid influx of volunteers into the city, including the irregular companies organized in the parishes, in mid-April the Metairie racecourse was converted into a military camp known as Camp Walker. It was a poorly chosen site. It lacked easy access to clean drinking water, the ground was marshy, and clouds of mosquitoes from the adjacent swamps swarmed over the men who bivouacked there. Because of these deficiencies, Camp Walker was abandoned in May and the men transferred to a new site, Camp Moore, eighty miles north of the city.[9]

Just prior to its occupation by the new recruits, Metairie had, on April 6, recently concluded its spring race meeting. Richards entered several horses in this meet under his silver gray and white colors, including Millington's debut on the first day of the month in a two-heat race over a mile distance, which the colt won handily. At the end of the spring races, Richards remained in New Orleans for some weeks, caught up in the fever of southern patriotism sweeping the city. In late April, impressed by the dash and spirit of a newly formed company known as the "Tiger Rifles," he dipped into his resources and outfitted the poorly clad men with new uniforms in the colorful Zouave style.[10]

The commander of the Tiger Rifles was Alexander White, though that was possibly an assumed name. Rumor had it that he was the son of a former Kentucky governor who had shot a man during a game of high-stakes poker and fled the state to avoid prosecution. Prior to the war, White operated the steamer *Magnolia,* transporting goods along the Mississippi between New Orleans and Natchez. In March 1861, following Louisiana's secession and the subsequent Union blockade of the river, White leased a recruiting station at 29 Front Levee Street, near the custom house, and began to organize a military company. The Tiger Rifles were formed around the nucleus of the crew of the *Magnolia,* and were a ragtag bunch of roughnecks: Irish immigrant ship hands, draymen, and stevedores from the docks of New Orleans. William R. Stone, a volunteer from Madison Parish who joined the Jeff Davis Guards, wrote home to his sister Kate that he had seen the Tiger Rifles, "recruited from the very dregs of the City." When the Tigers were mustered into Confederate service on April 25, the roster included Captain Alexander White, three lieutenants, four sergeants, four corporals, and fifty-five privates.[11]

The Tiger Rifles were part of a unit that came to be known as the 1st Louisiana Special Battalion, commanded by Major Chatham Roberdeau Wheat (1826– 1862), an even more colorful character than Alexander White. Roberdeau Wheat was a giant of a man, six foot four inches in height and weighing 275 pounds. A native of Virginia, Wheat served in the Mexican War and afterward moved to New Orleans, where he studied and practiced law. Between 1849 and 1857, Wheat organized and participated in filibuster expeditions against Cuba, Mexico, and Nicaragua, and in 1860 he set off for Europe, where he joined with General Giuseppe Garibaldi and Victor Emmanuel II in the last stages of the unification of the Italian peninsula, commissioned as a brigadier general in the Italian army.[12]

Learning of the secession of the southern states, Wheat, an ardent secessionist, returned to New Orleans in April 1861 and opened a recruiting station near the city's docks. Wheat's first recruiting notice appeared in the city's *Daily True Delta* on the eighteenth, and ran daily through the end of the month:

> Attention Volunteers!
>
> The undersigned has opened a Rendezvous, at 64 St. Charles street, first floor, up stairs, for the purpose of forming a company of VOLUNTEERS for active service. The time for action has now arrived. Let the chivalry of the city and State, then, rally to the standard of the Southern Confederacy. R.C. WHEAT

The editor of the *New Orleans Daily Crescent* took note, reporting, "We understand our friend Gen. C.R. Wheat, is about raising a company of volunteers, to serve in the army of Louisiana," and advised "all friends of a glorious cause to repair and enlist." Within a few days he formed an association with Alexander White, and on April 23 they began to recruit jointly, using White's headquarters on Front Levee Street as well as his original station on St. Charles.[13]

Wheat's military reputation was such that, in addition to the Tigers, he attracted several other companies then being raised in the city to form a proposed battalion. Like the Tiger Rifles, the men of the other companies were drawn from the lowest social echelons of New Orleans, the inhabitants of the southern edge of the city along the waterfront of the Mississippi River. On May 10, Wheat was elected as major and commanding officer of the five companies and the new battalion was officially sanctioned by the state. The men of the battalion, which later came to be generally referred to as Wheat's Tigers, were, like those of many of the other companies in the city, initially bivouacked at Camp Walker. On May 14, Wheat's battalion, along with several other companies, departed New Orleans for better quarters at Camp Moore.[14]

Exactly why Keene Richards selected Alexander White's Tiger Rifles to outfit, among all the companies then being raised in New Orleans, is not clear. The *New Orleans Bee* noted, "While in camp here they were accounted 'hard nuts to crack,' and no one doubted but that they would signalize themselves in battle. Their spirit so pleased A. Keene Richards, Esq., that he fitted them out in a dashing Zouave uniform at his own expense." This implies that Richards viewed the troops drilling at Camp Walker and singled out the Tiger Rifles for his support. Recruited from the waterfront and among the poorest residents of the city, the Tigers would certainly have been poorly clothed and obviously in need of military apparel. The Confederate government would not provide uniforms until late 1862, and in the meantime volunteers were expected to provide their own clothing, for which they would receive a small stipend. In practice, company captains, with the assistance of various aid societies and sponsors, generally furnished their men with uniforms. The commutation system, as it was known, led to a lack of standardization and encouraged adoption of a wide variety of uniform styles.[15]

Another possibility is that Keene Richards was previously acquainted with either Alexander White or Roberdeau Wheat and lent his support based on friendship. White may have carried bales of Transylvania cotton downriver for Richards aboard the *Magnolia.* Wheat was well known in the city as an accomplished military man and considered a hero by many. As a businessman who made frequent visits to New Orleans, Keene Richards would have been aware of Wheat's reputation.

The French-style Zouave uniforms in which Richards clothed White's company were both colorful and exotic in appearance. The men were outfitted with woolen Zouave jackets, the 1st Platoon in blue and the 2nd Platoon in brown, trimmed in red cotton and worn over loose-fitting red flannel shirts with white porcelain buttons; blue and white vertically striped pantaloons with white canvas leggings; and stockings with blue and white horizontal stripes. Covering their heads were red flannel fezzes with red tassels. To our modern perceptions, the men of White's company might appear to be dressed in clown suits, but in their own view they were elegantly clad and quite dashing. During the Civil War, multiple units both North and South were outfitted in Zouave uniforms, at least initially. The uniform style derived from the clothing worn by the Zouaoua tribe of North Africa, who, along with a number of French settlers, served with the French Army in the North African campaigns during the 1830s. Richards probably suggested the choice of Zouave uniforms for White's company, since, after all, he had seen authentic Zouave troops during his travels in North Africa in 1851 and the Crimea in 1855, but the men of the company would likely have been very receptive to the idea.[16]

Early in May, after providing uniforms for White's men and before the battalion was relocated to Camp Moore, Keene Richards went home to Kentucky. He was at Louisville on May 18 for the first day of the 1861 spring meeting at the Woodlawn course, and two weeks later he raced his horses at the Association track in Lexington. After half a year's absence, he returned to find the state sharply divided in its political opinions concerning the momentous events of previous months.[17]

During the recent presidential election, John Bell and the Constitutional Union party carried the state, indicating that most Kentucky voters supported preservation of the Union, but proslavery candidate John C. Breckinridge made a strong showing with 36 percent of the popular vote. Abraham Lincoln did not carry a single county in Kentucky, receiving only five votes in Fayette County, the home of his wife's parents. Governor Beriah Magoffin was a defender of slavery and supported the right of secession, but, fearing a Union invasion of the state if Kentucky appeared ready to secede, he rejected demands from both Lincoln and Davis to supply troops after the occupation of Fort Sumter. Magoffin's telegraphed reply on April 15, 1861, to Simon Cameron, Lincoln's secretary of war, was that "Kentucky will furnish no troops for the wicked purpose of subduing her sister Southern States." On May 16, the Kentucky House of Represen-

Members of Wheat's Tiger Rifles, 1st Louisiana Special Battalion, outfitted in Zouave uniforms purchased for them in 1861 by Keene Richards. The caps and shirts are red, with dark blue jackets and white trousers and leggings with blue stripes. Oil painting, 2000, courtesy of Don Troiani, a well-respected artist specializing in historical and military art for the Revolutionary and Civil War eras.

tatives resolved that Kentucky would take a position of strict neutrality. The Senate adopted a similar resolution, and on May 20 Magoffin issued a proclamation of armed neutrality, warning both the Union and Confederacy that Kentucky would resist invasion of her soil by troops from either side.[18]

Given the mounting pressures on the state to choose sides, few expected Kentucky's neutral stance to survive for long. Kentucky was a key state that occupied a strategic position at the junction of the Ohio and

Mississippi Rivers; if Kentucky should secede from the Union, the remaining three loyal slave states would likely follow suit. "I think to lose Kentucky is nearly the same as to lose the whole game," Lincoln wrote to a friend, and he tread carefully in his handling of the state during the spring and summer of 1861 so as not to push Kentucky toward the Confederacy. Despite official policy, many residents of the state made personal decisions on partisanship, slipping away to Tennessee to join with Confederate forces or to Ohio or Indiana to enlist with the Union army. Congressional and state elections during the summer strengthened the Unionist position in Kentucky, so that there was no longer any possibility of secession.[19]

John C. Breckinridge, the former vice president under James Buchanan and presidential candidate in the 1860 elections, returned from Washington to his Lexington home on August 15. Although the popular vote in Kentucky had gone to Bell and the Constitutional Union party, Breckinridge's popularity was such that, in the 1859 state elections, he was elected to represent the state in the U.S. Senate beginning in March 1861, thus becoming only the second man in history to go directly from the vice presidency to a Senate seat. Although under constant suspicion because of his southern sympathies, Breckinridge worked tirelessly both as vice president and as senator to avert a war between the states. He counseled against secession and hoped to see the Union restored, but he believed a peaceful separation was better than war.[20]

Kentucky's neutral status was shattered in late summer when Confederate troops under General Gideon Pillow invaded the western part of the state, occupying the strategic river towns of Columbus and Hickman on September 5. In response, Union forces commanded by General Ulysses S. Grant moved in and seized Paducah two days later. Receiving the news of these incursions, the Kentucky legislature ordered the American flag to be raised over the state capitol, and on September 18 it adopted a set of resolutions, passed over Governor Magoffin's veto, that placed Kentucky firmly in the Union camp and in a state of war against the Confederacy.[21]

Keene Richards now found himself in a difficult position in his home state, faced with the need to make some momentous personal decisions about his future. One of the leading citizens of the Bluegrass, his sympathies were wholly with the southern cause, a position that carried little risk while Kentucky remained neutral but now was increasingly untenable.

It was one thing to play the dilettante, supplying a Confederate company with fancy uniforms in the fever of the moment, but it would be an entirely different level of commitment to actually serve in the Confederate military or government. Transylvania Plantation, Richards's primary asset, was in the Deep South, now within the bounds of a separate nation, but Blue Grass Park and his valuable breeding and racing stock in Kentucky were vulnerable to confiscation by Federal authorities should he overtly commit to the Confederacy. Even if he remained loyal to the Union, a border state like Kentucky, with its strategic position on the Ohio River, was sure to be hotly contested ground during the war, placing his horses at risk from both sides in the conflict. His friend and fellow breeder Robert A. Alexander, a staunch Unionist, visited Illinois in mid-September to scout out possible locations for a safe haven for his stock should the war threaten Woodburn Farm.[22]

Although surely beset by misgivings, Richards prepared to leave Kentucky and fully embrace the southern cause. But first he arranged to protect his assets. On July 1, Richards borrowed nearly $60,000 from the estate of his late grandfather Keene, equivalent to more than $2 million in the present day. The loan was secured by a deed of trust for his property in Arkansas and Louisiana, including Transylvania Plantation, and named his cousin, Wallis Bodien Keene, as trustee. There could be no other reason for Richards to require such an enormous sum other than an intention to leave Kentucky for the duration of the war. He almost certainly would have arranged for most of this to be converted into letters of credit from a local bank—the traveler's check of the era—since it would have been both difficult and imprudent to carry this much money in gold coin.[23]

Either together or separately, Richards met with cousin Morris Keene, farm manager Frank Sherritt, and his friend Edward Troye, and to each man he gave careful instructions. Morris Keene was assigned the task of shepherding some of Blue Grass Park's most valuable horses, including Fysaul and the Knight of St. George, to Transylvania Plantation, along with many of the grooms and other enslaved persons on his Georgetown place. Richards mistakenly assumed that they would be secure from the hazards of war in the Deep South. Sherritt, who continued as manager of Blue Grass Park during Richards's long absence, was directed to sell many of the remaining horses. Robert A. Alexander, who stayed in Kentucky through the war, purchased Hillsborough, Target, Millington (subsequently renamed Australian), and several other horses from Sherritt for $5,000 during the late autumn of 1861. At about the same time, Alexander also acquired Richards's celebrated trainer Ansel, on loan for the duration of the war.[24]

Edward Troye was entrusted with the most important responsibility of all—possession of Blue Grass Park. On September 19, Richards visited the Scott County Clerk's office. There, he executed a deed for his home and farm to Troye for the sum of $12,200, and a further instrument conveying "all the interest I have in my Grand fathers Wm B Keenes Estate both real and personal & mixed in the State of Ky as devised to me by his last will and testament" to Troye for $3,000.[25]

The conveyance was no more than a legal fiction to forestall possible confiscation of Keene's estate—the property of an active southern sympathizer. It was made in the understanding that it would be sold back to Richards sometime in the future, when it was safe to do so. The rationale was that Union officers would be less likely to appropriate the land from Troye, who remained a British subject, particularly if he could produce a legal title. Troye, who had a farm of his own in Madison County, Alabama, where his wife and daughter lived, probably did not have the means to pay $15,200 outright for these Scott County properties, nor the financial wherewithal to maintain the estate. Troyes's biographer, Mackay-Smith, proposed that the conveyance was a three-way arrangement, by which the wealthy Robert A. Alexander could help his good friend Keene Richards without offending the latter's sense of honor: "Mr. Alexander may have seen his opportunity to kill two birds with one stone, to make it possible for Troye to pay the money to Richards and thus help his friend, and also to secure for himself portraits of his favorite horses by the most eminent equestrian portrait painter of the day." The deeds to Richards's properties stated that the money had been "to him in hand paid," and so Alexander likely put up the purchase price, which Troye repaid in installments as he executed paintings of the prize stock at Woodburn. Although the total sum was not inconsequential, to Richards the money was far less important than the fact that his Kentucky property was now safeguarded in friendly hands.[26]

In June 1861, Troye completed paintings of the Arabian horses Fysaul and Lulie for Richards, working at the studio his patron had built for him at Blue Grass Park. In October, shortly after Richards departed Kentucky for the south, General Winfield Scott, formerly the commanding general of the Union Army, arrived at Blue Grass Park to pose for an equestrian portrait. Troye originally received the commission during the summer of 1860 from the Alumni Association of the Virginia Military Institute and made a few sketches while in Lexington, Virginia. At Blue Grass Park, a tent was set up in a pasture near the garden, where the aging general, dressed in his military uniform, struck a heroic pose while mounted on one of

General Winfield Scott mounted on a bay gelding sired by Glencoe. This horse was subsequently presented by Keene Richards to Confederate cavalry raider John Hunt Morgan, and then presented to General Scott after Morgan's capture in 1863. Painted in 1861 by Edward Troye. Courtesy of the Virginia Military Institute Archives.

Keene Richards's horses. Troye completed two large paintings of General Scott, each featuring a different horse. In the smaller painting, the general is seated on an Arabian or part-Arabian steed, dark bay in color, and in the larger portrait he is on a bay gelding sired by the peerless Glencoe.[27]

The subsequent history of these two horses is striking for its irony. The gelding, generally known as Glencoe, Jr., was personally presented by Keene Richards to Confederate cavalry raider John Hunt Morgan on a visit home in 1862. Following Morgan's capture in July 1863, the horse was shipped as a gift to Winfield Scott by Union general James Shackleford. The Arabian horse was given by Richards to Basil Duke, Morgan's second in command, at the same time as the presentation of the Glencoe horse to Morgan. Both equestrian portraits of Scott are signed and dated December 1861. Not long after completion of this commission, Troye left the country for England, taking with him the originals of his five Oriental paintings for safekeeping. Troye remained in England until autumn 1864, when he returned to the United States. A marginal note on the property conveyances from Richards states that these documents were delivered to Troye on December 6, 1864. After Troye returned to Kentucky, his generous patron Robert A. Alexander provided him with one lucrative commission after another.[28]

Whatever plans Richards had for departing Kentucky were abruptly hastened by a developing threat to his friend John C. Breckinridge. Ever since his return to Kentucky a few weeks before, Breckinridge had been viewed by ardent Unionists as a "malign influence" whose presence might tilt the state into the secessionist camp. Although Breckinridge continued to condemn actions by Lincoln that he considered unconstitutional and illegal, he committed no overt act of disloyalty to the Union and still hoped for a peaceful resolution to the conflict. Even so, he fully expected to be arrested as soon as Kentucky abandoned its neutral stance and embraced the Union cause, a circumstance that seemed more likely with each passing day. On September 13, just as Keene Richards would do a few days later, Breckinridge transferred all his property by deed of trust to his friend Madison C. Johnson, an undisputed Unionist and cousin of Richards's deceased wife, Sallie.[29]

Breckinridge's fears were confirmed when the Kentucky legislature ended neutrality on September 18, siding with the Union. The arrests began that night. Among the first to be arrested were former Kentucky governor Charles S. Morehead, a southern sympathizer and outspoken critic of the Lincoln administration, and Reuben T. Durrett, acting editor of the pro-southern *Louisville Courier.* The same day, the leaders of the Kentucky legislature, John A. Fisk and Richard A. Buckner, directed General George H. Thomas, commandant at Camp Dick Robinson, to take action against "a gathering of the rebels in Lexington," by which they meant the peace meeting scheduled to take place on Friday, September 20. General Thomas ordered Colonel Thomas E. Bramlette of the 3rd Kentucky Volunteer Infantry to advance from Camp Robinson into Lexington, with orders to break up the proceedings if there should be demonstrations hostile to the Union, and to take Breckinridge into custody. At 11:30 p.m. on September 19, Bramlette, then at Nicholasville a dozen miles south of Lexington, dashed off a quick missive to Thomas, reporting that his men would be in Lexington within a few hours. "We are in advance of all expectation," he wrote, "and will take them by surprise."[30]

Colonel Bramlette's assurance was premature. A man identified only as "Smith," observing the military activities at Nicholasville, hurried to Lexington ahead of Bramlette's troops to warn Breckinridge, arriving at the senator's rooms in the Phoenix Hotel just before sundown. Receiving news of his imminent arrest, Breckinridge took a pencil and quickly wrote "Hawks are about" on a scrap of paper, leaving it unsigned. He sent a small boy running with the note to his cousin, William Preston, who was a few blocks away at Wickliffe, the family home of his wife. Preston took the note from the boy, who was breathless after his dash through the streets, and recognized the handwriting as that of Breckinridge. He set out immediately for the Phoenix, meeting privately with Breckinridge as the sky began to darken with the setting sun. Breckinridge informed him that there were Union troops on the way to Lexington with warrants for the arrest of himself and some of his friends; he would be leaving the city as soon as it was fully dark.[31]

Preston left shortly thereafter, concerned over the possibility of his own arrest and equally determined to escape from the city. Breckinridge quickly packed a few belongings, said goodbye to his family, and slipped out of the hotel. He rode through the darkness to a prearranged rendezvous at the Winton estate, some seven miles north of Lexington and the home of a distant relative, Letitia P. Dallam. The adjoining property was Cabell's Dale, the historic home of the Breckinridge family and his birthplace. Breckinridge was met at Winton by Keene Richards, who, accompanied by his distant cousin Samuel Y. Keene and a young enslaved boy, came from nearby Georgetown with a carriage to take them both to safety. Preston probably dispatched a messenger in haste to Richards upon leaving Breckinridge; both men knew Richards to be a dependable friend of the South with the resources to expedite an escape from the Bluegrass. Plans may have been in place for several days, ever since the threat of Breckinridge's arrest had become imminent. This would explain Richards's quick response.[32]

The men exchanged greetings and passed around a jug of "Old Crow" bourbon whiskey, contemplating the enormity of the step they were about to take, an irrevocable commitment to the Confederate cause. It was a sad occasion for John C. Breckinridge. In the words of biographer Davis, "He had fought for compromise and failed; he had sought peace and moderation and found only bitterness; he had proclaimed his devotion to the Union to the best of his ability and found, after all, that he had convinced only himself." Breckinridge had no intention of heading south until the threat of imprisonment forced him to take flight. Two alternatives were available to him at this point. He could maintain his neutral position and seek refuge somewhere in exile, or he could join the Confederacy and take up arms against the Union.[33]

There was a certain poignancy for Richards in these last moments in the Bluegrass. He still considered Kentucky to be home despite his many connections to Louisiana, but Union-controlled Kentucky was no longer a safe haven for a man who, having more than one hundred slaves, was among the larger enslavers of the rebellious states. During a brief span of years just prior to the beginning of the conflict, he had achieved his youthful ambition to become one of the most important horse breeders in the country, but now all his plans were disrupted by the uncertain conditions of a civil war. Richards's carefully structured breeding programs involving Arab horses and English Thoroughbreds imported by him at the cost of so much effort and treasure had just begun to bear fruit, but how could he continue to plan and supervise during this great national upheaval? What was to become of these irreplaceable bloodlines now that his position in Kentucky had become untenable?

As the three men passed around the jug of bourbon at Winton, working up the courage to take the next fateful step, the conversation perhaps naturally turned for a while to admiration of the striking team of matched horses hitched to Richards's carriage. The evidence suggests that these were the same pair of gray Anglo-Arab mares that Richards used as a carriage team beginning in 1859 and were listed in his 1866 catalog as both being the offspring of Mokhladi. Samuel Y. Keene referred to them as "two beautiful white match Arab mares" in a 1900 letter to horseman Randolph Huntington, a later breeder of Anglo-Arab horses. At last, they could delay no longer, and Breckinridge and Keene climbed into the carriage, taking what small luggage they had brought along. With Keene Richards holding the reins, the carriage lurched forward, bound eastward to the mountains of Kentucky.[34]

Another well-known citizen of the Bluegrass departed Lexington on the same day to avoid arrest, although he set out to the west, traveling directly to join the Confederate forces at Bowling Green. Captain John Hunt Morgan, commander of a volunteer company of the Kentucky militia known as the Lexington Rifles, made no secret of his inclinations, flying a Confederate flag over his hemp and woolen mill ever since the fall of Fort Sumter. The militia, or State Guard, was widely perceived as being pro-southern in its sympathies. When Kentucky declared for the Union on September 18, the legislature issued an order to disarm the State Guard. After sundown on September 20, Morgan and most of his troops slipped away in the darkness with two wagons loaded with rifles and covered with hay. They marched westward until they passed through the Confederate lines, arriving at Bowling Green by October 1.[35]

Even as Morgan led his men toward western Kentucky, Richards's Arab team took his carriage rapidly eastward across the state, arriving in Mount Sterling at four o'clock early Friday morning. They stopped briefly at the home of an unnamed "ex-official" and then continued on their way to Owingsville, in Bath County. Their passing on the state road was noted by several, who reported that "one of the travellers was closely muffled, and, whenever they were about meeting any one, the negro boy raised himself so as to cover the muffled figure." From here, Richards turned southeast, entering the Appalachian foothills and traveling deeper into the mountainous region until, on Sunday, September 22, they reached Prestonsburg in Floyd County, near the Virginia line. Breckinridge and Richards were among the first arrivals of a substantial outflow of armed Kentuckians from across the state moving through Prestonsburg and then southwest into Tennessee. Within four days, more than a thousand men passed through Cumberland Gap to join the Confederacy. Many of these men were well known to Keene Richards and his companions, among them George W. Johnson of Scott County, who reached Prestonsburg on Tuesday, and William Preston, who arrived on the following day.[36]

Within a few days, Breckinridge and Richards, along with many other southern partisans, passed through the Gap to Tazewell, Tennessee, and on to the nearest railroad junction, most likely the village of Morristown. From here the two men took the train into Knoxville on October 4, where Breckinridge "was greeted with great enthusiasm by the crowd assembled at the depot." From Knoxville, Breckinridge and William Preston traveled by rail to Bowling Green, Kentucky, the western part of the state then being in the hands of Confederate troops under Brigadier General Simon Buckner, former inspector general of the Kentucky State Guard and now commander of the 2nd Division of the Army of Central Kentucky. At Bowling Green on October 8, Breckinridge published an address "To the People of Kentucky" in which he resigned from the Senate, because "there is no longer a Senate of the United States within the meaning and spirit of the Constitution." Breckinridge soon met with General Buckner, expressing his desire to join the Confederate army in any capacity. He was subsequently appointed by Jefferson Davis as a brigadier general and assigned to the 2nd Division under Buckner. On November 16, he was given command of the 1st Brigade of Kentucky troops.[37]

After the war, Samuel Y. Keene recalled accompanying Richards and Breckinridge in their flight from Kentucky into Tennessee. Richards probably handed over his carriage and Arab team to Samuel Keene at the railroad station on October 4 and accompanied Breckinridge on the train at least as far as Knoxville, then continued on to his plantation in northeastern Louisiana by way of connections through Chattanooga, Memphis, and Vicksburg. Before the war, autumn was the season when he would visit

Transylvania to check on the cotton crop and arrange for its transport and sale, and this may have been one reason for his extended journey. He probably also wished to alert his overseer or farm manager as to the impending arrival of his valuable bloodstock, notify his friends at neighboring plantations of his full commitment to the Confederate cause, and consult with them about the security of the region and appropriate measures for home defense. Richards remained in Louisiana no more than a few weeks, and then headed back to Kentucky, rejoining Breckinridge in Bowling Green in November.[38]

Samuel Keene bade farewell to Richards and Breckinridge at the railway station and returned through eastern Kentucky to his grocer's business in Georgetown. He took no further part in the war. Forty-four years old in 1861, Samuel must have considered himself too old for military service and was over age by the time Union conscription laws were passed in 1863. The presence of the buggy team of Arab horses at Blue Grass Park after the war was noted in Richards's 1866 sale catalogue. There can be little doubt that these were the same horses that carried the two men out of Kentucky in 1861, since Richards noted he had been driving this particular team for the past seven years. In an 1868 letter to Breckinridge, then in self-imposed exile in Canada, Richards referred to one of the mares, "who carried us to Virginia," as being in his stable.[39]

In Bowling Green, General Breckinridge welcomed Richards and appointed him as a volunteer aide-de-camp on his personal staff, a civilian with the nominal rank of captain. Richards arrived in Confederate-occupied western Kentucky just in time to attend, as one of the representatives for Scott County, the "sovereignty" or secession convention held at Russellville on November 18–20. Although this gathering and its proceedings possessed no real legal authority, the leaders of the convention intended, by establishing a Confederate government in the state, to rally support among Kentuckians for the southern cause and to convey legitimacy to the occupation of western Kentucky by Confederate troops.[40]

After the Kentucky legislature declared for the Union side in mid-September, a stream of southern sympathizers from across the state converged on the Confederate headquarters at Bowling Green to enlist in the military or to volunteer their services in any needed capacity. George W. Johnson, who like Richards had fled through the Gap to Tennessee, arrived in Bowling Green in early October and joined the staff of General Buckner as a volunteer aide-de-camp. Johnson was an experienced politician, having served four terms in the Kentucky House of Representatives between 1838 and 1845, and so became one of the leaders of this relatively small group of self-imposed exiles. He was a defender of the institution of slavery, being one of the "Committee of Sixty" who, in 1845, seized the press of abolitionist Cassius M. Clay in Lexington and shipped it to Cincinnati. Although an ardent champion of states' rights, Johnson originally was opposed to secession.[41]

General Albert Sidney Johnston, in charge of the Confederacy's western operations, came to Kentucky and established his command at Bowling Green shortly after sending Buckner to occupy the city in mid-September. George W. Johnson was a distant relative, his oldest daughter being married to a nephew of the general. "Large majorities of the people have always been and now are in favor of a permanent connection with the South," Johnson informed the general, and in private conference he proposed the formation of a provisional government of Kentucky, representing the true sentiments of the people. Johnston was sympathetic, knowing that the establishment of a Confederate government in Kentucky would provide a boost in support for the southern cause and allow Kentuckians to join the Confederacy without viewing themselves as traitors to their state. At the same time, however, Johnston knew that if his troops were forced to retreat from their positions in Kentucky, the prospect of a government in exile would be a severe blow to the morale of Kentucky supporters. Despite misgivings, the general cooperated with George W. Johnson and his associates in the process of setting up a provisional government.[42]

George Johnson took the first step toward establishing a Confederate Kentucky by organizing a preliminary planning conference held October 29–30 at Russellville, Kentucky, about thirty miles southwest from Bowling Green. Sixty-three men from thirty-four counties assembled in the Odd Fellows Hall to air their grievances against the Lincoln government and the state legislature. Keene Richards was not present at this initial gathering, having not yet returned from Louisiana. Johnson introduced a set of resolutions that served as the focus of discussion for the gathering, and after minor revisions they were adopted unanimously. The resolutions denounced the Frankfort legislature as no longer representing the will of most Kentuckians. The 1792 Kentucky state constitution and all subsequent versions asserted that "all power is inherent in the people," who possessed the "inalienable and indefeasible right to alter, reform, or abolish their government, in such manner as they may think proper." Citing this constitutional right of revolution, the assembly called for a sovereignty convention to be held at Russellville on November 18 with the intended purpose of "severing forever" Kentucky's connection with the federal government.[43]

When the sovereignty convention convened on the morning of November 18, more than two hundred men, including Keene Richards, crowded into the second-floor ballroom of William Forst's elegant Russellville home. The Forst ballroom proved too small for the assembly, and so on the third day the convention was moved to Bethel College, which had been closed since May 1861. On the morning of November 20, the convention delegates drafted an ordinance of secession, which declared Kentucky to be a "free and independent state" severed from the United States and "absolved of all allegience [*sic*]" to the state government in Frankfort. A draft constitution appended to the ordinance adopted those sections of the existing state constitution "not inconsistent with the acts of this convention" and called for a regular election for the restoration of a permanent government to be held in the future at a time and place free from the "influence of the armies of the United States." Bowling Green was chosen as the new state capital, and George W. Johnson, in recognition of his leadership role and unwavering commitment to the cause, was unanimously elected governor and given authority to conclude a treaty with the Confederate States by which Kentucky could be admitted to the Confederacy.[44]

The convention sent three commissioners to Virginia to apply for admission of Kentucky into the Confederacy. Although President Jefferson Davis had some reservations about the irregularity of the secession process in Kentucky, he was convinced that the action represented the will of the majority of the citizens of the state. Accordingly, he recommended admission of Kentucky to the Confederate Congress on December 7, 1861. The proposal was approved, and three days later Davis signed an act admitting Kentucky as the thirteenth Confederate state, and the

Kentucky delegates were able to take their seats representing the state in the Confederate Congress. Ironically, Kentucky, along with Missouri, was now represented in both the United States and Confederate Congresses, and fielded regiments to both armies. Back in Kentucky, less than three months after its formation, Johnston's army was forced to evacuate the state in February 1862, and the Confederate shadow government followed to become a government in exile.[45]

14

A TASTE OF WAR

In November 1861, General Don Carlos Buell was appointed commander of Union forces in Kentucky, and early the next year the Confederate defensive line through Kentucky began to unravel. Federal troops scored a victory near Mill Springs in southeastern Kentucky in mid-January and Ulysses S. Grant captured Fort Henry on the Tennessee River in early February, with Fort Donelson on the Cumberland but a short march away for Grant's troops. Faced with the possibility of being caught between the advancing armies of Grant and Buell, the Confederate command in Kentucky ordered a withdrawal southward toward Nashville. The retreat began on Tuesday, February 11, as Johnston's troops marched out of the city on the Nashville Pike. The 1st Kentucky Brigade, to which Keene Richards was attached as aide to General John C. Breckinridge, rendezvoused with Johnston's army south of Bowling Green and served as rearguard during the march. Union troops occupied the capital city of Confederate Kentucky early in the morning on Saturday, February 15, and continued to advance, forcing Johnston to march his men into Alabama and then Mississippi, making camp in late March at Burnsville, near Corinth, a strategically important railroad junction.[1]

Earlier that month, Keene Richards took a temporary leave from Breckinridge, who tended to allow his friend considerable latitude. As a volunteer aide, he was not sworn to military service and remained essentially a civilian bound only by his sense of commitment to his friend and the cause they both served. Richards had some business to attend to in New Orleans and was anxious to learn if his cousin Morris Keene had brought his valuable equine stock safely to Transylvania. Rail lines passed through northern Alabama with connections to New Orleans, so he could visit the city and his plantation and return in a matter of days. Richards reached New Orleans about March 10 and, a few days later, sat down to pen the first of three letters he would send back to Breckinridge during the course of a single week. He entrusted these letters to various persons who were about to set out from the city to join Johnston's army. In this first missive, he noted:

> I have been here for a week on some business for myself and for the purpose of seeing what can be done about getting out some of my cotton for purchasing Armes in Europe for your Brigade. I have made my own arrangements here and have a permit from the proper authorities to take out a portion of my crop. I have been forced to take out an interest in a fast steamer in order that I may ship my cotton. She is to run the Blocade from here to Havana. My cotton will be sold there or shipped to Europe. The risk will be great and the profits not large.[2]

During the previous week, Richards had by chance encountered William L. Yancey, the Confederacy's former ambassador to England and France, who had just arrived in New Orleans on March 13. Yancey left London two weeks before, on the arrival of James Mason and John Slidell as his replacements. "I took him to dinner at my favorite Restaurant," Richards informed the general, "and at that time secured a great deal of information." Yancey provided him with letters of introduction to persons in England who might assist him with the purchase of weapons. "If I go myself, I will start in ten days or less time. I will select the best Armes in England for Sharp shooters for your Brigade. The ordinary Army Enfield is not acurate enough for the purpose." The fine English rifles, he wrote, were far more accurate and of longer range than any other: "If I could only arm two Companies with such guns I would be doing a great service. The Federals have them and are killing many of our best officers in every fight." He planned to take his old friend Joseph D. Pickett along with him to England. Pickett had accompanied Richards on the Grand Tour to Europe and into the desert lands of the Near East and was now serving as chaplain to the troops of the 1st Kentucky Brigade.[3]

Evidently Richards had previously discussed this plan with Breckinridge, for in his second letter, dated March 25, he noted that the steamer with its cotton cargo would set out from one of the bayous "in the way I suggested to you last fall." As this was written, Richards was already aboard a Confederate gunboat, the *J. A. Cotton,* which was then churning up the Mississippi River less than twenty-five miles south of Transylvania Plantation. He left it to the general's discretion as to whether Richards should himself travel to England with the cotton: "I feel confident in her getting out and I have made arrangements to go on her provided I don't hear from you. I wrote to you [in his previous letter] that if your Brigade was likely to have a fight soon that I would not go but would join you immediately. I will trust to your judgement and friendly feeling for me in giving me your advice in this Matter. The vessel will leave in about a week. It is more difficult to run the blockade now than it has been at any time during the winter." He concluded by stating simply, "If I don't hear from you in a few days I will join you and let the steamer and the cotton take its chances."[4]

At Transylvania on March 28, Richards handed a third letter for Breckinridge to his cousin Wallis Bodien Keene for personal delivery. "Body" Keene, twenty-one years old, was visiting his mother and stepfather, Horace B. Tebbetts, at Atherton Plantation in Carroll Parish not far away. Captain Keene was on leave from the 1st Regiment Mississippi Cavalry, commanded by Colonel Wirt Adams, which had participated in the long retreat from Bowling Green; he may, in fact, have accompanied Richards on the train to Louisiana. His cousin wished to form an artillery company with some of his friends, Richards informed Breckinridge, and would very much like to have the battery fielded as part of the 1st Kentucky Brigade. He referred again to his plan to secure English weapons, writing, "I ship some cotton today to New Orleans with permit from the Governor it will go out by fast steamer. I have written you several letters in reference to this matter and hope you will answer by telegraph. I will be governed by your advice." Richards then noted in a postscript, "All my horses and Negroes have arrived safe."[5]

Breckinridge did indeed respond by telegraph, probably a curt summons to return immediately. Johnston's army had broken camp and was marching toward the enemy, determined to wrest Tennessee from Union control. On April 6, two great armies would clash near a small town on the Tennessee River, twenty-three miles north of Corinth. By a matter of mere

(*Left*) General John C. Breckinridge, CSA, whom Keene Richards helped escape from imminent arrest in Kentucky and later served as volunteer aide-de-camp. Civil war photographs, 1861–1865, Library of Congress. (*Right*) Captain Alexander Keene Richards in Confederate uniform. Courtesy of Lowry Schneider.

days, Keene Richards would miss participating in one of the bloodiest conflicts of the entire war, known as the battle of Pittsburg Landing—or as Shiloh to the Confederates. Among the casualties were George W. Johnson, the Confederate governor of Kentucky, and Albert Sydney Johnston, one of the South's most able generals. The Union offensive drove a wedge deep into the Confederacy, gaining a vast amount of territory in the process. Federal troops now controlled the upper Mississippi and Tennessee valleys and were positioned to continue their advance into the southern heartland.[6]

Through two days of hell at Shiloh, John C. Breckinridge directed his troops with skill and courage, vindicating the faith and affection of the men of the Kentucky Brigade for their general and earning the esteem of his superiors. His performance during and after the battle (and his value to the Confederacy as a political asset) was rewarded by promotion to the rank of major general on April 18. Breckinridge announced his staff appointments on April 13, which once again included Keene Richards as one of three volunteer aides-de-camp. This reappointment indicates that, by this time, Richards must have returned from Louisiana and rejoined the general at his headquarters in Corinth.[7]

In the weeks following the clash at Shiloh, both armies were content to occupy their respective positions while they rested, tended to their casualties, and waited for reinforcements. At the end of the month came news that stunned the entire southland—New Orleans, the largest city and most important port in the Confederacy, had been captured. The Confederacy lost an irreplaceable resource capable of providing new ships and supplies for the defense of the Mississippi River valley, and the Federals were now free to use the city as a base from which to launch a campaign up the Mississippi to meet the advance coming down the river. If the Union were able to obtain complete control of the river, the Confederacy would be split, with the river a formidable barrier between the eastern and western sides.[8]

A few days after the battle, the Confederate troops marched uneventfully southward, going into camp near Tupelo, Mississippi, on May 8. Since it appeared that his men would now remain in camp for some time, Breckinridge, who had been mildly ill for several weeks, took a four-week leave of absence beginning June 8. He traveled to Carroll Parish in Louisiana to visit some distant relatives, the Carson family, who owned a great estate overlooking the Mississippi River known as Airlie Plantation. Almost certainly, the general was accompanied by his aide Keene Richards, especially since Richards's Transylvania Plantation was located less than two miles north of Airlie and the Carsons would have been well known to him as neighbors and friends.[9]

Dr. James Green Carson, a wealthy cotton planter, was one of the largest slaveholders in Louisiana, having nearly two hundred enslaved people in residence on his twenty-six hundred-acre plantation. When Breckinridge and Richards rode up the long, tree-lined avenue leading to the Carson mansion, with its acres of well-tended gardens, they were warmly welcomed. Breckinridge was a distant cousin to the doctor's wife, Catherine. The Carsons had five children, of whom the youngest and only daughter, Katie, was eight years old at the time of the general's visit. Long after the war ended, in 1876, Katie would marry Breckinridge's youngest son, Clifton.[10]

Richards would be an able guide for the general, providing introductions to some of the leading families of the area. Breckinridge probably did not spend all his leave time at Airlie, and likely was entertained at Transylvania on some occasions. Amanda Stone, owner of Brokenburn Plantation in nearby Madison Parish, was a frequent caller at Airlie Plantation, usually bringing her children along so that they could play and socialize with the Carson children while their elders visited. Amanda's eldest daughter, Kate, twenty-one years old, noted in her diary on June 17, "Yesterday we spent at Dr. Carsons. One of the hottest days possible. Gen. Breckinridge was in the neighborhood and was expected to dinner, but much to our regret did not come . . . he is said to be exceedingly handsome." Kate Stone was to be further disappointed in her desire to meet Breckinridge. The general's leave was cut short when bombardment of Vicksburg by Federal gunboats began on June 28. "Gen. Breckinridge started to Vicksburg yesterday [June 28] in a carriage," Kate wrote, "and he runs a great risk of being captured, as they have pickets across the point."[11]

Richards had more urgent reason to travel to Carroll Parish than simply to serve as companion to his general. On June 6, Union gunboats and rams had destroyed Confederate naval forces on the Mississippi at Memphis and captured the city, giving the Union navy control of the entire river save for a small section in the vicinity of Vicksburg. With Federal gunboats cruising the river and small landing parties coming ashore in the neighborhood, Transylvania Plantation no longer provided a safe refuge for his valuable breeding stock. The need to remove his stock was now undeniable, so Richards directed Morris Keene or another trusted representative to take his horses 150 miles southwest to Thomas J. Wells at Dentley Plantation in Rapides Parish, far distant from the Mississippi River.[12]

The five thousand men of Breckinridge's reserve corps were among the troops now assigned to defend Vicksburg, one of the last remaining Confederate bastions on the Mississippi. They arrived at the city on June 30. Vicksburg was located on the eastern side of the Mississippi, perched on high bluffs on the outside of a hairpin bend, and was nearly impregnable in its position. General Breckinridge joined his men shortly after their arrival, following what must have been a very hazardous crossing of the Mississippi since, by this time, Union mortar boats were bombarding the city.[13]

The Union high command believed that Vicksburg could be taken without difficulty by a naval attack alone, given the ease with which Baton Rouge and Natchez had been overcome. A naval assault by gunboats on June 13 failed, and it was now apparent that capture of the city would require substantial land forces operating in a joint army-navy assault. Even as the inhabitants of Vicksburg and the defending troops joyously celebrated their successful stand against the Yankee fleet, Breckinridge received a new set of marching orders for his corps. An assault upon Baton Rouge would divert Federal attention away from Vicksburg, and the recapture of the city would bring a two hundred-mile stretch of the Mississippi back under Confederate control. If Baton Rouge could be taken, this would be a significant step toward the important goal of liberating New Orleans from the Yankees. Combining his force with six thousand men under Daniel Ruggles, the Confederate expeditionary force launched its attack on the Louisiana capital city before dawn on August 5, 1862. With Keene Richards at his side, Breckinridge led charge after charge against the Union enemy. In his after-action report, the general commended Richards for his role in urging on the troops during the fiercest fighting. Despite initial success in forcing back the opposition, Federal gunboats on the river prevented the Confederates from cementing a victory, and they were forced to retreat from the city. Baton Rouge would remain in Union hands for the remainder of the war.[14]

The Kentucky Brigade was subsequently sent to help defend Port Hudson, one of the strongest points on the Mississippi. On the evening of August 10, Colonel L. Stoddard Johnston came to the camp and handed Breckinridge a letter from Braxton Bragg. Bragg was planning an offensive to regain Tennessee and Kentucky, and he wanted Breckinridge with his army, as much for his political influence in Kentucky as for the troops he could bring. "If you desire it, and General Van Dorn will consent, you will come at once," Bragg wrote. "A command is ready for you, and I shall hope to see your eyes beam again at the command 'Forward,' as they did at Shiloh, in the midst of our greatest success." Nothing would be closer to Breckinridge's own heart's desire than to participate in liberating Kentucky from its Union occupiers. His reply to Bragg, delivered by Johnston, made his sentiments perfectly clear, as well as his loyalty to his troops: "I would make any sacrifice to join you, except leaving the remnant of my command. I will remain with it under all circumstances."[15]

Breckinridge's self-imposed condition proved to be an obstacle, however, because his immediate superior in the theater, Major General Earl Van Dorn, would not release the Kentucky troops. So Breckinridge, true to his word, could do little but remain in camp with his troops, seething with frustration, while the Kentucky campaign began.[16]

During that summer of 1862, Confederate cavalry commander John Hunt Morgan launched a major raid from Tennessee into Kentucky. In the early afternoon of July 5, he forded the Cumberland River with his men and crossed into Kentucky. During the next twenty days, Morgan and his raiders cut an audacious lightning swathe across the state, deftly eluding pursuing Federal forces while burning bridges, destroying military stores and provisions, and generally confounding the Union high command in Kentucky. Morgan's exploits were reported daily in the press, and on July 13 Abraham Lincoln sent Henry Halleck, senior army commander in the West, a sharply worded telegram: "They are having a stampede in Kentucky. Please look into it."[17]

Morgan took his raiders northeast to the Bluegrass region. He bypassed Lexington and Frankfort as too well defended, and on the evening of July 15 rode into Georgetown, Keene Richards's hometown, dispersing a small force of Home Guards. Here, in a town considered "a very hotbed of Southern feeling" where many had family ties, the raiders halted for two days to rest and recover. His second in command, Basil Duke, who grew up in Scott County, observed that in all the region Georgetown was the one place where "sympathy for us was strongest," and was "an admirable selection as a resting point." The town was central between the two points from which they might expect attack, Lexington and Frankfort, and their presence in Georgetown would hinder communication between the two Union strongholds.[18]

In every town the raiders visited, friendly crowds thronged to see the famous Morgan and his men, extending the southern hospitality for which the region was famous. Their reception at Georgetown was all that could have been desired, and from pro-southern Scott County and from the surrounding region enough volunteers came to Morgan to form an additional mounted company. Encouraged by the success of the expedition, on July 16 Morgan sent a telegram from Georgetown to General Edmund Kirby Smith at Knoxville informing him that: "I am here with a force sufficient to hold all the country outside of Lexington and Frankfort. These places are garrisoned chiefly with Home Guards. The bridges between Cincinnati and Lexington have been destroyed. The whole country can be secured, and 25,000 or 30,000 men will join you at once." In his desire to "liberate" Kentucky, Morgan badly misjudged the sentiments of the population. The hospitable reception they enjoyed in towns throughout the state misled Morgan into believing that the majority of Kentucky's citizens favored the southern cause and needed only encouragement and support to rebel en masse against Union authority. The crowds who came to see him in the towns were drawn more by simple curiosity to meet this colorful character and his men, rather than from strongly held secessionist yearnings. In large part, Morgan's telegram helped precipitate a late summer Confederate invasion of Kentucky by armies commanded by Kirby Smith and Bragg.[19]

Kirby Smith fiercely longed to carry off some enterprise that would garner him more newspaper headlines and public recognition. He sent a copy of Morgan's telegram on July 24 to General Braxton Bragg at Tupelo, Mississippi, seeking the latter's cooperation in an invasion of Kentucky. Like many Confederate leaders, Kirby Smith believed that the citizens of the Bluegrass state were seething under the heel of their Union oppressors and needed only the encouragement of a strong Confederate military presence to flock to his banner and help expel the Federals from Kentucky. Kirby Smith led his army on a forced march northward out of Knoxville and into the Bluegrass region, routing a hastily assembled Union force a few miles south of Richmond. On the morning of September 2, Kirby Smith rode triumphantly into Lexington at the head of his troops, now numbering about twelve thousand men.[20]

His immediate goal achieved, Kirby Smith made his headquarters at Lexington, but now seemed to have lost the momentum that had carried him this far. He was disappointed by the response of Bluegrass residents to recruitment efforts. Although he expected his ranks to be swelled by thousands of eager volunteers, scarcely a man had enlisted in the Confederate infantry. Smith began to disperse his troops throughout the region, sending units to occupy cities and towns and obtain supplies while assuring the citizens that they came not as invaders, but as liberators, calling for patriotic Kentuckians to "join with us in hurling back from our fair and sunny plains the Northern hordes who would deprive us of our liberty, that they may enjoy our substance."[21]

As these events were unfolding, in late August Braxton Bragg moved his men out of Tennessee into Kentucky to reinforce Kirby Smith and secure the Confederate occupation of the state. Towing his field artillery, Bragg led a force of twenty-seven thousand infantry northward from Chattanooga on August 28, closely pursued by Don Carlos Buell, the Union commander, who took his troops out of Nashville on September 10 on a hard march into Kentucky. En route to Glasgow, Bragg became increasingly concerned by the failure of John C. Breckinridge to join his army. Not only were the five thousand troops under his command sorely needed in Kentucky, but he expected Breckinridge would be a great asset in his home state to rally large numbers of volunteers to the Confederate banner. On August 27, as he was preparing to set his force on the march, Bragg sent a telegram to Breckinridge at Jackson, Mississippi: "We leave for your beloved home. Would that you were with us. Your division is ready as soon as you join, but you must hurry up to overtake us." Bragg and Smith were fully confident that Breckinridge would very soon add his strength to the invasion force, but as days went by with no sign of the Kentucky general and his troops, confidence became concern.[22]

John C. Breckinridge was a very frustrated general officer. There was not a man of his command, himself included, who was not eager to join Bragg and Smith in Kentucky to purge their home state of the tyrannical Union presence, but instead they were stuck in Mississippi awaiting the pleasure of Breckinridge's immediate superior, Major General Earl Van Dorn. Despite the appeal of the Kentucky campaign, Breckinridge remained at Holly Springs with the remnants of his command because Van Dorn was unwilling to relinquish the Kentuckians, veterans all.[23]

By September 17, the long-suffering Breckinridge and his troops were finally released from Van Dorn's command by order of the Confederate secretary of war, George W. Randolph. Breckinridge immediately informed Bragg that he would soon be joining him in Kentucky. He summoned his aide, Captain Keene Richards, and told him that he had a special mission for him, one that was of great personal importance. Breckinridge wished Richards to set out in advance of the troops on a long solo journey to Lexington, by the fastest means possible. Once there, he was to contact Breckinridge's former law partner, James B. Beck, who would make the necessary arrangements to deal with the urgent matter. Richards packed and made an immediate departure. Breckinridge wasted no time in moving his troops out. "Embarked on a dawn train," John S. Jackman of the 9th Kentucky Regiment noted in his diary on the nineteenth, "going to Kentucky certain, this time."[24]

While Breckinridge's troops were in transit from northern Mississippi to Knoxville, events had been unfolding rapidly in the Bluegrass state. Braxton Bragg, acting as foil to Buell's Union army, marched his troops to Munfordville on September 17, accepting the surrender of the greatly outnumbered Union commander of the post, and then to Bardstown. His path now clear of Bragg's troops, Buell moved quickly, driving the Army of the Ohio up the Louisville Road in forced marches, the first units reaching the river city on September 25, where they were welcomed by cheering crowds.[25]

Kirby Smith was reluctant to merge the two Confederate armies, for this would place him subordinate to Bragg and bring an end to his independent command; he was content to let Bragg deal alone with Buell. Unable to decide the best place to concentrate his army, Bragg positioned his combined forces across the state in a line from Bardstown to Georgetown, intending to hold the Bluegrass region against any move from Buell. Contrary to Bragg's expectations, Buell did not tarry at Louisville after arriving there with his troops on September 25, but marched the Federal army out of the city in four columns, each following a separate road, intended to converge on Bardstown, cut Bragg off from any convenient line of retreat, and defeat the rebels somewhere south of Lexington.[26]

The two armies, blue and gray, finally met in battle on October 8 near the small crossroads town of Perryville, about ten miles southwest from Harrodsburg. Kirby Smith's troops were not present at the battle; self-serving as always and ever reluctant to relinquish the independence of his command, Kirby Smith halted his troops north of the Kentucky River, informing his superior that he felt he must protect Lexington. The battle that took place was one of the bloodiest of the entire war. Both armies took very heavy casualties. The outcome of the Perryville battle was unclear to either commander. As Buell biographer Stephen Engle observed, "Though neither side acknowledged defeat, neither knew who had won, either." Bragg was now forced to a bitter conclusion: he would have to abandon Kentucky. On October 13, the demoralized Confederate armies, now united, set out on a march through the mountains of eastern Kentucky toward Cumberland Gap, without pursuit by the shaken Union force. With Bragg's passage through the Gap a few days later, the grand adventure was over. Kentucky was forever lost to the Confederacy.[27]

Keene Richards arrived in Lexington a few days before the battle of Perryville. The task he had been given by his friend and commander, John C. Breckinridge, was to have the general's wife, Mary Cyrene Breckinridge, escorted to Richmond, there to await the arrival of her husband as he marched into Kentucky at the head of his army. John and Mary Breckinridge were deeply in love, and the couple had not seen each other since Breckinridge made his hasty departure from Lexington more than a year earlier. To accomplish his mission, Richards first went to see James B. Beck, who had been Breckinridge's law partner until 1861 and remained one of his closest personal friends. Beck was, however, not available at the time, so Richards rode north into Scott County to see Mary Breckinridge. Mary and her children were then living with the family of George W. Johnson, the ill-fated former provisional Confederate governor of Kentucky who had been killed at the battle of Shiloh in April 1862. Mary was overjoyed when Richards arrived at the Johnson's Scott County farm and gave her the news of her husband's imminent arrival in Kentucky and his desire for her to join him immediately. Leaving her children in care of the Johnsons, Mary promptly set off to Lexington to consult with James Beck about travel arrangements.[28]

Having complied with his general's request, Richards visited his home in nearby Georgetown. As he approached Blue Grass Park, the neatly fenced paddocks and the old Craig house on the hill above the spring, where he had been born, were welcome sights. Soon after his arrival, Richards was greeted by Frank Sherritt, his farm manager and agent for several years before the war and, during his recent absence, the man to whom he had entrusted the care of Blue Grass Park. Frank had much to tell him. During May of this year, on his own authority, Sherritt had organized a six-day spring race meeting held over Richards's private track, the first and only time such an event was held at Blue Grass Park. The meeting had been attended by large crowds on each day and attracted entries from many notable Bluegrass horsemen.[29]

As Richards inspected his estate in company with Sherritt, his attention was caught by one particular horse, a large bay gelding, sired by the celebrated Glencoe in summer 1857 and known affectionately as Glencoe, Jr. The horse was later described by cavalryman Basil Duke, John Hunt Morgan's second in command: "He stood sixteen hands, and perhaps half an inch in height, and was not only a strong, but a 'big horse.' He had the Thoroughbred points in nearly as marked degree [as Morgan's Black Bess], but in more robust proportion, and in gait and action he was almost her equal. . . . Big as he was, he was yet extremely nimble and sure-footed." Richards was struck by a sudden inspiration. Morgan's favorite mount, Black Bess, had been lost to him last spring, and he had made do with mediocre mounts ever since. This magnificent animal would make a splendid replacement for Bess! Morgan was now in Lexington, having arrived there on the afternoon of October 4 after a scouting mission through eastern Kentucky. Richards bade farewell to Sherritt, no doubt complimenting him on his astute management of the property during his absence, and rode away from Blue Grass Park leading two horses behind him, Glencoe, Jr., and a handsome dark bay part-Arabian that he intended to present to Basil Duke.[30]

Upon his arrival at Lexington, Richards found the city in a state of considerable excitement and confusion. Most of the Confederate troops had marched out of Lexington on Thursday, October 2. When John Hunt Morgan arrived two days later, as ranking officer he assumed command. He did not long remain in Lexington, for the unanticipated movement of Buell's Army of the Ohio meant that all available remaining soldiers would be needed for the looming confrontation. Morgan and Duke would depart Lexington on Monday as well, so Richards had a very narrow window in which to present his equine gifts. The meeting between Richards and Morgan may have taken place on Sunday, October 5, at Hopemont, Morgan's home in Lexington. Morgan was grateful for the gift and appreciated the many fine qualities of Glencoe, Jr., for the gelding became his constant companion during the remainder of his campaigning. Basil

Duke recalled, "I saw Morgan on one occasion, when we were in close and hot pursuit of a body of Federals, ride this horse over a steep 'bluff' or eminence along a small watercourse, which was at least thirty feet in height and almost precipitous, yet he went down it as surely and landed at the bottom as lightly as a cat could have done." The partnership between man and horse came to an end on July 26, 1863, when Morgan and most of his men were captured near West Point, Ohio, following an audacious raid across Indiana and Ohio. The son of Glencoe was later presented by General James M. Shackleford to Winfield Scott, who had been painted by Edward Troye in December 1861 seated on this very same horse, an irony savored by many at the time.[31]

Keene Richards probably lingered in the Bluegrass for another day or so, perhaps returning to his home, but after the battle of Perryville on October 8 it would have been clear that he must return immediately to his commanding general. He may have attached himself temporarily to Bragg's or Kirby Smith's army as they slowly retreated through eastern Kentucky, but more likely he would have spurred his horse directly for Cumberland Gap. At about the same time, James Beck escorted Mary Breckinridge to Richmond to meet her husband, but "He did not meet her, and I returned to Lexington," Beck recalled. "She went South with a friend." Exactly why Richards had not been given the task of taking Mary to Richmond himself is unclear, but possibly John Breckinridge had felt that Beck would be better acquainted with the current situation in Kentucky and had the connections to arrange transport.[32]

As Mary was traveling southward, her husband was on his way north. On the morning of October 15, Breckinridge and his command set out from Knoxville for Kentucky, intending to follow the old Wilderness Road through Cumberland Gap. "Our hearts were high with hope that we would join Genls Bragg & E Kirby Smith," wrote Private Johnny Green, "and redeem our state from the hands of the despoiler." Johnny would not see Kentucky again that year, nor for many yet to come. The men of the brigade had just set out from camp on the morning of October 17, and were still more than thirty miles short of the Gap, when a courier galloped up to Breckinridge and handed him a dispatch. Bragg had been defeated and was retreating from Kentucky. With heavy hearts, the Kentucky soldiers retraced their steps back to Knoxville. "The boys are not as cheerful today, as when going on the road the other way," Private Jackman observed to his diary on the nineteenth. The only bright note for John Breckinridge in the whole debacle was his reunion with his beloved wife, Mary, in Knoxville a few days later. Had his troops been present at Perryville, it might have made a difference in the outcome, but all he could do now was take the fight elsewhere.[33]

In late October, Breckinridge received orders to move his troops to Murfreesboro, Tennessee, southwest from Nashville, and direct military operations in that area. He once again appointed Keene Richards as one of his aides. Bragg arrived on November 30 with his troops and took command, and as the new year began the Confederates fought to a stalemate at Stones River against a Union force under William Rosecrans. Believing Union reinforcements were about to arrive, Bragg withdrew from the state. The battle of Stones River was one of the deadliest conflicts of the entire war; of the nearly one hundred thousand men engaged, almost twenty-four thousand were casualties, about evenly distributed on both sides. Keene Richards did not participate in this bloody conflict. When his commanding general went to Murfreesboro in late October, Richards was left behind in Knoxville, seriously ill and confined to bed. For Richards, the war was over, and he would not see his friend Breckinridge for many years.[34]

15
TRANSITIONS

In Knoxville on October 30, the ailing Keene Richards wrote to his commander to inform him that "I find that my health is not improving as fast as I expected and Dr. Luke Blackburn as well as Dr. Keene of Georgetown insist that it will not do for me to go into camp for some time. This is their suggestion and not mine." Blackburn was a well-respected physician from Woodford County, Kentucky, serving with the Confederate army. In his letter to Breckinridge, Richards declared his desire "to be with you to the end of this war" but felt that he might now better serve the southern cause by undertaking a different sort of work, one that would separate him from his friend for a considerable time. "I propose to go to Europe immediately," he wrote, "and employ my time getting up a Light Battery to be used in the spring campaign in Kentucky."[1]

Richards had previously suggested this plan to Breckinridge. Seven months before, while at New Orleans on personal business, Richards wrote to his general on March 18 proposing that he go to England to secure better rifles for the men of the brigade. Breckinridge declined the offer, wishing to keep Richards on his staff and near at hand, but evidently the idea lingered in Richards's mind. Perhaps it was again brought to the surface in conversations with Luke Blackburn, an ardent successionist who, in a rather odd occupation for a physician, served the Confederacy as a procurer of weapons during the first years of the war. Hearing of Blackburn's efforts to help the Confederacy in this way may have renewed Richards's ambition to do the same.[2]

Richards's desire to separate himself from Breckinridge's command and travel abroad may also have been fostered by a dampened enthusiasm for active service in the war. Like the other men of the brigade, Richards was bitterly disappointed by the failure of the Kentucky campaign. Only he, of all the men of Breckinridge's command, had been able to set foot inside his native state, and then only for a few days. Although Confederate armies scored many successes in the eastern theater during 1862, the story in the west was discouraging. Kentucky committed to the Union shortly after the onset of the war, and recent events had demonstrated that there was no real longing among the citizens to rise up and "overthrow their oppressors." Federal forces were building up in Tennessee, blocking future efforts to regain the state, and Union control of the Mississippi River was nearly complete. Only the fortress city of Vicksburg and the formidable guns at Port Hudson, twenty-five miles north of Baton Rouge, now stood against the bluecoats.[3]

Richards was no warrior at heart. Although during the past year he had often shared the hardships of campaigning with his fellow Kentuckians, and had fought bravely enough at Baton Rouge, circumstances often led to his absence from the battlefield when blood was being shed. As a volunteer aide on Breckinridge's staff, Richards had the freedom to slip away temporarily on personal missions, with the welfare of his vulnerable Mississippi riverfront plantation, Transylvania, and his horses always a concern equal to the conduct of the war. Upon his return to the army after a visit to Louisiana, Richards saw the bloody aftermath of Shiloh, an object lesson in just how horrifying the new "total warfare" could be and one that certainly left a lasting impression on the sensitive young man. In many respects, Richards was little more than a dilettante when it came to actual warfare, one who was willing to exercise his wealth and influence in support of the southern cause but who found the reality of field campaigning a difficult burden to shoulder.

"I now feel that I can use my time and means better in this way," Richards wrote, but "if you as my friend and Gen think differently write to me by Maurice [Morris] Keene and I will be with you sick or well." If the general approved of his mission, Richards asked him to send a letter of authorization by way of Morris Keene. This implies that Keene was then most likely with Richards at Knoxville, and would carry this letter to Breckinridge and return with a reply. Richards may have invited his cousin and best friend Keene to accompany him in the liberation of Kentucky. No military records have been found for Keene, and he evidently remained a civilian for the span of the war. During the fall of 1861, Keene shepherded a number of Richards's most valuable horses from Georgetown to Transylvania and perhaps remained there for some time, but no further indication of his location or travels appears until this letter placing him in Tennessee.[4]

Richards closed his letter by informing his commander that "Mrs Breckinridge is well and in fine spirits. I start this morning with Capt Johnson," and added a postscript, "I think it best that no one should know of my movements until I am safe in Europe if I am to go." Certain that permission would be granted, Richards was so eager to be off on his self-appointed mission that he intended to depart immediately, sick or well. Morris Keene brought the requested permission from Breckinridge, and the two men soon traveled together into the Deep South. Keene would accompany Richards to England and remain there with him until the conclusion of the war.[5]

Richards and Keene probably traveled by rail from Knoxville through Atlanta to Montgomery, thence on to Mobile by way of the Alabama River, and northward by rail again to Meridian, Mississippi. From Meridian it was a straight shot over the Southern Railroad line through Jackson to Vicksburg on the river. There was little hazard in crossing over to the Louisiana side beneath the eyes of the watchful gunners of Vicksburg, since Union gunboats had not operated in this section of the Mississippi River for several months following July's unsuccessful naval siege of the city. Once across, Richards rode northward over the old river road thirty-five miles to Transylvania Plantation. Although his cotton had been burned, he must have been relieved to find the property, with its tree-shrouded mansion and elegant gardens, still intact. The peace that now held along the riverfront was deceptive, he knew, for the Yankee invaders would soon be back. The capture of Vicksburg was the key to controlling the entire river.

Northeastern Louisiana was the core region for cotton production in the state, and Carroll Parish, where Transylvania was located, was second only to Tensas Parish in cotton harvested and baled. Great fortunes had been made by cotton, among them that of William B. Keene, whose lands and wealth had been inherited by Keene Richards. With the increasing Union presence on the river in 1862 and the loss of their harvest, most of these wealthy planters abandoned their plantations and fled. Wholesale destruction of baled cotton along the Mississippi began in spring of 1862, when Louisiana governor Thomas O. Moore issued orders on April 25 for the burning of all of the cotton in New Orleans and along the river to avoid confiscation. "As far as we can see are the ascending wreaths of smoke," Kate Stone noted in her journal on May 9 at Brokenburn, "and we hear that all the cotton of the Mississippi Valley from Memphis to New Orleans is going up in smoke. The planters look upon the burning of the cotton as almost ruin to their fortunes, but all realize its stern necessity."[6]

When Richards made a brief visit to Transylvania with Breckinridge in June, he must have gritted his teeth at the loss of his cotton, but was likewise resigned to the "stern necessity." Even more disturbing, while helping man the fortifications of Vicksburg during July as the city was besieged by Union gunboats, he must have heard reports of Union troops conscripting plantation slaves along the river at gunpoint, forcing them to labor on a canal intended to allow naval forces to bypass the fortress city. More cotton could be planted, but his enslaved workers represented an enormous capital investment that he could ill afford to replace.

Now, five months later, Richards was back at Transylvania and no doubt dismayed by the loss of many of his best enslaved workers. Kate Stone noted that Federal raiding parties had scoured the riverfront for slaves from Lake Providence to Pecan Grove. Transylvania was squarely in the middle of this zone and would have been a prime target. He had been wise to send his horses away from here to General Wells in Rapides Parish, for surely they would also have been taken. Richards and Morris Keene lingered at Transylvania for about two weeks before departing for Wells's plantation sometime in late November, where he could check on the well-being of his horses before continuing on to the coast. At the plantation gate, Richards may have turned in his saddle for one last, good look at the place that held so many fond memories. As he turned his horse toward Alexandria, located in the center of the state fifty miles west of the Mississippi, perhaps he wondered what would become of Transylvania Plantation in the months ahead and whether he would ever see it again.[7]

In late November, as Ulysses S. Grant was beginning to organize his campaign against Vicksburg, Richards and Keene rode southwest from Carroll Parish into the old pine flatwood terraces and bottomlands around the Red River in central Louisiana. Upon Richards's arrival at Dentley

Plantation, about fifteen miles south of Alexandria, he was warmly greeted by his old friend Thomas Jefferson Wells. Fifty-seven years old at the time of Richards's visit, Wells had strong ties to Kentucky. He was educated at Transylvania University in Lexington and, as the most notable horse breeder of Louisiana, had developed a system whereby he sent his best mares to board at the farm of Joseph R. Gross, on the Winchester pike a few miles outside Lexington. Here they were bred to some of the most outstanding horses of the Bluegrass. As soon as the foals were weaned, they were sent to Dentley to be broken, trained, and raced. At the center of the property stood the elegant Wells residence, and within sight of the house was a mile track that was generally used for training but sometimes hosted race meetings. This was sugar cane country, which had begun to replace cotton in the area during the 1850s following devastating cater-

Thomas Jefferson Wells, leading Louisiana turfman and a close personal friend of Keene Richards. Courtesy of the Alexandria Historical and Genealogical Library and Museum, Alexandria, Louisiana.

pillar infestations. His older brother, Monfort, was the largest sugar cane producer in Rapides Parish at Wellswood, his huge plantation on nearby Bayou Boeuf, but Jefferson Wells was passionately dedicated to raising Thoroughbred Running Horses at Dentley.[8]

Despite his optimistic assertion to Breckinridge that cannon obtained in England could be used for a renewed offensive into Kentucky during spring 1863, Richards seemed to be in no great hurry to be about this task and lingered at Dentley for several months. While enjoying the general's hospitality, his attention, and soon his affection, was captured by an attractive young woman who lived on Bayou Rapides west of Alexandria and was visiting the plantation. Mary Editha Winn, daughter of avid turfman Wade Hampton Bynum and Caroline LaMothe Bynum, was a second cousin to T. J. Wells. Mary was twenty-six years old and recently widowed when she met thirty-five-year-old Keene Richards for the first time. Her husband, Walter O. Winn, had passed away two years before. The young couple became so enamored of one another that when Richards returned to the United States after the war, he courted Mary assiduously and they were wed in Carroll Parish in January 1867.[9]

Richards was also captivated by another resident of Dentley Plantation. Wells was pleased to show off his Thoroughbred Running Horse stock to another turfman, and the two spent many hours examining the horses and discussing the fine points of breeding and racing, no doubt accompanied by Wells's trainer, an elderly slave known as Hawk. Richards's attention kept coming back to one high-spirited two-year-old colt, a rich golden chestnut in color with a large white star on his forehead and four white feet, standing just under sixteen hands in height. Foaled in April 1860, the young horse had an impeccable ancestry, sired by the celebrity horse Lexington, then standing at Robert A. Alexander's Woodburn Farm in Woodford County, Kentucky, out of Wells's prized mare, Reel. This was quite a match, since Reel, the mother of Lecomte and Starke, was considered the most outstanding mare in America, and Lexington the foremost stallion. The foal was named General Westmore by Wells to honor a friend and outstanding turfman, Samuel M. Westmore, considered to be "the best judge of horseflesh in the south." This was the last foal produced by Reel before her death. The portrait made of Reel by Edward Troye for Wells in 1859 or 1860 shows her in an apparently gravid condition, and she may well have been carrying General Westmore when painted. As was Wells's custom, once the foal was weaned, it was sent south to Dentley Plantation for training.[10]

Wells made some trials of the colt at his private track and concluded that this was an exceptional horse, "the best of Reel's produce"—quite a compliment considering the many other outstanding racers she had birthed. He had not yet been able to race General Westmore, since racing venues throughout the South had been shut down by the war, but Richards, watching the colt being exercised on the track, was convinced that here was a horse that he must have. The sale was made on February 23, 1863, Richards signing a note promising to pay, once the war had concluded, $5,000 in "legal Kentucky money," an astounding sum for the time, and the colt was turned over to the care of Richards's groom, who was in residence at Dentley to look after his other horses. The circumstances prompted Richards to rename his new horse War Dance, which commemorated not only the times but his descent from "a dancing family," by which Richards was referring to the names of the colt's dam, Reel, and granddam, Gallopede.[11]

The impulsive purchase of War Dance during the Civil War was, like so many of Richards's equine acquisitions, a demonstration of the Kentucky turfman's ability to select superior horses. After the war, when Richards resumed his breeding, War Dance would become one of the nation's leading sires of winning horses. Richards did not long remain at Dentley after finalizing the sale, but set out again, traveling west into Texas and then south to the border with Mexico, until he finally reached the city of Matamoros, across the Rio Grande from Brownsville, Texas, and near the coast. A small, sleepy town of little consequence before the war, with the imposition of the Union blockade of rebel ports in April of 1861 Matamoros became the "backdoor of the Confederacy" for blockade runners and grew into a bustling community with over thirty thousand inhabitants by the end of the war.[12]

The roads across Texas were busy with caravans bringing cotton, the South's most valuable asset, to the mouth of the Rio Grande, where it was loaded into fast-sailing schooners for shipment to the world market. The blockade runners returned with loads of war materials and other supplies badly needed by the Confederacy. Confederate ships left Matamoros bearing the flags of Mexico or England, the latter readily provided by accommodating British consuls in Havana and other foreign ports. The Lincoln administration was hesitant to provoke foreign powers and reluctantly adopted a position that trade between Matamoros and England did not violate the blockade; in consequence, the U.S. Navy generally avoided stationing warships at the mouth of the Rio Grande.[13]

Once into international waters, Confederate ships were liable to be stopped and inspected regardless of the flag they carried, but most blockade runners could slip through without interference. Richards would have little difficulty securing passage on a blockade runner, for there were often dozens of vessels at anchor waiting to unload or take on cargo, or for favorable conditions to make their run. Blockade runners preferred to set out on dark, moonless nights, particularly in fog or rain, and would sometimes remain at the river mouth for weeks until circumstances were nearly ideal. Surely on such a night the two cousins crossed the Gulf of Mexico aboard a fast schooner to Havana, where they boarded a ship that carried them safely to England, arriving about the first of May.[14]

As Richards and Keene sailed for England, events were unfolding in Louisiana that would threaten the safety of War Dance and the other horses at Dentley Plantation. In April 1863, Major General Nathaniel P. Banks led an expedition of Union troops up the Bayou Teche to Opelousas, opposed unsuccessfully by Confederate general Richard Taylor.[15]

The swift advance of Union troops into Rapides Parish and the temporary occupation of Alexandria created something of a panic at Dentley. The plantation was little more than a dozen miles south of the city, and the Federal troops were plundering the countryside on their march north, confiscating cotton, sugar and molasses, and thousands of cattle, horses, and mules. Thousands of enslaved persons were liberated and followed the army as best they could. Looting by individual soldiers was widespread, with homes being stripped of food and anything of value; what could not be carried off was destroyed. "Houses were entered and all in them destroyed in the most wanton manner," Union general William Dwight Jr. observed with considerable distaste. As the Federal army approached Alexandria, Wells's nephew, also named Jefferson Wells, quickly gathered up the most valuable of the horses, those of both his uncle and Keene Richards, and led them to safety in the interior of Texas.[16]

War Dance was in notable company on the trip to Texas. He was accompanied by Richards's prized stallion, the Knight of St. George, and the aging Arabian Fysaul along with Wells's mare Fanny Wells (by Sovereign out of Reel) and an unknown number of other horses. Jefferson Wells, a son of the general's brother Montfort, was twenty-nine years old and had spent much of his time at Dentley helping his uncle raise and train horses. Presumably Jefferson took along several grooms and other slaves to help handle the animals. The elder Wells most likely accompanied his nephew on this exodus, because records place him in Texas in July 1863. After a long and dusty journey stretching out nearly five hundred miles, they came to the ranch of Thomas F. McKinney, located along Onion Creek on what was then the outskirts of Austin on the opposite, or southern, side of the Colorado River. The region south of Austin is a landscape of rolling, wooded juniper-oak savanna, through which winds Onion Creek with long, quiet pools lined with bald cypress, occasional rapids, and two beautiful waterfalls pouring over limestone ledges. Raising livestock was the primary occupation at the McKinney ranch.[17]

At the age of twenty-two, Kentucky-born Thomas Freeman McKinney came to Texas in 1823 as a trader, entering into a brief partnership with cotton planter Jared E. Groce Jr. of Hempstead and then with Samuel May Williams. Relocating to Galveston Island, McKinney developed an interest in horse racing, acquiring several good horses that he ran at Velasco and Galveston. He continued his passion for racing and breeding horses at his ranch on Onion Creek, where McKinney purchased nine leagues (forty thousand acres) of land south of the Colorado River in 1839 for 11 cents per acre, or a total of $4,400. Although most of his horses were Quarter Horses and Saddlebreds, McKinney devoted considerable attention to breeding and training Thoroughbred Running Horses. These valuable equines were sheltered in a large two-story horse barn located about 250 feet west of the residence and grazed in pastures separate from the other horses. John Van Hagen lived on the property and trained horses for McKinney from about 1852 to 1873. Near Van Hagen's home were stone-walled corrals, and on the opposite side of Onion Creek, in a level stretch of bottom land between Onion and Williamson Creek, was McKinney's private training track, which hosted occasional racing events as late as the Civil War period.[18]

Thomas F. McKinney, who owned a large ranch near Austin, Texas, and provided refuge for many of Keene Richards's most valuable horses during the Civil War. Daguerreotype. Image no. 1946/001-67, courtesy of the Texas State Library and Archives Commission.

When the marauding Yankees of Banks's expedition threatened Alexandria and nearby plantations, it was only natural that Thomas Jefferson Wells would instinctively think to send the valuable horses at Dentley to McKinney's distant ranch for safekeeping. In autumn 1831, when McKinney and Jared Groce Jr. were partners in shipping cotton, Jared's older brother Leonard Waller Groce married fifteen-year-old Courtney Ann Fulton, first cousin to T. J. Wells. The Groce household near Hempstead, known as Bernando, developed a reputation for hospitality, and no doubt McKinney was a frequent visitor. In 1853 the Groces built an elegant mansion, Liendo, six miles northeast from Bernando on land Leonard purchased from McKinney in 1841. The community of Hempstead would be laid out nearby soon afterward. The last days of T. J. Wells were spent at Liendo. The aging turfman, fifty-seven years old, fell ill in July 1863, not long after arriving in Texas, and died on the fifteenth of the month. McKinney made frequent business trips to New Orleans, and almost certainly he would have attended the Metairie races and there become acquainted with Wells, one of the region's foremost turfmen. He was also a close friend of George A. Feris, who had long been a staunch supporter of Keene Richards.[19]

When Texas seceded from the Union on February 1, 1861, McKinney, a unionist by sentiment, chose loyalty to his state, although that loyalty would lead to financial ruin by the end of the war. He was more than willing to provide a haven for the prized Thoroughbred Running Horse stock of his friend. On February 22, 1865, McKinney's trainer, John Van Hagan, placed an advertisement in the *Texas State Gazette* of Austin for the stud services of "Gen. M. Wells colt" (War Dance): "Will stand the ensuing season, Gen. M. Wells colt, five years old, by Lexington out of Reel, at the stable of Thomas F. McKinney, on Onion creek, and will serve mares at $100 each, which may be discharged with a good $100 mule." This is the only advertisement for War Dance in Texas that could be located, although there may have been others. The colt's aristocratic bloodline would have been irresistible to any serious breeder, yet only one foal is known to have been sired by War Dance in Texas, a filly known as Lizzy G. That foal, doubly inbred to Reel, would have a significant impact on American Thoroughbred bloodstock in the decades after the war. Among her illustrious descendants was one of the century's stellar horses, Domino, foaled in 1891. Domino, a terrific sprinter, won nineteen of twenty-five races. His earnings totaled $193,650, a record that stood until broken by Man o' War in 1920.[20]

Of the other horses taken to Texas, there are no records of any progeny produced while in McKinney's care. The Knight of St. George sired three fillies while in Louisiana: Dixie, foaled in 1863, and Night Rose and Mary C, both foaled in 1864. No other offspring are reported for this stallion until 1867, by which time the Knight was back in service at Blue Grass Park. Thomas J. Wells's mare Fanny Wells, foaled in 1858, produced no progeny until 1868. As for Keene Richards's prized Arabian stallion Fysaul, a careful search of available records indicates that the horse did not sire any foals for more than a decade after 1862, the first of which was delivered at Georgetown in 1873.[21] Keene Richards's valuable stock, Thoroughbred, part-Thoroughbred, and Arabian, would remain safely at McKinney's ranch for the duration of the war and shortly thereafter, until he returned from overseas to reclaim them.

As his horses were being hastily escorted into Texas, in May 1863 Keene Richards and his cousin Morris Keene arrived in England by steamer from the port of Havana, Cuba, likely debarking at Liverpool before traveling on to London. His ostensible rationale for traveling to England was the purchase of artillery for Breckinridge's command. Arms purchases were not strictly legal, but Confederate agents were adept at exploiting loopholes in British law, British manufacturers were eager to sell ordnance to either side of the American conflict, and the government generally was willing to overlook arms deals while not actually endorsing such transactions. Richards was doubtless certain that the contacts and goodwill he had garnered on his several prewar visits would facilitate the necessary arrangements. As a prominent American breeder and turfman, he had been readily accepted into the social circles of the horse-minded British gentry, which included not only the aristocracy but also high-ranking military officials and members of Parliament. Upon his arrival, he thus became part of a little community of London Confederates having similar intentions.[22]

Before the commencement of hostilities, the Confederate government recognized that the success of the rebellion depended largely on securing support from the two most powerful nations in the world, Britain and France. Lacking the industrial capability of the northern states, the South hoped to secure arms and munitions from Britain. Equally important, southern leaders also sought diplomatic recognition, which would provide the Confederacy status as a nation rather than as an internal rebellion, and thus enable it to sign economic and military treaties with foreign governments. Southern cotton, they believed, would provide the necessary leverage to accomplish these very important goals, and could prompt direct European intervention on behalf of the South. The prevailing sentiment expressed by the politicians, planters, merchants, newspapermen, and the general population of the Confederacy was that "King Cotton" alone could overcome all obstacles to southern independence. Although never an official policy of the Confederate government, southern planters and state and local officials supported and established a widely popular embargo of cotton shipments to Europe to carry out economic coercion by means of a cotton famine.[23]

Southern cotton supplied the busy textile mills of Britain and was critical to the economy of the island nation. Cotton fabric was Britain's largest export. Nearly 4 million persons out of the total British population of 21 million depended on this single industry for their livelihood, and more than three-quarters of the cotton used in manufacturing came from the American South. The perceived power of King Cotton to influence British foreign policy would prove to be an illusion. At the start of the war, British textile mills had enough cotton on hand to support production for at least a year. The Confederacy soon realized that it had made a significant error by withholding cotton exports, which created tension between Britain and the South. As the only medium of exchange acceptable in Europe, cotton would have provided revenue to purchase arms and supplies early in the war. The embargo was gradually relaxed until, after 1863, the idea of King Cotton as a tool of diplomatic coercion had all but disappeared.[24]

British merchants were free to carry on a brisk business selling arms to both sides in the American war under the provisions of Britain's declaration of neutrality issued the previous spring. There were some limitations, although these primarily concerned outfitting vessels of war. There was, however, no specific ban against selling weapons to belligerents, whether for naval service or for armies on land. Although the British government could not sell arms, there was no restriction on private contractors.[25]

Both agents of the Confederate government and representatives of southern state governments purchased cannon, small arms and ammunition, and military supplies, as did private individuals seeking to equip specific units. Keene Richards was among the latter category. In his October 30, 1862, letter to John C. Breckinridge, he proposed "getting up a Light Battery" of artillery for the general's command, capable of being moved with the army in the field. British guns were the most modern artillery pieces in the world, and three manufacturing firms, Armstrong, Blakely, and Whitworth, supplied these weapons to the Confederacy. Smoothbore, muzzle-loading guns were the dominant type used in the war, but rifled pieces, with far greater accuracy, were highly regarded. Confederate artillerymen considered the Whitworth rifled artillery to be the best available, and so at the top of Richards's shopping list might have been the Whitworth twelve-pounder breech-loading field piece, a rifled gun capable of a range and accuracy that would not be exceeded until World War I. Blakely guns were also very popular. Light in weight and firing ten-pound projectiles, they were eminently practical weapons.[26]

Whether or not Keene Richards carried out his plan to purchase artillery for General Breckinridge can only be a matter for speculation. He did state, in his petition for amnesty after the war, that "[I] never at any time sent any thing from England or elsewhere to the so called Confederate States of America," though he might not have been willing to admit, on the record, if he had. Records of purchases and shipments of weapons and military supplies from Britain to the Confederacy are incomplete, and even less information is available regarding purchases made by private individuals. He probably retained most of the funds he had set out with from Kentucky in September 1861, in the form of letters of credit that would be honored by British banks. This would cover his living expenses while abroad and still leave more than enough to purchase a battery of artillery.[27]

We may not know if Richards purchased weapons for Breckinridge, but he certainly had an interest in the design of field artillery. On June 30, 1863, he applied to the British Patent Office for a patent on innovations in "Ordnance and Fire-Arms, and Projectiles to be Used Therewith." The document was accompanied by a series of meticulous engineering drawings. Since he had just arrived in England a few weeks before submitting them to the Patent Office, he must have been working on refining his ideas for some time, perhaps while in the field with the Confederate army, or during his stay at Dentley Plantation in Louisiana, perhaps at Galveston while awaiting transport on a blockade runner, or even while at sea en route to Liverpool or Southampton from Havana. In his patent application, Richards described a method for construction of cannon and mortars that he claimed would allow them to be taken apart and reassembled in a matter of minutes, but to be as strong as weapons built by conventional means. At my request, Lawrence E. Babits, an Army veteran, military historian, and editor of *Artilleryman Magazine,* carefully examined the patent sketches and concluded that Richards's design concept was fundamentally flawed because the barrel would likely burst when fired. The only one ever built was a prototype, for which he borrowed heavily from a London bank.[28]

Richards also designed an "Improvement in Traction Engines," although this was not submitted to the Patent Office until July 11, 1865, by which time he had returned to America. The patent was, instead, granted to Morris Keene, still in the country, as "a communication from abroad by Alexander Keene Richards, residing in Kentucky, United States of America." In agriculture, steam engines used to power farm equipment were drawn by teams of horses until, in 1858, British inventor Thomas Aveling attached a chain drive to an engine so that it could move itself. Traction engines were generally too heavy to work in soft ground and often bogged down, a problem compounded by having smooth-surfaced iron wheels that provided no grip. Richards attempted to solve this problem with spring-loaded blades along the perimeter of the wheel. This approach was unnecessarily complicated and was never adopted; instead, a simple solution was later devised in the form of angled cleats on the wheels.[29]

Richards's 1863 patent application indicated that he was living at Berners Street and Oxford in London's West End. He probably stayed at the Berners Hotel, 10 Berners Street, a large structure with a row of columns across the front converted from a bank to a hotel in 1826 after it failed notoriously when one of the partners, Henry Fauntleroy, was hanged for forgery in 1824. A postwar London guidebook noted that visitors "from America and the Colonies, and in fact from all quarters of the globe, are very fond of 'putting up' at the Berners Hotel, and fully appreciate its homely comforts and general air of quiet refinement." Here was one of the busiest streets in the West End, and from the hotel Richards could observe the "mighty tide of life that rolls along Oxford Street [and] unceasingly passes but a few yards from its doors." Regent's Park, with its botanical and zoological gardens, was but a few blocks to the north of the hotel, and, given his interest in antiquities, Richards certainly must have spent many hours viewing exhibits at the British Museum, a short stroll to the east. Travel was facilitated by easy access to railway stations, and the numerous horse-drawn cabs would carry a fare for sixpence per mile. London at the time was the largest city in the world, having a population of nearly 3 million persons, of whom some two thousand of the forty thousand foreign residents were American or Confederate. It was a dirty, congested, noisy, exuberant city, disrupted by construction of the main drainage system and the new underground railway, and subject to dense "pea soup" fogs rendered noisome by the stench of millions of coal fires.[30]

His traveling companion, Morris Keene, perhaps stayed with Richards initially. Apparently having little taste for London life, he eventually struck out on his own and relocated to the city of Croydon in the northeastern part of the county of Surrey, about nine miles south of London Bridge. Proximity to the capital stimulated development of Croydon as an agricultural and industrial center early in the nineteenth century, and construction of a railroad link to London in 1839 promoted rapid population growth. By the time Keene became a resident, the city had a population of over thirty thousand inhabitants and was known for extensive iron works. Keene took employment with the Victoria Iron Works, which manufactured "highway locomotive engines." These were used in agriculture and to pull wagons on public roads, but his workplace suggests he may have had an important role in Richards's traction engine design. No information is available as to what position he occupied at the works.[31]

Some Confederates residing in London had visited the city before the war, but many had not. Keene Richards was quite familiar with the city, having come to London as a launch point for his Near East expeditions of 1851 and 1854, and for extended stays in 1858 and 1859. As a prominent turfman of substantial means, he had been welcomed into the elite social circles of London, and now, having decided to remain in London for an indefinite period, he would have quickly reestablished contacts among the aristocrats of the turf. Although slavery was regarded by the people of Great Britain with considerable distaste, there was nevertheless widespread sympathy for the Confederacy among the English upper and middle classes. The ruling classes harbored considerable resentment against the democratic system and the growing economic power of the United States, and the southern lifestyle with its planter aristocracy was perceived by British elites to resemble more closely that of the mother country than that of the industrial North. In contrast, the working class of England tended to be more supportive of the Union, seeing the American Civil War as "a struggle between free, egalitarian laborers in the North fighting against a South that sought to preserve a structured society headed by a landed aristocracy." Under the circumstances, Richards had every reason to believe that he would be warmly welcomed by former acquaintances.[32]

His first approach would have been Richard Ten Broeck, a close friend who was still in England and would remain there until 1867. Ten Broeck still carried on an active racing program, and so Richards very likely was his guest at many racing events. Richards's social interactions were not limited to turf circles. The Confederates in the city were a relatively small community, most residing in the West End, and thus there were plenty of opportunities for socializing with compatriots. On one such occasion, a few of the leading London Confederates and, by invitation, Keene Richards gathered at St. James Church in Piccadilly on August 25, 1864, for the wedding of Samuel W. Hardinge (a former ensign in the U.S. Navy) and the notorious Confederate spy Belle Boyd, who began her career in espionage at the tender age of seventeen. Hardinge, serving on the USS *Greyhound,* had been among her captors in May 1864 when Belle attempted to flee the United States on a blockade runner. Smitten by her charms, Hardinge fell deeply in love and proposed marriage. Belle recalled, "I said I would if he would agree to give me his signal book covering every flag of the U.S. Naval code, leave the navy [and] enter the service of the Confederacy." The turncoat officer was arrested by order of the secretary of the Navy on June 8 and dismissed from the service early in July. Recently released from Federal prison in Boston, Belle came to England by way of Bermuda, arriving during the early summer.[33]

Belle was staying at the Brunswick Hotel at 52 Jermyn Street, Piccadilly, and it was here that she was finally reunited with her lover. They quickly made wedding plans, and on August 25 the *Morning Post* announced that the nuptials for "Miss Belle Boyd, the Southern heroine," would take place that very morning. The British press had followed the exploits of Boyd since the summer of 1862, and her courage and audacity had captured the public imagination. The wedding took place at St. James Church, within sight of the Brunswick Hotel. While not a large ceremony, it was attended by some of the more prominent Confederate officials in London, along with sympathizers, both British and American. Among the London Confederates present were Caleb Huse, Henry Hotze, James Williams, and John Louis O'Sullivan. Caleb Huse, appointed by Jefferson Davis as the Confederacy's principal arms procurement agent in Europe, was responsible for obtaining most of the weapons imported by the South from Britain and other foreign powers during the war. Hotze had

Belle Boyd, Confederate spy. As an expatriate in London, England, in August 1864, Keene Richards attended her wedding in company with prominent Confederate officials then abroad. Library of Congress, Brady-Handy photograph collection.

been sent by the Confederate government with instructions to carry out a vigorous propaganda campaign in Britain to sway public opinion and the government in support of the Confederacy. Williams, a former U.S. ambassador to the Ottoman empire, was an experienced journalist who aided Hotze in his efforts, as did O'Sullivan, who originated the concept of "manifest destiny" in an 1845 magazine article arguing that the United States had a divine right to expand throughout North America. Keene Richards's invitation to the wedding was a measure of the esteem in which he was held by his countrymen in Britain.[34]

On April 23, 1865, the British mail steamer *Asia* from Boston arrived at London with news of Lee's surrender of the Army of Northern Virginia two weeks earlier. Taking advice from the American foreign minister, Keene Richards departed Liverpool, England, on June 16, aboard the Cunard steamer *Cuba.* Arriving in New York on June 28, he came back to Kentucky, where he reported himself "ready to abide by the laws of the United States of America and the Military laws of Kentucky." His petition was supported by several outstanding Kentuckians, including former governor James F. Robinson (1862–1863), who asserted that "He is a man of honor and integrity and we believe he will scrupulously comply with any promise which he may make." This was endorsed by current governor Thomas E. Bramlette, who noted that, although he did not know Richards personally, the recommendations made by "men of responsibility and high social position" were ample authority for him. Richards signed the oath of allegiance to the Union at Lexington on July 11 and submitted his application for clemency to President Andrew Johnson. On September 8, 1865, Richards was pardoned for his actions during the war. His cousin Morris Keene lingered a bit longer in England, but finally arrived at New York on October 2, 1865, aboard the *City of Cork.*[35]

16

STUNNED BY MISFORTUNE

Now that he was back in Kentucky and once again a citizen of the United States in good standing, Keene Richards immediately set about rebuilding his equine enterprise. More than anything, he wished to resume the lifestyle he had known before the war. This would require an infusion of cash, and for this he called upon his old friend Edward Troye, to whom he had signed over the Blue Grass Park property in 1861 before departing to serve with John C. Breckinridge and the Confederacy. With Troye and his wife, Cornelia, as cosigners, in October 1865 Richards took out a mortgage on the home place for $4,400 with the Lexington banking firm of Grinstead and Bradley. (Grinstead was an old family friend and well-known horse breeder.) The first and most important step was to retrieve the valuable bloodstock, Running Horse, Thoroughbred, and Arabian, that he had sent west for safety four years earlier.[1]

On November 3, 1865, a newspaper report from New Albany, Indiana, informed readers that the *Rebecca,* a sidewheel riverboat, "came in from below yesterday, having on board a lot of fine blooded horses belonging to Mr. Keene Richards, of Kentucky. The stock has been in Texas for a long season." These included his prize stallion, the Knight of St. George, as well as his last remaining Arabian stallion, Fysaul. The retrieval was probably accomplished by a telegram to a trusted friend in the South. By January 1866, the sportsman's magazine *Turf, Field and Farm* was able to write that Richards "again has collected at his beautiful home, at Georgetown, Ky., a magnificent stable of racing stock. He will reappear upon the turf in the spring with some of the finest colts that ever strided around a race course." There was a significant omission in the stock that came back to Kentucky in the autumn of 1865: War Dance, the spirited colt he purchased from Thomas J. Wells in February 1863. War Dance would not return to Kentucky until spring of the following year, because Madison Wells, brother to the late General Wells, had begun training and racing this horse on his own initiative.[2]

Madison Wells, acting governor of Louisiana since March 1865, sent to Texas for War Dance after the war ended and brought him to New Orleans. He wrote to Richards to inform him of this and suggested that he come to the city or send for the horse. The governor then turned War Dance over to Samuel M. Westmore, for whom the five-year-old colt had originally been named, for training. Despite his reputation as a knowledgeable horseman, Westmore made "but a hasty effort" to train War Dance before entering him into competition, a three-mile dash race at the New Orleans Crescent track on April 17, 1866. Wells's decision to race War Dance was ill-considered. The horse had been favoring a leg in the days just prior to the race, and he broke down before the half-way point. Richards arrived in New Orleans on the day of the race to discover the unauthorized entry of his prized horse and was unable, or unwilling, given the esteem in which he had held the governor's late brother, to withdraw his horse. This was the first and only race of War Dance's career. Immediately afterward, Richards shipped his lamed horse up the Mississippi to Louisville and home.[3]

On arrival at Georgetown, War Dance would be in good hands. Steadfast Frank Sherritt, who had scrupulously managed Blue Grass Park during the years of Richards's absence, was still in charge, and two other valued members of his prewar staff were now again in residence, the master trainer Ansel and the jockey John. Both men, enslaved persons before the war and now free men working as paid employees, spent the war years in Woodford County at Robert A. Alexander's Woodburn Farm, an arrangement made between Alexander and Richards before the latter's departure from Kentucky in the autumn of 1862. While at Woodburn, Ansel was in charge of the racing stable and had trained Asteroid, sired by Lexington out of a Glencoe mare. Asteroid was one of the century's greatest running horses, undefeated in twelve races during 1864–1865. On February 2, 1865, at considerable risk to himself, quick-thinking Ansel saved this valuable horse from Confederate guerrilla raiders who asked for Asteroid by name, by substituting another horse in the darkened stable.[4]

Before leaving Georgetown for the south, Richards arranged for $5,500 in additional capital by mortgaging his best horses to Grinstead and Bradley on March 28, 1866. These included those currently at Blue Grass Park, notably the Knight of St. George, Blonde, Sister to Pryor #1, Transylvania, Fysaul, several brood mares, and War Dance, which he noted was presently at New Orleans. This money was essential if he was going to be able to return Transylvania Plantation, the source of his prewar wealth, to productivity. On July 21, a correspondent for the *Vicksburg Times* reported having the pleasure of meeting Richards, who "is now at work cultivating the famous Transylvania Plantation in Carroll Parish, Louisiana, having 'turned the sword into a pruning hook.' We wish the gallant major the highest success, both as a planter and breeder of noble equine stock." Success as a planter in the Reconstruction South was a daunting task, for no longer did Richards have the benefit of enslaved labor. He would be required to pay wages.[5]

He had been prudent to send his valuable bloodstock to General Wells in Rapides Parish in early June 1862. Only days later, the war came to northeast Louisiana as Union forces attempted to capture or bypass the fortress city of Vicksburg, Mississippi, one of the last Confederate strongholds blocking Federal control of the Mississippi River. As Admiral David Farragut began bombarding Vicksburg on June 26 with his fleet of ironclads, General Thomas Williams, waiting for his turn in a land assault, began to excavate a canal across the narrow spit of land, DeSoto Point, formed by a hairpin curve of the Mississippi River as it swept past Vicksburg, perched high on the bluffs overlooking the water. If the Mississippi could be diverted through a canal dug across the neck of the curve, Vicksburg would become irrelevant and the river opened to Union navigation. To aid in this effort, Federal raiding parties scoured the riverfront for enslaved workers from Lake Providence to Pecan Grove; Transylvania was squarely in the middle of this zone and would have been a prime target. "The Negroes are eager to go, leaving wife and children and all for freedom promised them," Kate Stone recorded, "but we hear they are being worked to death on the canal with no shelter at night and not much to eat." It quickly became apparent that Vicksburg, undamaged by the bombardment, could not be taken by a naval assault. As to the canal, the work proved much more difficult than had been expected in the tropical heat and malarial swamps. In late July, Williams gave up on the project and returned to Baton Rouge with nearly two-thirds of his command sick and unfit for duty. Soon afterward, a party of Confederates rowed across to river to inspect the abandoned works and found more than five hundred fresh graves and about six hundred slaves that had been abandoned there, ill and malnourished.[6]

Vicksburg remained key to control of the river, and so in January 1863 the Federals returned in far greater numbers with Major General Ulysses S. Grant in overall command. The capture of Vicksburg was one way to achieve the objective, but there were alternatives. The bayou country of the Mississippi floodplain was a vast network of interconnecting waterways, and if a route could be found that would bypass the Confederate stronghold, Vicksburg could be left to wither on the vine, a prize to be plucked when convenient to do so. Grant therefore set in motion his "bayou operations," sending out work brigades to develop bypass routes in several different locations and reactivating the old canal project across DeSoto Point. With a massive Union presence in northeast Louisiana, thousands of enslaved people fled the nearby plantations and sought refuge with the soldiers working at Lake Providence. On March 3, Kate Stone recorded that "A great many Negroes have gone to the Yankees from this section. Keene Richards has lost 160 from Transylvania and fifty of them are reported dead. The Negroes at work on the canal have what they call black measles, and it is very fatal to them." A few days later, she estimated that there were five thousand former enslaved persons camped at Lake Providence, "taken from places up the river." None of these efforts to create a bypass were successful. In April, U.S. Adjutant General Lorenzo Thomas came to Lake Providence and began organizing volunteers from among the former enslaved persons into soldiers of the newly formed African Brigade, who would begin their training and occupy the region when Grant's troops crossed the Mississippi on April 30 to assault Vicksburg from the rear.[7]

Hordes of northern speculators descended on the appropriated Louisiana cotton lands. While at Lake Providence, Lorenzo Thomas appointed a three-man commission to oversee leasing of plantations "to persons of proper character and qualifications." One of the commissioners, George B. Field, a New York attorney who toured the lower Mississippi valley on behalf of Edwin M. Stanton, informed the secretary of war in March 1863 that there were no less than 150 plantations on the west bank of the Mississippi River between Vicksburg and the mouth of the Arkansas River, most of which were abandoned. If these were rented out to persons who agreed only to use black workers, nothing could better demonstrate that "free negro labor under good management can be made a *source of profit* to the *employer*." A plantation bureau for Louisiana was created at New Orleans, and Samuel W. Cozzens was detailed from the quartermaster corps to take charge of the agency as superintendent of plantations, directing a team of agents and inspectors to oversee the lessees and collect the rents. By mid-May 1863, Cozzens had responsibility for fifty-seven abandoned plantations, including a number in Carroll Parish. The army furnished black laborers to pick the cotton, and the lessees agreed to feed and clothe the workers, pay them a wage, and "treat [them] humanely"; it was made clear that slavery was not to be reinstated. The speculators who leased the plantations were only interested in harvesting the immediate crop, with little interest in the upkeep of the property. Neglect of improvements, dilapidation of buildings, and deterioration of the land resulting from inexperience in farming were widespread.[8]

On October 10, 1863, one of Cozzens's agents, Julian E. Bryant, reported to his district headquarters on the condition of leased plantations in Carroll Parish. While a few of the properties were in good condition, many had been quite neglected, especially after a Confederate raid on June 29 during which workers' quarters and cotton gins had been burned and the workers captured or driven from the premises. Exceptions were the Mounds Plantation and Transylvania Plantation, leased by the partnership of Montague & Clary, and subleased by a "Mr. Campbell." Bryant reported that "The contrabands on these places seem much better cared for than on the others, are all at work and quite well supplied with rations." The inspector noted that there were 117 contrabands at these two plantations, of which ninety-seven were field hands. He continued in his appraisal, noting that "About three hundred and fifty acres of cotton are being gathered."[9]

The Mounds Plantation was bequeathed in 1857 by the will of William B. Keene to the five minor children of his deceased son, John Wallis Keene, to be administered by one of his executors, Horace B. Tebbetts, until the eldest, Wallis Bodien Keene, reached the age of twenty-one. Wallis reached the age of majority in March 1862 but was now absent from Carroll Parish, having enlisted with his younger brother Benjamin in the Confederate army in 1861, the two serving together in the same units. Tebbetts, a former New Englander who came south before the war, married the widow of John Wallis Keene in December 1858. In April 1863, he leased two of his plantations to Judge Lewis Dent, and he asked the Lake Providence commissioners recently appointed by Lorenzo Thomas to appoint agents to manage four others. Tebbetts departed Carroll Parish on April 15 and took his family and the minor heirs of Alexander Keene, for whose estates he was responsible, north for safety. Alexander Keene had died in 1855, and his widow, Julia Morgan, subsequently remarried to a cousin, Oliver T. Morgan. Presumably, Oliver was not present in Carroll at the time. Tebbetts wrote to Abraham Lincoln from New York in September 1863, asking to regain possession of his plantations from the government lessees on his planned return to Carroll Parish in February 1864.[10]

After Grant and the bulk of his troops departed northeast Louisiana for the assault on Vicksburg, the mettle of the occupying forces left behind, including the half-trained African Brigade, would be tested by Confederate raiders sent by Edmund Kirby Smith, recently transferred to command the Trans-Mississippi Department. These raids, under the command of Major Generals Richard S. Taylor and John G. Walker, were intended to capture Federal outposts, cut the Union supply line across the river, and at the very least break up some of the Union-occupied plantations growing cotton to finance the northern war effort and capture many of the former enslaved persons now working on the leased properties. These incursions were largely unsuccessful, but on June 29 the 12th and 19th Texas Cavalry, a brigade of seasoned veterans commanded by Colonel William H. Parsons, went on a rampage of destruction through Carroll Parish. The Texas cavalry burned nearly every structure they came across for ten miles along the Tensas River, from the DeSoto mound to Lake Providence. They burned slave cabins, cotton gin buildings, outbuildings of all kinds, and even the elegant plantation houses, and captured hundreds of Black field hands. Taking pleasure in destroying the property of alleged Union sympathizers, plantations leased to the Federals, the raiders spared only two of the mansions in their path, which "sheltered ladies who had not left their homes." Even on these properties, however, all other buildings were set afire. Returning to their camp, the Texans passed through what one participant said "was once the garden spot of the great Mississippi valley, now reduced almost to a wilderness." The house at Transylvania Plantation survived the ire of the raiders; even though it was then a Federal leased property, Richards was a well-known Confederate sympathizer. Minor partisan raids and skirmishes continued during the remainder of 1863 and into the summer of 1864.[11]

The world of Thoroughbred racing had changed dramatically during Richards's absence, and for the remainder of his life it would continue to rapidly evolve as control of the American turf and the shaping of its future passed from the South to the North. On the eve of the Civil War, racing and breeding of running horses was concentrated in the southern states, with only a scattering of tracks in the North. In the great internecine conflict that followed, racing was suspended nearly everywhere in the nation. Kentucky was the only state on either side of the conflict that continued to host racing meetings every year for the duration of the war. Racing was slow to revive in the southern states after the war. The southland was the primary theater of the war, and the equine establishments of the region were utterly devastated. Much of the finest bloodstock in the nation trotted off to war under Confederate banners and was subsequently killed or captured, and both armies confiscated horses from stud farms for remounts. The southern economy was in ruins, its infrastructure destroyed, and the planter class that had supported the racing establishment was impoverished. It would be more than a decade before racing resumed in the South with even a shadow of its former vigor. The famous Metairie track of New Orleans, which dominated American racing prior to the war, reopened in autumn 1865 but struggled financially until it permanently closed in 1872, its fate sealed by a schism in the membership and competition from the recently established rival Louisiana Jockey Club.[12]

At the commencement of the war, Kentucky's economy was primarily agricultural, producing livestock, wheat, corn, tobacco, and hemp. Most of the farms in the state were of relatively small size compared to the large slavery-based cotton, rice, and sugar plantations of the South, and the average Kentucky slaveholder possessed five or fewer slaves. The greater diversity of the Kentucky agricultural economy, with less reliance on slave labor, left landowners in the state in better postwar condition than southern planters, who not only experienced destruction of property but lost considerable capital invested in slaves. Equine breeding operations in the state, however, were severely damaged by the war. In consequence, the Bluegrass state slipped from prominence, becoming something of a backwater in the breeding industry as primacy transferred to New York. Historian Maryjean Wall attributed the postwar decline to three developments: depletion of the breeding stock, depletion of the farm labor pool, and the great disparity between the agricultural wealth of Kentucky and the Wall Street and industrial wealth of New York.[13]

As a border state, Kentucky was the scene of persistent and violent guerrilla warfare. Frequent raids upon Bluegrass breeding farms by Confederate partisans and by cavalry commanders such as John Hunt Morgan resulted in the loss of much of the region's prime breeding stock. After the war, with so many southern courses no longer operating, the regional market for Thoroughbred bloodstock was depressed and many Kentucky breeders shipped their best horses north to find buyers at higher prices. In Kentucky and the southern states, thorough-bred breeding and racing had been wholly dependent on Black labor ever since the colonial period. The enslaved were customarily occupied in caring for their enslaver's bloodstock, and as jockeys and trainers. The most talented were viewed as valuable assets and often granted extraordinary privileges and authority not allowed to other slaves. During the war, many Kentucky slaves fled the farms to enlist in the Union army and to seek refuge in the army camps. Afterward, many migrated in large numbers to Lexington and Louisville, hoping to find employment and safety from the widespread racial violence that marked the postwar rural areas. In Kentucky, the abundant antebellum labor pool of enslaved Blacks evaporated.[14]

Following the war, when New York capitalists set about to restore racing in the North, Kentucky horsemen were at a significant disadvantage because the wealth generated by agriculture in the Bluegrass could not compete with the far greater wealth derived from northern finance and industry. The new titans of the turf used their vast wealth to build on a grand scale, setting up lavish racing stables and breeding farms in the northeast on a scale that could not be equaled by Kentucky gentry. As Wall observed, "verdant, woodland pastures were the hallmark of Kentucky farms, material excess characterized the new farms in the northeast." These modern horse estates were built to evoke a nostalgic rural charm and not only provided their owners with refuges from the noise and pollution of city life but enhanced and certified their elite status.[15]

The resurrection of northern racing began amid the turbulence of the early years of the war. Racing entrepreneur John L. Cassady traveled from Cincinnati to the northeast in the summer of 1862 and ignited a revival of racing running horses in that region. Cassady met with leading citizens in Philadelphia, Boston, and New York, who agreed to put up prize money for racing events in each city in exchange for a share of the proceeds. In New Jersey, a group of wealthy capitalists established the Riverside track on the Passaic River in May 1863. Its success prompted the building of a luxurious new track at Saratoga Springs, north of Albany in New York. These venues proving popular and profitable, a group of wealthy New Yorkers, led by Wall Street speculator Leonard P. Jerome, founded the first American Jockey Club during the spring of 1866 (the modern Jockey Club was established in 1894), and in the city's suburbs they built Jerome Park, the most modern and lavish racing establishment in the nation. As northeastern capitalists began to lay out grandiose breeding farms and racing stables, New York and the northeast became the new focus of breeding and racing American Thoroughbreds.[16]

The nature of Thoroughbred racing also evolved during the postwar era. The new magnates of the northern turf, rather than adopting traditional southern customs, looked across the Atlantic to Britain for their model. Among the most conspicuous of the changes established in the North was the style of racing. Heat racing was the most common type of competition at American tracks prior to the Civil War, grueling long-distance events that tested a horse's stamina more than its speed. Heat racing in America began to decline in favor of dash races shortly before the war, and as shorter races became the preferred mode in the North, it spread from there to the rest of the country. As endurance was gradually eliminated as a prime consideration in the success of racehorses, the underlying rationale for Keene Richards's prewar breeding program became no longer relevant.[17]

During the remainder of the nineteenth century, racing venues became increasingly dependent upon public patronage for their financial well-being. Jockey clubs traditionally covered the expenses of conducting race meetings through member subscriptions and entry fees. Since most clubs had relatively few members, revenues were usually barely sufficient to break even, even with gate receipts added. The small scale of racing programs posed another financial difficulty, since race meetings were generally held for a single week in the spring and fall and tracks generated little income during the remainder of the year. Economic necessity required track operators to develop new sources of revenue to support their programs. One way to do this was to attract a greater public patronage, with a more diverse class attendance, and this was in large part accomplished by moving wagering on races from the private realm to the public, from wagers made between individuals to trackside betting. In this way, tracks could attract the masses, who could only afford to place small bets and were thus unable to participate in the usual forms of wagering. Jockey clubs traditionally barred public gambling from the tracks, but now began to embrace it wholeheartedly, the fees collected from pool-sellers and bookies becoming a substantial revenue stream. The new dash system of racing was facilitated by overt gambling, since shorter races allowed more events per day and increased the opportunities for wagering. The ability to offer the largest purses in the nation was among the factors that led to the dominance of New York racing in the period after the Civil War.[18]

Keene Richards returned to the turf with vigor in May of 1866, entering young horses from his stable that had been foaled while he was abroad. His silver gray and white racing colors appeared at Louisville's Woodlawn track on May 7 and 8, at the Association track in Lexington in midmonth, and at the Buckeye track in Cincinnati at the end of the month. Richards's reappearance was welcomed by his peers, as neither his support for the rebellious Confederacy nor his prolonged absence from the country had in any way diminished his reputation as a prominent American turfman. Such was his prestige that Richards, along with his close friend Robert A. Alexander, were invited to become founding members of the American Jockey Club in New York, both honored with the distinction as one of the fifty Life Members out of a total membership of more than a thousand. Appointed as race steward for the grand opening meeting at Jerome Park in early October, Richards entered War Dance, listed simply as "ch. h. by Lexington, out of Reel, 6 years," for the Inauguration Race, but withdrew when he learned that Kentucky, the famed horse belonging to William R. Travers and George Ormsby, was also an entry. Kentucky had such a formidable reputation that, of twenty-nine horses entered for this race, all but two were withdrawn by their owners. Kentucky, who had lost only one race, in 1864, and thereafter racked up a string of nineteen wins in a row before coming to Jerome Park, won the race handily, and was afterward purchased by Leonard Jerome for the unprecedented sum of $40,000.[19]

After the New York races, Richards came back to Kentucky. On October 3 of that year, Richards exhibited the Knight of St. George at the St. Louis agricultural fair, for which he received a $700 premium. At the October races at Louisville and Cincinnati, he again entered horses from his Georgetown stable. His experience earlier in the year attempting to put his Louisiana plantation in order for cotton production made it clear that a great deal of capital would be required. On October 13, 1866, Richards took the desperate step of mortgaging virtually all the property he owned, including his home estate of Blue Grass Park, all his land in Louisiana, including Transylvania Plantation, and the tract of 1,780 acres in Phillips County, Arkansas, owned jointly with Morris Keene, for a loan of $44,000 from the estate of his deceased grandfather, William B. Keene. Some of this money may have been used for resuming breeding operations at Georgetown, but most probably went to propping up his efforts to bring Transylvania back into profitability. Trying to make Transylvania productive again with paid labor proved to be a money pit into which Keene Richards would keep pouring an ever-increasing amount of borrowed capital. This would soon lead to financial disaster.[20]

He did not tarry long in Kentucky, for he had urgent personal business in the southland. Accompanied by Morris Keene, Richards arrived at the St. Charles Hotel in New Orleans on November 13. From here, it appears, he traveled to Rapides Parish and proposed to the attractive southern belle who had caught his eye in December 1862 while he lingered at Dentley Plantation before resuming his journey to Mexico and ultimately to England. Mary Editha Winn spent the latter part of the war in Texas, probably traveling there with General Thomas J. Wells when he fled the approaching Yankees in the late spring of 1863, and likely resided with him at Liendo, the estate of Leonard and Courtney Ann Groces in present-day

Waller County. She returned to Rapides Parish in December 1865. On Saturday, December 22, Keene Richards was united with Mary Winn in a wedding held at Winn Forest Plantation, the estate she had inherited from her late husband, Walter O. Winn. Winn Forest was located on the Mississippi floodplain in Madison Parish near Transylvania and Brokenburn plantations.[21]

Mary Richards initially took up residence at Transylvania Plantation. Although her new husband was busy getting the plantation ready for cotton planting, which in the region typically began in March, he was also traveling much of the time. Seed and other agricultural supplies had to obtained from New Orleans, and he greatly increased his indebtedness in 1867 by signing more than $50,000 in notes for them. He also went to Louisville to purchase saddles and an expensive piece of jewelry for

Mary Winn Richards, second wife of Alexander Keene Richards.
Private collection.

Mary—likely his wedding gift to her—and to Lexington and Cincinnati, where he entered horses in the May races at each track. The plantation occupied most of his attention, however, so that he did not have time to participate in racing elsewhere during the year. Mary befriended Kate Stone, of nearby Brokenburn plantation, who noted in her journal that "We had many visitors: the Bynums, now living at Transylvania with Mrs. Richards, the Keenes, Mary Keene such a nice girl and to think she married a Yankee." The Bynums were, of course, Mary Richards's family, formerly resident in Rapides Parish, and those temporarily living at Transylvania included her parents, Wade H. and Caroline La Mothe Bynum, and two younger sisters, Emily and Caroline. Keene Richards being preoccupied with plantation affairs and often absent, Kate wrote, "[Mary Richards] and I, having no lovers on hand, enjoyed a nice time going around together."[22]

Mary brought her own financial troubles into the marriage. When her former husband, Walter O. Winn, died in Rapides Parish in 1861, Mary became his sole heir and executrix. The estate was a large one, valued at over $500,000, with debts against it amounting to about $120,000. Among these debts were nine promissory notes, executed by Walter in 1860 to the New Orleans firm of Rotchford and Brown, cotton brokers, each for the sum of $5,000 and thus totaling $45,000. Despite the apparent size of the estate, Mary was unable to repay these debts, initially because of the turbulence of the war in Louisiana and her removal to Texas, but later because she had no assets but the land itself. As her attorney, Michael Ryan, testified in the Parish Court at Alexandria, Mary Richards had inherited from her husband "a large succession of lands and slaves and mules. The slaves were set free during the war, the mules perished, the dwelling house was burned by Federal Army in 1864. She was left nothing but tracts of land in Madison & Carroll & Rapides in this state." According to Ryan, cutting of the levees by Federal troops during the war flooded the lands and rendered them worthless.[23]

Keene Richards was heavily indebted, and the only way to extricate himself from his financial predicament would be if bumper crops of cotton could be grown at Transylvania. The price for cotton was high after the war, and most planters, like Richards, were able to borrow enough money to put in their crops and pay the field workers. Instead, many soon found themselves in dire straits, for the years 1866 and 1867 were disastrous for cotton planters along the lower Mississippi. In 1866, a major flood destroyed a great deal of cotton and kept the fields inundated until it was too late to plant a second crop. Those few who were able to put in a second crop could not harvest it because an invasion of armyworms destroyed the plants before they could mature. The following year witnessed an almost identical sequence of events, and many of the planters faced ruin. Kate Stone later recalled the agricultural devastation of 1867, writing, "The cotton planted was very late, and when it was looking as luxuriant and promising as possible and we saw ease of mind before us, the worms came. In a few days the fields were blackened like fire had swept over them. We made about twenty bales and spent $25,000 doing it. All in this section have suffered in the same way, and for awhile they seemed stunned by their misfortunes." With little to show for all his effort and expense, Richards was facing a financial crisis.[24]

Richards brought Mary and her family to his home in Georgetown, and here Mary would remain as a permanent resident, with occasional visits south. Temporary relief from his troubles was provided by wedding ceremonies at Blue Grass Park in September 1867. On the twenty-third day of the month, the Richards and Bynum families were further linked through a double wedding involving Mary's two younger sisters. United in marriage were Richards's twenty-six-year-old first cousin Wallis Bodien Keene and Mary's twenty-five-year-old sister Caroline Atherton Bynum together with Dr. Colin Beverly Buckner, of Vicksburg, who wed Mary's other sister, Emily Elizabeth Bynum, who was twenty-eight. Dr. Buckner, who owned a drugstore in Vicksburg, had served as the captain of Company C in the 28th Mississippi Calvary during the war. Forty-four years old at the time of his nuptials, Buckner had been married before, to Kate Stone's aunt Laura Ragan Buckner, but Laura died at Bladen Springs, Alabama, in February 1865. Dr. Buckner was well known in Carroll Parish, and he appears many times in the pages of Kate's Civil War diary. Keene Richards would soon have reason to be very thankful that Dr. Buckner was his brother-in-law.[25]

As the year 1868 began, Richards was in a desperate situation, having failed to make a cotton crop at Transylvania because of the vicissitudes of nature. Writing to his old friend John C. Breckinridge on July 8 to inform him of his circumstances since they parted in 1862, Richards stated: "I got my property back, and got credit and tried to make cotton without any portions and in two years I lost about $75,000. The consequence of this was the Bank forced me to put in a claim of voluntary Bankruptcy." With great reluctance, on February 25, he filed a bankruptcy petition in the U.S. District Court at Louisville. In his petition, he itemized debts totaling a little more than $200,000, equivalent to more than $4.3 million in 2024. His unsecured debts, promissory notes given for a variety of purchases dating back as far as 1858, amounted to about $84,000, mostly for plantation supplies obtained in 1867. Secured debts, primarily mortgages made on land in Kentucky, Louisiana, and Arkansas to Harvey Graves, came to another $120,000. Hearings on the matter were held at Winchester, Kentucky, and on July 4 Richards received a discharge of his debts from the court.[26]

The personal cost was a heavy one. To pay his indebtedness, the court ordered his Louisiana and Arkansas property to be auctioned off. The sale was held in Lexington "before the courthouse door" on November 9, 1868, at 11:00 a.m., where "the plantation known as Transylvania" and 640 acres of "wild land, known as Section 13" were sold to the highest bidder, along with a one-half interest in 1,780 acres of land "situated on the Oldtown Ridge, near Helena, Phillips County, Arkansas." The Arkansas property had been jointly owned with Morris Keene, but in November 1866 the two cousins had partitioned the land. Since his return to America, Morris had also plunged into a financial abyss, filing for bankruptcy in Arkansas on February 4, 1868, shortly before his cousin Richards.[27]

Transylvania was Keene Richards's second home, and the old plantation was dear to his heart. It was at the plantation in 1868 that Mary Richards presented her husband with Eleonora ("Nora"), the first of their three children. Two more girls were born at Georgetown: Emily ("Emma") in 1869 and Caroline in 1871. At the courthouse auction in Lexington, the purchaser, doubtless by prior arrangement, was none other than his new brother-in-law, Dr. Colin Buckner. The Vicksburg doctor and pharmacist had emerged from the war in good financial condition and had sufficient wealth that he was willing to expend a small fortune, $25,000, to rescue the property of his wife's sister and husband. Buckner held on to Transylvania and the other tract until April 1870, when Richards purchased it back from him for $25,000 in cash. Buckner also bought the Arkansas land, which he sold to Morris Keene in 1869, who was then attempting to regain the lands he lost in consequence of their separate bankruptcies.[28]

Richards would remain in financial distress for the rest of his life. There would be no more trips to foreign lands to import noteworthy Thoroughbreds, or to the East to purchase pureblooded Bedouin Arabians. Such indulgences were now forever beyond his means. His breeding experiment, intended to infuse new Arabian blood into the Thoroughbred Running Horse and thereby improve stamina, was no longer even particularly relevant to the new style of "dash" racing that was becoming dominant, even in Kentucky. As one Memphis commentator observed in 1873:

> In racing, as in everything else, the world moves. It is only a few years since dash races were first introduced into this country. Like every innovation upon established usages, the change met with the bitter opposition of the old fogies. Now dashes are becoming the fashion. Think of the Kentucky Association running a programme with three dashes in a single day! Only a few years ago the order of exercises at Lexington ran: mile heats, two mile heats, three mile heats, mile heats, best three in five, and four mile heats. It was nothing but heats. Now the tendency is all the other way.[29]

17
WINS AND LOSSES

Keene Richards was now, for a time, propertyless but back in residence at Blue Grass Park through the kindness of friends. In 1861 he had sold Blue Grass Park to his friend Troye in order to avoid possible Federal confiscation. In his July 1868 letter to Breckinridge, he wrote, "I am still living in the old House at Georgetown where I was born. The deed made Troye the day we had to start for the Mountains has stood the test of Law and reconstruction and I am working hard to get a little clear from Troye before either of us dies. My friends that I like come here to see me I give them some of the best Whiskey they ever drank. We talk Horse go to see the stallions then over to the Training Stable to see the Race Horses." Richards appears to have been successful in this, for in December of that year Troye and his wife, Cornelia, conveyed Blue Grass Park, "upon which A. K. Richards resides," to Harvey Graves for the sum of $1. Troye subsequently purchased a large block of farmland in Madison County in northern Alabama for $4,000 to provide a home for his family. Troye applied himself diligently to his property, but neither his heart nor talent lay in agriculture, and he spent much of the ensuing years as he always had, traveling about the country to paint on commission. Subsequent land transactions imply that Graves returned ownership of Blue Grass Park to Richards while retaining an interest in the property. Despite his role as estate administrator, this was likely due to his close relationship with Richards.[1]

Richards's only source of income to support his family would now have to come from breeding and racing Thoroughbred horses. Blue Grass Park was in good condition, thanks to the able management of Frank Sherritt. Bereft of capital and lacking the formerly substantial cash flow from his plantation cotton, Richards was forced to take on a business partner, John C. Kilgour of Cincinnati.[2]

John Kilgour (1834–1914) was a wealthy businessman who was relatively new to Thoroughbred racing. In 1880, the worth of John and his brother, Charles, was estimated to be about $2 million, equal to about $60 million today. Prior to his involvement with Keene Richards, he did not own any racehorses, but participated in the founding of the racing association in Cincinnati in January 1866, known as the Buckeye Club, and served as third vice president. In July 1868, the sporting magazine *Spirit of the Times,* in a report on Blue Grass Park, noted that "In the last year, Mr. John Kilgour, of Cincinnati, has become joint owner with Mr. Richards in the broodmares and racing stock of this establishment." Kilgour even bought a farm of his own in Scott County, nearly five hundred acres on the Lexington road a little south of Georgetown.[3]

Kilgour first appears in the racing record with a report of the Cincinnati races on May 29, 1868, entering several horses from the Georgetown stables in his name but under Richards's silver gray and white racing colors. His neophyte status was confirmed by the *Spirit* writer, who observed that, at Louisville in June, Kilgour "won several races . . . certainly very encouraging for a beginner." Richards named a two-year-old colt for his new partner. Sired by imported Mickey Free, the horse John Kilgour had a rather successful racing career. Beginning in September, numerous entries at race meetings across the country were made under the name of "Richards & Kilgour," although Richards also put up horses under his name alone in many of the same meetings. This partnership designation continued for several years, but in 1871 there was only one such entry, in June at Jerome Park, and none thereafter. Kilgour's personal interest in horse racing ended at about that time, although he continued to back Richards financially for a few more years. Shortly after disengaging from the partnership, in 1883 Kilgour disposed of his Scott County farm, selling it off in parcels.[4]

At about the same time that Richards associated with Kilgour, or possibly a little earlier, his celebrated trainer Ansel—who took the surname of Williamson upon gaining his freedom—departed from Bluegrass Park. "Uncle Ansel," as he was often referred to by admiring turfmen, was "the most popular, polite, and, at the same time, the most intelligent of colored trainers, whose only fault is a tendency to be too lenient with his stock." Now free to choose his own employment, he was considered one the best trainers in the business. During the remainder of his life he worked for some of the nation's most prominent turfmen. In late June 1868, Ansel was at Dexter Park in Chicago caring for the horses of James Conlisk. In 1871, he was employed by Abraham Buford of Woodford County, Kentucky, and soon thereafter he spent four years at Henry Price McGrath's McGrathiana Farm near Lexington, where he trained Aristides, winner of the first Kentucky Derby in 1875. The following year found Ansel at Stony Brook Stud, near Princeton, New Jersey, hired for the season to train for David McDaniel, and the next year he moved on to the stable of Carr & Company at Jerome Park. This firm was rebranded as the "Manhattan Stable" of J. G. Nelson & Co. in 1878. McGrath lured Ansel back into his employ early in 1879. This was the trainer's last season working with horses. In poor health, he retired and came back to Lexington during the summer, where, at the age of seventy-five, he passed away at his home on June 25, 1881. Richards would replace Ansel first with George H. Rice, early in 1868, and later with John McClelland, who trained for him at Blue Grass Park until 1881.[5]

Despite involvement in the founding of the first American Jockey Club in New York and serving as permanent steward for Jerome Park in that state, Keene Richards seemed to have no particular interest in racing his horses at northern tracks. He entered and withdrew only a single horse, War Dance, at the Jerome Park inaugural meeting in 1866, and afterward his horses only appeared on the northern turf on a few occasions, most of these being in 1870 and 1871. Richards competed at Saratoga (New York) in the summer of both years, at Monmouth Park (New Jersey) only in summer 1870, and on a single occasion at the Pimlico track in Maryland in fall 1870. The record shows an entry for "Richards & Kilgour" at Jerome Park in 1871, although Richards may not have attended, and in 1879 at a new track in Chicago. Instead, Richards preferred to follow the familiar old southern circuit, much as he had done in the years before the war. His busiest years were 1868 through 1871, during which he participated in an average of nine different race meetings each year, peaking in 1870 with a dozen meets. The racing season began in March with meetings held at tracks in the Deep South cities of Mobile, New Orleans, and Memphis, moving north in late spring to Nashville, Lexington, Louisville, and Cincinnati, and to the northern turf during the summer months. Fall meetings reversed the pattern, beginning with meets in Kentucky and Tennessee during September and October and moving southward in November and December for tracks in Alabama and Louisiana. After 1873, Richards attended fewer race meetings due to personal and financial difficulties.[6]

His income was provided by stud fees, sales of yearlings and older horses, and prize money from race meetings. His most valuable stallions commanded significant stud fees. The services of the Knight of St. George were advertised as $100 during the breeding season, Mickey Free and War Dance, each $50, and the Arabian Fysaul, who was still hale despite his age, $30. No data is available to indicate the exact number of mares serviced by these horses, but given the large number of offspring reported in the stud books and race entries, his income from this source must have amounted to several thousand dollars per year. His breeding stock was relatively limited, for as one visitor observed, "By action of the war the brood mares at Blue Grass Park were reduced in numbers, and Mr. Richards has been dependent upon his few remaining mares, and the few sent by [other] breeders." He could no longer afford to purchase top-quality mares, domestic or imported, and had to make do with those he still owned. Sales of Richards's colts, fillies, and brood mares were held at Blue Grass Park in June and generally featured about two dozen animals. The accommodations and feast offered to guests were described in an account of the 1874 sale: "The sale took place under a spacious canvass, spread for the purpose, around which comfortable seats were arranged. At the close of the sale a bountiful dinner was served, consisting of a splendid burgoo, choice beef, mutton, bacon, bread, buttermilk and ice water." The 1873 sale brought $6,790, and in 1874 and 1875, $5,270 and $5,850, respectively. The horses of Richards's racing stable often competed against their relatives, the offspring of his prized stallions, bred at Blue Grass Park and purchased at these sales. His own racehorses did well enough that he was consistently among the highest national earners each year. In 1870, August Belmont topped the list, having won $34,755 from racing, with Keene Richards in eleventh place with $7,280. For the following year, David McDaniel was the top earner, with $58,755, and Richards tenth, having taken $7,000 from his racing string. From this information, it would appear that

Richards was able to achieve an annual gross income of about $15,000, no mean sum considering that the average daily wage for an unskilled worker in 1879 was $1.89, or less than $600 per year.[7]

Richards's postwar income was but a shadow of the wealth he had once commanded, and indeed a paltry sum compared to the resources of most of the turfmen of the Bluegrass, men such as Robert A. Alexander, Abe Buford, Frank Harper, and James A. Grinstead. The wealth of these men, affluent as they might be, paled against that of the new turf magnates of the North. Most Kentucky breeders, except for Alexander, depended mainly upon their farms for income. The wealth generated by agriculture in the Bluegrass could not compete with the far greater wealth derived from northern finance and industry. The new northern titans of the turf used their vast wealth to build grandly, setting up lavish racing stables and breeding farms on a scale that could not be equaled by Kentucky gentry. Unlike Kentucky farms, however, where raising horses was but one of many agricultural operations, the new farms established by northeastern capitalists such as Milton H. Sanford, August Belmont, and the Lorillard brothers were devoted entirely to breeding Thoroughbreds.[8]

Prior to the war, Keene Richards counted the Bluegrass horsemen as his friends and social equals, and in Kentucky this was still the case. His established reputation as a knowledgeable and successful breeder now gained him entry into the social circles of the northern turf as well. However, feeling the need to keep up appearances as a member of elite society, he lived far beyond his means. Although able to reestablish Blue Grass Park as a nationally famous breeding establishment, he was forced to depend upon the bloodstock that he had acquired before the war, since he could no longer afford to purchase expensive horses to supplement his operation. Richards's lifestyle was a house of cards, and the expenses associated with breeding and racing along with those inherent with maintaining the overt appearance of Bluegrass gentry kept him heavily indebted and would soon lead to a collapse of the framework he had so desperately patched together.

After his bankruptcy was finalized and his existing debts discharged, Richards needed a constant infusion of cash to maintain his lifestyle and stave off creditors, so he continued to borrow heavily. During 1870 to 1872, he executed six promissory notes to Harvey Graves totaling about

$19,000, and in 1870 or 1871 he mortgaged his recently reacquired Louisiana property to the New Orleans firm of Renshaw and Cammack, commission merchants, for $17,100 in cash. This was probably, at least in part, to pay for plantation supplies. Feeling perhaps a little desperate under such a crushing burden, Richards appointed Morris Keene his agent to rent or sell these properties, including Winn Forest. His cousin already had a buyer lined up, and promptly made a conveyance of Transylvania Plantation and Section 13 to Thomas Oliver Meaux for $47,000. Richards, however, found himself unable to part with the land, and the sale was subsequently revoked. In December 1873, Keene and Mary executed a second mortgage on Transylvania Plantation to Graves in exchange for $10,000. This sum was paid over by Graves to Renshaw and Cammack. In addition, Richards pledged to set aside all profits from the plantation to Renshaw and Cammack until the balance of his debt to them was paid. Even if Richards had managed, since the disastrous years of 1866 and 1867, to put the plantation back into profitable condition, there could be no cotton income available to him for some time. At the same time, Richards was also under siege by many suits brought against him for other debts.[9]

The next two years were quite possibly the worst of Richards's life, marred by personal and financial distress. On July 25, 1874, Edward Troye, one of Richards's closest friends, died suddenly of pneumonia, "hastened by heart disease," while visiting Blue Grass Park. Richards wrote a lengthy tribute to his friend for the *Georgetown Times,* noting that "for forty years, there have been few animals of any great merit in America that have not stood before his easel to be placed on canvas by his truthful brush." He was a prolific artist. Troye's biographer, Alexander Mackey-Smith, catalogued 356 paintings and eleven drawings known to have been made by Troye, and estimated that this was probably less than half of the artist's actual production. Richards was his primary patron, having commissioned twenty-seven paintings. They included ten portraits of his Arabians, nine of Thoroughbred Running Horses, and eight scenes of Syria and the Holy Land. He had also collected eighteen additional works by the artist. Woodburn Farm was another important client. Troye executed eighteen paintings for Robert A. Alexander and six for his brother, Alexander John Alexander. The last works made by Troye were portraits in the fall of 1872 for his friend James A. Grinstead of two horses at his Walnut Hills Farm near Lexington, the chestnut mare Mary Hadley and the two-year-old colt Waverly. Troye was buried in the Georgetown cemetery, his grave marked by an eight-foot-high marble monument topped by the figure of a Muse holding a banner inscribed "Sacred to the Memory of E. Troye Artist." Richards designed the monument but, because he lacked the money to pay for it, Grinstead covered the costs.[10]

Richards's mounting debts and past-due notes now began to catch up with him again. On August 10, 1874, Richards was at last forced to sell Transylvania Plantation and the nearby Section 13 for the sum of $42,000, with little prospect of retrieval. He was, at least, able to keep it in the family, as the purchaser was his first cousin, Narcissa Keene Johnson, daughter of his uncle Alexander Keene. Only a month later, after Harvey Graves signed a quitclaim on the property, Richards lost Blue Grass Park as a result of a suit brought against him by the Sayre Bank in the Scott County District Court. This was immediately followed by a cross-petition filed by the firm of Grinstead and Bradley. Richards was indebted to Grinstead and Bradley for $4,400, having, as cosigner, assumed responsibility for the Troye's mortgage of Blue Grass Park on October 16, 1865, obligated by a promissory note payable within twelve months and now long overdue. Richards also owed $10,000 to Sayre for a second mortgage of the Georgetown property made in October 1871, the note now being a year overdue. On September 12, 1874, the court determined that Richards remained indebted by the full amount of both mortgages and ordered the Blue Grass Park properties to be sold at public auction and the proceeds applied to the debts. In December 1875, nearly two hundred acres of Richards's estate, including the homestead tract beside Royal Spring, went under the gavel to Sayre for $17,000. The forced sale from Richards to Sayre was recorded in July 1876, and within a matter of weeks Sayre sold the eighty-acre homestead tract adjoining Royal Spring to James A. Grinstead of Lexington for $2,500. A close friend, Grinstead allowed Richards to remain on the property and to continue his equine operations.[11]

Equally devastating, on County Court Day, April 19, 1875, the elegant brick house above Royal Spring where Richards had been born and made his home caught fire and was gutted, leaving nothing behind but "bare, black, smoking walls." According to a report in the *Georgetown Times*, the fire was first discovered in the roof and was probably the result of a spark from the kitchen. "The contents of the house, including many rare and valuable paintings, quaint old silver ware and china, and curious articles of ornament and use gathered from foreign lands, were generally saved, though some of the goods were considerably damaged in removal, as is always the case on such exciting occasions," the account noted. All of Troye's work was rescued, this being the highest priority, but "all of the clothing of the children, save what they had on, was burned, and a number of books are missing from the library." As the house was at the edge of town, the blaze quickly drew a crowd from those attending Court Day, who immediately pitched in to try to save as much as possible. Richards published a card in the paper thanking all those who came to assist: "My wife and myself feel that when we have such friends, we desire to live out our days, even though it be in a humble shelter made from the ruins of our old homestead." The house, erected as a residence in 1808 by Georgetown founder Elijah Craig, was not rebuilt. James Grinstead, his friend and principal creditor, kindly rented a farm near Georgetown for Richards and his family to use as a residence.[12]

The final blow in these two miserable years came but weeks later, with the death of John C. Breckinridge, Richards's friend and former commander. In April 1865, as the Confederacy crumbled, Breckinridge fled the country and spent nearly four years in exile, first in Canada and later, for the sake of Mary's health, in Europe. In the political climate of the immediate postwar Reconstruction period, he was fearful of being arrested and hanged if he returned to the United States. The unforgiving attitude began to shift after a few years, aided by the efforts of his numerous friends, including several northern men of significance. In December 1868, President Andrew Johnson issued a proclamation granting full pardon and amnesty to all persons who had participated in the rebellion. Breckinridge returned to Kentucky in March 1869 and took up his old law practice as a resident of Lexington. Richards had sent many messages to his old general by way of friends traveling abroad, and in his lengthy letter to Breckinridge of the previous year he urged him to come to Blue Grass Park for a visit. "We will have some of Jesse Woods Old Crow. The same we had before we started for the Mountains. My Wife and Myself have provided a Room for you and she will be so glad to see you as Myself and we will drive about Scott and town."[13]

Whether Breckinridge took Richards up on his offer to visit him in Georgetown is unknown, but certainly the old friends socialized on many occasions after his return. One such occasion was an outdoor dinner "under the stately locust trees" at McGrathiana Farm in May 1872, given by Henry P. McGrath for his many friends. Present were not only Richards and Breckinridge, but also Richard Ten Broeck, former Kentucky governor James F. Robinson and his son, Union general James F. Robinson Jr., former Confederate generals Abe Buford and Basil Duke, and many other prominent men who had supported opposite sides during the war. Breckinridge, since his return, had dedicated his influence toward North-South reconciliation, but here on the lawn under the trees no such effort was necessary among these friends and acquaintances.[14]

By this time in Kentucky, service with the defeated Confederate cause had actually become a social and political asset rather than a hindrance. Although the Kentucky legislature declared for the Union cause in September 1861 and the state supplied far more volunteers to the Union army than to the Confederacy, the border state was occupied by Federal troops and by the following year had evolved into what amounted to a police state. In a state abounding with southern sympathizers and rampant guerrilla activity, the military government became increasingly heavy-handed in its treatment of civilians. Civil liberties essentially disappeared; citizens could be arrested for aiding the Confederacy or even expressing sympathy for the southern cause, and in some cases were executed. Regardless of sectional loyalty, most white Kentuckians were outraged by a government that treated the population as though it were part of the rebellion rather than part of the Union. Many slaveholders in the state had initially sided with the Union, believing the U.S. government would protect their property rights, but they felt betrayed by the Emancipation Proclamation and the enlistment and arming of free blacks in the army. After the war, widespread resentment against the federal government united former Kentucky Confederates and Unionists, so that "Democratic politics enveloped in a Lost Cause narrative . . . came to define Kentucky in the years following the war." During the Reconstruction period, it was often remarked that Kentuckians had "waited until after the war to secede" from the Union. Always popular and well-respected, had Keene Richards sought state or local political office after the war, very likely he would have been elected.[15]

Breckinridge's health began to decline soon after the dinner at McGrathiana, and on May 17, 1875, the former statesman-soldier passed away at his Lexington home from cirrhosis, brought about from injuries to his liver suffered during the war. He was laid to rest in Lexington Cemetery, the procession led by Basil Duke and followed by a crowd estimated at more than twenty thousand mourners. Keene Richards was one of sixteen pallbearers, aided by William Preston and Stoddard Johnson.[16]

From 1872 through 1880, Richards stayed fairly close to home, abandoning the southern circuit to race his horses mainly in Lexington and occasionally in Louisville, Nashville, or Cincinnati. With the closing of the Metairie track and the loss of Transylvania, Louisiana had perhaps lost much of its appeal. He went to New Orleans on only two occasions, in 1876 and 1877. On northern tracks, Richards appeared once at Jerome Park in 1873 and at Chicago in 1879. Most of his entries were offspring of War Dance, and his horses competed successfully much of the time. For 1875, Richards's earnings from the track, $10,995, placed him ninth among American horsemen, and in 1876 his earnings of $8,120 put him in sixth place, the top earner being August Belmont of New York in both years. The horse Australian, imported by Richards in 1858 and still at Woodburn in 1876, was fourth nationally among leading sires, and his War Dance ranked sixth. In May 1876, Richards's horse Bullion very nearly won the second running of the Kentucky Derby at Churchill Downs. There were eleven entries in the race, which was won by Vagrant. Bullion, a three-year-old, was perhaps denied victory only due to an injury inflicted by another horse. The *Louisville Courier-Journal* described the incident that ended Bullion's racing career:

> Bullion was pushing Vagrant very closely for the championship, and was only second to him for the half-mile stretch from the three-quarter pole to the first quarter pole. Shortly after passing the latter place, however, one of the horses engaged in the race, thought to be Harry Hill, ran upon him, and striking his left hind foot, cut him down, almost entirely severing the tendon of that leg. The noble ani-

mal, notwithstanding the wound, ran on and scarcely fell behind the body of horses as they came in, though, after the race, he came dragging his foot in scarcely able to walk.[17]

In the mid-1870s Richards developed an interest in hurdle racing, this being an early form of steeplechase, in which horses leap over a series of wooden fences spaced along the course of a dirt track ordinarily used for flat racing. The first hurdle race in America took place in 1834 at the National Course in Washington, D.C., and the first true steeplechase at the Riverside track in New Jersey in 1865. A steeplechase involves a variety of obstacles, including brush fences, timber rails, stone fences, and water jumps. Richards's first venture into the sport occurred at the spring races at Louisville in 1876, where hurdles were set up for the first time at this track and the race was won by his four-year-old horse Redman, sired by War Dance. Hurdle or steeplechase racing became a minor American obsession for about two decades after the Civil War, but was controversial due to the large number of injuries to horses and riders. In that same year, of 412 race events analyzed by the *New York Herald*, nearly 70 percent were dashes ranging from a half-mile to four miles, 20 percent were heat races, and hurdles and steeplechases each accounted for about 5 percent, indicating the decline of heat racing and the inroads made by jumpers. In 1879, a writer for the *New York Sun* observed, "More first-class steeplechasers have been sent from Blue Grass Park than from any other breeding establishment in America." During this period Richards also developed an interest in breeding his Arabians with Trotting and Saddle horses, acquiring the noted Trotting stallion Norman for the former.[18]

With the house at Blue Grass Park destroyed by fire, hosting the June yearling sales became more of a challenge for Keene Richards, requiring him to move his annual sale to different venues. Immediately after the fire, the event took place at Montague and Brown's stable in Lexington, fetching $5,280 for two dozen animals, an average of $244. In the following year, 1876, the sale was again held at Lexington, but prices had greatly declined. Richards was able to dispose of sixteen animals for an average of $209, the sale totaling $3,350. The 1877 sale was held before the Phoenix Hotel in Lexington, with his stock prices further depressed, averaging only $163. This was probably quite a shock to Richards, considering that fifteen of the twenty-three animals sold had been sired by War Dance. The *Cincinnati Enquirer* noted that in previous years Richards had held his sale at John Kilgour's farm, but found the location to be too distant from the railroad; this suggests that sales may have been moved from Blue Grass Park to the Kilgour property prior to the fire, at least on some occasions. Hoping to draw a larger crowd of potential purchasers with deeper pockets, Richards held a joint sale of stock at Lexington with James A. Grinstead in 1878 on the grounds of the Kentucky Association track. The "stock was in good order, and the attendance of turfmen, from a distance as well as from this State, was large," wrote the correspondent for the *New York Times.* The sale bought better prices for Richards than in the previous year, but the average of $213 was still greatly reduced from just a few years before. This was the last yearling sale by Richards.[19]

In 1878, Richards suffered another great personal loss with the suicide of his best and oldest friend, Morris Keene. After the war, Keene took up residence in Phillips County, Arkansas, but suffered financial difficulties that forced him into bankruptcy in 1868, the same year as his cousin Keene Richards. By November of 1869, he apparently moved back to Louisiana, being described as a resident of that state in a property transaction, where in 1872 Richards gave him power of attorney to handle affairs related to the Transylvania and Winn Forest plantations. After the sale of Richards's land to Thomas Meaux fell through, Keene relocated back to the state of his birth, settling at Pooles Island in Maryland. Keene had purchased the remote island in Chesapeake Bay in 1871, in partnership with George A. Merritt, for $14,000. In an apparent effort to restore his fortunes, in November 1876 he attempted to purchase the north half of Winn Forest Plantation from Dr. Colin Buckner, executing five notes for $5,100, each payable over a period of five successive years. Evidently unable to meet financial obligations, on April 30, 1878, having returned to Carroll Parish, Keene took a fatal overdose of morphine. Morris Keene was "a gentleman well-connected and much respected in this parish," observed the *Carroll Conservative.* "We are not fully informed as to the cause of his hurrying out of existence, but it was supposed to be depression of mind produced by reversals of fortune."[20]

More unpleasant news was in store in the following year. On October 22, 1879, a blaze broke out in one of the buildings on the campus of Bethany

College, Richards's alma mater. This building housed the library and the copies of Troye's Oriental paintings that Richards donated to the college in 1860. The fire was discovered at about 3:00 a.m. by a student, who gave the alarm, and immediately the entire neighboring village rushed to the scene with buckets in hand as well as ladders and blankets that could be wetted down to fight the fire. Fortunately, the library building was separated from the main building by a thick, fireproof wall, and the blaze was soon extinguished by heroic efforts on the part of the populace. All the Troye paintings were rescued, this being the highest priority of those battling the conflagration. Investigation afterward determined that the fire was the result of arson. The southwest end of the main building had also been set afire, but the flames did not make any headway before they were discovered and extinguished. At this location, a jug was found containing coal oil, some of which had been poured around the premises.[21]

The identity of the culprit or culprits responsible for setting the fire was not immediately known, but it was suspected to be the work of a gang of arsonists who had set several barns and other structures ablaze recently in the neighborhood. Within a matter of days, suspicion fell upon several men. Dr. David Parkinson, a dentist, and Thomas Cheek were both arrested for the Bethany arson, and three other men were arrested for setting fires in other locations. An indictment was handed down against these men by a grand jury on December 9, and they were later tried and convicted.[22]

As the year 1881 began, Alexander Keene Richards was fifty-three years old. Recently described as an "agreeable and scholarly gentleman . . . a little above the medium height, strongly built, large head, intellectual features, short gray hair, and long gray whiskers," he was weary and saddened after fifteen years of loss. Since his return to the United States after the war, he had lost all his property, all his wealth, and his family home was reduced to blackened walls and ashes. His closest friends were gone as well; Edward Troye, Morris Keene, John C. Breckinridge, and Robert A. Alexander had all been laid to rest. All of the imported English Thoroughbreds and Arabians that he had so carefully selected for their bloodlines and potential and had shipped home at great expense were now gone, felled by age or illness. Mickey Free, sired by Irish Birdcatcher, had been one of the first to go, in early 1868 at the age of twenty-nine. No death date is recorded for the Knight of St. George, once Richards's favorite stallion, but he was likely buried beneath the sod in 1871 or 1872 because there are no documented progeny beyond 1872. All of his prized imported Arabians were now gone as well, the last, Fysaul, having expired in August 1877. Only a few months before his death, the *Georgetown Times* reported that the elderly Arabian stallion "frisks about like a four-year-old." During the previous three years, Richards's energy and enthusiasm for the racing circuit was considerably diminished. In 1878 he appeared only at Lexington, Louisville, and Cincinnati, with one entry at each location, and in 1879 at Lexington, Louisville, and Chicago, each time represented by a single horse—Round Tree. In his last year of racing, Richards took three horses to the spring meeting in Lexington and remained at home for the remainder of the year. All of his entries in these years were sired by War Dance.[23]

There were still some bright spots in his life, notably his wife and children. From all appearances, he was a happily married man, and his three girls had survived the vicissitudes of childhood and were now thriving adolescents. Although his imported stallions were gone, he had others with good bloodlines and some respectable mares. Richards could take particular pride in the accomplishments of War Dance at stud, for he ranked consistently among the top American sires in terms of the victories and earnings of his progeny. In 1879, War Dance ranked sixth nationally, and in fifth place in 1880. The Thoroughbred database of Pedigree Online lists 185 known offspring for War Dance. Benjamin Bruce observed, "War Dance has never had a large number of choice mares during his career at the stud, but has had to make his name as a sire upon untried mares. With such material he has made a reputation second to no son of Lexington." He was, according to Bruce, "one of the best representatives of a racing and winning family in the Stud Book." The *Spirit of the Times* stated that "his grand appearance, and his blood, Lexington, the king of racers, crossed upon Reel, the ex-queen of the turf, brought him plenty of patronage," and that "next to the Lexingtons no strain of mares are more deservedly popular." Hamilton Busbey, publisher of *Turf, Field and Farm,* echoed this sentiment in his 1904 book on the *Trotting and the Pacing Horse:* "War Dance himself ranks second only to Lexington as a sire of brood mares. His blood is now valued highly in a pedigree."[24]

Richards could also take pride in Australian, who was then the property of Woodburn Stud. His pride was perhaps mixed with regret at having

War Dance, an outstanding stud horse purchased by Keene Richards from Thomas Jefferson Wells of Louisiana in the summer of 1863. War Dance raced only once and was retired to Kentucky, where he became one of America's leading sires. Painted by Edward Troye in 1869 at Blue Grass Park. Photograph courtesy of Sotheby's, 2024.

sold the promising little imported colt Millington to Robert A. Alexander in 1861, who gave him a new name and almost immediately retired him to the stud. Australian's record was even more impressive than that of War Dance, rarely far from the top spot and second only to Lexington from 1871 to 1875. When this outstanding stallion died at Woodburn Stud in October 1879, *Turf, Field and Farm* commented, "Australian has sired more real good racehorses of both sexes than almost any other horse in America, either native or imported." Richards could also feel some small measure of vindication in the career of Limestone, one of his Arabian-Thoroughbred Running Horse crosses. Although his Arabian experiment was now producing third- and fourth-generation foals, none had proved of particular note on the racecourse. The best of the lot was the second-generation chestnut horse Limestone, sired by War Dance out of Transylvania, who was herself the product of a match between Massoud and Peytona. "It is sufficient to say," one writer observed, "that he won twenty races, and $15,000 for his owner, as a four-year-old." He was considered by many to be the best jumper of his day: "Although a good horse on the flat, his greatest excellence was exhibited in running cross-country, steeplechases and hurdle-races." When, in 1879, Richards was asked about his Arabian experiment, he still retained some optimism, informing the interviewer that he firmly believed "that judicious handling of the best Arab blood will yet produce flyers who will leave our modern racehorses nowhere at the end of long races."[25]

The career of this prominent and well-liked Kentuckian came to an unexpected end before he could truly evaluate the outcome of his life's work. On the morning of March 18, 1881, fifty-three-year-old Richards succumbed to pneumonia at his home on the farm now rented for him by Grinstead. "The death of Mr. Richards was brought on by carelessness and unnecessary, if not reckless, exposure," the *Louisville Courier-Journal* observed in a lengthy tribute to the deceased turfman.

> He was in the habit of riding about at all hours of the night in an open vehicle in all sorts of weather. He thought his constitution could withstand almost every trial of strength. He had visited Mr. H. P. McGrath only a few days before, and advised him to get up and dress himself, that he would feel the better for it, and slapping his own chest added: "I feel as if I could live for fifty years." When attacked with the malady which carried him off, he refused for a day or two to see a physician, and consented at last with reluctance. His fine constitution rallied under proper treatment, and he was enabled to get up and walk about. Then, with the characteristic disregard of himself, he went into his library, where there had been no fire for several days, and sat there for several hours without a fire, thus encouraging the relapse from which he never rallied.[26]

On March 21, a large procession, including many notables, friends, and neighbors, followed Keene Richards as he was borne to Georgetown Cemetery and laid to rest, in a severe snowstorm, within sight of the grave of his old friend Edward Troye. By unhappy coincidence, within a matter of weeks Ansel Williamson, celebrity trainer at Blue Grass Park before the war, and Richards's prized horse War Dance followed him in death. Mary Richards survived her husband by more than forty years, passing away at New Orleans in 1923 at the age of eighty-six. She was laid to rest at Georgetown Cemetery.[27]

Keene's three daughters all married prominent men and lived comfortable lives. Nora, the eldest, married Edward G. Swarz (1866–1944) on July 23, 1903, a New Orleans businessman originally from Georgetown, Kentucky, who operated a lumber mill at Burton, Louisiana, and would inherit substantial wealth from his father in 1915. Nora was his second wife, and the couple had no surviving children. Nora survived her husband's death in 1944, but her date of passing is undetermined. Emily, the middle daughter, was wed circa 1898 to Francis "Frank" P. Stubbs (1872–1933) of Monroe, Louisiana, where they made their residence. Frank was a well-known lawyer and banker who made an unsuccessful bid for the governorship of Louisiana in 1920 and rose to command of the state National Guard. Emily was the first of the Richards children to pass away, succumbing on September 28, 1910, at the age of forty-one years following a severe illness. The Stubbs had two children, Frank Jr., born in 1900, and his baby sister, Mary, who died of the croup as a toddler in 1908. Frank would be the only surviving grandchild of Keene Richards. Like his father, he attended Tulane Law School and the Virginia Military Institute. The youngest of the sisters, Caroline, married Dr. John E. Pack (1849–1931) of Georgetown on July 14, 1898, also his second marriage. There were no children from this union, and Dr. Pack died from a stroke on October 31, 1931. Caroline was very socially active and served as an officer in the local chapter of the Daughters of the American Revolution. She passed away on November 24, 1962, aged ninety-one. The sisters remained very close after their respective marriages. There are numerous notices in the pages of the *Georgetown Times* over the years indicating that the sisters in Louisiana regularly visited Caroline in Kentucky, together or separately, often accompanied by their mother, and would spend the summer in the Bluegrass escaping the tropical heat of their home state. Caroline, in turn, made many trips to visit her family in Louisiana. Regardless of where they made their residence, upon passing all were interred at the Georgetown Cemetery.[28]

Richards was eulogized in the newspapers and the sporting magazines of the day. *Turf, Field and Farm* noted that he was a "courteous, pure minded, noble hearted gentleman" who had never been known to utter an oath or to wager a single dollar on a horse race. "The turf and breeding interests of America owe much to the memory of A. Keene Richards," the editor, Hamilton Busbey, concluded. James A. Grinstead was the actual owner of Richards's property and livestock, and so, after Richards's death, the remaining stock and breeding records of Blue Grass Park were removed to his Walnut Hills Farm, a few miles north of Lexington. John McClelland, Richards's trainer, came to Walnut Hills with the horses and was employed in the same capacity by Grinstead. Because of the resulting overcrowding, most of the brood mares and young stock were sold at public auction in May 1882. Grinstead held on to Blue Grass Park until January 1885, assigning it to John T. Shelby, who conveyed it to John B. Graves of Scott County for $10,124. Graves immediately sold the property to William Payne of Scott County, taking a $500 profit on the transaction. Payne held on to the land for only four years, selling it in April 1889 to Jefferson D. Grover of Georgetown for exactly the same price he had paid. Five years later, in October 1894, Grover conveyed the property to his older sister, Alice P. Montgomery, for $14,000. The following year, Alice and her husband, Henry P. Montgomery, founding president of the First National Bank of Georgetown, built a house on the high ground overlooking the spring. The Montgomerys soon began subdividing the property and selling the lots, marking the end of Blue Grass Park as farmland.[29]

18
LEGACY

Keene Richards and Robert Alexander are often considered to be the most influential Kentucky horsemen of the nineteenth century. The first-class Thoroughbreds these gentlemen imported from England were of great significance in establishing modern bloodlines. Richards's greatest contribution was the importation of the little colt that became Australian in Alexander's stud. Among the top sires of the nineteenth century, Australian established one of the oldest male lines still in existence, through his descendants Spendthrift, Hastings, Fair Play, and Man o' War, the latter widely regarded as the greatest racehorse of all time. Spendthrift, foaled in 1876, was a champion running horse and the best son of Australian. He was the sire of Hastings, foaled in 1893, who had a combative temperament that did not keep him from a successful career on the turf. In residence at August Belmont's Nursery Stud, Hastings topped the American sire list in 1902. The most famous son of Hastings was Fair Play, born in 1905, who led the sire list in 1920, 1924, and 1927 as well as the broodmare sire list three times. According to one modern writer, "today one can scarcely find a North American or European stakes winner free of his blood." Fair Play's greatest legacy was the legendary Man o' War, foaled in 1917, who produced no fewer than sixty-four stakes winners and became a leading sire in 1926, largely due to the dominance of his son Crusader on the racing scene. Another son, War Admiral, captured the Triple Crown in 1937. Though diminished, Australian's bloodline has made a "resurgence in these early years of the twenty-first century" with the appearance of a number of champion horses of this strain.[1]

Aside from his important contributions to the bloodlines of the modern Thoroughbred horse, Keene Richards is probably best known to those interested in equine history for his daring ventures among the Bedouin tribes of the Syrian desert. The globetrotting chronicle of his travels, both in 1851–1853 and again in 1855–1856, reads like an epic adventure novel set in strange and distant lands. Although much of the credit must be given to his companions Edward Troye and Morris Keene for their extended sojourn among the tribes in 1856, it was Richards who conceived the quest and made the first pioneering probes into the desert with his Lebanese translator, Yusef Badra, and Bedouin guide, Sheikh Abdul Medjuel el Mezrab. No westerner before Richards had ever sought out pureblooded Arabian horses among the desert tribes, though others would soon follow in his footsteps.

Richards should also be remembered for his unwavering support of Edward Troye, the most noteworthy animal painter of the nineteenth century. Richards and his fellow Kentucky turfman, Robert A. Alexander of Woodburn Farm, were his greatest patrons, and the generous fees paid to Troye allowed him to follow his muse without hindrance while living in comfort. The paintings Troye created of notable landscapes of the Holy Land, made during the second expedition, must be considered among his greatest works and demonstrate the artist's skill in landscape rendition.

Most writers who have assessed the results of Richards's experiment in breeding Arabian horses to Thoroughbred Running Horses, both during his lifetime and in the years since, have expressed admiration for his knowledge of horses and the great lengths to which he went to secure pureblooded Arabians from the desert. With few exceptions, however, all have dismissed his project as a dismal failure, the foolish waste of a great fortune. John H. Wallace, editor and publisher of the racing journal *Wallace's Monthly* (1875–1894) and author of *The Horse of America* (1897) and other influential equine publications of the latter nineteenth century, was among his harshest critics. In his book, he dedicated a considerable part of the chapter on Arabian horses to debunking the notion that Thoroughbred performance could be improved by an infusion of Arabian blood. "The most notable example of the folly of attempting to regenerate the American race horse by the introduction of the 'blood of the desert' is furnished in the sad experience of the late A. Keene Richards, of Kentucky," he wrote. "We must conclude that the whole scheme is mere moonshine, and that Arabian blood as a means of improvement has failed to develop the value that enthusiasts and dreamers have claimed for it." A review of *The Horse of America*, published in 1898 in *The Nation*, took issue with Wallace's general dislike of Arabians, observing that "The inoffensive Arab-steed seems particularly odious to Mr. Wallace . . . [who makes] various assertions and statements all tending to belittle the supposed virtues of the Arab horse and to cast ridicule and discredit on those, including notably Mr. Wilfred B. Blunt and Mr. A. Keene Richards, who have imported these horses to England and America."[2]

Nevertheless, rejection of the Anglo-Arab cross as a means to improve the Thoroughbred has persisted to the present day. Well-known equine author and blogger Kathleen H. Kirsan recently stated, "Richards was a good breeder, and he knew that returning to the original power bloodlines can rejuvenate bloodstock. Because he had the resources, he was able to travel to Arabia twice where he purchased the best Arabian racers money could buy. This, however, was a disastrous assumption for him as both experiments ended in failure and great financial loss because the Arabian additions to his herd actually decreased the natural speed of his racing stock." Kirsan is correct in this summation. Although Richards's goal primarily was to increase endurance, speed was also essential for a successful racehorse; his experiment was terminated without any of the offspring having demonstrated notable performance in either aspect.[3]

There were others, however, who were convinced that the Arabian horse was a truly beautiful and noble animal worth breeding for its own sake, not as a means to improve the Thoroughbred horse. Like Richards, they believed that the only way to obtain pureblooded Arabians was to go among the Bedouin tribes, and so they, more or less, followed his footsteps into the Syrian desert. Among the first of these was Roger D. Upton, who made two trips into the Syrian desert, the first in 1874, to obtain Arabian horses from the Anizah Bedouins. Upton was greatly impressed by the performance of Turkish cavalry horses he encountered serving with British forces in the Crimean War, and he became convinced that Arabian horses were far superior to, in his opinion, degenerate English Thoroughbreds. Aided and encouraged by the British consul, James H. Skene, he returned with three Arabian mares and two stallions. Upton believed that cavalry and saddle horses could be improved by an admixture of Arabian blood. He advocated—unsuccessfully—for a national replacement of the

Thoroughbred by pure Arabians rather than attempting to improve them with Arabian blood.[4]

A few years later, James Skene would again prove helpful to British travelers seeking Arabian horses. In 1877, Wilfrid and Lady Anne Blunt, who developed an interest in Arab culture and horses during previous travels to the East, came to Syria on the first of three trips to the Near East. On these expeditions, they traveled widely through the region, first to Syria and Lebanon, then to Saudi Arabia, Iraq, and Iran, and later into Algeria and Egypt. Shortly after arriving at Aleppo on their first trip, the Blunts conceived the idea of visiting the Bedouins after discussions with Skene. "We have made a plan . . . of importing some of the best Anazeh blood to England and breeding it pure there," Anne wrote in her journal on December 14, 1877. "It would be an interesting and useful thing to do and I should very much like to try it." Their journey to the East took on new purpose, becoming a mission to preserve the increasingly rare and endangered Arabian horse. With their first acquisitions, the Blunts founded Crabbet Arabian Stud in Sussex, which came to dominate Arabian bloodlines globally. Most of the registered Arabians today contain one or more Crabbet bloodlines. Following these Britons, in 1906 an American, Homer Davenport, came to the desert lands of the Near East in search of pure Arabian horses. Davenport had been fascinated by Arabians since childhood, and with the backing of millionaire Peter Bradley he was able to purchase ten mares and seventeen stallions from the Anizah Bedouins to establish the Davenport Desert Arabian Stud in Massachusetts. In his subsequent catalog, Davenport referred to Keene Richards's ill-fated project; in contrast to the latter's ambitions, he noted, "it was [my] purpose . . . to produce anything but racehorses." Instead, like the Blunts, he intended to breed only pure Arabian horses, rather than use them in an effort to improve other breeds.[5]

Richards's Arabian experiment failed to enhance the racing characteristics of Thoroughbred Running Horses, but the bloodlines of his imported Arabian horses continue to the present day, although few in number and, of course, genetically diminished to traces in passing through many generations. In all cases, the lines transitioned to Standardbreds and trotting and pacing horses. Research using the website of Pedigree Online suggests that the line of Massoud seems to have ended about the beginning of the twentieth century. This may not be entirely accurate, because the mare Transylvania was the daughter of Massoud and Peytona, and she was an amazingly fertile mare. Although bred two or more times each to Richards's imported English stallions, the Knight of St. George and Mickey Free, to War Dance and Melbourne, Jr., and twice to Mambrino Patchen, sire of many famous Trotters, only two of her nineteen subsequent progeny are listed on the site. According to the website, the lines of Fysaul and Sacklowie appear to have disappeared during the late twentieth, with no new descendants listed for Fysaul after 1968 or after 1985 for Sacklowie. Listings for registered horses descended from Mokhladi, however, can still found in the twenty-first century, in the sixteenth generation removed from the Syrian desert stallion.[6]

The real significance of Richards's Arabian importations lies in their important contribution to the development of the American Saddlebred horse, derived from the breed known as the Kentucky Saddler or American Saddle Horse. The original Saddle Horse, now extinct, was developed by breeders in Kentucky and Tennessee early in the nineteenth century by continuous crossing of the American Running Horse with imported English Thoroughbreds to provide a gaited horse that became the most popular riding horse of the century and was favored during the Civil War as a cavalry mount. The American Saddle Horse Association today recognizes two foundation sires for the breed, Denmark (foaled in 1839) and Harrison Chief (foaled in 1872). It is within the more influential Denmark line that a Richards Arabian mare had a minor, if significant, effect. Denmark, an American Running Horse, was the sire of Gaine's Denmark (foaled in 1851), the most important of his sons in the future development of the Saddle Horse. Among Gaine's Denmark's numerous progeny was the horse known as (Adam's) Pilot Denmark, who was bred to one of Richards's "arabian mares," unidentified, although most likely Sadah or Lulie, and the product was Arabian Denmark, who thus became part of the Saddle Horse lineage. Most of Arabian Denmark's line ended during the 1970s, but it is carried on in the present day by at least two Saddlebred horses, Dream's Darling Lady (foaled in 2003) and Attache's Sweet Sea (foaled in 2004).[7]

Dr. George A. Feris, a rancher from the Fort Bend region of Texas, was one of the most enthusiastic supporters of Richards's plan to reinvigorate the Thoroughbred Running Horse with Arabian blood. The two first met in 1855 at the Metairie track in New Orleans, where the two men had jointly and vainly tried to convince other horsemen of the benefit that would be gained by importing Arabians for this purpose. Richards later sold a number of his imported Arabian stallions to Feris, initially Boherr, Hamdan, and Abdel-Kadir, and later Bazar, sired by Fysaul out of the Barb mare Zariphe. Abdel-Kadir was the pride of the Feris stud, an American-born pure Arabian, son of Massoud out of Sadah. In 1875, Feris placed an advertisement in the Texas *Immigrant's Handbook* in which he noted, "I have been engaged in breeding horses in Texas for thirty seven years, and now have a few young stallions of the Arabian, crossed with Lexington, Wagner, Eclipse, Woodpecker, and Leviathan mares," thus evoking some of the most respected Thoroughbred Running Horse bloodlines known. He informed readers that he had brought three of Keene Richards's Arabian stallions to Texas and that he "considered their produce better adapted to the climate and uses of Texas than any other blood."[8]

Feris was conducting an ambitious breeding experiment of his own, similar in nature to Keene Richards's project, but involving the Spanish horses of Mexico rather than Thoroughbred Running Horses. Most of the horses of Mexico were of Andalusian stock, descendants of the thousands of Andalusian horses brought to the New World by the Spanish. "The ordinary Mexican pony, so common in western and southwestern Texas and along the Rio Grande border, is the most blue-blooded animal in all this land," observed the *Dallas Morning News* in 1897. "He is a descendant of the pure Barbs brought by Cortez to Mexico when he invaded that country, but the stock has been bred until it has degenerated into the light but wiry, tough little animals known today as Spanish stock. Dr. Ferris believed an infusion of Arabian blood would develop this stock to its normal condition." Feris purchased outstanding "Spanish" mares from Mexican stockmen for his experiment, and also frequently sold the produce of his own stud, having Arabian bloodlines, to these same horsemen as well as to his own countrymen. His experiment was apparently far more successful than that of Richards, since he was not trying to improve speed or endurance, but simply produce a better horse, and those who purchased such horses from him were quite satisfied with the outcome. Writers for the *Morning News* concluded in 1888 that the hybrids were "the equal in all respects of any Arabian or Barb horse," and in 1897 that "his experiments proved he was not far wrong."[9]

Feris died in 1898, and his unmarried daughter, Sarah Lavinia Feris, assumed management of the ranch, although she made her residence in nearby Richmond. Responding to Thornton Chard's inquiries about the Feris Arabians, she replied on January 20, 1934. She had inherited her father's love of the Arabian blood, she informed him, and the last two stallions of pure Arabian blood, Shepherd and Moor, bred by her father, had died in his possession. "We lived in a community that only cared to raise a cowpony that would respond to the dig of a spur and the swish of a rawhide quirt," she wrote. "Competent help could not be procured so the herd was turned on the open range and soon nearly all were lost." Thus it would seem that traces of the Arabian blood and spirit imported by Keene Richards are also to be found in the work and saddle horses of the American West and southward across the border, and in the wild horses of the region. Somewhere in the shortgrass prairie and scrublands, a mustang stallion, protective of his harem, today paws the ground and screams his rage at a would-be usurper, the blood flowing in his veins connecting him to his ancestors of the Syrian desert across a great ocean and nearly two centuries of time.[10]

NOTES

INTRODUCTION

1. Mangum, *A Kingdom for the Horse,* 7–12.

2. Mangum, *A Kingdom for the Horse,* 12–21 (quotation, 19).

3. Coleman, *Three Kentucky Artists,* 53 (first quotation), 70–71; Mackay-Smith, *Race Horses of America,* 371 (second quotation), 402–3, 405, 409–36; *Turf, Field and Farm,* August 14, 1874, 116.

4. Hillenbrand, *Seabiscuit;* Clee, *Eclipse;* Kirsan, *Legacy of Lexington;* Kim Wickens, *Lexington;* Bowen, *Man o' War;* Boyd, *Native Dancer;* Capps, *Secretariat;* Hotaling, *The Great Black Jockeys;* Mooney, *Race Horse Men;* Hotaling, *Wink;* Drape, *Black Maestro;* McDaniels, *Prince of Jockeys;* Mooney, *Isaac Murphy.*

5. Welch, *Who's Who in Thoroughbred Racing;* Bowen, *Legacies of the Turf;* Johnson and Crookshanks, *Virginia Horse Racing;* Harrison, *The Belair Stud;* Harrison, *The Roanoke Stud;* Harrison, *The John's Island Stud;* Auerback, *Wild Ride;* Black, *The King of Fifth Avenue;* Kamoie, *Irons in the Fire;* Johnson, *John Randolph of Roanoke;* Vosburgh, *Cherry and Black.*

1. REINVENTING THE AMERICAN THOROUGHBRED

1. Passport application for A. Keene Richards, July 6, 1855, "Passport Applications," NARA, roll 51; Borden, *Arab Horse,* 24–28.

2. Gaines, *History of Scott County,* 2:418–19; Apple, Johnson, and Bevins, *Scott County,* 127–28.

3. Kentucky bluegrass was not native to the state but was introduced by early settlers.

4. Hervey, *Racing in America,* 1:223–26; O'Dell, "At the Starting Post," 30–33; Campbell, *Horse in Virginia,* 31–32, 35, 41. For a detailed analysis of the evolution of Thoroughbred racing in Kentucky, see O'Dell, "At the Starting Post," and O'Dell, "Under Siege."

5. Hervey, *Racing in America,* 1:226–33; Kirsan, *Sport Horse Breeder,* 4–30; Denbo and Wharton, *Horse World,* 10–17; O'Dell, "At the Starting Post," 33–73; *Kentucky Gazette* (Lexington), May 13 and October 21, 1797.

6. Hervey, *Racing in America,* 2:339; Riess, "Cyclical History," 31–34; Adelman, *A Sporting Time,* 42–52; O'Dell, "At the Starting Post," 74, 78.

7. Weeks, *American Turf,* 51–52; Youatt, *Obligation and Extent,* 98; "Decline of the English Race Horse," *Porter's Spirit of the Times* 2 (June 20, 1857), 249 (first quotation); One Who

Loves the English Horse [pseud.], "'American' Horses," *Bell's Life* (February 22, 1857), 9 (second quotation).

8. Anderson, *Making the American Thoroughbred,* 208–18; Hervey, *Racing in America,* 2:168–74.

9. Buffon, *Histoire Naturelle,* 9:103 (quotations, translated).

10. Jefferson, *Notes on the State of Virginia,* 64–112; Dugatkin, *Mr. Jefferson and the Giant Moose,* 20–24, 55–80, 89–100, 129.

11. Youatt, *The Horse: With a Treatise on Draught,* 44 (first quotation); Youatt, *The Horse: Its History,* 50 (second quotation).

12. Skinner, "The Horse, in England and America," introduction to Youatt, *The Horse,* 31–33 (first quotation, 31; third quotation, 32); Brown, *Biographical Sketches,* 257 (second quotation).

13. Smith, *Observations on Breeding,* 46–68; Walsh and Lupton, *The Horse in the Stable,* 139–40; Bruce, *The Thoroughbred Horse,* 71

14. *A Comparative View,* 56; Mackay-Smith, *Speed and the Thoroughbred,* 107–16.

15. *A Comparative View,* 31–57 (first quotation, 52; second quotation, 53); *On the Deteriorated Condition,* 15–27; Nolan, *Cavalry, History and Tactics,* 334 (third quotation); Cecil [pseud. for Cornelius Tongue], "Horses, Ancient and Modern," *Spirit of the Times* 25 (December 8, 1855), 513.

16. Herbert, *Forester's Horse and Horsemanship,* 353–77 (quotation, 353). On Herbert, see Judd, *Life and Writings of Frank Forester.*

17. Youatt and Cecil, *The Horse,* 37; Lynghaug, *Official Horse Breeds Standards,* 638; Whyte, *History of the British Turf,* 425 (quotation); "Exploits of the English Race Horse," *The Sporting Magazine* 2 (September 1793), 362; L., "To the Editor," *The Sporting Magazine* 39 (November 1811), 53–54; Bruce, *Horse-Breeders Guide,* 198.

18. Pick, *Pedigrees and Performances,* 25–26, 41–42; Youatt, *The Horse: With a Treatise on Draught,* 46–47 (first quotation, 47); "Exploits of the English Race Horse," 362; D.P., "Observations on the American Turf," *Spirit of the Times* 24 (February 3, 1855), 606 (second quotation); Herbert, *Forester's Horse and Horsemanship,* 354–77 (third quotation, 369; fourth quotation, 377).

19. Richards, "The Arab Horses," 6 (first quotation), 2 (second quotation).

20. Richards, "The Arab Horses."

21. Cavendish, *A New Method,* 73 (first quotation); Stark, *Elements of Natural History,* 1:145 (second quotation); Burckhardt, *Notes on the Bedouins,* 308 (third quotation); Layard, *Discoveries Among the Ruins,* 281 (fourth quotation); Daumas, *Les Chevaux du Sahara,* 36.

22. Lawrence, *Practical Treatise on Horses,* 180 (first quotation); Layard, *Discoveries Among the Ruins,* 274 (second quotation).

23. Cecil [pseud.] "Has Our Breed of Horses Deteriorated?" *Farmer's Magazine,* 3rd series, 4 (December 1853), 548 (first quotation); Spectator [pseud.]. "Breeding of Horses," *Spirit of the Times* 25 (March 24, 1855), 65 (second quotation); Speed, *Horse in America,* 14 (third quotation), 15 (fourth quotation).

24. Review of "The Deteriorated Condition of Our Saddle-Horses, the Causes and the Remedy," *The Veterinarian,* 3rd series, 26 (November 1853), 624 (first quotation), 625 (second quotation); Speed, *Horse in America,* 29 (third quotation).

25. Elisha I. Winter, "The Thorough Bred and Imported Oriental Horse, Winter Arabian," (advertisement) *Kentucky Reporter,* March 21, 1825; Richards, "The Arab Horses," 2, 5, 6. The

"Levant" was a term used in nineteenth-century travel writing to refer to the lands of the eastern Mediterranean currently or recently governed by the Ottoman empire.

26. Keene Richards to John W. Keene, November 6, 1851. Author's collection.

2. INVENTING THE THOROUGHBRED

1. Franck, "Beiträge zur Rassekunde unserer Pferde," 33–51.

2. Kavar and Dovč, "Domestication of the Horse," 1–14; Olsen, "Early Horse Domestication," 245–72; Levine, "Early History of the Horse," 5–22; Bowling and Ruvinsky, "Genetic Aspects," 26–29; Clutton-Brock, *Natural History of Domesticated Mammals,* 106, 108; Anthony, "Bridling Horse Power," 59–82.

3. Wagoner, *Equine Genetics,* 20–21, 28–29; Golshan, *Introduction to the Turkmen Horse in Iran,* 23–48, 75–81. For a general account of the spread of horsemanship through ancient cultures, see Hyland, *Horse in the Ancient World,* 1–32. The Turkoman is also referred to as the Turcoman, Turkmen, or simply as the Turk horse.

4. Leo Africanus, *Description of Africa,* 3:942–43; Buffon, *Histoire Naturelle,* 4:237. See also the English translation by Barr, *Buffon's Natural History,* 5:150.

5. Morland, *English Race Horse,* 2–3; Upton, *Newmarket and Arabia,* 108–34 (quotation, 126).

6. Youatt, *The Horse: With a Treatise on Draught,* 4; Ammon, *Historical Reports,* 65–68; Smith, *Natural History of Horses,* 90–91, 100 (quotation); Wallace, *Horse of America,* 25–27.

7. Youatt, *The Horse: With a Treatise on Draught,* 2–4; Smith, *Natural History of Horses,* 97–101; Blunt, *Bedouin Tribes,* 1:419–20; Wentworth, *Authentic Arabian Horse,* 29, 81–86, 96, 134; Ridgeway, *Influence of the Thoroughbred Horse,* 5 (first quotation), 425–77; Borden, *Arab Horse,* 40 (second quotation); Thornton Chard, "The Arabian and the Barb," *Western Horseman* 2 (January 1937), 5–7.

8. Ammon, *Historical Reports,* 71–72 (quotation, 72); Wallace, *Horse of America,* 27–31, 36–44. Ammon also noted the gift of the Cappadocian horses, but did not place as much weight upon this as a foundation for the Arabians.

9. Klynstra, *Nobility of the Desert,* 7–16; Azzaroli, *Early History of Horsemanship,* 180–81; Deb Bennett, "The Arabian Horse," *Equus,* no. 441 (June 2014), 62 (quotation); Wagoner, *Equine Genetics,* 38; Epstein and Mason, *Domesticated Animals of Africa,* 2:426, 439–40; Jansen et al., "Mitochondrial DNA," 10908; Levine, "Early History of the Horse," 198.

10. Bowling and Ruvinsky, "Genetic Aspects," 38 (quotation).

11. Cavendish, *A New Method,* 63, 73; Rice, *History of the British Turf,* 2:129–31; Youatt, *The Horse: With a Treatise on Draught,* 28.

12. Kirsan, *American Running Horse,* 5–18; Kirsan, *Sport Horse Breeder,* 7, 8, 27, 328; Richey, *History of Ireland,* 53–54 (first quotation, 54); Mackay-Smith, *Speed and the Thoroughbred,* 19–29, 53–94; Markham, *Cavelarice,* 45 (second quotation); Mackay-Smith, *Colonial Quarter Race Horse,* 25–29, 31–32. According to Youatt, *The Horse: With a Treatise on Draught,* 24, the first so-called Arabian horse was brought to England in 1121 during the reign of Henry I, though there seems to be some doubt as the authenticity of the claim.

13. Kirsan, *American Running Horse,* 18–23; Richard Stanyhurst, "Perfect Description of Irelande," 9 (quotations); Mackey-Smith, *Speed and the Thoroughbred,* 7, 23; Mackay-Smith, *Colonial Quarter Race Horse,* 34, 37; Richardson, *Horse and Pony Breeds,* 68, 154.

14. Mackay-Smith, *Speed and the Thoroughbred,* 3, 42, 126; *General Stud Book* (1891), 14.

15. Youatt, *The Horse: With a Treatise on Draught,* 44, 48; Whyte, *History of the British Turf,* 79–90; Prior, *Royal Studs,* 83; Mackay-Smith, *Speed and the Thoroughbred,* 147–50; Weatherby, *General Stud Book,* 516; Wallace, *Horse of America,* 71; Jansen et al., "Mitochondrial DNA," 907; Wallner et al., "Y Chromosome," 2029–35; Wallner et al., "Identification of Genetic Variation," e60015. Haplogroup classification of the male Y chromosome is currently used to estimate the population group of the paternal line.

16. For example, in 1831 Youatt, in *The Horse: With a Treatise on Draught,* 44, noted that "The English trained horse is more beautiful, and far swifter and stouter than the justly-famed coursers of the desert."

17. Cunningham et al., "Microsatellite Diversity," 360–63; Hill et al., "Equine mtDNA Variation," 287–94; John Lawrence, *The Horse,* 9 (first quotation); Rous, *Laws and Practice,* vi (second quotation); Wallace, *Horse of America,* 51 (third quotation).

18. Weatherby, *Introduction to a General Stud Book.*

19. Hill et al., "Equine mtDNA Variation," 291–93. The definition, which applies to horses foaled in the United States, is indicated in the "American Stud Book Principal Rules and Requirements, Section V: Rules for Registration, Genetic Typing and Parentage Verification: 1. Eligibility for Foal Registration," http://www.jockeyclub.com; Willett, *Classic Racehorse,* 65–70.

20. John Lawrence, *History and Delineation of the Horse,* 109 (first quotation); Willett, *Classic Racehorse,* 21 (second quotation). The 1809 edition of Lawrence's book differed significantly from the second edition of 1829, cited previously.

21. Bennett, *Roots of New World Horsemanship,* 172, 193–207; Harrison, *Early American Turf Stock,* 1:23–26; Wallace, *Horse of America,* 105; Kirsan, *Sport Horse Breeder,* 5. A good discussion of horse evolution is provided by Hulbert, "The Ancestry of the Horse," 11–34. Horses were first brought to the New World in 1493 on Columbus's second expedition, but remained confined to islands of the Caribbean for twenty-six years until Cortes landed at Mexico.

22. Harrison, *Early American Turf Stock,* 27–32; Ramage, *John Wesley Hunt,* 43–47; *Kentucky Gazette* (Lexington), March 15, 1788 (quotation).

23. Harrison, *Early American Turf Stock,* 31–33; Anderson, *Making the American Thoroughbred,* 1–17; Hervey, *Racing in America,* 2:339–42.

24. Mackay-Smith, *Colonial Quarter Race Horse,* xxix–xxx, 5–17; Wallace, *Horse of America,* 105–6; Kirsan, *Sport Horse Breeder,* 5–6, 10–28, 328.

25. Speed, *Horse in America,* 40; Harrison, *Early American Turf Stock,* 27–32.

26. Kirsan, *Sport Horse Breeder,* 13–17 (first and second quotations, 17); Kirsan, *American Running Horse,* 319–30; Edgar, *American Race-Turf Register.*

27. Kirsan, *Sport Horse Breeder,* 26, 30, 321 (quotation, 26); Kirsan, *American Running Horse,* 317.

28. Kirsan, *Sport Horse Breeder,* 26; Kirsan, *American Running Horse,* 319–30; Wallace, *American Stud-book;* Bruce, *American Stud Book.*

3. BLUE GRASS PARK AND TRANSYLVANIA PLANTATION

1. H. B. [Hamilton Busby], "Closing Notes of a September Holiday," *Turf, Field and Farm* 37 (October 4, 1872), 209–10 (quotation, 209).

2. Jensen, *Maryland Physicians,* 81–82; Jones, *History of Dorchester County,* 335–37; Cordell, *Medical Annals of Maryland,* 21–24, 53, 64, 464, 705; *Georgetown Telegraph* (Kentucky), March 19, 1812; Jones, *Keene Family History,* 202–5. Thomas B. Keene died at Georgetown in 1804.

3. Scott County (Kentucky) Deed Book B, 137–42, June 24, 1813, deed, William Shortridge, Deputy Sheriff, to William B. Keene (fragmentary, recopied from records burnt in 1837 courthouse fire; a replacement deed was issued in 1837 and is recorded in Deed Book N, 23–24).

4. Information on attendance at Transylvania from student files, Betty Jean Gooch, Special Collections Librarian, Transylvania University Library, to Gary O'Dell, personal communication, August 7, 2008; "Medical Obituary: William Richards, M.D.," *Western Journal of the Medical and Physical Sciences* 7 (June 30, 1833): 159–60 (quotation).

5. U.S. Bureau of Land Management, *Louisiana Tract Book 40* (Monroe District), 165. The sale date was recorded as March 15, 1828; Certificate No. 90, signed by Andrew Jackson, was issued during the following year by the U.S. General Land Office. Tract books and plat maps are housed by the Louisiana Office of State Lands at Baton Rouge and are also available through their online database, accessible at https://www.doa.la.gov/doa/osl/. The land certificates or patents are archived by the U.S. Bureau of Land Management as "General Land Office Records 1796–1907" and are available through their online database, accessible at http://www.glorecords.blm.gov/. For more information about the Land Act of 1820 and public land policies in Louisiana, see Treat, *National Land System,* and Poret, *History of Land Titles.* Carroll Parish was created from Ouachita Parish in 1838, and divided into East Carroll Parish and West Carroll Parish in 1877.

6. Pinkston, *Place to Remember,* 8–9, 237–40; *U.S. Tract Book* 40 (Monroe District), 71, 85, 87, 90, 93, 160, 165, 167, 169, 171.

7. Cohn, *King Cotton,* 103–17; Passell, "Cotton Land Distribution," 917–37.

8. Delcourt, "Presettlement Vegetation," 122–39; Clark, "Slave Trade," 331–42; Deyle, *Carry Me Back,* 44–45; 1850 U.S. Census, Slave Schedules.

9. Murphy, "Old Houses of East Carroll Parish," 1–2 (quotations, 1).

10. Gunn diaries, vol. 6, October 28, 1853, 178–81 (quotation, 179–80). The Thomas Butler Gunn diaries are archived at the Missouri History Museum in St. Louis, and are available online in their entirety through a link to LeHigh University in Bethlehem, Pennsylvania, https://pfaffs.web.lehigh.edu/node/60175.

11. Murphy, "Old Houses of East Carroll Parish," 3.

12. Gunn diaries, vol. 6, October 28, 1853, 182–83 (quotations).

13. Gunn diaries, vol. 6, November 2, 1853, 184 (first, second and fifth quotations), 187 (third and fourth quotations). Morris Keene was Keene Richards's second cousin and best friend, being the son of Thomas Keene, brother to Dr. William B. Keene. He was one year younger than Richards.

14. Gunn diaries, vol. 6, November 2, 1853, 183 (first quotation), 185 (second and third quotations); Yarema, *American Colonization Society,* 1–48.

15. Gunn diaries, vol. 6, November 3–12, 1853, 188–90. In 1860, Thomas Gunn was sent undercover by the editor of the *New York Evening Post* to Charleston, South Carolina, posing as a British correspondent from a London newspaper. He received a friendly reception from local elites because, at the time, the South viewed Great Britain as a potential ally. He kept a phony diary, should anyone search his room, and his actual reports on secession were sent to New York in the mail and published as columns in the *Post.* After the commencement of hostilities, Gunn was engaged as a war correspondent by the *New York Tribune* and covered the war until March 1863, when he returned to England to care for his sick father.

16. Woodman, *King Cotton;* Stephenson, "Ante-Bellum New Orleans," 161–74. The *Times-*

Picayune (New Orleans) for October 23, 1849, noting the arrival of the steamer *Courtland* from Louisville, reported Morris H. Keene, Wm. B. Keene, and J. Wallace Keene as passengers.

17. Agricultural statistics, U.S. Censuses of 1830, 1840, 1850; Hilgard, "Cotton Production in Louisiana"; Gray, *History of Agriculture,* 1:533; Menn, *Large Slaveholders of Louisiana,* 170–86. All economic adjustments in this book are derived from the online calculation tool available at "Inflation Calculator," U.S. Official Inflation Data, Alioth Finance, https://www.officialdata.org.

4. THE HORSE WHISPERER

1. Hamilton Busby, "Denton Offutt and His Book," *Turf, Field and Farm* 26 (January 4, 1878), 8 (quotation). A more complete biography of Offutt can be found in O'Dell, "Denton Offutt."

2. James S. Offutt, "Denton Offutt"; Offutt, *New and Complete System,* front matter (quotation); Townsend, *Lincoln and the Bluegrass,* 30–31. Both James S. Offutt and Townsend drew upon the same source, family records of Offutt descendant Martha B. Cheek of Lexington, for information about Denton Offutt's early life. Townsend, however, unlike James Offutt, placed Denton among the Offutt children who came to Kentucky with their parents in 1801—an error, given Denton Offutt's autobiographical statement as to his Kentucky birth.

3. Townsend, *Lincoln and the Bluegrass,* 30–45, 150–53; Library of Congress, Abraham Lincoln Papers, series 1, General Correspondence, 1833–1916, Abraham Lincoln (May–June, 1860), Autobiographical Notes; Library of Congress, Abraham Lincoln Papers, series 1, General Correspondence, 1833–1916, Howard, James Q., Biographical Notes, May 1860 (Abraham Lincoln); Herndon and Weik, *Herndon's Lincoln,* 72–86; Denton Offutt, "To People a Warning Against Swindlers in the Teaching of the Art of Taming Horses Selling a Book," *Spirit of the Times* 20 (June 25, 1859), 230; Denton Offutt, "Secret for Taming Vicious Horses, Etc.," *Spirit of the Times* 11 (September 18, 1841), 343 (quotation).

4. Offutt, "Secret for Taming Vicious Horses," 343 (quotation).

5. Library of Congress, Offutt, Denton, "Best and Cheapest Book on the Management of Horses, Mules, Etc.," Broadsheet (1843), Printed Ephemera Collection, portfolio 197, folder 34 (quotation); Offutt, *Method of Gentling Horses;* Offutt, *New and Complete System;* Offutt, *The Educated Horse,* 36–46; "Discoveries in Animal Physiology," *The Valley Farmer* 5 (April 1853), 144; Denton Offutt to Abraham Lincoln, September 7, 1859, and February 11, 1861, Library of Congress, Abraham Lincoln Papers, series 1, General Correspondence 1833–1916; Offutt, "To People a Warning"; Offutt, *The Educated Horse,* 36–46.

6. Offutt, *Method of Gentling Horses,* front matter; Offutt, *New and Complete System,* front matter (quotation); Busby, "Denton Offutt and His Book."

7. Offutt, "Best and Cheapest Book"; Library of Congress, Offutt, Denton, "Phrenology & Physiology of Animals," printed advertisement, Abraham Lincoln papers, series 1, General Correspondence. 1833–1916; Denton Offutt to Abraham Lincoln, September 7, 1859. The Henry Clay endorsement was also reprinted in "The Horse-Tamers in Court: Mr. Offutt's Suit Against Mr. Rarey," *New York Times,* February 5, 1861, 6. The address heading Clay's letter, "Ashland," does not refer to the city of Ashland, Kentucky, but to Clay's Lexington estate, which was named Ashland.

8. Offutt, "To People a Warning" (first quotation); Offutt, "Best and Cheapest Book" (second quotation); Busby, "Denton Offutt and His Book," (third quotation, 8); "Horse-Tamers in

Court," *New York Times,* February 5, 1861; "Rarey Compelled to Look After His Laurels," *Daily Milwaukee Press and News* 13 (February 8, 1861), 1.

9. Thomas B. Thorpe, "Rarey, the Horse Tamer," *Harper's New Monthly Magazine* 22 (April 1861), 616–18; Sara L. Brown, "Rarey, the Horse's Master and Friend," *Ohio Archaeological and Historical Quarterly* 25 (October 1916): 488–91; Busby, "Denton Offutt and His Book."

10. Rarey, *Art of Taming Wild Horses.* Rarey's practice of requiring a pledge of secrecy is noted in the preface to an 1858 edition published in Columbus. A complete publication history for Rarey's works, including pirated editions, can be found in Henderson, *Early American Sport,* 204–9.

11. Thorpe, "Rarey, the Horse-Tamer," 615–22; Brown, "Rarey, the Horse's Master and Friend," 491–99, 503–25.

12. "Look Out, England!" *Spirit of the Times* 29 (April 23, 1859), 26 (quotation).

13. Busby, "Denton Offutt and His Book," 8.

14. Brown, "Rarey, the Horse's Master and Friend," 525, 527; "Rarey the Horse-Tamer in New York," *Harper's Weekly* 5 (January 19, 1861), 36–37; *Denton Offutt v. John S. Rarey,* New York Supreme Court, index no. LJ1863024, Division of Old Records, New York County Clerk, New York, N.Y.; *Brooklyn Daily Eagle,* January 31, 1861; "The Secret of Horse-taming—Rarey's Case Before the Court," *New York Times,* February 2, 1861; Townsend, *Lincoln and the Bluegrass,* 263; Busby, "Denton Offutt and His Book," 8; "Sudden Death of Prof. J.S. Rarey," *New York Times,* October 8, 1866, 5.

15. Busby, "Denton Offutt and His Book," 8 (quotations); E. J. Edwards, "Robert Bonner," *American Monthly Review of Reviews* 20 (August 1899), 161–65.

16. Busby, "Denton Offutt and His Book," 8 (first and second quotations); Denton Offutt, "The Educated Horse" (first installment), *Turf, Field and Farm* 26 (January 11, 1878), 17–18 (third quotation, 17).

17. Offutt, *The Educated Horse,* 25 (quotation).

5. THE GRAND TOUR

1. "Paintings from the Holy Land," *Millennial Harbinger,* series 5, vol. 3 (August 1860), 455 (quotation).

2. Stone, *Barton Warren Stone,* 75–79; Stevenson, *Bacon College Story,* 7–16.

3. 1850 U.S. Decennial Census, including Slave Schedules; Harrison and Klotter, *New History of Kentucky,* 168–69.

4. Harrell, "Disciples of Christ," 191.

5. Jennings, *Disciples of Christ,* 286; Foster, *Life of Alexander Campbell,* xii (first quotation); Alexander Campbell, "The Crisis," *Millennial Harbinger,* series 1, vol. 1 (January 2, 1832), 86–88 (third quotation, 87); Alexander Campbell, "Tracts for the People," no. 33, "Tract for the People of Kentucky," *Millennial Harbinger,* series 3, vol. 4 (May 1849), 241–49; Alexander Campbell, "Tracts for the People," no. 8, "Our Position to American Slavery," *Millennial Harbinger,* series 3, vol. 2 (June 1845), 259 (second quotation); Fife, "Alexander Campbell," 23–100; Harrell, "Disciples of Christ," 191–92.

6. Gunn diaries, vol. 6, November 2, 1853, 186–87 (quotations); "Residence of A. K. Richards, Georgetown," *Spirit of the Times* 30 (July 28, 1860), 299.

7. Gunn diaries, vol. 6, November 2, 1853, 187 (first and second quotations), 196 (third and fourth quotations).

8. Power, *William Kimbrough Pendleton,* 133; Benjamin B. Bruce, "Death of Col. A. Keene Richards," *Kentucky Live Stock Record* 13 (March 26, 1881), 200; *General Catalogue of Princeton University,* 161; McAllister, *Bethany,* 456; "Report of Examinations," *Millennial Harbinger,* series 3, vol. 5 (September 1848), 531–34; Perrin, Battle, and Kniffin, *Kentucky: A History,* 831. The *Kentucky Live Stock Record* was renamed in 1895 as the *Thoroughbred Record,* under which name it was published until folding in 1990.

9. "Pickett's Administration," 149–50; "Graduating Classes," *Millennial Harbinger,* series 3, vol. 6 (August 1849), 466–67; "Appointment," *Millennial Harbinger*, series 5, vol. 1 (September 1858), 540; Keene Richards to John W. Keene, November 6, 1851, "News from Jerusalem," *Millennial Harbinger,* series 4, vol. 3 (June 1853), 357 (quotations); passport application for A. Keene Richards, February 17, 1851, "Passport Applications," NARA, roll 35.

10. Gunn diaries, vol. 6, October 4, 1853, 154 (quotations); "Report of Examinations," *Millennial Harbinger,* series 3, vol. 5 (September 1848), 533.

11. Morgan and Kellam genealogy obtained from the Familysearch website of the Genealogical Society of America, https://www.familysearch.org/en. Additional information was obtained from the U.S. Supreme Court case *Mellen v. Buckner* 139 U.S. 388 (1891). Gunn diaries, vol. 10, November 18, 1858, 13.

12. Boisseau, "Grand Tour," 1–2; Kilbride, *Being American in Europe,* 11.

13. "Obituary: Alexander Keene Richards," *New York Herald,* March 20, 1881 (quotation); Keene Richards to John W. Keene, November 6, 1851.

14. "Obituary: Alexander Keene Richards," *New York Herald,* March 20, 1881; Keene Richards to John W. Keene, November 6, 1851.

15. "Obituary: Alexander Keene Richards," *New York Herald,* March 20, 1881; Keene Richards to John W. Keene, November 6, 1851 (quotation).

16. "Obituary: Alexander Keene Richards," *New York Herald,* March 20, 1881; Keene Richards to William K. Pendleton, June 26, 1860, reprinted in *Millennial Harbinger,* series 5, vol. 3 (August 1860), 456 (quotation, emphasis in the original).

17. Richards, "The Arab Horses," 2; Bruce, "Death of Col. A. Keene Richards"; "Obituary: Alexander Keene Richards," *New York Herald,* March 20, 1881.

18. Bruce, "Death of Col. A. Keene Richards"; "Obituary: Alexander Keene Richards," *New York Herald,* March 20, 1881.

19. "Obituary: Alexander Keene Richards," *New York Herald,* March 20, 1881; Von Orlich, *Travels in India,* 14–17 (quotation, 16); Fahmy, *All the Pasha's Men,* 10. The description of the canja is from Head, *Life and Adventures of Bruce,* 58.

20. "Obituary: Alexander Keene Richards," *New York Herald,* March 20, 1881; Porter, *Handbook for Travellers in Syria,* xlix–1;"American Travelers in the East," *New York Journal of Commerce,* August 25, 1856. The three Roman provinces of Arabia were known as Arabia Petraea, Arabia Deserta (central and northern Arabia), and Arabia Felix (the modern region of Yemen).

21. "Obituary: Alexander Keene Richards," *New York Herald,* March 20, 1881.

22. Finkel, *Osman's Dream,* 413–57 (quotation).

23. Richards, "The Arab Horses," 2, 7; Keene Richards to William K. Pendleton, June 26, 1860, 456 (first quotation), 457 (second quotation); Coleman, *Light from the East,* 490 (third quotation); "Obituary: Alexander Keene Richards," *New York Herald,* March 20, 1881.

6. THE LAND OF ARABIAN HORSES

1. Durbin, *Observations in the East,* 2:48–61 (quotation, 50–51).

2. "Obituary: Alexander Keene Richards," *New York Herald,* March 20, 1881; Yusef Badra, Transylvania Plantation, Louisiana, to John Ross Browne, January 16, 1854, John Ross Brown Collection, Bancroft Library, University of California, Berkeley, California.

3. Browne, *Yusef,* 177–78 (first quotation, 178; second quotation, 177).

4. Blowers, "'Living in a Land of Prophets,'" 494–513; Lewis, "James Turner Barclay," 163–70; Barclay, *City of the Great King;* Burnet and Barclay, *Jerusalem Mission,* 111–19; Johnson, *Hadji in Syria,* 23–25 (quotation). Barclay refers to "Joseph Bodra" as "the faithful attendant of the unfortunate Molyneux, in defense of whom he had killed and wounded several Arabs, near the Dead Sea" (*Jerusalem Mission,* 123). In late August 1847, Lieutenant Thomas Howard Molyneux of the HMS *Spartan* led a brief expedition from Beirut to explore the Dead Sea using a dinghy from the ship transported for the purpose. He was accompanied by three seamen and a dragoman hired in Beirut to serve as guide and interpreter, and several skirmishes were fought with unfriendly Arabs. In his account of the journey Molyneux referred to his dragoman by name as "Toby." Whether Badra was in fact the dragoman Toby, and a recommendation from Molyneux was among his possessions, or this was a spurious claim intended to impress Barclay, cannot now be determined. See Molyneux, "Expedition to the Jordan," 104–30.

5. Browne, *Yusef,* 417–21.

6. Badra to Browne, January 16, 1854 (quotation). This letter, in conjunction with Browne's *Yusef,* contains important clues as to the chronology of Richards's activities in the Levant. The book states that Browne met Yusef on November 23, 1851, and was guided by him for a period "less than forty days," until Yusef's incarceration in Beirut, which would be in the first week of January 1852. Yusef, in his letter to Browne, states that a few days after Browne's departure from Beirut, he was freed by the pasha, and that "a few weeks after" his release he was engaged to "take some Horses to America for an American gentleman," first traveling with him to Palmyra. The pasha's concluding remarks referred to one of the "Turkish" bath houses in the city, built by the Ottomans.

7. Farley, *Resources of Turkey,* 229–32; Durbin, *Observations in the East,* 2:62–63; Walpole, *The Ansayrii, and the Assassins,* 94 (quotation).

8. "Obituary: Alexander Keene Richards," *New York Herald,* March 20, 1881.

9. Burton, *Romance of Isabel Lady Burton,* 393–95 (quotation, 394); Lovell, *Rebel Heart,* 155–56, 161.

10. Berman, *American Arabesque,* 21 (first quotation), 72–80; Ernst, *Following Muhammad,* 192 (second quotation).

11. "Obituary: Alexander Keene Richards," *New York Herald,* March 20, 1881; Lovell, *Rebel Heart,* 155–200; Burton, *Romance of Isabel Lady Burton,* 194.

12. Blunt, *Bedouin Tribes,* 1:371–76; Raswan, "Tribal Areas and Migration Lines," 494–502.

13. Badra to Browne, January 16, 1854; "Obituary: Alexander Keene Richards," *New York Herald,* March 20, 1881.

14. Badra to Browne, January 16, 1854; Coleman, *Light from the East,* 491; Browne, *Yusef,* 183 (first quotation), 312–13 (second quotation); Richards, "The Arab Horses," 2 (third quotation).

15. Coleman, *Light from the East,* 490–91; Badra to Browne, January 16, 1854.

16. "Cartoonist Favored by Sultan," *Evening Mail* (New York), June 7, 1906; Davenport, *Quest of the Arab Horse,* 9–18.

17. Davenport, *Quest of the Arab Horse,* 9–18 (quotation, 12).

18. Badra to Browne, January 16, 1854 (quotation). Although Badra was apparently fluent in spoken English, his long and chatty letter was probably dictated to Morris Keene, Richards's cousin, to which he appended his signature in Arabic script. Badra was still in Beirut on April 19, 1852, on which day he visited Bayard Taylor, an American traveler. See Taylor, *Lands of the Saracen,* 29.

19. Badra to Browne, January 16, 1854 (quotation); [Morris Keene], "The Late Arabian Importations," *Spirit of the Times* 26 (November 22, 1857), 482; Coleman, *Light from the East,* 491; Bruce, *American Stud Book,* 1:149.

20. [Keene], "The Late Arabian Importations," (quotation); Badra to Browne, January 16, 1854.

21. Badra to Browne, January 16, 1854 (quotations). During October 1907, President Theodore Roosevelt came to northeastern Louisiana, parking his private rail car on a siding at Stamboul Plantation, and spent two weeks hunting black bear in East Carroll and Madison parishes. He wrote about his experience here in the chapter titled "In the Louisiana Canebrakes" in his book *Outdoor Pastimes of an American Hunter,* 360–90.

22. John Ross Browne, New Orleans, to Lucy Browne, January 12 (quotation) and March 31, 1854, published in Browne, *J. Ross Browne,* 162, 169.

23. Browne, *Yusef,* 416 (quotation). In referring to Badra's weapons, Browne probably means "yataghan," a long, curved Turkish dagger, rather than "atagar" (atgeir, aetgar, ategar) since the latter was a short spear with a slightly curved blade used by medieval Scandinavian warriors.

24. Coleman, *Light from the East,* 491. Coleman stated that the Richards party departed Beirut for Smyrna, which strongly suggests a direct route by sea.

25. Durbin, *Observations in the East,* 2:101–9 (first quotation, 101; second quotation, 109).

26. "Obituary: Alexander Keene Richards," *New York Herald,* March 20, 1881; Burton, *Richard F. Burton,* 30 (quotation).

27. Hendricks, *Encyclopedia of Horse Breeds,* 328–29, 421–23; U.S. Bureau of Foreign Commerce, *Consular Reports,* 176,

28. Harter, *World Railways,* 135–70.

7. SETTING UP THE EXPERIMENT

1. "Arrival of the Crescent City," *Daily Picayune* (New Orleans), March 12, 1853; Gunn diaries, vol. 6., September 30–October 5, 1853, 130–55.

2. "Peytona," *Thoroughbred Heritage,* https://www.tbheritage.com/Portraits/Peytona.html.

3. *Spirit of the Times* 8 (May 19, 1838), 108; Anderson, *Making the American Thoroughbred,* 194–96.

4. Anderson, *Making the American Thoroughbred,* 197–202.

5. *Spirit of the Times* 9 (March 23, 1839), 30; Owen, *History of Alabama,* 3:987–88; Anderson, *Making the American Thoroughbred,* 124–26.

6. "The Great Peyton Stake," *Spirit of the Times* 13 (October 28, 1843), 411 (quotation).

7. Struna, "The North-South Races," 28–57.

8. Struna, "The North-South Races," 28–57; Eisenburg, *Great Match Race,* 25, 30 (first quotation), 149 (second quotation).

9. "Defeat of Fashion by Peytona," *Spirit of the Times* 15 (May 17, 1845), 34–35; Anderson, *Making the American Thoroughbred,* 208–10.

10. *Charleston Courier,* May 19, 1845 (quotations); "Defeat of Fashion," 34–35.

11. "Defeat of Fashion," 34–35; "Fashion Again a Winner!" *Spirit of the Times* 15 (May 24, 1845), 146; "Philadelphia and Camden Spring Races," *Spirit of the Times* 15 (May 31, 1845), 158; Hervey, *Racing in America,* 2:173–75.

12. Gunn diaries, vol. 6, November 13–16, 1853, 162–63 (quotations, 162).

13. Gunn diaries, vol. 6, October 16–19, 1853, 165–68.

14. Richards, *Catalogue of Blood Horses,* 5–6 (quotation, 6); *American Stud Book,* 1:248, 274, 295, 343, 359, 418.

15. "Memoir of Grey Eagle," *Spirit of the Times* 12 (June 18, 1842), 186–89; Hervey, *Racing in America,* 2:103, 122–23 (quotation, 123), 133, 221.

16. Richards, "The Arab Horses," 8; "Death of Old Glencoe," *Porter's Spirit of the Times* 3 (September 5, 1857), 13.

17. Wallace, *The Horse of America,* 65 (quotation).

18. Bruce, *American Stud Book,* 1:149, 2:189; Bruce, "Death of Col. A. Keene Richards," *Kentucky Live Stock Record* 13 (March 26, 1881), 200 (quotation).

19. Richards, "The Arab Horses," 2 (quotation).

20. George A. Feris to Randolph Huntington, November 30, 1887, quoted in Thornton Chard, "Keene Richards' Arabian Importations," part 1, 14; Dizikes, *Sportsmen and Gamesmen,* 144–45; Hervey, *Racing in America,* 2:189, 193, 238–39 (quotation, 238).

21. George A. Feris to Randolph Huntington, November 30, 1887.

22. Richard Ten Broeck, "Some Personal Reminiscences, Incidents and Anecdotes," *Spirit of the Times* 120 (December 27, 1890), 872–75; Hervey, *Racing in America,* 2:190–93, 239 (first quotation, 191; second quotation, 239).

23. Hervey, *Racing in America,* 2:292.

24. Hervey, *Racing in America,* 2:216–24; Herbert, *Forester's Horse and Horsemanship,* 276–83.

25. Hervey, *Racing in America,* 2:198; Stafford, *Wells Family of Louisiana,* 91–92; Eakin and Barber, *Rapides Parish,* 22, 30–31. Hervey incorrectly identifies Wellswood Plantation, owned by Monfort Well, as the site of Thomas J. Wells's equine operations. The outline of the former racetrack is today marked by an oval of scattered crepe myrtle trees at Dentley.

26. Hervey, *Racing in America,* 2:200–202; Bruce, *American Stud Book,* 2:240; Stafford, *Wells Family of Louisiana,* 92.

27. Hervey, *Racing in America,* 2:273–84; *Spirit of the Times* 23 (June 4, 1853), 186; *Spirit of the Times* 23 (June 11, 1853), 198; Ten Broeck, "Some Personal Reminiscences," 872 (quotation).

28. Hervey, *Racing in America,* 2:286–89.

29. Hervey, *Racing in America,* 2:289–90.

30. Hervey, *Racing in America,* 2:291–99 (quotation, 298).

31. Hervey, *Racing in America,* 2:300.

32. Danielle, "Dr. Geo. A. Feris," *Types of Successful Men of Texas,* 429.

33. George A. Feris to Randolph Huntington, December 1, 1887, quoted in Chard, "Keene Richards' Arabian Importations," part 2, 14–15 (first quotation, 14; second quotation, 15); stud bill for part-Arabian horses owned by Feris, with notations on reverse in Feris's handwriting,

dated November 20, 1887, reproduced in Chard, "Keene Richards' Arabian Importations," part 2, 23.

34. Lawrence, *The Horse,* 266 (first quotation); Rous, *Laws and Practice,* vii (second quotation).

35. Hervey, *Racing in America,* 2:239–40, 300. Lexington, who was progressively going blind, was permanently retired to stud after his race with Lecomte, and in the summer of 1856 was sold to Robert A. Alexander of Woodford County, Kentucky.

8. RETURN TO THE EAST

1. William T. Porter, "Animal Painting," *Spirit of the Times* 12 (March 12, 1842), 13 (first quotation); Coleman, *Three Kentucky Artists,* 53, 70–71; Mackay-Smith, *Race Horses of America,* xxviii (second quotation). Mackay-Smith provides an extended discussion of the characteristics of Troye's work (358–88) and a chronological list of all known paintings and drawings by the artist (409–36).

2. Mackay-Smith, *Race Horses of America,* 1–4; Keene Richards, "Death of Edward Troye, Esq.," *Georgetown Times* (Kentucky), July 29, 1874; Troye, *Troye's Oriental Paintings,* 1–2. An original copy of Troye's pamphlet could not be located but is photographically reproduced in its entirety in Mackay-Smith, *Race Horses of America,* 437–43.

3. Mackay-Smith, *Race Horses of America,* 51–59; "Animal Painting," advertisement by Edward Troye, *Lexington Intelligencer* (Kentucky), November 8, 1834.

4. Mackay-Smith, *Race Horses of America,* 90–97.

5. *Observer and Reporter* (Lexington, Kentucky), July 20, 1839; Mackay-Smith, *Race Horses of America,* 123–25.

6. Mackay-Smith, *Race Horses of America,* 127–28, 139–54.

7. Richards, "Death of Edward Troye, Esq.," *Georgetown Times* (Kentucky), July 29, 1874 (quotation).

8. Mackay-Smith, *Race Horses of America,* 168, 203–7 (quotation, 203).

9. Mackay-Smith, *Race Horses of America,* 422, 425, 426.

10. Richards, "The Arab Horses," 2 (quotation).

11. Layard, *Discoveries Among the Ruins,* 280–81 (first quotation, 280); Richards, "The Arab Horses," 2 (second quotation). Additional works consulted by Richards for information in preparation for his second trip to the East, according to his own statements, included: Burckhardt, *Notes on the Bedouins;* Drummond-Hay, *Western Barbary;* Sue, *The Godolphin Arabian;* Nolan, *Cavalry: Its History and Tactics;* and Charles J. Apperley, "Nimrod's German Tour," *The Sporting Magazine* 24 (September 1829), 321–29. Richards also noted having read Richard F. Burton's *Personal Narrative of a Pilgrimage to El-Medina and Meccah,* but as the first edition (London) was published in 1855, he may not have seen it until his return from the Levant. He probably also read many other authors whom he did not mention specifically.

12. Mackay-Smith, *Race Horses of America,* 174; Hervey, *Racing in America,* 2:302; passport application of Edward Troye, June 26, 1855, "Passport Applications," NARA, roll 51 (quotation).

13. Passport application of Maurice [Morris] Keene, April 24, 1855, "Passport Applications," NARA, roll 50; Browne, ed., *J. Ross Browne,* 159–60, 181, 182.

14. "Hadjee" [Morris Keene], "Arab Horses and Dromedaries for the United States," *Spirit of the Times* 26 (August 23, 1856), 326 (quotations).

15. *Journal of Edward Troye,* typescript, copy in Keeneland Library, Lexington, Kentucky, 10–11 (quotations, 10). The pages in Troye's journal are not in chronological sequence; it begins with his arrival in Constantinople, whereas the earlier visit to Paris is several pages further along. Page numbering in citations is that used internally (that of the original ms.), rather than the page numbers of the typescript. For quotations, I have inserted occasional punctuation for clarity but have left spelling as in the original transcript.

16. Troye, journal, 11 (quotations); Royle, *Great Crimean War,* 490–501; Baumgart, *Crimean War 1853–1856,* 211–16.

17. Finkel, *Osman's Dream,* 455–58; Grenville, *Europe Reshaped, 1848–1878,* 166–79; Baumgart, *Crimean War 1853–1856,* 3–8, 93–126; Royle, *Great Crimean War,* 15–133.

18. Baumgart, *Crimean War 1853–1856,* 121–65.

19. Troye, journal, 12–13 (quotation, 12).

20. Troye, journal, 13–14 (quotations, 13).

21. Troye, journal, 1, 14, 19–20.

22. Troye, journal, 1–3, 20–22. According to *Murray's Hand-Book for Travellers in the Ionian Islands, Greece, Turkey, Asia Minor and Constantinople,* 171, European travelers to Constantinople "land at the Custom-house quay, which is much encumbered by bales of goods."

23. Hornby, *Constantinople During the Crimean War,* 35–36 (quotations, 35).

24. *Hand-Book for Travellers in the Ionian Islands,* 171; "Some Account of Constantinople," *The Saturday Magazine,* supplement 657 (September 1842), 121–28; Karpat, "Istanbul in the Nineteenth Century," 272–78.

25. Hornby, *Constantinople During the Crimean War,* 34 (first quotation); Thornbury, *Turkish Life and Character,* 1:48–49 (second quotation).

26. Troye, journal, 5–6, 23; Dicey, *The Morning Land,* 1:121; White, *Three Years in Constantinople,* 1:12–13.

27. Thornbury, *Turkish Life and Character,* 2:169–71 (quotation, 170).

28. Troye, journal, 14 (quotation); [Henry Wood], "Letter from Syria," *New York Journal of Commerce,* August 28, 1856.

29. Wood, "Letter from Syria," (quotations).

30. Troye, journal, 7; Russell, *The War,* 167–252.

31. Troye, journal, 9 (quotation). According to information provided on the website of Ferrylines.com, travel time at sea by conventional ferry from Istanbul to Sevastopol in the modern era is about thirty-two hours. Steamship travel during the mid-nineteenth century was probably very similar in duration.

32. Russell, *The War,* 175–78.

33. Russell, *The War,* 179 (first quotation), 191–220.

34. Troye, journal, 8 (first quotation); Russell, *The War,* 209, 257 (second quotation); Wood, "Letter from Syria," (third quotation).

35. "Death of Yusef," *Georgetown Herald* (Kentucky), December 20, 1855; Wood, "Letter from Syria," (quotation).

36. Richards, "The Arab Horses," 2 (first and second quotations); Wood, "Letter from Syria" (third quotation); Mackay-Smith, *Race Horses of America,* 175, 425 (fourth quotation).

37. Wood, "Letter from Syria," (quotation).

38. Troye, *Troye's Oriental Paintings,* 2. This pamphlet, issued to visitors to an exhibition at Odd Fellows Hall, New Orleans, in April 1857 notes the outfitting of Troye's studio in Damas-

cus. Wood, "Letter from Syria"; Lovell, *Rebel Heart,* 187–205; Jane Elizabeth Digby, October 24, 1855, bound diary, September 1855–July 1881, Minterne House Collection, Dorset, Great Britain (quotation). The diary entry was provided through the courtesy of Mary S. Lovell.

39. Mackay-Smith, *Race Horses of America,* 176, 426; Troye, *Troye's Oriental Paintings,* 5; Wood, "Letter from Syria," (quotations). Jane Digby was in fact a gifted artist, and her sketchbooks are filled with many excellent pencil drawings of landscapes in the Middle East (Lovell, *Rebel Heart,* figures 29–31).

40. Wood, "Letter from Syria," (quotation).

41. Wood, "Letter from Syria." My interpretation of events, in which Richards left Syria very early and returned home, differs significantly from that of other writers, notably Troye's biographer, Alexander Mackay-Smith (1981), who assumed that the three men remained together for the duration of the visit to the East. It is quite clear that only Morris Keene accompanied Troye on a long expedition through the desert beginning in February 1856; Troye's journal states that he was in company with "Mr. Keene," and makes no mention of Richards. The consul, Henry Wood, in his letter to the *Journal of Commerce,* stated that one of the three men returned home after visiting Baalbec and Damascus, "committing his enterprise to a friend who accompanied him, and the other two, after spending eight months in Damascus, Palestine, on the shores of the Dead Sea, and in the Desert, left a short time since for America." Since Morris Keene was definitely with Troye during these journeys, the one who returned home must have been Keene Richards.

42. Troye, journal, 26–27; Conder, *Palestine, or the Holy Land.*

43. Keene, "Arab Horses and Dromedaries"; Troye, journal, 32 (quotation); Cumpston and Bates, *Percussion Pistols and Revolvers,* 84–89; Taffin, *Gun Digest Book,* 11–14. It is not clear what Troye meant by a "Remic" rifle; possibly he was referring to the Minié rifles.

44. Duckers, *British Military Rifles,* 16–18; Bilby, *Civil War Firearms,* 42–71; Nosworthy, *Bloody Crucible of Courage,* 27–34 et passim.

45. Wishart, *Fur Trade,* 18–19; Berman, *American Arabesque,* 99.

46. Troye, journal, 27–37.

47. Troye, journal, 37–38.

48. Troye, journal, 37–47 (quotations, 40, 45).

9. BARGAINING WITH BEDOUINS

1. Wood, "Letter from Syria" (quotations).

2. Keene, "Arab Horses and Dromedaries," (first quotation); Porter, *Giant Cities of Bashan,* 17 (second quotation).

3. Wood, "Letter from Syria."

4. Tristram, *Bible Places,* 305–54; Aharoni, *Land of the Bible,* 36–42; Ben-Arieh, "Geographies of the Holy Land," 69–79.

5. Collelo, *Syria: A Country Study,* 74–77; Porter, *Five Years in Damascus,* 271–72 (first quotation, 271); Libbey and Hoskins, *Jordan Valley and Petra,* 1:107 (second and third quotations). On the biblical fertility of Bashan and Gilead, see, for example, Numbers 32:1–42; Deuteronomy 3:12–17; Jeremiah 50:19; Micah 7:14 (KJV).

6. Wood, "Letter from Syria," (quotations). In his biography of Troye, Mackey-Smith associates Troye and Keene's description of the grasslands and numerous ruined cities in

Wood's letter with their earlier journey along the Jordan River valley to the Dead Sea. It is clear, however, from the context, that they were referring to their later travel through Bashan, particularly in the reference to the ruins of Gadara, located east of the Sea of Galilee. See Mackay-Smith, *Race Horses of America*, 176–77.

7. Silberman, "Desolation and Restoration," 76–87.

8. Porter, *Giant Cities of Bashan*, 49 (first quotation), see also 49–55, 69–70, 80–81; Silberman, "Desolation and Restoration," 81 (second quotation); Rodinson, *Mystique of Islam*, 11–13. Additional biblical references to the desolation of the Holy Land include Isaiah 24:3; Leviticus 26:31–35; Deuteronomy 29:22–28.

9. Schumacher, *The Jaulân*, 1–4, 9–12.

10. Wood, "Letter from Syria"; Ball, *Rome in the East*, 181–82, 196–97; Parker, "Decapolis Reviewed," 437–41; Kulling and Vasudevan, "Gadara," 284–86.

11. Wood, "Letter from Syria," (quotations).

12. Wood, "Letter from Syria," (first quotation); Keene, "Arab Horses and Dromedaries," (second quotation). The tribes from which horses were purchased, sometimes named, more commonly indicated only as northern or southern Anizah, were noted in Richards, "The Arab Horses," and Keene, "Arab Horses and Dromedaries."

13. Burckhardt, *Notes on the Bedouins*, 1:1–3 (first quotation, 2; second quotation, 2–3), 32–33.

14. Addison, *Journey to the East*, 2:112; Blunt, *Bedouin Tribes*, 1:43–46, 363–65; Schumacher, *Across the Jordan*, 108–9.

15. Richards, "The Arab Horses," 2; Keene, "Arabian Importations"; Burckhardt, *Notes on the Bedouins*, 23–24; Upton, *Gleanings from the Desert*, 233; Post, "Races and Relations of Syria," 182.

16. Merrill, *East of the Jordan*, 492 (first quotation); J. W. Thompson, "Horse-Dealing in Syria, 1854," Part 2, *Blackwood's Edinburgh Magazine* 86 (October 1859), 420–21 (second quotation, 421). Merrill (1837–1909) was the U.S. consul at Jerusalem in 1882–1885, 1891–1893, and 1898–1907. Captain Thompson was assistant to the expert cavalryman Captain Louis E. Nolan in this endeavor, author of *Cavalry: Its History and Tactics*. Together the two men managed to acquire and ship nearly three hundred Arabian and part-Arabian horses and a few mules to Varna, Bulgaria, by July, for use in the Crimea. Very likely, some of these horses along with their riders were subsequently slaughtered at Balaklava on October 25, 1854, during the ill-fated charge of the Light Brigade. Nolan was responsible for launching the charge and, killed by shrapnel, was the first casualty. Moyse-Bartlett, *Louis Edward Nolan*, 158–74, 215–21.

17. Keene, "Arab Horses and Dromedaries," (quotations).

18. Wallace, *The Horse of America*, 65 (first quotation); Wood, "Letter from Syria," (second, third, and fifth quotations); Burckhardt, *Notes on the Bedouins*, 1:57–65 (fourth quotation, 64).

19. Upton, *Newmarket and Arabia*, 156 (quotation). For a good discussion of beliefs concerning Arabian horses during the first half of the nineteenth century, see Ammon's *Historical Reports*, published in 1834.

20. Schofler, *Flight Without Wings*, 3–4, 10–12; Forbis, *Classic Arabian Horse*, 274–89.

21. Schofler, *Flight Without Wings*, 10; Keene, "Arab Horses and Dromedaries"; Burckhardt, *Notes on the Bedouins*, 2:57–58 (quotation, 58). Names and terms in the Arabic language were necessarily rendered phonetically by English writers, so there was considerable variety in the spelling of the Arabian bloodlines. For example, the "Sacklowee" referred to by Morris Keene

was written as "Sacklowie" by Keene Richards, "Sakláwye" by Burckhardt, "Seglawee" by Upton, and "Seglawi" by Lady Ann Blunt.

22. Burckhardt, *Notes on the Bedouins,* 2:56; Roger D. Upton, "Arabian Horses, Studied in their Native Country in 1874–75," *Fraser's Magazine* 14 (September 1876), 401 (first quotation); Keene, "Arab Horses and Dromedaries," (second quotation).

23. Keene, "Arab Horses and Dromedaries," (quotations); Burckhardt, *Notes on the Bedouins,* 2:60–61.

24. Keene, "Late Arabian Importations," (quotations); Richards, "The Arab Horses," 4. The bloodline for Fysaul is a little uncertain; Morris Keene noted that he was "Coyhelan," whereas Keene Richards described his line as "pure Sacklowie," but also noted that the "Koheyl" was often crossed with the Sacklowie. These contradictory statements are probably the reason why the *American Stud Book* (1:144) attributes a Keheilan-Seglawi mix to this horse. Strictly speaking, Fysaul's family association, according to Bedouin custom, would be that of the dam, but this has not been recorded.

25. Richards, "The Arab Horses," 4–5 (quotations); Keene, "Late Arabian Importations."

26. Blunt, *Bedouin Tribes,* 1:345, 382, 426; Lancaster, *The Rwala Bedouin Today,* 8–9. At the time of the Blunts' visit (1877–1878), the Rwala had just been soundly defeated in a war they had instigated against the Sba'a; see Blunt, *Bedouin Tribes,* 1:59–63, 311–12.

27. Upton, "Arabian Horses," 389; Blunt, *Bedouin Tribes,* 1:426, 437; Forbis, *Classic Arabian Horse,* 131–34.

28. Richards, "The Arab Horses," 7 (first quotation); Keene, "Late Arabian Importations," (second quotation).

29. Burckhardt, *Notes on the Bedouins,* 1:10 (first quotation); Upton, "Arabian Horses," 389; Blunt, *Bedouin Tribes,* 2:190 (second quotation).

30. Keene, "Late Arabian Importations," (quotation); Burckhardt, *Notes on the Bedouins,* 1:209–11; Blunt, *Bedouin Tribes,* 1:430.

31. Wood, "Letter from Syria," (quotations); Sanders Bruce, "Death of Edward Troye," *Turf, Field and Farm* 19 (August 7, 1874), 100.

32. Troye, *Troye's Oriental Paintings,* 3 (quotation).

33. Troye, *Troye's Oriental Paintings,* 3 (first quotation); Keene, "Arab Horses and Dromedaries," (second and third quotations).

34. Wood, "Letter from Syria," (quotation); Keene, "Arab Horses and Dromedaries."

35. Keene, "Arab Horses and Dromedaries"; Keene, "Late Arabian Importations," (quotations); *American Stud Book,* 1:149. The Dongolese are Nubian people of northern Sudan, at the time ruled by Egypt.

36. Mackay-Smith, *Race Horses of America,* 177, 184, 426.

37. Keene, "Arab Horses and Dromedaries"; Mackay-Smith, *Race Horses of America,* 192; Bruce, "Death of Edward Troye"; "Paintings from the Holy Land," *Millennial Harbinger,* series 5, vol. 3 (August 1860), 455. The final versions of his Oriental paintings, executed in Antwerp, were quite large: *Bazaar in Damascus* (84 by 64 inches); *Sea of Tiberias or Galilee* (66 by 44 inches); *River Jordan—Bethabara* (66 by 44 inches); *The Dead Sea* (120 by 72 inches); and *The Syrian Ploughman* (120 by 72 inches).

38. "Arrival of Mr. Troye, the Artist," *Porter's Spirit of the Times* 1 (January 24, 1857), 337 (first quotation); "Mr. Troye, the Artist," *Spirit of the Times* 26 (January 31, 1857), 606 (second, third, and fourth quotations); Mackay-Smith, *Race Horses of America,* 238 (fifth quotation). The

weekly sporting newspaper *Spirit of the Times* was known by three different names during its history, and in fact, for a brief time, all three were published simultaneously in competition against one another. In 1856, the original *Spirit of the Times,* founded in 1831 by John T. Porter, was acquired in a hostile takeover by John Richards, and Porter, sponsored by George Wilkes, began to publish a competing paper known as *Porter's Spirit of the Times.* In 1859, George Wilkes withdrew from the partnership with Porter and began to publish *Wilkes' Spirit of the Times.* Neither *Porter's* nor the original *Spirit,* both of which had mainly a southern subscriber base, survived the beginning of the Civil War, leaving *Wilkes' Spirit of the Times* alone in the field after 1861 until the advent in 1863 of a new and similar journal, *Turf, Field and Farm,* edited by former Lexington, Kentucky, resident Hamilton Busby and published in New York. See Wallace, *The Horse of America,* 97–99, in this regard.

39. Richards, "The Arab Horses," 8; *American Stud Book,* 1:150 (first quotation); Keene, "Arab Horses and Dromedaries," (second quotation); Keene, "Late Arabian Importations," (remaining quotations); "Residence of A. Keene Richards," *Spirit of the Times* 30 (July 28, 1860), 300.

40. Edward Troye, *Paintings of the Holy Land;* Mackay-Smith, *Race Horses of America,* 192–202; Richards, "Death of Edward Troye"; Troye, *The Dead Sea,* dedication (quotation). A copy of the shorter version of the New York exhibition pamphlet, *Troye's Oriental Paintings,* archived at Yale University Library, has a label affixed across the front stating "Alumni Hall, Yale College, Entrance on High Street," indicating that an exhibition was also made at New Haven, Connecticut.

10. BECOMING A HORSEMAN

1. *American Stud Book,* 1:149, 295, 343, 2:189, 274, 418.

2. Richards, *Catalogue of Blood Horses,* 8; *American Stud Book,* 2:367, 3:324; Mackay-Smith, *Race Horses of America,* 184–85.

3. George A. Feris to Randolph Huntington, December 2 and 3, 1887, letters quoted in Chard, "Arabian Importations," part 1, 15–17 (first and second quotations, 16; third quotation, 17); Chard, "Arabian Importations," part 1, note 21, and reproduction of marginal notes by Huntington on these letters; *American Stud Book,* 1:150. Information on the death of Hamdan was written by Feris on the back of a crayon copy of an oil painting of Hamdan (the original destroyed in a fire), a photograph of which was supplied by Feris's daughter, S. Lavinia Feris, to Randolph Huntington, and quoted in Chard, "Arabian Importations," part 1, 17. The article "The Arabian Horse in Texas," *Galveston Daily News,* March 31, 1877, states that Hamdan died in 1861, but this is probably an error.

4. *American Stud Book,* 1:149, 2:189, 3:131; Richards, "The Arab Horses," 4; Herbert, *Forester's Horse and Horsemanship,* 1:354–57. Spencer Borden, in *The Arab Horse* (1906), 84, and in "No Clay-Arab Mixture," *The Country Gentleman* 69 (September 22, 1904), 870, asserts that Richards imported the Arabian mare Zilcaadi, grandsire of the famed Kentucky Morgan horse Dorsey's Golddust. This is an error. Zilcaadi was one of four Arabian stallions presented by Sultan Mohmond in 1830 to Charles S. Rhind, U.S. consul to Constantinople, and subsequently sold at auction in New York; see Brenda L. Tippin, "Golddust: Rare Line of the Gifford Family," *The Morgan Horse* 77 (June/July 2018), 58–59, 64–65, 68, 72–77.

5. O'Dell, "Under Siege," 397; Mooney, *Race Horse Men,* 3–9 (first quotation, 6), 38–40 (second quotation, 40), 44; Hotaling, *Great Black Jockeys,* 13, 69–73, 77, 106–7.

6. Hervey, *Racing in America,* 250; Keene, "Late Arabian Importations."

7. Mooney, *Race Horse Men,* 12 (first quotation), 44–50 (second quotation, 50).

8. *Porter's Spirit of the Times* 2 (March 14, 1857), 111 (quotation).

9. "The U.S. Agricultural Society, Fifth Annual Fair," *Louisville Daily Journal,* September 5, 1857 (first quotation); "The U.S. Agricultural Exhibition," *New York Times,* September 5, 1857; "United States Agricultural Society: Fifth Annual Fair at Louisville," *Spirit of the Times* 27 (September 19, 1857), 374 (second quotation).

10. *Porter's Spirit of the Times* 4 (March 20, 1858), 145 (quotation).

11. Richards, "The Arab Horses," 8 (quotation).

12. Hervey, *Racing in America,* 2:107, 204, 205; Mackay-Smith, *Race Horses of America,* 76.

13. Hervey, *Racing in America,* 2:143–49.

14. Hervey, *Racing in America,* 2:139–42; *Spirit of the Times* 18 (February 26, 1848), 6; *Spirit of the Times* 18 (May 6, 1848), 126.

15. Abe Buford, "Death of Old Gipsey—Sale of Glencoe," *Porter's Spirit of the Times* 2 (July 4, 1857), 285 (first quotation); Richards, "The Arab Horses," 7, 8 (second quotation).

16. Mackay-Smith, *Race Horses of America,* 238–41.

17. Mackay-Smith, *Race Horses of America,* 143 (first and second quotations); A. Keene Richards, "Death of Old Glencoe," *Porter's Spirit of the Times,* September 5, 1857, 13 (third, fourth, and fifth quotations); "Glencoe and His Grave," *Turf, Field and Farm* 15 (October 25, 1872), 264; *Turf, Field and Farm* 57 (August 4, 1893), 99 (sixth quotation); "Breeding Establishments of Kentucky: A. Keene Richards' Stud," *Spirit of the Times* 18 (July 11, 1868), 370 (seventh quotation); Anderson, *Making the American Thoroughbred,* 218.

18. Jensen, *Maryland Physicians,* 82; Will of William B. Keene, September 27, 1856, Scott County (Kentucky) Will Book M, 666–70, probated May 1856. Alexander's wife, Julia (Morgan) Keene, remarried on October 18, 1856, to her cousin, Oliver T. Morgan. Her father, Oliver J. Morgan, was one of the largest land and slave holders in northern Louisiana. His plantations bordered Transylvania and other Keene properties to the west and south.

19. Will of William B. Keene (quotations); 1860 U.S. Census, Slave Schedules, Carroll Parish, Louisiana, NARA, microfilm archive, M653, roll 427. The Mounds Plantation was located on Sections 20, 27–29 of Township 20 North, Range 12 E, about three miles west of present-day Transylvania, Louisiana.

20. Will of William B. Keene. The separate section specified in Keene's will is identified as Section 13, Township 20 S, Range 12 E, "district north Red River." This is obviously a misprint, since the coordinates place the location on Atchafalaya Bay on the Gulf coast of Louisiana, far removed from the north Red River. The correct location is Section 13, Township 20 N, Range 12 E. On the 1853 La Tourrette map of Louisiana, this section is labeled as the property of "Dr. Wm. B. Keene," La Tourette, State of Louisiana.

21. *Observer and Reporter* (Lexington, Kentucky), October 24, 1857; Connelley and Coulter. *History of Kentucky,* 4:310.

22. "Residence of A. Keene Richards," 299 (quotation).

23. "Residence of A. Keene Richards," 299 (first quotation); Hamilton Busby, "Closing Notes of a September Holiday," *Turf, Field and Farm* 37(October 4, 1872), 209–10 (second quotation, 210), Bruce, "A. Keene Richards," *Turf, Field and Farm* 32 (March 25, 1881), 184.

24. Scott County (Kentucky) Deed Book T, September 15, 1845, 172; Scott County (Ken-

tucky) Deed Book 3, October 14, 1857, 375; Scott County (Kentucky) Deed Book 5, December 1, 1859, 254.

25. "Residence of A. Keene Richards" (quotations, 300).

26. "Breeding Establishments of Kentucky," 370; "Residence of A. Keene Richards," 299; "Visit to A.K. Richards' Racing Stables, Near Georgetown, Ky.," *Wilkes' Spirit of the Times* 1 (January 21, 1860), 306 (first, second, third, and fourth quotations); Richards, *Catalogue of Blood Horses,* 10 (fifth quotation). The presence of the training stables and racetrack on the Ross tract is noted in Scott County (Kentucky) Mortgage Book 4, October 6, 1871, 32.

27. "Breeding Establishments of Kentucky: A. Keene Richards' Stud," 370 (quotation); H.B. [Hamilton Busby], "Sad Recollections," in William O. Gaines, B.O. *Gaines History of Scott County,* vol. 2 (Georgetown, Ky.: B.O. Gaines Printery, 1905), 446; Mackay-Smith, *Race Horses of America,* 403. "Residence of A. Keene Richards," 300. The *Louisville Courier-Journal* for March 22, 1881, states in "Keene Richards" that Troye's studio was next to Richards's home and was burned in the same fire that destroyed the house in 1879; they may have confused the studio with the house built for Pompey, then deceased. I have relied primarily on Busby's eyewitness description of the farm layout in Gaines's 1905 *History of Scott County,* written after Richards's death: Traveling "from the training stable near the centre of Blue Grass Park to the gate which opens on the road at the mouth of the Royal Spring. First you pass the old studio of Troye, a circular building. . . . Next we pass a stable . . . which was the imperial home of the Knight of St. George. . . . A little further on is the ruin of the family mansion" (446). Busby was a frequent visitor to Blue Grass Park.

28. "Visit to A. K. Richards' Racing Stables," 306 (quotation); "Residence of A. K. Richards, Georgetown," 300.

29. "Residence of A. K. Richards, Georgetown," 300 (first quotation). "Visit to A. K. Richards' Racing Stables," 306 (second quotation).

30. "Visit to A. K. Richards' Racing Stables," 306 (quotations).

31. "Love for the Horse," *New Orleans Daily Democrat,* July 6, 1879 (first quotation); "Georgetown, Ky, Spring Meeting," *Wilkes' Spirit of the Times* 6 (June 7, 1862), 219 (second quotation).

32. "A. Keene Richards," *Turf, Field and Farm* 32 (March 25, 1881), 184 (first quotation); "Sale of Blood Stock Belonging to A. K. Richards," *Wilkes' Spirit of the Times* 3 (October 13, 1860), 85 (second quotation); "Death of Yusef," *Georgetown Herald,* December 20, 1855 (third quotation); "Residence of A. Keene Richards," 299–300.

33. Whayne, Deblack, and Sabo, *Arkansas: A Narrative History,* 140–41.

34. U.S. Bureau of Land Management, "General Land Office Records 1796–2015," Ancestry.com. Richard M. Johnson and Leonidas L. Johnson each obtained dozens of Arkansas land parcels, too numerous to list here. Whitley, *Kentucky Ante-Bellum Portraiture,* 563, 565, 570.

35. Phillips County (Arkansas) Deed Book Q, September 28, 1859, deed, Leonidas L. Johnson and Irene E. Johnson to A. Keene Richards and Sallie Richards, 507 (first quotation); Scott County (Kentucky) Mortgage Book 3, October 13, 1866, Mortgage, A. Keene Richards to Harvey C. Graves, 250–51 (second quotation, 251). The technical description of the 1,760 acres in Arkansas is sections 24, 25, and the north half and southwest quarter of 36, Township 2 South, Range 3 East.

36. Denhardt, *Foundation Dams,* 34; *American Turf Register* (1857), 3, 13, 14, 28.

37. *American Turf Register* (1858), 5, 12, 26, 27, 34, 35, 36, 37. The *American Stud Book,* 1:486, states that Glycera was bred by A. Keene Richards, foaled in 1855. This seems unlikely because of the chronology involved. The dam, Sister to Pryor #1, bred by Ten Broeck, could not have been acquired by Richards as early as 1854.

11. THE "AMERICAN INVASION" OF ENGLAND

1. Hervey, *Racing in America,* 2:263; Thomas B. Merry, "Ten Broeck's Great Coup," *Thoroughbred Record* 88 (November 30, 1918), 254; Walter S. Vosburgh, "The Passing of Jerome Park," *Outing* 38 (August 1901), 518–91; *Spirit of the Times* 111 (April 3, 1886), 298.

2. "American Horses for England," 367; Herbert, *Forester's Horse and Horsemanship,* 312, 322, 345–52; Hervey, *Racing in America,* 2:300.

3. "American Race Horses Going to Europe," *New York Herald,* July 10, 1856; "Death of Lecomte and Pryor," *Spirit of the Times* 27 (December 5, 1857), 510; Bird, *Admiral Rous,* 200; "Littlefield, Once Noted Jockey, Dead," *New York Times* (July 9, 1915), 9; "The American Horses in England," *Spirit of the Times* 27 (April 25, 1857), 126; "The English Turf and American Horses," *Spirit of the Times* 27 (May 2, 1857), 138.

4. Dizikes, *Sportsmen and Gamesmen,* 123–29.

5. Dizikes, *Sportsmen and Gamesmen,* 123–29; Ten Broeck, "Some Personal Reminiscences," 873 (quotation).

6. Dizikes, *Sportsmen and Gamesmen,* 123–29; Chambers and Chambers, *Chamber's Encyclopaedia,* 799; Ten Broeck, "Some Personal Reminiscences," 873 (quotation). See also Rous, *Laws and Practice,* passim.

7. Earl of Suffolk and Berkshire [Henry Charles Howard], "Ascot Reminiscences," *Badminton Magazine of Sports and Pastimes* 1 (September 1895), 177–78 (first quotation, 177); Ten Broeck, "Some Personal Reminiscences," 872–73 (second quotation, 873).

8. Salvatore [pseud. for John Hervey], "Barbarity and the Two Umpires—Lexington's Half-Brother and the Irishman," *Thoroughbred Record* 121 (March 30, 1935), 212 (quotations). See William J. Minor, "Age of the Race-Horse Pryor," *Spirit of the Times* 27 (April 4, 1857), 91, and various issues of *Spirit of the Times* during the period for examples of the attacks on Ten Broeck.

9. Hervey, *Racing in America,* 2:325; Sanders D. Bruce, *Horse-Breeder's Guide and Hand-Book* (New York: Turf, Field and Farm, 1883), 198, 200.

10. "Our Horses in England," *Spirit of the Times* 27 (June 13, 1857), 210; "Mr. Richard Ten Broeck," *Baily's Magazine of Sports and Pastimes* 8 (May 1864), 56; *Spirit of the Times* 111 (April 3, 1886), 298; Merry, "Ten Broeck's Great Coup"; Anon., "Richard Ten Broeck," *Bailey's Monthly Magazine of Sports and Pastimes* 8 (May 1864), 56 (first and second quotations); "The Late Wm. Brown and Parole," *Turf, Field and Farm* 72 (March 28, 1903), 295–96 (third quotation).

11. Woodruff, *Trotting Horses of America,* 88; "The Turf of 1854," *New York Times* (May 1, 1854), 1; *American Turf Register* (1854), 3, 4, 12, 13, 25, 28, 30; DuBose, *Notable Men of Alabama,* 384; Fry, *Memories of Old Cahaba,* 67; Custance, *Riding Recollections,* 14–15; Nicholson, *Notorious John Morrissey,* 67–69.

12. John Hervey, "Barbarity and the Two Umpires," *Thoroughbred Record* 121 (March 30, 1935), 212; Hervey, *Racing in America,* 2:284; "The American Horses in England, 1860," *American Turf Register* (1860), 76; Custance, *Riding Recollections,* 15.

13. Custance, *Riding Recollections,* 14 (first quotation); Edward Spencer, "The Old Style and the New," *Fores's Sporting Notes and Sketches* 20 (1903), 162–63 (second and third quotations, 162).

14. "The American Horses in England," *American Turf Register* (1857), 58–59; "Death of Lecomte and Pryor."

15. Ten Broeck, "Some Personal Reminiscences," 873 (quotations).

16. Ten Broeck, "Some Personal Reminiscences," 873; Merry, "Ten Broeck's Great Coup"; Bird, *Admiral Rous,* 200; *American Turf Register* (1857), 29.

17. Merry, "Ten Broeck's Great Coup," 254 (quotation).

18. "Foreign Sporting Intelligence," *Spirit of the Times* 27 (August 15, 1857), 319 (quotations); *American Stud Book* 2:290; *American Turf Register* (1857), 58–59; Merry, *American Thoroughbred,* 101–2.

19. "An English Turfman on Ten Broeck's Tactics," *Wilkes' Spirit of the Times* 1 (September 10, 1859), 11; *American Stud Book*, 1:479–80, 482; Mackay-Smith, *Race Horses of America,* 258.

20. Bruce, "Death of Col. A. Keene Richards"; *American Stud Book,* 2:240; *American Turf Register* (1858), 12–14; *American Turf Register* (1859), 3.

21. *American Turf Register* (1859), 56–57; *American Stud Book,* 1:163; Hervey, *Racing in America,* 2:277–78.

22. "Sporting Intelligence," *New York Herald,* September 12, 1859; Satellite, "Stock on the Farm of A. Keene Richards," *Wilkes' Spirit of the Times* 2 (July 28, 1860), 327 (quotations).

23. Ten Broeck, "Some Personal Reminiscences," 873–75; Hervey, "Barbarity and the Two Umpires," 211–13; *Famous Horses of America,* 15; "Mr. Richard Ten Broeck," 57.

24. Ten Broeck, "Some Personal Reminiscences," 873–75 (quotation, 873); "Starke the Winner of the Goodwood Cup," *New York Times* (August 17, 1861), 3; *Famous Horses of America,* 19.

25. Ten Broeck, "Some Personal Reminiscences," 873–75; Merry, "Ten Broeck's Great Coup"; "Marriages," *London Times* (June 23, 1857), 1.

26. Hervey, *Racing in America,* 2:252.

27. Hervey, *Racing in America,* 2:265–68.

28. Hervey, "Barbarity and the Two Umpires," 211; *Spirit of the Times* 111 (April 3, 1886), 298; "Death of John A. Morris," *New York Times,* May 27, 1895, 1; Paul Cervin, "The Valley of the Pedernales," *Turf and Sport Digest* 11 (September 1934), 26–28; Di Brino, *History Morris Park Racecourse,* 2–3; Vosburgh, *Racing in America,* 13.

29. Rollins, *Hurstbourne Country Club,* 15–16; Ten Broeck, "Some Personal Reminiscences," 873–75; Merry, "Ten Broeck's Great Coup."

12. SOME NEW BLOOD

1. Busby, "Denton Offutt and His Book," (quotations).

2. Busby, "Residence of A. Keene Richards," 300; Satellite, "Stock on the Farm of A. Keene Richards," 327; *American Stud Book,* 1:100; Merry, *American Thoroughbred,* 40, 50.

3. Taunton, *Portraits of Celebrated Racehorses,* 149, 153; Merry, *American Thoroughbred,* 42 (quotation); Richardson, *The English Turf,* 330–33.

4. *American Stud Book,* 1:84; "The Earl of Derby," *Baily's Magazine of Sports and Pastimes* 2 (October 1860), 5.

5. Merry, *American Thoroughbred,* 50 (quotation).

6. "Death of Imp. Australian," *Kentucky Live Stock Record* 10 (October 18, 1879), 248; Bruce, *Horse-Breeder's Guide,* 146; Merry, *American Thoroughbred,* 42 (quotations).

7. "Turf History: Imp. Knight of St. George," *Turf, Field and Farm* 2 (April 21, 1866), 241–42; "Return of Knight of St. George to England," *York Herald* (Great Britain), November 30, 1861. The Knight was not, in fact, sent back to England.

8. "Personal," *Kentucky Statesman* (Lexington), June 14, 1859, 2; "Residence of A. Keene Richards," 299 (quotation).

9. Passport application of Alexander Keene Richards, 15 July 1859, "Passport Applications," NARA, roll 81; passport application of Lewis L. Herndon, July 15, 1859, "Passport Applications," NARA, roll 81; Whitley, *Ante-Bellum Portraiture,* 566 (first quotation); Perrin, *History of Bourbon,* 593 (second quotation), 630.

10. "Arrival of the Persia," *New York Times,* September 20, 1859, 1 (quotation).

11. "Arrival of the Persia."

12. "Visit to A. K. Richards' Racing Stables," 306 (quotation).

13. "Visit to A. K. Richards' Racing Stables," 306 (quotations); Busby, "Residence of A. Keene Richards"; *American Stud Book,* 3:104, 113, 5:863, 868.

14. Satellite, "Stock on the Farm of A. Keene Richards," 327 (quotation); "Obituary," *American Stud Book,* 3:367. The year 1877 witnessed not only the death of Fysaul, but also Rarey's Cruiser, imported Sovereign, and imported Phaeton, the latter being one of Ten Broeck's imports shipped with Eclipse and Barbarity to America. The *American Trotting Register* commenced publication in 1871.

15. *American Stud Book,* vols. 1 and 2; "Residence of A. Keene Richards"; Satellite, "Stock on the Farm of A. Keene Richards," (quotation).

16. 1860 U.S. Census; *American Turf Register* (1859), 20.

17. *American Stud Book,* 1:236; *American Turf Register* (1860), 3, 20, 22, 24, 26, 50, 52, 63, 65, 71, 73, 74.

18. The place and date of death for Sallie Richards and her son, Lonnie, are recorded in family papers, provided by Richards's descendant Lowry Schneider of Louisiana.

19. Satellite, "Stock on the Farm of A. Keene Richards," 327 (first quotation); "Visit to A. K. Richards' Racing Stables," 307 (second quotation); Scott, *Kentucky Agricultural Society,* 153 (third quotation).

13. CHOOSING SIDES

1. McPherson, *Battle Cry,* 213–21; Roland, *American Iliad,* 24–25.

2. McPherson, *Battle Cry,* 223, 228–31 (first quotation, 187; second quotation, 230–31).

3. "A. Keene Richards Sale," *Kentucky Statesman* (Lexington), September 14, 1860; *American Turf Register* (1860), 50–52, 63–65.

4. McPherson, *Battle Cry,* 232; "Present State of the Country," *New Orleans Daily Crescent,* November 9, 1860 (quotations). From 1844 to 1846, John C. Breckinridge was a resident of Georgetown, Kentucky, where he practiced law with his partner and cousin, Thomas Bullock. See Davis, *Breckinridge,* 29–32.

5. *American Turf Register* (1860), 70–71, 73–74; Crickmore, *Racing Calenders 1861,* 1–3.

6. McPherson, *Battle Cry,* 234–35.

7. Roland, *American Iliad,* 28; Winters, *Civil War in Louisiana,* 4–9 (quotation, 4).

8. Winters, *Civil War in Louisiana,* 9–13, 19–20; McPherson, *Battle Cry,* 254, 257–59, 272–84; Roland, *American Iliad,* 35–40 (quotation, 40).

9. Winters, *Civil War in Louisiana,* 20–21; "Camp Life," *New Orleans Daily Crescent,* May 7, 1861.

10. Crickmore, *Racing Calenders 1861,* 3–5; "Spring Meeting, 1861: Second Day," *New Orleans Daily Crescent,* April 2, 1861; "Wheat's Battalion at Stone Bridge," *New Orleans Bee,* August 1, 1861.

11. Schreckengost, *Wheat's Tigers,* 36–38; "Another Company," *New Orleans Daily Crescent,* April 19, 1861; DeLeon, *Four Years in Rebel Capitals,* 66; Anderson, *Brokenburn,* 16–17 (quotation, 17); "Wheat's Battalion," *New Orleans Bee,* August 1, 1861; "New Orleans Tiger Rifles," *Daily True Delta* (New Orleans), April 23, 1861; "Notice," *Daily True Delta,* April 25, 1861.

12. Schreckengost, *Wheat's Tigers,* 5–30; Dufour, *Gentle Tiger,* 6, 21–119; Anon., "Sketch of Major Chatham Roberdeau Wheat," *Southern Bivouac* 2 (May 1884), 385–89; Wheat, "Memoir of Gen. C. R. Wheat," 47–54.

13. "Attention, Volunteers," *Daily True Delta,* April 18, 1861 (first quotation); *Daily Crescent,* April 18, 1861 (second quotation); Schreckengost, *Wheat's Tigers,* 35–36; "New Orleans Tiger Rifles," *Daily True Delta,* April 23, 1861.

14. "Wheat's Battalion," *New Orleans Bee,* August 1, 1861; "Removal of Camp Walker," *New Orleans Bee,* May 13, 1861.

15. "Wheat's Battalion," *New Orleans Bee,* August 1, 1861 (quotation); Field and Smith, *Uniforms of the Civil War,* 261–67.

16. Schreckengost, *Wheat's Tigers,* 41; Field and Smith, *Uniforms of the Civil War,* 57–58; Winters, *Civil War in Louisiana,* 16–17.

17. Crickmore, *Racing Calendars 1861,* 15–18. The 1st Louisiana Special Battalion shipped out from Camp Moore by train on June 13 to Virginia. Having recovered from a severe wound suffered at Manassas (Bull Run) in July 1861, Major Chatham Roberdeau Wheat was killed on June 27, 1862, at the battle of Gaines' Mill, Virginia. His battalion was disbanded shortly afterward and the men assigned to other units in the Army of Virginia (Schreckengost, *Special Battalion,* 76, 145–55, 168–70).

18. Harrison, *Civil War in Kentucky,* 4–9 (quotation, 8); Harrison and Klotter, *New History of Kentucky,* 186–89; Federal Writers' Project, *Military History of Kentucky,* 151–57.

19. Harrison, *Civil War in Kentucky,* 9–12; Harrison and Klotter, *New History of Kentucky,* 189–91 (quotation, 190).

20. Davis, *Breckinridge,* 202–5, 248–80.

21. Simon, "Lincoln, Grant, and Kentucky," 9–20; Federal Writers' Project, *Military History of Kentucky,* 162–64.

22. Mangum, *A Kingdom for the Horse,* 47.

23. Scott County (Kentucky) Conveyance Book M, 388, deed of trust, A. Keene Richards to Wallis Bodien Keene, recorded August 6, 1865.

24. Richards, *Catalogue of Blood Horses,* 2, 4, 5; Neptunus [Benjamin Bruce], "War Dance," *Kentucky Live Stock Record* 3 (June 17, 1876), 392; "Death of Imp. Australian," *Kentucky Live Stock Record,* 248; "Death of Ansel Williamson," *Kentucky Live Stock Record* 13 (June 25, 1881), 409; Mangum, *A Kingdom for the Horse,* 115. Morris Keene's role in taking the horses from Kentucky to Louisiana is assumed, as there is no documentary evidence. Keene, then living in the Richards household, was the obvious choice for this important assignment. Richards's closest

friend, Keene was the former manager or overseer at Transylvania and had proved worthy of trust on many previous occasions. There is no documentation to show that Ansel was sold to Robert A. Alexander. Ansel's obituary in the *Live Stock Record* notes only that "about 1861 he took charge of the late Mr. R.A. Alexander's stable," and other published accounts mention only that Ansel trained for Alexander during the war and afterward, a free man, returned briefly to work for Keene Richards.

25. Scott County (Kentucky) Deed Book 6, September 19, 1861, deed, A. Keene Richards to Edward Troye, 17; Scott County (Kentucky) Deed Book 6, September 19, 1861, deed, A. Keene Richards to Edward Troye, 18 (quotation).

26. Mackay-Smith, *Race Horses of America,* 226, 229 (quotation).

27. Mackay-Smith, *Race Horses of America,* 265–66, 269–71; Wyeth, *Roose's Companion and Guide,* 26.

28. Duke, *General Basil W. Duke,* 292; Brown, *Morgan's Raiders,* 123–24, 225; Richards, "Death of Edward Troye"; Mackay-Smith, *Race Horses of America,* 222.

29. Davis, *Breckinridge,* 280–85; Smith, *History of Kentucky,* 828.

30. U.S. War Department, *War of the Rebellion: Official Records* [hereafter *O.R.*], series 1, vol. 4, 262–63 (first quotation, 262), John Fisk and Richard A. Buckner to George H. Thomas, September 18, 1861; 263 (second quotation), Thomas E. Bramlette to Thomas, September 19, 1861; series 2, vol. 2, 805–6, Case of Charles S. Morehead, Reuben T. Durrett, and M. W. Barr; Davis, *Breckinridge,* 285.

31. *O.R.*, series 1, vol. 4, 267, Bramlette to Thomas, September 22, 1861; "Breckinridge," *Louisville Courier-Journal,* June 18, 1875 (quotation); Davis, *Breckinridge,* 285–86.

32. Davis, *Breckinridge,* 286; Maltby, "Civil War Times," 227; R. L. McClure, "Marked by Striking Events Is Career of World's Oldest Active Turfman," *Atlanta Constitution,* May 24, 1902; Connelly, *History of Kentucky,* 4:12. The 1861 map of Fayette County shows "Mrs. L.P. Dallam" as resident at Winton; Hewitt and Hewitt, *Topographical Map.* Dr. William B. Keene (Keene Richards's grandfather) and Greenup Keene (Samuel Y. Keene's father) were cousins; see Gaines, *History of Scott County,* 1:81.

33. Keene Richards to John C. Breckinridge, July 8, 1868, Library of Congress, Breckinridge Family Papers, MSS13698, Manuscript Division; Davis, *Breckinridge,* 287–88 (quotation, 287).

34. Richards, *Catalogue of Horses,* 10; Samuel Y. Keene to Randolph Huntington, March 24, 1900, quoted in Chard, "Keene Richards' Arabian Importations," part 1, 18 (quotation). Davis, in his otherwise excellent biography of Breckinridge, assumed that Richards brought only a single half-Arab horse to this meeting (Davis, *Breckinridge,* 286–87). That Richards drove a team of Anglo-Arabs taking Breckinridge to safety is clear from several sources, including Samuel Y. Keene's statement and Richards's 1881 obituary.

35. Stickles, *Simon Bolivar Buckner,* 56–57, 67–69, 79; Duke, *History of Morgan's Cavalry,* 88–91; Ramage, *Rebel Raider,* 44–45.

36. "John C. Breckinridge on the Wing," *Louisville Daily Journal,* September 25, 1861 (quotation); "Whereabouts of Senator Breckinridge," *Louisville Daily Journal,* October 2, 1861, 3; Davis, *Breckinridge,* 287–88; Collins, *History of Kentucky,* 1:94–95; Kettell, *History of the Great Rebellion,* 167; Sehlinger, *General William Preston,* 132; Thompson, *First Kentucky Brigade,* 527.

37. "Reception of Mr. Breckinridge in Knoxville," *Daily Dispatch* (Richmond, Virginia), October 7, 1861 (first quotation); "Address of John C. Breckinridge," 254–59 (second quotation, 254); *O.R.*, series 1, vol. 4, 445, Simon B. Buckner to Samuel Cooper, October 13, 1861; 504, Judah P.

Benjamin to Albert Sidney Johnston, November 3, 1861; 552, Johnston, Special Orders No. 89, November 14, 1861; 556, Buckner, General Orders No. 18, November 15, 1861.

38. Amnesty application by A. Keene Richards, NARA, "Case Files of Applications from Former Confederates for Presidential Pardons ('Amnesty Papers'), 1865–1867," Record Group 94, M1003, roll 26 (also available at KDLA). Although, according to witnesses, the carriage contained only "two gentlemen and a negro boy" as it passed through eastern Kentucky ("John C. Breckinridge on the Wing," *Louisville Daily Journal,* September 25, 1861), it is difficult to conceive how the Arabian horses could have been brought back as an intact team to Blue Grass Park unless some friend, such as Samuel Y. Keene, drove the carriage back to Georgetown from eastern Tennessee. Possibly Keene managed to conceal his presence in the carriage, or he accompanied the carriage on his own horse.

39. Richards, *Catalogue of Blood Horses,* 10; Richards to Breckinridge, July 8, 1868.

40. Harrison, "Government of Confederate Kentucky," 136.

41. George W. Johnson, Bowling Green, to Ann Johnson, October 20, 25, 1861, reproduced in Porter, "Letters of George W. Johnson," 342–43; Harrison, "Governors of Confederate Kentucky," 6–11. Johnson's wife, Ann, was the daughter of Scott County horseman Willa Viley.

42. *O.R.*, series 1, vol. 4, 450–51, George W. Johnson to Albert Sydney Johnston, October 15, 1861 (quotation, 40); Johnston, *Albert Sydney Johnston,* 381; Coulter, *Civil War and Readjustment,* 136–37; Harrison, "Governors of Confederate Kentucky," 11–12.

43. "Conference at Russellville, KY," 259–61 (third quotation, 260); Harrison, *Kentucky's Road to Statehood,* 164 (first and second quotations).

44. *Journal of the Congress of the Confederate States,* 1:536–37, Jefferson Davis to Howell Cobb, president of the Congress, December 2, 1861; 537–40 (first and second quotations, 537; third and fourth quotations, 538), George W. Johnson to Jefferson Davis, November 21, 1861; Coffman, *The Story of Logan County,* 189; Clark, "William Forst House"; "Proceedings of the Convention"; Spencer and Spencer, *History of Kentucky Baptists,* 1:731–32.

45. *Journal of the Confederate Congress,* 1:536–37, Johnson to Davis, November 21, 1861; 541–43, Johnson to Davis, November 21, 1861; 546–47, vote on bill to admit Kentucky to Confederacy, December 9, 1861; 554, act of admission signed by Davis, December 10, 1861; 574, Kentucky delegates seated, December 16, 1861.

14. A TASTE OF WAR

1. McPherson, *Battle Cry,* 392–98; Johnston, *Life of General Johnston,* 484–522; Nicholas, "Mill Springs," 48–73; George W. Johnson to Ann Johnson, February 15, 1862, in Porter, "Letters of George W. Johnson," 346; Thompson, *First Kentucky Brigade,* 79–83; Duke, *History of Morgan's Cavalry,* 110–36; Daniel, *Days of Glory,* 61–70.

2. Keene Richards (New Orleans) to John C. Breckinridge, March 18, 1862, "Carded Records," NARA, Record Group 109, M331, roll 211 (quotation). On the duties and responsibilities of volunteer aides-de-camp, see Eicher, *Civil War High Commands,* 40.

3. Walther, *William Lowndes Yancey,* 333–34; Richards to Breckinridge, March 18, 1862 (quotations).

4. Richards (aboard steamer *J.A. Cotton*) to Breckinridge, March 25, 1862, "Carded Records," NARA, Record Group 109, M331, roll 211 (quotations).

5. Richards (Transylvania Plantation) to Breckinridge, March 28, 1862, NARA, "Confeder-

ate Papers," (quotations). If Captain Wallis B. Keene returned immediately to the brigade, he was likely present for the battle of Shiloh and, as a member of Wirt Adams's cavalry regiment, would have participated in the subsequent withdrawal from Corinth and detachment to Vicksburg in June 1862. There is no documentation as to whether Captain Keene was able to raise an artillery company, and his name does not appear in the records of the Kentucky Brigade. Keene's scant surviving service record shows only that he was among the troops surrendered at Galveston, Texas, on May 26, 1865, by Confederate general E. Kirby Smith to Union major general Edward R. S. Canby; this was the last Confederate force to surrender. See Parole of W. B. Keene, June 17, 1865, "Compiled Records," NARA, Record Group 94, M1003, Record Group 109, M258, roll 43; *O.R.*, series 1, vol. 48, pt. 2, 600–602, terms of surrender.

6. McPherson, *Battle Cry,* 413–14; Daniel, *Shiloh,* 305; Thompson, *First Kentucky Brigade,* 530–31; Pollard, *Southern History of the War,* 305; Alexander M. McCook, June 20, 1894, reproduced in Porter, "Letters of George W. Johnson," 349–51. In a March 24, 1900, letter to Randolph Huntington, Samuel Y. Keene stated that "Mr. Richards was at the battle of Shiloah, and was taken through the lines after the battle to identify the body of Geo. W. Johnson then provisional Governor of Ky" (Samuel Y. Keene to Randolph Huntington, March 24, 1900, quoted in Chard, "Keene Richards' Arabian Importations," part 1, 18). This is the only account to make such a claim. All other accounts indicate that Johnson was found on the battlefield by Alexander McCook. Although Keene Richards did not return from Louisiana in time to participate in the battle of Shiloh, he may have confirmed McCook's battlefield identification.

7. *O.R.*, series 1, vol. 10, pt. 1, 613–21, Report of Colonel Robert P. Trabue, April 15, 1862; "Confederate Rag-Bag," *Historical Magazine,* series 3, vol. 2 (August 1873), 92; statement of promotion, John C. Breckinridge, NARA, Record Group 109, M331, roll 32; Thompson, *First Kentucky Brigade,* 107; *O.R.*, series 1, vol. 52, pt. 2, 302, Breckinridge, General Orders No. 9, April 13, 1862; Keene Richards appointment, "Carded Records," NARA, Record Group 109, M331, roll 211.

8. Smith, *Untold Story of Shiloh,* 74–75; Fowler, *Under Two Flags,* 111–27; "Capture of New Orleans," *Rebellion Record,* 4:510–25; Winters, *Civil War in Louisiana,* 76–102; Cumming, *Journal of Hospital Life,* 20.

9. Smith, *Untold Story of Shiloh,* 81–82; Grant, *Memoirs of U.S. Grant,* 1:379–81; Thompson, *First Kentucky Brigade,* 115–18; Williams, *P.G.T. Beauregard,* 152–54; Statement of twenty-eight-day leave, Breckinridge, "Carded Records," NARA, Record Group 109, M331, roll 32; Anderson, "Dr. James Green Carson," 251.

10. Menn, *Large Slaveholders of Louisiana,* 175–76; Anderson, "Dr. James Green Carson," 251–54; Breckinridge, *Wide Neighborhoods,* 6–7; Brown, *Cabells and Their Kin,* 496.

11. Anderson, *Brokenburn,* 120 (first quotation), 126 (second quotation).

12. Fowler, *Under Two Flags,* 172–92; Neptunus, "War Dance," 392; Salvatore [John Hervey], "A Famous but Mysterious Mare," *Thoroughbred Record* 109 (May 25, 1929), 568–69. Postwar accounts of the removal of Richards's stock claim they were taken to Thomas J. Wells at Wellswood Plantation. Wellswood, however, was the estate of Monfort Wells, the brother of Thomas, and so it is more likely that they were quartered at nearby Dentley Plantation, where Thomas J. Wells had long operated a Thoroughbred Running Horse breeding establishment.

13. *O.R.*, series 1, vol. 17, pt. 2, 601, P. G. T. Beauregard to Samuel Cooper, June 15, 1862; 606, Bragg, General Orders No. 76, June 17, 1862; 614, Jefferson Davis to Bragg, June 20, 1862; 622, Daniel Ruggles to William Preston, June 23, 1862; *O.R.*, series 1, vol. 15, 761, Earl Van Dorn

to Daniel Ruggles, June 22, 1862; 761–62, Daniel Ruggles to Braxton Bragg, June 22, 1862; Williams, *Beauregard,* 157–59; Ballard, *Vicksburg,* 44–45; Thompson, *First Kentucky Brigade,* 118–19; Jackman, *Diary of a Confederate Soldier,* 47.

14. Ballard, *Vicksburg,* 38–39, 46–62; Davis, *Breckinridge,* 318–23; Winters, *Civil War in Louisiana,* 120; *O.R.*, series 1, vol. 15, 6–12, Martin L. Smith to Manning M. Kimmel, August [n.d.], 1862; 15–19, Earl Van Dorn, September 9, 1862; 786, Van Dorn to John C. Breckinridge, July 26, 1862; 76, Breckinridge to Kimmel, September 30, 1862; 51–53, Godfrey Weitzel to Benjamin Butler, August 7, 1862; Se De Kay [pseud.], "Battle of Baton Rouge," *Memphis Daily Appeal,* August 11, 1862; "Breckinridge at Baton Rouge," *Athens Post* (Tennessee), August 22, 1862. For a more detailed account of the events leading to the battle of Baton Rouge, and of the battle itself, see Bearss, "The Battle of Baton Rouge," 77–128.

15. *O.R.*, series 1, vol. 15, 797, Van Dorn to Breckinridge, August 13, 1862, 80–81, Breckinridge to Kimmel, September 30, 1862; 800, Breckinridge, General Orders No. 23, August 15, 1862; Cunningham, *Port Hudson Campaign,* 6–8; Bonham, "Man and Nature at Port Hudson," 372–77; Jackman, *Diary of a Confederate Soldier,* 54–55; *O.R.*, series 1, vol. 16, pt. 2, 995 (first quotation), Braxton Bragg to John C. Breckinridge, August 8, 1862; *O.R.*, series 1, vol. 12, pt. 2, 340 (second quotation), John C. Breckinridge to Braxton Bragg, August 10, 1862.

16. Davia, *Breckinridge,* 326.

17. *O.R.*, series 1, vol. 16, pt. 1, 767–70, John H. Morgan to Edmund K. Smith, July 30, 1862; 738 (quotation), Abraham Lincoln to Henry W. Halleck, July 13, 1862; Duke, *History of Morgan's Cavalry,* 163–82; Ramage, *Rebel Raider,* 85–93.

18. *O.R.*, series 1, vol. 16, pt. 1, 767–69, Morgan to Smith, July 30, 1862; Duke, *History of Morgan's Cavalry,* 187, 195–96 (quotations, 196).

19. *O.R.*, series 1, vol. 16, pt. 1, 769, Morgan to Smith, July 30, 1862; *O.R.*, series 1, vol. 16, pt. 2, 733–34 (quotation), John H. Morgan to Edmund K. Smith, July 16, 1862; Duke, *History of Morgan's Cavalry,* 184–97; Ramage, *Rebel Raider,* 100–102; Connelly, *Army of the Heartland,* 195.

20. *O.R.*, series 1, vol. 16, pt. 1, 933, Kirby Smith to Samuel Cooper, August 30, 1862; *O.R.*, series 1, vol. 16, pt. 2, 730–31, Smith to Cooper, July 21, 1862; 733–34, Hugh L. Clay to Carter L. Stevenson, July 24, 1862; 734–35, Edmund K. Smith to Braxton Bragg, July 24, 1862; 741, Bragg to Cooper, August 1, 1862; 766–67, Smith to Bragg, August 20, 1862; 775–76, Smith to Bragg, August 24, 1862; 777–78, Smith to Cooper, August 24, 1862; *O.R.*, series 1, vol. 52, pt. 2, 330, Bragg to Jefferson Davis, July 21, 1862; Hammond, "Campaign of General E. Kirby Smith," Part One, 227–33, Part Two, 248–54, Part Three, 291–92; Connelly, *Army of the Heartland,* 193–216; Parks, *Edmund Kirby Smith,* 200–295; Peter, *Diary of Frances Peter,* 29–31.

21. Hammond, "Campaign of General E. Kirby Smith," Part Three, 296–97; Proclamation urging Kentuckians to support the Confederacy, n.d., Gilder Lehrman Institute of American History, Collection #GLC02502 (quotation); Connelly, *Army of the Heartland,* 217–19.

22. Connelly, *Army of the Heartland,* 223–24; Engle, *Don Carlos Buell,* 287–90; *O.R.*, series 1, vol. 16, pt. 1, 40, Military Commission, Buell Court of Inquiry, Cincinnati, Ohio, Statement of Major General Buell, May 5, 1863; 932, Smith to Braxton Bragg, September 3, 1862; *O.R.*, series 1, vol. 16, pt. 2, 470–71, Don C. Buell to Henry W. Halleck, September 2, 1862; 501–2, Thomas J. Wood to Buell, September 10, 1862; 512, Lovell H. Rosseau to Buell, September 13, 1862; 515, Buell to Halleck, September 19, 1862; 775, Bragg to Kirby Smith, August 24, 1862; 779, Bragg, General Orders No. 124, August 25, 1862; 798, Samuel Jones to Bragg, September 6, 1862; 805–6, Jones to Bragg, September 9, 1862; 809–10, Jones to Bragg, September 10, 1862; 815,

Bragg to Samuel Cooper, September 12, 1862; 996 (quotation), Bragg to John C. Breckinridge, August 27, 1862.

23. Davis, *Breckinridge,* 326; *O.R.,* series 1, vol. 12, pt. 2, 350, Breckinridge to J. P. Johnson, September 13, 1862; vol. 15, 81, Report of Maj. Gen. John C. Breckinridge, September 30, 1862; vol. 16, pt. 2, 809–10, Samuel Jones to Bragg, September 10, 1862; vol. 17, pt. 2, Van Dorn, Special Orders No. 59, September 4, 1862.

24. *O.R.,* series 1, vol. 16, pt. 2, 852, George W. Randolph to Earl Van Dorn, September 19, 1862; 996 (first quotation), Braxton Bragg to John C. Breckinridge, September 17, 1862; 996 (second and third quotations), Breckinridge to Bragg, September 17, 1862; vol. 17, pt. 2, 703, Bragg to Randolph, September 15, 1862; 706, Van Dorn to Sterling Price, September 18, 1862; Jackman, *Diary of a Confederate Soldier,* 57 (fourth quotation). The conversation between Breckinridge and Richards depicted here is based on circumstantial evidence and inference, since no direct documentation could be located. Eyewitness testimony by James Beck on February 20, 1863, at a military court of inquiry into Buell's conduct during the Kentucky campaign placed Keene Richards in Lexington anywhere from a few days to as much as a week prior to the October 8, 1862, battle of Perryville (*O.R.,* series 1, vol. 16, pt. 1, 455, 460). Breckinridge and his staff and troops did not arrive at Knoxville until October 3 (*O.R.,* series 1, vol. 16, pt. 2, 997); if Richards had accompanied Breckinridge, this would not have allowed him time to make the approximately two hundred-mile journey by horseback from Knoxville over rough terrain in time to be present at Lexington several days before Perryville. Accordingly, I have concluded that Richards must have departed Holly Springs before Breckinridge, and, as an individual, would have been able to travel from there to Knoxville more quickly than the Kentucky troops.

25. Connelly, *Army of the Heartland,* 231–33; Engle, *Don Carlos Buell,* 290–93; Noe, *Perryville,* 72–79; Brown, "Munfordville," 143–67; Johnston, "Bragg's Campaign in Kentucky: No. 3, Munfordville to Frankfort."

26. *O.R.,* series 1, vol. 16, pt. 2, 850, Edmund K. Smith to Braxton Bragg, September 19, 1862; 861, Smith to Bragg, September 21, 1862; 897, Bragg to Leonidas Polk, October 2, 1862; Johnston, "Bragg's Campaign in Kentucky: No. 2, Munfordville to Frankfort" and "No. 4, From Frankfort to Perryville"; McWhiney, *Bragg and Confederate Defeat,* 293–308; Engle, *Don Carlos Buell,* 302–3; Connelly, *Heartland,* 241–46; Noe, *Perryville,* 124–25.

27. O.R., series 1, vol. 16, pt. 1, 1092–94, Bragg to Samuel Cooper, May 20, 1863; Noe, *Perryville,* 130–33, 344–53, 327–37, 369, 373; McWhiney, *Bragg and Confederate Defeat,* 302–24; Cameron, *Staff Ride Handbook,* 95–101, 191; Johnston, "Bragg's Campaign in Kentucky: No. 5, Battle of Perryville"; Engle, *Don Carlos Buell,* 310 (quotation).

28. *O.R.,* series 1, vol. 16, pt. 1, 454–57, 460–61, Buell Court of Inquiry, testimony of James B. Beck, February 20, 1863; Davis, *Breckinridge,* 330–31; Maltby, *Mary Cyrene Breckinridge,* n.p.; Bevins, "Leonidas Johnson House," National Register of Historic Places; Porter, "Letters of George W. Johnson," 338, 340. After the Civil War, James Beck embarked upon a successful political career. He was elected as a Democrat to the U.S. House of Representatives in 1867 and to three succeeding terms, and then served as a U.S. senator from Kentucky from 1876 until his death in Washington, D.C., in 1890.

29. "The Georgetown Races," *Louisville Daily Democrat,* May 24, 1862; "Georgetown Correspondence," *Louisville Daily Democrat,* May 28, 1862; "Georgetown, Ky, Spring Meeting," *Wilkes' Spirit of the Times* 6 (June 7, 1862); Crickmore, *Racing Calenders 1861,* 33–34.

30. Duke, *Reminiscences,* 292 (quotation); Duke, *History of Morgan's Cavalry,* 259–60; Peter,

Diary of Frances Peter, 51; O.R., series 1, vol. 16, pt. 2, 903–4, Braxton Bragg to Leonidas Polk, October 3, 1862. Keene Richards and Basil Duke almost certainly knew each other. Duke was born in southern Scott County, a few miles from Georgetown, and after the death of his parents during his childhood he continued to reside in the same house under the care of his uncle, the well-known Thoroughbred Running Horse breeder James K. Duke, until 1858.

31. *O.R.*, series 1, vol. 16, pt. 1, 528, Buell Court of Inquiry, testimony of Oliver P. Beard, February 28, 1863; Ranck, "Lexington: War History," 462; Davis and Swentor, *Bluegrass Confederate*, 154; Duke, *History of Morgan's Cavalry*, 260–61; Duke, *Reminiscences*, 292 (quotation); Peter, *Diary of Frances Peter*, 52; John Hervey, "Among My Correspondents: Harness Racing Notes and Notions Suggested by their Letters," *Harness Horse* 4 (March 1, 1939), 478; Brown and Banash, *Dee Brown's Civil War Anthology*, 159; Mowery, *Morgan's Great Raid*, 146–62.

32. *O.R.*, series 1, vol. 16, pt. 1, 455 (quotations), testimony of James B. Beck.

33. *O.R.*, series 1, vol. 16, pt. 2, 1000, George W. Brent to John C. Breckinridge, October 14, 1862; 1001, Breckinridge, Special Orders No. 47, October 18, 1862; Green, *Johnny Green*, 50 (first quotation); Jackman, *Diary of a Confederate Soldier*, 61 (second quotation); Mary Breckinridge to John C. Breckinridge, October 31, 1862, "Carded Records," NARA, Record Group 109, M331, roll 32; Davis, *Breckinridge*, 330–31.

34. *O.R.*, series 1, vol. 16, pt. 2, 1003, George W. Brent to John C. Breckinridge, October 23, 1862; *O.R.*, series 1, vol. 20, pt. 2, 421–22, Braxton Bragg to Jefferson Davis, November 24, 1862; *O.R.*, series 1, vol. 20, Additions and Corrections, 781–88, Report of John C. Breckinridge, January [n.d.], 1863; Davis, *Breckinridge*, 329, 334–48 (quotation, 347); Thompson, *History of the Orphan Brigade*, 150, 168–83; Daniel, *Battle of Stones River*; Keene Richards to John C. Breckinridge, October 30, 1862, "Carded Records," NARA, Record Group 109, M331, roll 211.

15. TRANSITIONS

1. Keene Richards to John C. Breckinridge, October 30, 1862, "Carded Records," NARA, Record Group 109, M331, roll 211 (quotations); Baird, *Luke Pryor Blackburn*, 1–2, 20. After receiving public acclamation for combating yellow fever epidemics during the 1870s, Blackburn was elected as the Democratic governor of Kentucky in 1879, his term distinguished primarily by significant reforms to the penal system. The identity of the "Dr. Keene" to whom Richards refers is unknown but may have been Benjamin O. Keene of Georgetown—almost certainly a relative, although the family connection has not been determined. In *The American Turf*, 139, John H. Davis refers to Dr. Benjamin Keene of Georgetown, a "leading man of his day" and a well-known racehorse breeder.

2. Keene Richards to John C. Breckinridge, March 18, 1862, "Carded Records," NARA, M331, roll 211; Baird, *Luke Pryor Blackburn*, 20–21; Van Horne, *Army of the Cumberland*, 1:10; "Telegraphed to the New Orleans Picayune," *Daily Picayune* (New Orleans), April 25, 1861; "Immense Meeting in Lafayette Square," *Daily Picayune*, April 26, 1861; Luke P. Blackburn to Sterling Price, August 20, 1862, "Carded Records," NARA, M331, roll 24; *O.R.*, series 1, vol. 17, pt. 2, 676–77, Sterling Price to George W. Randolph, August 11, 1862.

3. See Cunningham, *The Port Hudson Campaign*, 1–16, and McPherson, *Battle Cry of Freedom*, 575–90, on the status of the western war at this point.

4. Richards to John C. Breckinridge, October 30, 1862 (quotation).

5. Richards to John C. Breckinridge, October 30, 1862 (quotations). "Capt Johnson" pos-

sibly refers to Jilson P. Johnson, Breckinridge's chief of staff, who may have come to Knoxville to escort Mary Breckinridge to her husband in Murfreesboro.

6. Holley, *The Second Great Emancipation,* 22; Pinkston, *A Place to Remember,* 251; Winters, *Civil War in Louisiana,* 102; *O.R.,* series 1, vol. 6, 883, George W. Randolph to Mansfield Lovell, April 25, 1862; *O.R.,* series 1, vol. 15, 459–60, John G. Pickett, General Orders No. 17, May 3, 1862; Anderson, *Brokenburn,* 100–101 (quotation, 101).

7. Keene Richards, amnesty application; Anderson, *Brokenburn,* 128.

8. Stafford, *Wells Family of Louisiana,* 91–94 (quotation, 91); Eakin and Barber, *Rapides Parish,* 28; Salvator, "A Famous but Mysterious Mare," 568; "War Dance," *Kentucky Live Stock Record* 13 (January 29, 1881), 73; Champomier, *Sugar Crop of Louisiana,* 1–2; Daigle et al., *Ecoregions of Louisiana.* The site of the former Dentley Plantation is on Highway 112, about halfway between town of Lecompte and the village of Forest Hill, the location now occupied by a large plant nursery. The town of Lecompte, originally White's Landing, was renamed in the late 1850s after T. J. Wells's horse Lecomte defeated the famous Lexington. According to local tradition, the "p" was inserted by a painter lettering the sign on the railroad depot in 1882 and the community has been Lecompte ever since. See Eakin, *Lecompte: Plantation Town,* 14. Wellswood was located along Bayou Boeuf about two miles south of Lecompte.

9. Stafford, *Wells Family of Louisiana,* 206–8; "Mayfield v. Richards," 137; "Married," *Daily Advocate* (Baton Rouge), January 4, 1867.

10. Neptunus, "War Dance," 391–92; "War Dance," 13 (January 29, 1881), 73; Allerdice, *More Generals in Gray,* 234–35; "Gen. Westmore Finds Rest in the River," *Daily Picayune* (New Orleans), February 5, 1896 (quotation); Mackey-Smith, *Race-Horses of America,* 263–64. The portrait of Reel was left to Keene Richards by the will of Jefferson Wells.

11. Neptunus, "War Dance," 391–92 (first and third quotations, 392; second quotation, 391).

12. "Winning Sires of 1882," *Spirit of the Times* 105 (February 3, 1883), 1–2; Richards, amnesty application; Delaney, "Matamoros, Port for Texas," 473–74, 486; Ellis, "Maritime Commerce," 199 (quotation).

13. Delaney, "Matamoros, Port for Texas," 475–79, 483–85; Ellis, "Maritime Commerce," 198–99, 204–5.

14. Ellis, "Maritime Commerce," 185, 194, 197, 210; Richards, amnesty application.

15. Hollandsworth, *Pretense of Glory,* 108–17; Dupree, *Union Flag in Texas,* 35–45; Irwin, *Nineteenth Army Corps,* 86–150; Taylor, *Destruction and Reconstruction,* 129–37.

16. Hollandsworth, *Pretense of Glory,* 115–16; U.S. Congress, *Report of the Joint Committee,* 345; Beecher, *Record of the 114th Regiment,* 148–50; *O.R.,* series 1, vol. 15, 370–74 (quotation, 373), William Dwight Jr. to Cuvier Grover, April 29, 1863; Neptunus, "War Dance"; Salvator, "More of the Wells Fables," *Daily Racing Form* 28 (May 14, 1922), 14; Salvator, "A Famous but Mysterious Mare," 577.

17. Neptunus, "War Dance"; Henson, *McKinney Falls,* 1; *Texas State Gazette* (Austin), February 22, 1865.

18. Henson, *McKinney Falls,* 6–11, 14–24; Henson, *Samuel May Williams Home,* 4–11; Hogan, "Amusements," 415–19; Sheridan, *Galveston Island,* 49–50; "American Racing Calendar for 1839," *American Turf Register* 10 (1839), 28, 66.

19. Stafford, *Wells Family of Louisiana,* 94, 183; Bertleth, "Jared Ellison Groce," 364, 367; Crimmins, "Leonard Waller Groce," 99–104, 107; Jan I. Fortune, "Rebels in the Wilderness: The Story of Liendo," *Dallas Morning News,* July 19, 1931; Danielle, *Successful Men of Texas,*

430. Bertleth erroneously states that Courtney Ann Wells was Thomas Jefferson Wells's sister. With the mansion house carefully restored, Liendo Plantation is listed on the National Register of Historic Places.

20. Henson, *McKinney Falls*, 31–35; *Texas State Gazette* (Austin), February 22, 1863 (quotation); Salvatore, "A Famous but Mysterious Mare," 577; "Death of Mannie Gray," *Courier Journal* (Louisville), October 15, 1895; "Mannie Gray," *Thoroughbred Heritage*, http://www.tbheritage.com/Portraits/MannieGray.html; Floyd Oliver, "The Breeding Behind Domino," *Bloodhorse*, https://www.bloodhorse.com/horse-racing/articles/154278/the-breeding-behind-domino. Hervey ("A Famous but Mysterious Mare") points out inconsistencies in various editions of the *Stud Book* as to the foaling date for Lizzie G and concludes that Lizzie G could only have been mated to War Dance during his stay in Texas.

21. Bruce, *American Stud Book*, 3:223, 263, 4:156; progeny reports, *Pedigree Online Thoroughbred Database*, http://www.pedigreequery.com. Records for the progeny of Fysaul were compiled from entries for individual offspring listed in volumes 1–6 of the *American Stud Book*.

22. Richards, amnesty application; Boaz, *Guns for Cotton*, 19–22.

23. Owsley, *King Cotton Diplomacy*, 2–50; Hubbard, *Burden of Confederate Diplomacy*, 21–23; Boaz, *Guns for Cotton*, 3.

24. Owsley, *King Cotton Diplomacy*, 2–39; Boaz, *Guns for Cotton*, 2–3, 5.

25. Boaz, *Guns for Cotton*, 21–22.

26. Boaz, *Guns for Cotton*, 46; Richards to Breckinridge, October 30, 1862 (quotation); Diamond, "Imports of the Confederate Government," 478; Weller, "Confederate Use of British Cannon," 137–45; Hazlett, Olmstead, and Parks, *Field Artillery*, 194–213.

27. Keene Richards, amnesty application (quotation); "Concerning Fire-Arms: Field Artillery," *Harper's Weekly* 5 (August 10, 1861), 510.

28. Richards, "Ordnance and Fire-Arms"; Lawrence E. Babits to Gary O'Dell, personal communication, March 30, 2020. A line item in Richards's 1868 bankruptcy application refers to the debt incurred for the prototype.

29. Keene, "Improvements in Traction Engines" (quotations); Fletcher, *Development of Steam Locomotion*, 211–24; Wik, *Steam Power on the American Farm*, 60–81; Dieffenbach and Gray, "Development of the Tractor," 25–45.

30. Cunningham, *Illustrated London*, 275 (first and second quotations); Bennett, *The London Confederates*, 5–13, 20–21.

31. Keene, "Improvements in Traction Engines"; Anderson, *Parish of Croydon*, 228; *London and Croydon Railway Companion*, 7–13; *Directory of the Town of Croydon*, 240; "Steam on the Highway," *The Engineer* 20 (October 6, 1865), 219. Residence information for Morris Keene was obtained from the patent.

32. Boaz, *Guns for Cotton*, 19 (quotation); Bennett, *The London Confederates*, 135–51.

33. Whitehair, *Belle Boyd*, 232–35; Sigaud, *Belle Boyd: Confederate Spy*, 157–73; Charles F. W. Archer, "Belle Boyd: The Romantic Story of the Girl Spy of the Shenandoah," *Boston Journal*, April 1, 1893 (quotation); "Local and Provincial," *Liverpool Mail*, July 9, 1864.

34. *Morning Post* (London), August 25, 1864 (quotation); "Confederate Wedding," *Morning Post* (London) August 26, 1864; Bennett, *The London Confederates*, 40–41, 43, 45–48; Huse, *Supplies for the Confederate Army*, 10, 18–36; Oates, "Henry Hotze," 131–50; Burnett, *Henry Hotze*, 16–22; Armstrong, *History of Hamilton County*, 1:324; Williams, *Letters on Slavery;* Williams, *The South Vindicated;* Sigaud, *Belle Boyd: Confederate Spy*, 177; Harris, "John L. O'Sullivan," 275–90.

35. *London Evening Standard,* April 24, 1865; Ship *Cuba,* June 28, 1865, "Passenger Lists," NARA, M237, roll 253; Ship *City of Cork,* October 2, 1865, "Passenger Lists," NARA, M237, roll 257; Keene Richards, amnesty application (quotations). Keene Richards was granted pardon by President Andrew Johnson on September 8, 1865, although technically he was exempt from eligibility by virtue of possessing assets in excess of $20,000.

16. STUNNED BY MISFORTUNE

1. Scott County (Kentucky) Mortgage Book 3, 218, October 16, 1865, mortgage, J. E. Troye to Grinstead and Bradley.

2. "Gleanings from Our Exchanges," *Daily Missouri Democrat,* November 3, 1865 (first quotation); "The Georgetown Stable," *Turf, Field and Farm* 2 (January 6, 1866), 9 (second quotation).

3. Salvatore, "A Famous but Mysterious Mare," 569 (quotation); Neptunus, "War Dance," 391–92; Henry G. Crickmore, *Racing Calendars 1866,* 4. James Madison Wells was appointed governor when Michael Hahn resigned to become a U.S. senator: see Cowan and McGuire, *Louisiana Governors,* 96.

4. "The Georgetown Stable," *Turf, Field and Farm* 2 (January 6, 1866), 9; Mangum, *A Kingdom for the Horse,* 80, 115, 120.

5. Scott County (Kentucky) Mortgage Book 3, 231, March 28, 1866, mortgage, Keene Richards to Grinstead and Bradley; "Personal," *Vicksburg Daily Times,* July 18, 1866.

6. Ballard, *Vicksburg,* 38, 46–62; *O.R.,* series 1, vol. 15, 25–29, Thomas Williams to Robert S. Davis, July 4, 1862; 31–33, Williams to Davis, July 4, 1862; Benedict, *History of the Seventh Regiment,* 12–17; Anderson, *Brokenburn,* 125, 127–28 (quotation, 128); Brady, *War Upon the Land,* 39–40; "Vicksburg," *Harper's Weekly* 6 (August 2, 1862), 482.

7. Simon, *Papers of Ulysses S. Grant,* 7:233–34, 399; *O.R.,* series 1, vol. 24, pt. 1, 10, Henry W. Halleck to Ulysses S. Grant, January 25, 1863; 10, Grant to Halleck, January 31, 1863; 14, Grant to John C. Kelton, February 4, 1863; vol. 24, pt. 3, 125–26, Grant to Nathaniel P. Banks, March 22, 1863; *O.R.,* series 3, vol. 3, 121, Lorenzo Thomas to Edwin M. Stanton, April 9, April 12, 1863; *O.R.,* series 1, vol. 14, pt. 3, 205–6, Grant, Special Orders No. 108, April 18, 1863; 403–4; Grant to Elias S. Dennis, June 11, 1863; Grant, *Personal Memoirs,* 445–56; Bastion, *Grant's Canal,* 27–46; Ballard, *Vicksburg,* 157–60, 171–72; Anderson, *Brokenburn,* 173 (first quotation), 176 (second quotation); "The Arming of Negroes: Speech of Adjutant-General Lorenzo Thomas at Lake Providence, Louisiana," *The Liberator* (Boston), May 1, 1863; "Conversations with Gen. Thomas," *New York Times,* July 20, 1863.

8. Lorenzo Thomas to Edwin M. Stanton, April 12, 1863, in Berlin, *Wartime Genesis,* 699–701 (first and third quotations, 700); Barnickel, *Milliken's Bend,* 51; McCrary, *Lincoln and Reconstruction,* 140; Randall, "Captured and Abandoned Property," 69–70; Eaton, *Grant, Lincoln, and the Freedmen,* 59; Pinkston, *A Place to Remember,* 261–62; George B. Field to Edwin M. Stanton, March 20, 1863, NARA, "Colored Troops Division, Letters Received," series 360, RG94 (second quotation, emphasis in the original). The Campbell referred to may have been John A. Campbell of Carroll Parish.

9. Julian E. Bryant to Captain, Headquarters of District of Northeastern Louisiana, October 10, 1863, in Berlin, *Wartime Genesis,* 728–35 (first and second quotations, 734).

10. Will of William B. Keene; Pinkston, *A Place to Remember,* 238–39; Horace B. Tebbetts to

Abraham Lincoln, September [n.d.] 1863, in Berlin, *Wartime Genesis,* 726–28; Williams, "Johnson v. Waters," 547–59. One of the wealthiest planters in the parish, Tebbetts and his wife, Frances, together owned more than 350 slaves and plantations valued in excess of $400,000. Following the war, Tebbetts was reimbursed more than $19,000 for cotton seized by the government. See Menn, *Large Slaveholders of Louisiana,* 181–82; U.S. Congress, *Cotton Claims,* 16, 28.

11. Prushankin, *Crisis in Confederate Command,* 15, 22–24; Bragg, *Letters of a Confederate Surgeon,* 143; Soldat, "Col. Parsons' Cavalry Raid in the Valley of the Mississippi Nearly Opposite Vicksburg," *Houston Weekly Telegraph,* August 4, 1863 (first and second quotations); *O.R.N.,* series 1, vol. 25, 415–16, Alfred W. Ellet to David D. Porter, July 3, 1863, 215–16; Pinkston, *A Place to Remember,* 265–66. Anne J. Bailey identified "Soldat" or "Solidat" as a member of the 12th Texas and a frequent correspondent to the *Telegraph,* whose letters "have proved quite accurate" (Bailey, "Texas Cavalry Raid," 31n12); Murphy, "Old Houses of East Carroll Parish," 4.

12. Hervey, *Racing in America,* 2:340–55; O'Dell, "Under Siege," 393; Paskoff, "Measures of War," 35–62; McPherson, *Second American Revolution,* 11–12, 38; Mooney, *Race Horse Men,* 128–33; Somers, *Sports in New Orleans,* 92–95.

13. O'Dell, "Under Siege," 396, 399; Wall, *How Kentucky Became Southern,* 56–67.

14. O'Dell, "Under Siege," 397–98.

15. O'Dell, "Under Siege," 399; Wall, *How Kentucky Became Southern* (quotation, 74).

16. O'Dell, "Under Siege," 394–95; Vosburgh, *Racing in America,* 3–13; Adelman, *A Sporting Time,* 80–81; Riess, *Sport of Kings,* 23–28; "The American Jockey Club," *New York Herald,* April 22, 1866.

17. O'Dell, "Under Siege," 399–400; Hervey, *Racing in America,* 2:340–42; Adelman, *A Sporting Time,* 84–85.

18. O'Dell, "Under Siege," 401–2; Adelman, *A Sporting Time,* 49–50, 84–89; Wall, *How Kentucky Became Southern,* 176; Robertson, *History of Thoroughbred Racing,* 91–93, 194–95; Reiss, *Sport of Kings,* xii; Weeks, *American Turf,* 42–43.

19. Crickmore, *Racing Calendars 1866,* 9, 11–12, 17–18; Vosburgh, *Racing in America,* 5; Hollingsworth, *The Kentucky Thoroughbred,* 160–66; "The Racing Week," *The World* (New York), September 24, 1866; "American Jockey Club," *New York Herald,* October 1, 1866; "Kentucky," National Museum of Racing and Hall of Fame, https://www.racingmuseum.org/hall-of-fame/horse/kentucky-ky. Kentucky was inducted into the Racing Hall of Fame in 1983.

20. Collins, *History of Kentucky,* 1:174; Crickmore, *Racing Calendars 1866,* 62–65, 69; Scott County (Kentucky) Mortgage Book 3, 250, mortgage, Alexander Keene Richards to Harvey C. Graves, October 13, 1866.

21. "Arrivals at the Principal Hotels," *Daily Picayune* (New Orleans), November 14, 1866; "Mayfield v. Richards," 140; "Married," *Daily Advocate* (Baton Rouge), January 4, 1867

22. Petition by debtor, National Archives and Records Administration, Alexander Keene Richards, Bankruptcy Case File, Record Group 21, Records of the U.S. District Court, U.S. District Court for the District of Kentucky, Louisville Term, Bankruptcy Act of 1867 Case Files 1867–1879, National Archives Identifier 719123, Case Number 842; Anderson, *Brokenburn* (first quotation, 372; second quotation, 371); Jones, *Keene Family History,* 205; *Banner-Democrat* (Lake Providence), September 24, 1898. Mary Keene was the daughter of John Wallis Keene, an uncle of Keene Richards, and co-owner of Atherton Plantation and half of Sauve Terre with her brother Bodien Keene. In 1867, she married Edward W. Constant of New York, and afterward the couple resided at Atherton. The *Mary E. Keene,* a palatial Mississippi steamboat

built in 1860, was named for her. She was lauded as the "belle of the ball" and considered to be an outstanding example of southern womanhood. See *Banner-Democrat,* cited above. Wade Hampton Bynum passed away at Transylvania Plantation on May 15, 1868. See Baird, *Bynum and Baynham Families,* 56.

23. "Wells v. Wells," 935; "Mayfield v. Richards," 137; testimony of M. Ryan, "Succession of Walter O. Winn on Petition of John S. Mayfield to Destitute Mary E. Richards Executrix," 43, handwritten case file, Historical Archives of the Supreme Court of Louisiana, Earl K. Long Library, University of New Orleans (quotation).

24. Taylor, *Louisiana: A History,* 126; Anderson, *Brokenburn,* 369 (quotation).

25. "Married," *Baton Rouge Tri-Weekly Gazette and Comet,* October 8, 1867; Anderson, *Brokenburn,* xxvi–xxvii, 349.

26. A. Keene Richards to John C. Breckinridge, July 8, 1868, Breckinridge Family Papers 1752–1904, vol. 261, Library of Congress (quotations); Petition by debtor, National Archives and Records Administration, Alexander Keene Richards, Bankruptcy Case File, Record Group 21, Records of the U.S. District Court, U.S. District Court for the District of Kentucky, Louisville Term, Bankruptcy Act of 1867 Case Files 1867–1879, National Archives Identifier 719123, Case Number 842; "Bankruptcy," *Louisville Daily Courier,* February 28, 1868; *Georgetown Weekly Times,* March 11, 1868; "Bankruptcy," *Louisville Daily Journal,* July 4, 1868.

27. "Assignees Sale of Southern Plantation," *Kentucky Statesman,* October 17, 1868 (quotations); Phillips County (Arkansas) Deed Record T, 219–20, November 25, 1866, Deed of Partition, A. Keene Richards and Morris H. Keene; Phillips County Deed Record W, 174, January 22, 1870, Deed in Bankruptcy, A. Keene Richards to William Preston; *Weekly Bankruptcy Register* 1 (March 30, 1868), 101.

28. U.S. Decennial Censuses of 1870 and 1880; Carroll Parish (Louisiana) Conveyance Book N, 473, January 20, 1869, F. H. Dudley, Assignee in Bankruptcy of A. Keene Richards, to C. B. Buckley; Carroll Parish (Louisiana) Conveyance Book N, 473, April 22, 1870, deed, C. B. Buckner to A. Keene Richards; Phillips County (Arkansas) Deed Record V, 620–21, March 13, 1869, deed, Colin B. and Emily E. Buckner to Morris H. Keene; Phillips County (Arkansas) Deed Record W, 589, November 1, 1869, deed, George Hancock to Morris H. Keene.

29. "Turf Matters," *Memphis Avalanche,* May 16, 1873 (quotation).

17. WINS AND LOSSES

1. Mackey-Smith, *Race Horses of America,* 309–10; Richards to Breckinridge, July 8, 1868 (first quotation); Scott County (Kentucky) Deed Book 9, 363 (second quotation), December 22, 1868, Edward and Cornelia A. Troye to Harvey C. Graves; Madison County (Alabama) Deed Book OO, 377–79, May 6, 1870, Northern Bank of Alabama to Edward Troye. In March 1872, Troye advertised the services of the twelve-year-old Thoroughbred stallion "Richards," sired by Mickey Free, at Mayslick and at Drake's Mill on the Deposit Road north of Huntsville; the horse was probably a gift from Richards to his friend. See the advertisement in the *Weekly Huntsville Advocate,* March 8, 1872.

2. "Breeding Establishments of Kentucky," 370 (quotation).

3. Cutter, "Kilgour, John"; "Cincinnati's Rich Men," *New York Times,* December 10, 1880; "Faro on Tick," *Illustrated Police News,* 11 (December 28, 1871), 7; "Organization of the Buckeye Club," *Wilkes' Spirit of the Times* 8 (January 27, 1866), 340; "Breeding Establishments of

Kentucky," 370 (quotation); Scott County (Kentucky) Deed Book 9, 380, deed, Executors of Thomas Smarr to John Kilgour.

4. "Breeding Establishments of Kentucky," 370 (quotation); "The Turf," *New Orleans Crescent,* March 21, 1869; "The Dead Turfman," *Cincinnati Enquirer,* March 22, 1881; "Public Sales," *Georgetown Times* (Kentucky), November 13, 1883; Scott County (Kentucky) Deed Book 20, 448, 449, 450, 476. The imported Thoroughbred stallion Mickey Free was a half-brother to the Knight of St. George, being also sired by Irish Birdcatcher. A successful racer in England, Mickey Free was imported in 1857 by Jason Fullington of the Ohio Importing Company and purchased in 1863, during Keene Richards's absence, by his farm manager, Frank Sherritt. See "Death of a Noted Racer," *Georgetown Times,* February 26, 1868; Scythian [pseud.], "Stallion Show at Lexington," *Wilkes' Spirit of the Times* 8 (May 2, 1863), 135.

5. "The Turf," *Chicago Tribune,* June 30, 1868; "Racing Notes," *New York Herald,* July 25, 1871; "Tom Bowling," *Cincinnati Enquirer,* November 13, 1873; "Turf Intelligence," *St. Joseph Gazette,* March 6, 1875 (quotation); "Turf Notes," *New York Herald,* February 15, 1876; "Turf Notes," *Daily American* (Nashville), February 8, 1877; "The Manhattan Stable," *New York Times,* April 22, 1878; "Turf Notes," *Public Ledger* (Memphis), March 22, 1879; "Track Talk," *Chicago Tribune,* August 10, 1879; "Turf Notes," *Daily American* (Nashville), June 21, 1881; "Flyers of the Turf," *The American* (Nashville), October 3, 1875; "Movements of American Trainers," *Sporting Gazette* (February 15, 1868), 8; "Blue Grass Park Stable," *Georgetown Times,* March 22, 1876. Ansel Williamson was inducted into the Racing Hall of Fame in 1998. See Dave Koerner, "Old Anse to Gain Unsought Fame: Hall Will Induct Aristides' Trainer," *Courier-Journal* (Louisville), August 9, 1998. In 1879, George H. Rice was the trainer and co-owner with George W. Darden, Nashville, of Lord Murphy, winner of the Kentucky Derby in that year. See Bolus, *Derby Dreams,* 75–84.

6. Information on Keene Richards's participation in race meetings is taken from newspaper accounts of race meetings and from volumes of the *American Turf Register and Racing Calendar* (published by the sporting magazine *Turf, Field, and Farm*) and *Krik's Guide to the Turf* for the respective years. Henry G. Crickmore, sports editor for the *New York World,* published *Krik's Guide* (New York) from 1878–1884 as the successor to the *Racing Calenders* he produced for 1861–1869.

7. Keene Richards, *Catalog of Blood Horses,* 3, 12; "Blue Grass Park," *Kentucky Live Stock Record,* 5 (June 23, 1977), 392 (first quotation); "Annual Stock Sale," *Georgetown Weekly Times,* June 11, 1873; "A. K. Richards' Sale of Thoroughbreds, and Other Stock," *Georgetown Times,* June 25, 1873; "A. K. Richards' Sale of Thoroughbreds," *Georgetown Times,* June 24, 1874 (second quotation); "Sale of the Bluegrass Yearlings," *Kentucky Live Stock Record* (June 25, 1875); "The Profits of Horse-Racing," *Chicago Tribune,* February 9, 1871; "Sporting Notes," *Chicago Evening Post,* February 9, 1872; Abbott, "Wages of Unskilled Labor," 363.

8. Wall, *How Kentucky Became Southern,* 74–78, 159–60; Adelman, *A Sporting Time,* 83. Robert Alexander's wealth was based on iron mining and refining, which he used to establish Woodburn Farm in Kentucky as a premier breeding establishment for superior cattle and Thoroughbred horses. See Wall, *How Kentucky Became Southern,* 42–43; Mangum, *A Kingdome for the Horse,* 9, 11–17.

9. Carroll Parish (Louisiana) Conveyance Book O, 575, December 11, 1873, Mortgage, A. Keene Richards to Harvey C. Graves; Carroll Parish (Louisiana) Conveyance Book O, 371, February 23, 1872, power of attorney, A. Keene Richards to Morris Horsey Keene; Carroll Parish

(Louisiana) Conveyance Book O, 574, February 20, 1872, deed, A. Keene Richards to Thomas Oliver Meaux; Carroll Parish (Louisiana) Conveyance Book O, 574, December 6, 1873, Reconveyance, Thomas Oliver Meaux to A. Keene Richards. The mortgage to Renshaw and Cammack could not be located but is referenced in other land transactions.

10. [Keene Richards], "Death of Edward Troye, Esq.," *Georgetown Times*, July 29, 1874 (quotation); Mackey-Smith, *Race Horses of America*, 346, 355, 403, 405, 409–36.

11. Carroll Parish (Louisiana) Conveyance Book O, 780, August 10, 1874, deed, A. Keene Richards and Mary E. Richards to Narcissa K. Johnson; Scott County (Kentucky) Order Book 31, 519–21, September 12, 1874, *Sayre v. Richards;* Scott County (Kentucky) Mortgage Book 3, 218, October 16, 1865, mortgage, J. E. Troye to Grinstead and Bradley; Mortgage, Scott County (Kentucky) Mortgage Book 4, 32, October 6, 1871, mortgage, A. K. Richards and Harvey C. Graves to E. D. Sayre; Scott County (Kentucky) Deed Book 15, 55–57, July 22, 1876, deed, A. Keene and Mary E. Richards and Harvey C. and Martha Graves to E. D. Sayre; Scott County (Kentucky) Deed Book 15, 90, August 29, 1876, deed, E. D. Sayre to James A. Grinstead; Scott County (Kentucky) Deed Book 15, 278–79, October 18, 1876, quit claim, W. B. Keene [junior] of Louisiana to James A. Grinstead.

12. "Fire," *Georgetown Times*, April 21, 1875 (first three quotations); A. Keene Richards, "Card of Thanks," *Georgetown Times*, April 21, 1875 (fourth quotation); "The Horse Show: Court Day at Georgetown," *Kentucky Live Stock Record* 1 (April 23, 1875), 186; "Keene Richards," *Courier-Journal* (Louisville), March 22, 1881.

13. Davis, *Breckinridge*, 479–82, 501–40, 548–624; President Andrew Johnson, December 25, 1868, "Granting Full Pardon and Amnesty to all Persons Engaged in the Late Rebellion," https://www.loc.gov/resource/rbpe.23602600/; Richards to Breckinridge, July 8, 1868 (quotation).

14. John Morris [John O'Conner], *Wanderings of a Vagabond: An Autobiography* (New York: self-pub., 1873), 261–62 (quotation, 262).

15. Marshall, *Creating a Confederate Kentucky*, 10–54 (first quotation, 34); Coulter, *Civil War and Readjustment*, 457 (second quotation).

16. Davis, *Breckinridge*, 606, 616–24; "Breckinridge: Death of the Great Kentuckian at Lexington," *Courier-Journal* (Louisville), May 18, 1875; "Dust to Dust: Funeral Services Over the Remains of Gen. John C. Breckinridge at Lexington Yesterday," *Courier-Journal* (Louisville), May 20, 1875.

17. Crickmore, *The American Turf, 1876*, 54; Watson, *Watson's Racing Guide*, 31–32; "The Derby," *Courier-Journal* (Louisville), May 16, 1876 (quotation).

18. Winants, *Steeplechasing: A Complete History*, 15–24; Adelman, *A Sporting Time*, 264; "A Day of Dashes," *Courier-Journal* (Louisville), May 20, 1876; "Racing in 1876," *New York Herald*, November 6, 1976; "Great Love for the Horse," *The Sun* (New York), June 15, 1879 (quotation).

19. "Sale of the Blue Grass Yearlings," *Kentucky Live Stock Record* 1 (June 25, 1875), 322; "Horse Sales at Lexington," *Kentucky Advocate* (Danville), June 30, 1876; "A. Keene Richards' Sale," *Georgetown Times*, July 4, 1877; "Lexington," *Cincinnati Enquirer*, June 26, 1877; "The Value of Race Horses," *New York Times*, June 26, 1878 (quotation).

20. *Weekly Bankruptcy Register* 1 (March 30, 1868), 101; Phillips County (Arkansas), Deed Record W, 589, deed, George Hancock to Morris H. Keene; Carroll Parish (Louisiana) Conveyance Book O, 371, February 23, 1872, power of attorney, A. Keene Richards to Morris Horsey Keene; "Kent," *The Cecil Whig* (Elkton, Maryland), July 15, 1871; Carroll Parish (Louisiana)

Conveyance Book P, 706, deed, C. B. Buckner to Maurice H. Keene; *Donaldsonville Chief* (Louisiana), May 4, 1878 (quotation). The *Donaldsonville Chief* reprinted the news item from the *Carroll Conservative*, a copy of which could not be located.

21. "Incendiary Fire," *Wheeling Intelligencer* (West Virginia), October 24, 1879.

22. "Neighborhood News," *Wheeling Intelligencer* (West Virginia), November 8, 1879; "Incendiary Incarcerated," *Wheeling Intelligencer*, November 10, 1879; "Indictment of the Suspected Fire Bugs Yesterday," *Wheeling Intelligencer*, December 10, 1879.

23. "Great Love for the Horse," *The Sun* (New York), June 15, 1879 (first quotation); "Death of a Noted Racer," *Georgetown Times*, February 26, 1868; "Death of Fysaul," *Georgetown Times*, August 15, 1877; "Imported Arabian Horses," *Georgetown Times*, February 21, 1877 (second quotation). Progeny sired by the Knight of St. George are reported on the Pedigree Online Thoroughbred Database: https://www.pedigreequery.com/progeny/knight+of+st+George. Richards's racing activity is reported by Crickmore, *Krik's Guide to the Turf*, for the respective years.

24. Crickmore, *Krik's Guide to the Turf* (1879–80), 281; Crickmore, *Krik's Guide to the Turf* (1880–81), 355; Neptunus, "War Dance," 392 (first and second quotations); "The Winning Sires of 1882: War Dance," *Spirit of the Times* 105 (February 3, 1883) 2 (third and fourth quotations); Busby, *Trotting and the Pacing Horse*, 147 (fifth quotation). Progeny sired by War Dance are reported on the Pedigree Online Thoroughbred Database: https://www.pedigreequery.com/progeny/war+dance. The most significant of War Dance's offspring to modern Thoroughbred bloodlines is Lizzy G, from whose female family came such influential sires as Domino, Hamburg, and Affirmed, the latter the Triple Crown winner for 1978. See information on the Thoroughbred Bloodlines website: https://www.bloodlines.net/TB/Families/Family23bLizzyG.htm.

25. "Death of Imp. Australian," *Turf, Field and Farm* 24 (October 24, 1879), 280 (first quotation); Arzt (pseud., German for "Physician"], "A Sire for Carriage Horses," *Wallace's Monthly* 3 (April 1877), 223–25 (second quotation, 224); United States Centennial Commission, *International Exhibition, 1876*, 6 (third quotation); "Great Love for the Horse," *The Sun* (New York), June 15, 1879 (fourth quotation). Limestone was purchased by Lyman A. Hitchcock in 1874 and retired to stud on his Massachusetts farm in 1876.

26. "Keene Richards," *Courier-Journal* (Louisville), March 22, 1881.

27. "Mrs. Mary E. Richards," *Lexington Herald*, March 22, 1923.

28. Jones, *Keene Family History*, 205, 212, 223, 232; "Swartz [sic], Edward George," *National Cyclopedia of American Biography* 27 (New York: James T. White, 1927), 8; "Native of Georgetown Dies in Louisiana," *Lexington Leader*, July 19, 1944; "Stubbs," *Georgetown Times*, February 9, 1933; "Births," *Georgetown Times*, November 14, 1900; "Births," *Georgetown Times*, August 2, 1905; "Personal Mention," *Georgetown Times*, January 22, 1908; "Death of Mrs. Stubbs," *Georgetown Times*, October 5, 1910; "Social Notes," *Georgetown Times*, November 6, 1927; "Frank Stubbs Dies at His Monroe Home," *Shreveport Times*, February 1, 1933; "Personal Mention," *Georgetown Times*, October 22, 1931; "Georgetown News," *Lexington Herald*, November 1, 1931; "Mrs. Caroline B. R. Pack," *Lexington Leader*, November 26, 1962; "Mrs. Mary E. Richards," *Lexington Herald*, March 22, 1923.

29 *Turf, Field and Farm* 32 (May 27, 1881), 329 (quotations); Samuel Y. Keene, "Lecomte—Edith Filly," *Thoroughbred Record* 63 (June 16, 1906), 394; "A. Keene Richards," *Turf, Field and Farm* 32 (March 25, 1881), 184; A. K. S., "A Noted Turfman," *Courier-Journal* (Louisville), January 28, 1883; "The Turf," *Nashville Banner*, October 6, 1881; Scott County (Kentucky) Deed Book 21, 442, January 8, 1885, deed, John T. Shelby, assignee of James A. Grinstead, to John B.

Graves; Scott County (Kentucky) Deed Book 21, 449–50, January 22, 1885, deed, John B. and Mary Graves to William Payne; Scott County (Kentucky) Deed Book 25, 85–86, April 9, 1889, deed, William and Elizabeth Payne to Jeff D. Grover; Scott County (Kentucky) Deed Book 29, 203–4, October 9, 1894, deed, J. D. Grover to Alice P. Montgomery; Bevins, *History of Scott County*, 236–37.

18. LEGACY

1. Hunter, *American Classic Pedigrees*, 80–81 (first quotation, 81), 15 (second quotation). Additional information is taken from portraits on the Thoroughbred Heritage website, http://www.tbheritage.com, for "Australian," "Fair Play," and "Man o' War" by Anne Peters, and "Spendthrift" and "Hastings" by Liz Martiniak.

2. Wallace, *Horse of America*, 61–66 (first quotation, 64; second quotation, 66); Anon., review of *The Horse of America*, by John H. Wallace, *The Nation* 66 (February 10, 1898), 116 (third quotation).

3. Kirsan, *Sport Horse Breeder*, 31 (quotation).

4. Upton and Amirsadeghi, *Arabians*, 32–33; Upton, *Newmarket and Arabia*, 163–200; Upton, *Gleanings from the Desert.*

5. Upton and Amirsadeghi, *Arabians*, 33–38; Blunt, *Bedouin Tribes;* Blunt, *A Pilgrimage to Nejd;* Anne Blunt, journal entry for December 14, 1877, British Library, Diaries of Lady Anne Blunt, Add MS 53889, ff. 56v–62v. (first quotation, f. 62r); Derry, *Bred for Perfection*, 103–55; Davenport, *My Quest of the Arab Horse;* Davenport, *Davenport Desert Arabian Stud*, 5 (second quotation). Lady Anne Blunt developed a lasting friendship with Jane Digby and Sheikh Medjuel, the latter having assisted Keene Richards on his first trip to the Syrian desert. See Lacy, *Lady Anne Blunt*, 16–17, 209. In the preface to *Bedouin Tribes* (vol. 1, page 8), Wilfrid Blunt states that, to his knowledge, he and Anne were the first to visit the Anizah Bedouins in the Hamad, apparently unaware of Edward Troye and Morris Keene's travels among the tribes there in 1856.

6. Bloodlines were traced using the databases of Pedigree Online (All Breed): https://www.allbreedpedigree.com and (Thoroughbred) https://www.pedigreequery.com.

7. Hendricks, *Encyclopedia of Horse Breeds*, 23–25; Speed, *Horse in America*, 33, 148–66; Lawrence, *Pure Arabians and Americo-Arabs*, 20, 63; Kirsan, *North American Sport Horse Breeder*, 35–37; Nall, ed., *Register of the American Saddle-Horse Breeders' Association*, 3:95; Sarah Gaddy, American Saddle Horse Museum (Lexington), personal communication, February 28, 2023.

8. "Blood Stock," advertisement in Burker, *The Texas Rural Register and Immigrants' Handbook for 1875*, 86 (quotations).

9. Hendricks, *Encyclopedia of Horse Breeds*, 28–33; "Imported Arabs," *Galveston Daily News*, April 4, 1874; "The Herds and the Flocks," *Dallas Morning News*, March 9, 1888 (second quotation); C. L. M., "Horse Talk of Interest," *Dallas Morning News*, December 31, 1897 (first and third quotations).

10. Wharton, *History of Fort Bend County*, 123; Chard, "Keene Richards' Arabian Importations," part 2, 23 (quotations).

BIBLIOGRAPHY

PRIMARY SOURCES

Manuscript Collections

Blunt, Anne. Diaries of Lady Anne Blunt. British Library, Add MS 53889, ff. 56v–62v.

Denton Offutt v. John S. Rarey. New York Supreme Court, index no. LJ1863024, Division of Old Records, New York County Clerk, New York, New York.

Digby, Jane Elizabeth. Bound diary, September 1855–July 1881. Minterne House Collection, Dorset, Great Britain.

Gunn, Thomas Butler. Diaries, 1849–1863. The Gunn diaries are archived at the Missouri History Museum in St. Louis, and are available online through LeHigh University (Bethlehem, Pennsylvania) at https://pfaffs.web.lehigh.edu/node/60175.

John Ross Brown Collection. Bancroft Library, University of California, Berkeley, California.

Johnston, J. Stoddard. "Bragg's Campaign in Kentucky, by a Staff Officer." Typed transcription in six parts. J. Stoddard Johnston Papers, 1850–1912, Filson Historical Society, Louisville, Kentucky.

Keene, Morris Horsey. "Improvements in Traction Engines." Patent No. 1836, July 11, 1865, Intellectual Property Office, United Kingdom.

Library of Congress. Abraham Lincoln Papers, series 1. General Correspondence, 1833–1916: Abraham Lincoln (May–June, 1860), Autobiographical Notes.

Library of Congress. Abraham Lincoln Papers, series 1. General Correspondence, 1833–1916. Howard, James Q. Biographical Notes, May 1860 (Abraham Lincoln).

Library of Congress. Breckinridge Family Papers, MSS13698, Manuscript Division.

Library of Congress. Offutt, Denton. "Best and Cheapest Book on the Management of Horses, Mules, Etc." Broadsheet (1843). Printed Ephemera Collection, portfolio 197, folder 34.

Library of Congress. Offutt, Denton. "Phrenology & Physiology of Animals." Printed advertisement. Abraham Lincoln Papers, series 1. General Correspondence, 1833–1916. Denton Offutt to Abraham Lincoln, September 07, 1859.

Murphy, Minnie S. "Old Houses of East Carroll Parish," draft 2. Typescript. N.d., Federal Writers' Project, Ouachita Parish Public Library, Monroe, Louisiana.
National Archives and Records Administration. Alexander Keene Richards, Bankruptcy Case File. Record Group 21, Records of the U.S. District Court, U.S. District Court for the District of Kentucky. Louisville Term, Bankruptcy Act of 1867 Case Files 1867–1879. National Archives Identifier 719123. Case Number 842.
National Archives and Records Administration. "Carded Records Showing Military Service of Soldiers who Fought in Confederate Organizations." Record Group 109, M258, roll 43; M331, rolls 24, 32, 211.
National Archives and Records Administration. "Case Files of Applications from Former Confederates for Presidential Pardons ('Amnesty Papers'), 1865–1867." Record Group 94, M1003, roll 26.
National Archives and Records Administration. "Colored Troops Division, Letters Received." Series 360, Record Group 94.
National Archives and Records Administration. "Confederate Papers Relating to Citizens or Business Firms, 186165." M346, roll 855.
National Archives and Records Administration. "Passenger Lists of Vessels Arriving at New York, New York, 18201897: 1865." M237, rolls 237, 253, 257.
National Archives and Records Administration. Passport Applications, compiled 10/31/1795–12/31/1905. M1372, rolls 35, 50, 51, 81.
"National Register Database and Research." National Register of Historic Places. https://www.nps.gov/subjects/nationalregister/database-research.htm#table.
Offutt, James S. "Denton Offutt: Employer and Friend of Lincoln at New Salem." Typescript, n.d., n.p. Abraham Lincoln Presidential Library, Springfield, Illinois.
"Petition of Denton Offutt, Relative to Improving the Breed of Domestic Livestock." Records, Governor Peter H. Bell, box 301-20, folder 16, Archives and Information Services Division, Texas State Library and Archives Commission, Austin, Texas.
"Proceedings of the Convention Held at Russellville Nov. 18th, 19th & 20th." Typed transcript. Special Collections, Filson Historical Society, Louisville, Kentucky.
Richards, Alexander Keene. "Ordnance and Fire-Arms, and Projectiles to be Used Therewith." Patent No. 1628, December 29, 1863, Intellectual Property Office, United Kingdom.
Smith, Edward Kirby. Proclamation urging Kentuckians to support the Confederacy, October 9, 1862. Gilder Lehrman Institute of American History, Collection #GLC02502.
"Succession of Walter O. Winn on Petition of John S. Mayfield to Destitute Mary E. Richards Executrix." Manuscript. Historical Archives of the Supreme Court of Louisiana, Earl K. Long Library, University of New Orleans.
Troye, Edward. Journal. Typescript. Keeneland Library, Lexington, Kentucky.

Published Primary Sources

Addison, Charles G. *Damascus and Palmyra: A Journey to the East, with a Sketch of the State and Prospects of Syria, Under Ibrahim Pasha.* 2 vols. Philadelphia: E. L. Carey and A. Hart, 1838.

"Address of John C. Breckinridge to the People of Kentucky." In *Rebellion Record,* vol. 3, section 2, "Documents," compiled by Frank Moore, 254–59. New York: G. P. Putnam, 1862.

American Turf Register and Racing and Trotting Calendar. Edward E. Jones, ed. New York: John Richards, 1856–1857.

American Turf Register and Racing and Trotting Calendar. Edward E. Jones, ed. New York: Jones, Thorpe and Hays, 1858–1859.

American Turf Register and Racing and Trotting Calendar. New York. 1845–1860. Editor and publisher varies.

"American Horses for England." *American Veterinary Journal* 1 (September 1856): 367.

Ammon, Karl W. *Historical Reports on Arab Horse Breeding and the Arabian Horse.* Translated by H. Stäubli. Hildesheim: Olms Presse, 1993. First published in Nürnberg, 1834.

Anderson, J. Corbet. *A Short Chronicle Concerning the Parish of Croydon in the County of Surrey.* London: Reeves and Turner, 1882.

Anderson, John Q., ed. *Brokenburn: The Journal of Kate Stone 1861–1868.* Baton Rouge: Louisiana State Univ. Press, 1995.

Apperley, Charles J. "Nimrod's German Tour." Serialized monthly in *The Sporting Magazine,* February 1829–February 1830, vols. 23–25.

Barclay, James T. *The City of the Great King.* Philadelphia: James Challen and Sons, 1858.

Beecher, Harris H. *Record of the 114th Regiment.* Norwich, N.Y.: J. F. Hubbard, 1866.

Benedict, George G. *History of the Seventh Regiment Vermont Volunteers.* Burlington, Vt.: Free Press, 1891.

Berlin, Ira, Thavolia Glymph, Steven F. Miller, Joseph P. Reidy, Leslie S. Rowland, Julie Saville, eds. *The Wartime Genesis of Free Labor: The Lower South.* Series 1, vol. 3, of *Freedom: A Documentary History of Emancipation 1861–1867.* Cambridge: Cambridge Univ. Press, 1990.

"Blood Stock." Advertisement in J. Burker Jr., *The Texas Rural Register and Immigrants' Handbook, for 1875.* Houston: B. F. Hardcastle, 1875.

Blunt, Anne. *Bedouin Tribes of the Euphrates.* 2 vols. New York: Harper and Brothers, 1879.

———. *A Pilgrimage to Nejd,* 2 vols. London: John Murray, 1881.

Bragg, Junius Newport. *Letters of a Confederate Surgeon 1861–1865.* Edited by Helen Bragg Gaughan. N.p., n.p. 1982.

Brown, Thomas. *Biographical Sketches and Authentic Anecdotes of Horses, and the Allied Species.* Edinburgh: Daniel Lizars, 1830.

Browne, John R. *Yusef, or The Journey of the Frangi: A Crusade in the East.* New York: Harper and Brothers, 1853.

Browne, Lina F., ed. *J. Ross Browne: His Letters, Journals and Writings.* Albuquerque: Univ. of New Mexico Press, 1969.

Bruce, Benjamin. "Death of Col. A. Keene Richards." *Kentucky Live Stock Record* 13 (March 26, 1881), 200.

Bruce, Sanders D. *American Stud Book.* New York: Sanders D. Bruce. Vol. 1. (1868); Vol. 2 (1873); Vol. 3 (1873); Vol. 4 (1884).

———. *The Horse-Breeder's Guide and Hand Book.* New York: Turf, Field and Farm, 1883.

———. *The Thoroughbred Horse: His Origin, How to Breed and How Select Him, with the Horse Breeder's Guide.* New York: Turf, Field and Farm, 1892.

Buffon, Georges Louis Leclerc. *Histoire Naturelle, Générale et Particulière,* vol. 4. Paris: L'Imprimerie Royale, 1753.

———. *Histoire Naturelle, Générale et Particulière,* vol. 9. Paris: L'Imprimerie Royale, 1761.

Burckhardt, John L. *Notes on the Bedouins and Wahábys, Collected During His Travels in the East.* 2 vols. London: H. Colburn and R. Bentley, 1831.

Burnet, David S., and James T. Barclay. *The Jerusalem Mission, Under the Direction of the American Christian Missionary Society.* Cincinnati: American Christian Publication Society, 1853.

Burton, Isabel. *The Life of Captain Sir Richard F. Burton.* London: Chapman and Hall, 1893.

———. *The Romance of Isabel Lady Burton: The Story of Her Life.* London: Hutchinson, 1898.

Burton, Richard Francis, and Edward Weller. *Personal Narrative of a Pilgrimage to El-Medinah and Meccah.* 3 vols. London: Longman, Brown, Green, and Longmans, 1855.

"Capture of New Orleans." In *Rebellion Record,* vol. 4, section II, "Documents," compiled by Frank Moore, 510–25. New York: G. P. Putnam, 1862.

Cavendish, William. *A New Method, and Extraordinary Invention, to Dress Horses, and Work Them According to Nature.* London: Tho. Milbourn, 1667.

Champomier, Pierre A. *Statement of the Sugar Crop of Louisiana of 1860–1861.* New Orleans: Cook, Young, 1861.

Coleman, Henry R. *Light from the East.* Louisville: privately printed, 1881.

Collins, Richard H. *History of Kentucky.* 2 vols. Covington, Ky.: Collins, 1874.

Commercial and General Directory of the Town and Parish of Croydon, 6th ed. Croydon, England: F. Warren, 1865.

A Comparative View of Form and Character of the English Racer and Saddle-Horse During the Last and Present Centuries. London: Thomas Hookham, 1836.

Conder, Josiah. *Palestine, or the Holy Land.* Vol. 1 of *The Modern Traveller.* London: James Duncan, 1824.
"Conference at Russellville, KY." In *Rebellion Record,* vol. 3, section 2, "Documents," compiled by Frank Moore, 259–61. New York: G. P. Putnam, 1862.
Crickmore, Henry G. *The American Turf, 1876: A Recapitulation of the Gross Earnings of All Sires, Horses and Stables, Number of Races Run, etc.* New York: Russell, 1877.
Crickmore, Henry G. *Krik's Guide to the Turf.* New York: H. G. Crickmore, 1875–1876, 1876–1877, 1877–1878, 1878–1879, 1879–1880, 1880–1881, 1881–1882.
———. *Racing Calenders 1861, 1862, 1863, 1864, 1865.* New York: W.C. Whitney, 1901.
———. *Racing Calendars 1866, 1867.* New York: W. C. Whitney, 1901.
———. *Racing Calendars 1868, 1869.* New York: W. C. Whitney, 1901.
Cumming, Kate. *A Journal of Hospital Life in the Confederate Army of Tennessee.* Louisville: John P. Morton, 1866.
Cunningham, Peter. *Illustrated London and Its Representatives of Commerce,* vol. 1. London: London Printing and Engraving, 1893.
Daumas, Eugène. *Les Chevaux du Sahara.* Paris: F. Chamerot, 1851.
Davenport, Homer. *Davenport Desert Arabian Stud, 1909–1910.* Hingham, Mass.: Self-published, 1910.
———. *My Quest of the Arab Horse.* New York: B. W. Dodge, 1909.
Davis, William C., and Meredith L. Swentor, eds. *Bluegrass Confederate: The Headquarters Diary of Edward O. Guerrant.* Baton Rouge: Louisiana State Univ. Press, 1999.
DeLeon, Thomas C. *Four Years in Rebel Capitals: An Inside View of Life in the Southern Confederacy, From Birth to Death.* Mobile, Ala.: Gossip Printing, 1890.
Dicey, Edward. *The Morning Land.* 2 vols. London: Macmillan, 1870.
Drummond-Hay, John H. *Western Barbary: Its Wild Tribes and Savage Animals.* London: John Murray, 1846.
Duke, Basil W. *A History of Morgan's Cavalry.* Cincinnati: Miami Printing, 1867.
———. *Reminiscences of General Basil W. Duke, C.S.A.* Garden City, N.Y.: Doubleday, Page, 1909.
Durbin, John P. *Observations in the East.* 2 vols. New York: Harper and Brothers, 1845.
Edgar, Patrick N. *American Race-Turf Register, Sportsman's Herald, and General Stud Book.* New York: Henry Mason, 1833.
Famous Horses of America. Philadelphia: Porter and Coates, 1877.
Farley, J. Lewis. *The Resources of Turkey.* London: Longman, Green, Longman, and Roberts, 1862.
Franck, Ludwig. "Beiträge zur Rassekunde unserer Pferde." *Landwirtschaftliche Jahrbücher,* vol. 4. Berlin: Wiegandt, Hempel and Parey, 1875. 33–51.
General Stud Book, Containing Pedigrees of Race Horses from the Earliest Accounts, 5th ed. London: J., E., J. P. and C. T. Weatherby, 1891.
Grant, Ulysses S. *Personal Memoirs of U.S. Grant.* 2 vols. New York: J. J. Little, 1885.
Grant, Ulysses S, and Ulysses S. Grant Association. *The Papers of Ulysses S. Grant.*

Vol. 7, *December 9, 1862–March 31, 1863*. Edited by John Y. Simon. Carbondale: Southern Illinois Univ. Press, 1979.

Green, Johnny. *Johnny Green of the Orphan Brigade: The Journal of a Confederate Soldier.* Edited by Albert D. Kirwan. Lexington: Univ. Press of Kentucky, 1984.

Hammond, Paul F. "Campaign of General E. Kirby Smith in Kentucky, in 1862." Part One. *Southern Historical Society Papers* 9 (May 1881): 227–33. Part Two, 9 (June 1881): 248–54. Part Three, 9 (July–August 1881): 291–92.

Head, Francis B. *The Life and Adventures of Bruce, the African Traveller.* New York: Harper and Brothers, 1840.

Herbert, Henry W. *Frank Forester's Horse and Horsemanship of the United States and the British Provinces of North America.* 2 vols. New York: Stringer and Townsend, 1857.

Hewitt, Earl A., and George Washington Hewitt. *Topographical Map of the Counties of Bourbon, Fayette, Clark, Jessamine, and Woodford, Kentucky from Actual Surveys.* New York: Smith, Gallup, 1861.

Hornby, Emilia B. *Constantinople During the Crimean War.* London: Richard Bentley, 1863.

Huse, Caleb. *The Supplies for the Confederate Army: How They Were Obtained in Europe and How Paid For.* Boston: T. R. Marvin, 1904.

Irwin, Richard B. *History of the Nineteenth Army Corps.* New York: G. P. Putnam's Sons, 1892.

Jackman, John S. *Diary of a Confederate Soldier: John S. Jackman of the Orphan Brigade.* Columbia: Univ. of South Carolina Press, 1990.

Jefferson, Thomas. *Notes on the State of Virginia.* London: John Stockdale, 1787.

Johnson, Sarah Barclay. *Hadji in Syria, or, Three Years in Jerusalem.* Philadelphia: James Challen and Sons, 1858.

Kettell, Thomas P. *History of the Great Rebellion.* Hartford, Conn.: F. A. Howe, 1865.

La Tourette, John. *La Tourette's Reference Map of the State of Louisiana.* New Orleans: John La Tourette, 1853.

Lawrence, James. *The Pure Arabians and Americo-Arabs (Huntington Horses).* Columbus, Ohio: Hartman Stock Farm, 1908.

Lawrence, John. *The History and Delineation of the Horse in All His Varieties.* London: James Cundee, 1809.

———. *The Horse, in All His Varieties and Uses.* London: M. Arnold, 1829.

———. *A Philosophical and Practical Treatise on Horses, and on the Moral Duties of Man Towards the Brute Creation,* 2nd ed. London: J. D. Symonds, 1802.

Layard, Austen H. *Discoveries Among the Ruins of Ninevah and Babylon.* New York: Harper and Brothers, 1853.

Leo Africanus [pseud.]. *The History and Description of Africa.* 3 vols. London: Hakluyt Society, 1896.

Libbey, William, and Franklin E. Hoskins. *The Jordan Valley and Petra.* 2 vols. New York: G. P. Putnam's Sons, 1905.

London and Croydon Railway Companion, 2nd ed. London: J. T. Norris, 1839.
Markham, Gervase. *Cavelarice, or The English Horseman Contayning All the Arte of Horsemanship.* London: Edward Allde and W. Jaggard, 1607.
"Medical Obituary: William Richards, M.D." *Western Journal of the Medical and Physical Sciences* 7 (June 30, 1833): 159–60.
Mellen v. Buckner, 139 U.S. 388 (1891).
Merrill, Selah. *East of the Jordan: A Record of Travel and Observation in the Countries of Moab Gilead and Bashan During the Years 1875–1877.* New York: Charles Scribner's Sons, 1881.
Molyneux, [William]. "Expedition to the Jordan and the Dead Sea." *Journal of the Royal Geographical Society of London* 18 (1848): 104–30.
Morland, T. Hornby. *The Genealogy of the English Race Horse, with the Natural History of His Progenitors.* London: J. Barfield, 1810.
Morris, John [John O'Conner]. *Wanderings of a Vagabond, an Autobiography.* New York: Self-published, 1873.
Murray's Hand-Book for Travellers in the Ionian Islands, Greece, Turkey, Asia Minor and Constantinople. London: John Murray, 1845.
Nall, I. B., ed. *Register of the American Saddle-Horse Breeders' Association*, vol. 3. Louisville: Courier-Journal Job Printing, 1900.
Nolan, Louis E. *Cavalry: Its History and Tactics.* London: Thomas Bosworth, 1853.
Offutt, Denton. *Denton Offutt's Method of Gentling Horses, and Curing Their Diseases.* Lexington: n.p., 1846.
———. *The Educated Horse: Teaching Horses and Other Animals to Obey at Word, Sign, or Signal, To Work or Ride; Also, the Breeding of Animals, and Discovery in Animal Physiology, and the Improvement of Domestic Animals.* Washington, D.C.: n.p., 1854.
———. *A New and Complete System of Teaching the Horse on Phrenological Principles.* Cincinnati: Appleton's Queen City Press, 1848.
Perrin, William H. *History of Bourbon, Scott, Harrison, and Nicholas Counties, Kentucky.* Chicago: O. L. Baskin, 1882.
Perrin, William H., J. H. Battle, and Gilbert C. Kniffin, eds. *Kentucky: A History of the State.* Louisville: F. A. Battey, 1887.
Peter, Frances D. *A Union Woman in Civil War Kentucky: The Diary of Frances Peter.* Edited by John D. Smith and William Cooper Jr. Lexington: Univ. Press of Kentucky, 2000.
Pick, William. *Pedigrees and Performances of the Most Celebrated Race-Horses, That Have Appeared Upon the English Turf.* Coppergate, York, England: W. Blanchard, 1785.
Pollard, Edward A. *Southern History of the War: The First Year of the War.* Richmond, Va.: West and Johnston, 1862.
Porter, Josias L. *Five Years in Damascus.* London: John Murray, 1855.
———. *The Giant Cities of Bashan and Syria's Holy Places.* London: T. Nelson and Sons, 1865.

———. *A Handbook for Travellers in Syria and Palestine.* 2 vols. London: John Murray, 1858.

Post, George E. "The Races and Relations of Syria and Palestine." *Transactions of the New York Academy of Sciences,* vol. 7. New York: New York Academy of Sciences, 1888.

Ranck, George W. "Lexington: War History." In *History of Fayette County, Kentucky,* edited by William H. Perrin, 452–69. Chicago: O. L. Baskin, 1882.

Rarey, John S. *The Modern Art of Taming Wild Horses.* Columbus: Ohio State Journal, 1856.

Review of *The Deteriorated Condition of Our Saddle-Horses, the Causes and the Remedy.* In *The Veterinarian,* Series 3, 26 (November 1853): 617–26. (Both the book author and review author are unknown.)

Review of *The Horse of America,* by John H. Wallace. *The Nation* 66 (February 10, 1898): 116–17.

Richards, Alexander Keene. "The Arab Horses, Mokhladi, Massoud and Sacklowie; Imported by A. Keene Richards, Georgetown, Kentucky." Lexington: Kentucky Statesman Printing, 1857.

———. "Catalogue of Thoroughbred English, also Arabian and Other Blood Horses, Imported and Bred by A. Keene Richards, Georgetown, Kentucky." Lexington: Observer and Reporter Printing, 1866.

Roosevelt, Theodore. *Outdoor Pastimes of an American Hunter.* New York: Charles Scribner's Sons, 1908.

Rous, Henry J. *On the Laws and Practice of Horse Racing.* London: Bailey Brothers, 1850.

Russell, William H. *The War: From the Death of Lord Raglan to the Evacuation of the Crimea.* London: George Routledge, 1856.

Schumacher, Gottlieb. *Across the Jordan: Being an Exploration and Survey of Part of Hauran and Jaulan.* London: Richard Bentley and Son, 1886.

———. *The Jaulân, Surveyed for the German Society for the Exploration of the Holy Land.* London: Richard Bentley and Son, 1888.

Scott, Robert W. *Report on the Kentucky Agricultural Society to the Legislature of Kentucky.* Frankfort: A. G. Hodges, 1857.

Sheridan, Francis C. *Galveston Island, or, A Few Months off the Coast of Texas: The Journal of Francis C. Sheridan, 1839–1840.* Austin: Univ. of Texas Press, 1992.

Skinner, John S. "The Horse, in England and America, as He has Been, and as He is." Introduction to *The Horse,* by William Youatt. New York: Leavitt and Allen, 1843.

Smith, Charles H. *The Natural History of Horses.* Edinburgh: W. H. Lizars, 1841.

Smith, Nicholas H. *Observations on Breeding for the Turf.* London: G. Whittaker, 1825.

Stanyhurst, Richard. "A Treatise Contayning a Playne and Perfect Description of Irelande." In *The Firste Volume of the Chronicles of England, Scotlande, and Irelande,* by Raphael Holinshed. 2 vols. London: John Hunne, 1577.

Stark, John. *Vertebrata*. Vol. 1 of *Elements of Natural History*. Edinburgh: Adam Black and John Stark, 1828.

Stone, Barton W. *The Biography of Eld. Barton Warren Stone*. Cincinnati: J. A. and U. P. James, 1848.

Sue, Eugene. *The Godolphin Arabian, or, The History of a Thoroughbred*. London: Chapman and Elcoate, 1845.

Taunton, Thomas H. *Portraits of Celebrated Racehorses of the Past and Present Centuries*. 4 vols. London: Sampson Low, Marston, Searle and Rivington, 1888.

Taylor, Bayard. *The Lands of the Saracen, or, Pictures of Palestine, Asia Minor, Sicily, and Spain*. New York: G. P. Putnam, 1855.

Taylor, Richard. *Destruction and Reconstruction: Personal Experiences of the Late War*. New York, 1879.

Thompson, Edwin P. *History of the First Kentucky Brigade*. Cincinnati: Caxton Publishing, 1868.

Thornbury, Walter. *Turkish Life and Character*. 2 vols. London: Smith, Elder, 1860.

Transactions of the New York State Agricultural Society for the Year 1860. New York: New York State Agricultural Society, 1861.

Tristram, Henry B. *Bible Places, or The Topography of the Holy Land*. London: Society for Promoting Christian Knowledge, 1875.

Troye, Edward. *The Dead Sea and the Ruins of Sodom and Gomorrah*. New York: W. A. Townsend, 1858.

———. *Troye's Oriental Paintings*. New Orleans, 1857. Reproduced in Mackay-Smith, *Race Horses of America*, 437–43.

———. *Troye's Paintings of the Holy Land, Illustrating Life in the East*. New York: W. A. Townsend, 1858.

United States Centennial Commission. *International Exhibition, 1876: Reports and Awards, Live Stock*. Edited by Francis A. Walker. Philadelphia: J. B. Lippencott, 1878.

Upton, Roger D. *Gleanings from the Desert of Arabia*. London: C. Kegan Paul, 1881.

———. *Newmarket and Arabia: An Examination of the Descent of Racers and Coursers*. London: Henry S. King, 1873.

Van Horne, Thomas B. *History of the Army of the Cumberland*, vol. 1. Cincinnati: Robert Clarke, 1875.

Von Orlich, Leopold. *Travels in India, Including Sinde and the Punjab*. Translated by H. Evans Lloyd. London: Longman, Brown, Green and Longman, 1845.

Wallace, John H. *Wallace's American Stud-book, Being a Compilation of the Pedigrees of American and Imported Blood Horses*. New York: W. A. Townsend and Adams, 1867.

Walpole, Frederick. *The Ansayrii, and the Assassins, with Travels in the Further East, in 1850–1851, Including a Visit to Nineveh*. London: Richard Bentley, 1851.

Walsh, John H., and James I. Lupton. *The Horse, in the Stable and the Field: His Varieties, Management in Health and Disease, Anatomy, Physiology*. London: Routledge, Warne, and Routledge, 1861.

Warren, F. *Commercial and General Directory of the Town and Parish of Croydon*, 6th ed. Croydon: F. Warren, 1865.

Watson, James. *Watson's Racing Guide for 1876–1877*. New York: D. W. Higgins, 1877.

Weatherby, James. *General Stud Book, Containing Pedigrees of Race Horses from the Earliest Accounts to the Year 1807, Inclusive*. London: Henry Reynell, 1808.

———. *An Introduction to a General Stud Book*. London: Henry Reynell, 1791.

White, Charles. *Three Years in Constantinople*. 3 vols. London: Henry Colburn, 1846.

Whyte, James C. *History of the British Turf, from the Earliest Period to the Present Day*. 2 vols. London: Henry Colburn, 1840.

Williams, James. *Letters on Slavery from the Old World*. Nashville: Southern Methodist Publishing House, 1861.

———. *The South Vindicated*. London: Longman, Green, Longman, Roberts and Green, 1862.

Winter, Elisha I. *The Thorough Bred and Imported Horse, Winter's Arabian*. Handbill. Lexington, March 1824. Univ. of Kentucky Special Collections, Lexington.

Woodruff, Hiram. *Trotting Horses of America*. New York: J. B. Ford, 1877.

Wyeth, Samuel D. *Roose's Companion and Guide to Washington and Vicinity*. Washington, D.C.: Gibson Brothers, 1892.

Youatt, William. *The Horse*. New York: Leavitt and Allen, 1843.

———. *The Horse: Its History, Management, and Treatment*. London: George Routledge, 1853.

———. *The Horse: With a Treatise on Draught*. London: Baldwin and Cradock, 1831.

———. *The Obligation and Extent of Humanity to Brutes, Principally Considered with Reference to the Domesticated Animals*. London: Longman, Orme, Brown, Green, and Longman, 1839.

Youatt, William, and Cecil [Cornelius Tongue]. *The Horse, A New Edition, Reedited and Revised*. London: George Routledge, 1855.

Government Documents

Hilgard, Eugene W. "Report on Cotton Production of the State of Louisiana." *Report on Cotton Production in the United States*. Washington, D.C.: Government Printing Office, 1884.

Journal of the Congress of the Confederate States of America, 1861–1865. Multivolume. Washington, D.C.: Government Printing Office, 1904.

"Mayfield v. Richards." *Cases Adjudged in the Supreme Court at October Term, 1884 and October Term, 1885. United States Reports*, vol. 115. New York: Banks and Brothers, 1886: 137–42.

President of the United States of America. "A Proclamation Granting Full Pardon and Amnesty to all Persons Engaged in the Late Rebellion." In *Statutes at Large, Treaties and Proclamations of the United States of America from December 1867, to March 1869*, vol. 4, edited by George P. Sanger, 711–12. Boston: Little, Brown, 1869.

"Wells v. Wells." *Reports of Cases Argued and Determined in the Supreme Court of Louisiana, for the Year 1878*, vol. 30, pt. 2. New Orleans: F. F. Hansell, 1879.

U.S. Bureau of Foreign Commerce. *Consular Reports, January 1900: Commerce, Manufactures, Etc.*, vol. 62. Washington, D.C.: Government Printing Office, 1900.

U.S. Bureau of Land Management. "General Land Office Records 1796–2015." https://ancestry.com/search/collections/1246/.

U.S. Bureau of Land Management. *Louisiana Tract Book 40* (Monroe District). Louisiana State Land Office database. http://www.doa.la.gov/slo/.

U.S. Congress. "Cotton Claims" (document 189). *Executive Documents, Printed by Order of the House of Representatives 1875–1876*, vol. 14. Washington, D.C.: Government Printing Office, 1877.

———. *Report of the Joint Committee on the Conduct of the War: Red River Expedition.* Washington, D.C.: Government Printing Office, 1865.

U.S. War Department. *Official Records of the Union and Confederate Navies in the War of the Rebellion* [O.R.N.]. Multivolume. Washington, D.C.: Government Printing Office, 1894–1922.

———. *War of the Rebellion: A Compilation of the Official Records of the Union and Confederate Armies* [O.R.]. Multivolume. Washington, D.C.: Government Printing Office, 1880–1901.

Williams, Steven K. "Johnson v. Waters." In *Cases Argued and Decided in the Supreme Court of the United States in the October Terms, 1883, 1884*, book 28. Rochester, N.Y.: Lawyers' Cooperative Publishing, 1886.

British Newspapers and Periodicals

Badminton Magazine of Sports and Pastimes.

Baily's Magazine of Sports and Pastimes.

Bell's Life in London and Sporting Chronicle.

Blackwood's Edinburgh Magazine.

The Engineer.

The Farmer's Magazine.

Fores's Sporting Notes and Sketches.

Fraser's Magazine.

Liverpool Mail.

London Evening Standard.

London Times.

Morning Post.

Sporting Gazette.

The Sporting Magazine.

Kentucky Newspapers and Periodicals

Courier-Journal.

Georgetown Herald.

Georgetown Times.

Georgetown Weekly Times.

Kentucky Advocate.

Kentucky Live Stock Record.

Kentucky Reporter.
Kentucky Statesman.
Lexington Herald.
Lexington Intelligencer.
Louisville Daily Courier.
Louisville Daily Democrat.
Louisville Daily Journal.
Observer and Reporter.

Louisiana Newspapers and Periodicals

Baton Rouge Tri-Weekly Gazette and Comet.
Daily Advocate.
Daily Picayune.
Daily True Delta.
New Orleans Bee.
New Orleans Daily Crescent.
New Orleans Daily Democrat.
Shreveport Times.

New York Newspapers and Periodicals

American Monthly Review of Reviews.
The Country Gentleman.
The Evening Mail.
Harper's New Monthly Magazine.
Harper's Weekly.
The Historical Magazine.
New York Herald.
New York Journal of Commerce.
New York Times.
Porter's Spirit of the Times.
Spirit of the Times.
The Sun.
Turf, Field and Farm.
Wallace's Monthly.
Weekly Bankruptcy Register.
Wilke's Spirit of the Times.

Tennessee Newspapers and Periodicals

The American (*Nashville*).
Athens Post.
Daily American (*Nashville*).
Memphis Avalanche.
Nashville Banner.
Public Ledger.

Texas Newspapers and Periodicals

Dallas Morning News.
Galveston Daily News.
Houston Weekly Telegraph.
Texas State Gazette.

Other Newspapers and Periodicals

Boston Journal.
The Cecil Whig (*Elkton, Md.*).
Charleston Courier (*Charleston, S.C.*).
Chicago Evening Post.
Chicago Tribune.
Cincinnati Enquirer.
The Constitution (*Atlanta, Ga.*).
Daily Dispatch (*Richmond, Va.*).
Daily Milwaukee Press and News.
Daily Missouri Democrat.

Daily Racing Form (Chicago, Ill.).
Equus.
Harness Horse.
The Horse.
Illustrated Police News (Boston, Mass.).
The Liberator (Boston, Mass.).
Millennial Harbinger (Bethany, W.Va.).
The Morgan Horse.
Outing.
St. Joseph Gazette.
The Saturday Magazine.
Southern Bivouac.
Turf and Sport Digest.
The Valley Farmer.
Vicksburg Daily Times.
Weekly Huntsville Advocate.
Western Horseman.
Wheeling Intelligencer.

SECONDARY SOURCES

Books and Articles

Abbott, Edith. "The Wages of Unskilled Labor in the United States 1850–1900." *Journal of Political Economy* 13 (June 1905): 321–67.

Adelman, Melvin L. *A Sporting Time: New York City and the Rise of Modern Athletics 1820–1870*. Urbana: Univ. of Illinois Press, 1986.

Aharoni, Yohanan. *The Land of the Bible: A Historical Geography*. Philadelphia: Westminster Press, 1979.

Allerdice, Bruce S. *More Generals in Gray*. Baton Rouge: Louisiana State Univ. Press, 1995.

Anderson, James D. *Making the American Thoroughbred, Especially in Tennessee, 1800–1845*. Norwood, Mass.: Plimpton Press, 1916.

Anderson, John Q. "Dr. James Green Carson: Antebellum Planter of Mississippi and Louisiana." *Journal of Mississippi History* 18 (October 1956): 243–67.

Anthony, David W. "Bridling Horse Power: The Domestication of the Horse." In *Horses Through Time*, edited by Sandra L. Olsen. Boulder, Colo.: Roberts Rhinehart for Carnegie Museum of Natural History, 1996.

Apple, Lindsey, Frederick A. Johnson, and Ann B. Bevins. *Scott County: A History*. Georgetown, Ky: Scott County Historical Society, 1993.

Armstrong, Zella. *History of Hamilton County and Chattanooga, Tennessee*. 2 vols. Chattanooga, Tenn.: Lookout Publishing, 1931.

Auerback, Ann H. *Wild Ride: The Rise and Tragic Fall of Calumet Farm, Inc., America's Premier Racing Dynasty*. New York: Henry Holt, 1994.

Azzaroli, Augusto. *An Early History of Horsemanship*. Leiden: E. J. Brill, 1985.

Bailey, Anne J. "A Texas Cavalry Raid: Reaction to Black Soldiers and Contrabands." In *Black Flag Over Dixie: Racial Atrocities and Reprisals in the Civil War*, edited by Gregory J. W. Urwin. Carbondale: Southern Illinois Press, 2005.

Baird, Nancy D. *Luke Pryor Blackburn: Physician, Governor, Reformer*. Lexington: Univ. Press of Kentucky, 1979.

Baird, Robert W. *Bynum and Baynham Families of America 1616–1850*. Baltimore, Md.: Gateway Press, 1983.

Ball, Warwick. *Rome in the East: The Transformation of an Empire*. London: Routledge, 2000.

Ballard, Michael B. *Vicksburg: The Campaign That Opened the Mississippi*. Chapel Hill: Univ. of North Carolina Press, 2004.

Barnickel, Linda. *Milliken's Bend: A Civil War Battle in History and Memory*. Baton Rouge: Louisiana State Univ. Press, 2013.

Bastion, David F. *Grant's Canal: The Union's Attempt to Bypass Vicksburg*. Shippensburg, Pa.: Burd Street Press, 1998.

Baumgart, Winfried. *The Crimean War 1853–1856*. New York: Oxford Univ. Press, 1999.

Bearss, Edwin C. "The Battle of Baton Rouge." *Louisiana History* 3 (spring 1962): 77–128.

Ben-Arieh, Yehoshua. "Nineteenth-Century Historical Geographies of the Holy Land." *Journal of Historical Geography* 15 (January 1989): 69–79.

Bennett, Deb. *Conquerors: The Roots of New World Horsemanship*. Solvary, Calif.: Amigo Publications, 1998.

Bennett, John D. *The London Confederates: The Officials, Clergy, Businessmen and Journalists Who Backed the American South During the Civil War*. Jefferson, N.C.: McFarland, 2007.

Berman, Jacob R. *American Arabesque: Arabs, Islam, and the 19th-Century Imaginary*. New York: New York Univ. Press, 2012.

Bertleth, Rosa G. "Jared Ellison Groce." *Southwestern Historical Quarterly* 20 (April 1917): 358–68.

Bevins, Ann B. *A History of Scott County, as Told by Selected Buildings*. Georgetown, Ky.: Kreative Grafiks Ink, 1981.

———. "Leonidas Johnson House (Clifon)." National Register of Historic Places Nomination Form, Reference No. 76000943, National Register of Historic Places.

Bilby, Joseph G. *Civil War Firearms: Their Historical Background and Tactical Use*. Conshohocken, Pa.: Combined Publishing, 1996.

Bird, Thomas H. *Admiral Rous and the English Turf 1795–1877*. London: Putnam, 1939.

Black, David. *The King of Fifth Avenue: The Fortunes of August Belmont*. New York: Dial Press, 1981.

Blowers, Paul M. "'Living in a Land of Prophets': James T. Barclay and an Early Disciples of Christ Mission to Jews in the Holy Land." *Church History* 62 (December 1993): 494–513.

Boaz, Thomas. *Guns for Cotton: England Arms the Confederacy*. Shippensburg, Pa.: Burd Street Press, 1996.

Boisseau, Tracy J. "Grand Tour." In *Encyclopedia of the United States in the Nineteenth Century*, vol. 2, edited by Paul Finkelman. New York: Charles Scribner's Sons, 2001: 1–2. New York: Charles Scribner's Sons, 2001.

Bolus, Jim. *Derby Dreams.* Gretna, La.: Pelican Publishing, 1996.

Bonham, Milledge L., Jr. "Man and Nature at Port Hudson, 1863, 1917." Part 1. *Military Historian and Economist* 2 (October 1917): 372–84.

Borden, Spencer. *The Arab Horse.* New York: Doubleday, Page, 1906.

Bowen, Edward L. *Legacies of the Turf: A Century of Great Thoroughbred Breeders,* 2 vols. Lexington, Ky.: Blood Horse Publications, 2005.

———. *Man o' War.* Lexington, Ky.: Eclipse Press, 2000.

Bowling, Ann T., and Anatoly Ruvinsky. "Genetic Aspects of Domestication, Breeds and Their Origins." In *The Genetics of the Horse,* edited by A. T. Bowling and A. Ruvinsky. Wallingford, UK: CABI Publishing, 2000.

Boyd, Eva J. *Native Dancer.* Lexington, Ky.: Eclipse Press, 2000.

Brady, Lisa M. *War Upon the Land: Military Strategy and the Transformation of Southern Landscapes During the American Civil War.* Athens: Univ. of Georgia Press, 2012.

Breckinridge, Mary. *Wide Neighborhoods: A Story of the Frontier Nursing Service.* Lexington: Univ. Press of Kentucky, 1952.

Brown, Alexander. *The Cabells and Their Kin.* Boston: Houghton Mifflin, 1895.

Brown, Dee A. *Morgan's Raiders.* New York: Smithmark Publishers, 1959.

Brown, Dee, and Stan Banash, ed. *Dee Brown's Civil War Anthology.* Santa Fe, N.Mex.: Clear Light, 1998.

Brown, Kent M., ed. *The Civil War in Kentucky: Battle for the Bluegrass State.* Mason City, Iowa: Savas Publishing, 2000.

———. "Munfordville: The Campaign and Battle along Kentucky's Strategic Axis." In *The Civil War in Kentucky: Battle for the Bluegrass State,* edited by Kent M. Brown, 137–74. Mason City, Iowa: Savas Publishing, 2000.

Brown, Sara L. "Rarey, the Horse's Master and Friend." *Ohio Archaeological and Historical Quarterly* 25 (October 1916): 487–539.

Burnett, Lonnie A. *Henry Hotze, Confederate Propagandist: Selected Writings on Revolution, Recognition and Race.* Tuscaloosa: Univ. of Alabama Press, 2008.

Busby, Hamilton. *The Trotting and the Pacing Horse in America.* New York: MacMillan, 1904.

Cameron, Robert S. *Staff Ride Handbook for the Battle of Perryville, 8 October 1862.* Fort Leavenworth, Kans.: Combat Studies Institute, 2005.

Campbell, Julie A. *The Horse in Virginia: An Illustrated History.* Charlottesville: Univ. of Virginia Press, 2010.

Capps, Timothy T. *Secretariat: Racing's Greatest Triple Crown Winner.* Lexington, Ky.: Eclipse Press, 2003.

Chambers, William, and Robert Chambers. *Chamber's Encyclopaedia: A Dictionary of Universal Knowledge.* London: J. B. Lippincott, 1890.

Chard, Thornton. "The Arabian and the Barb." *Western Horseman* 2 (January 1937): 5–7.

———. "Keene Richards' Arabian Importations." Part 1. *The Horse,* American Remount Association, 15 (Nov.–Dec. 1934): 12–18.

———. "Keene Richards' Arabian Importations." Part 2. *The Horse,* American Remount Association, 15 (January–February 1935): 21–25.

Clark, Granville. "William Forst House." National Register of Historic Places Nomination Form, Reference No. 73000816, National Register of Historic Places.

Clark, Thomas D. "The Slave Trade Between Kentucky and the Cotton Kingdom." *Mississippi Valley Historical Review* 21 (December 1934): 331–42.

Clee, Nicholas. *Eclipse: The Horse That Changed Racing History Forever.* London: Bantam, 2009.

Clutton-Brock, Juliet. *A Natural History of Domesticated Mammals.* Cambridge: Cambridge Univ. Press, 1999.

Coffman, Edward. *The Story of Logan County.* Nashville, Tenn.: Parthenon Press, 1962.

Cohn, David L. *The Life and Times of King Cotton.* New York: Oxford Univ. Press, 1956.

Coleman, J. Winston. *Three Kentucky Artists: Hart, Price, Troye.* Lexington: Univ. Press of Kentucky, 1974.

Collelo, Thomas, ed. *Syria: A Country Study,* 3d ed. Washington, D.C.: Library of Congress, Federal Research Division, 1988.

Connelly, Thomas L. *Army of the Heartland: The Army of Tennessee, 1861–1862.* Baton Rouge: Louisiana State Univ. Press, 1967.

Connelley, William Elsey, and E. Merton Coulter. *History of Kentucky.* Edited by Charles Kerr. 5 vols. Chicago: American Historical Society, 1922.

Cordell, Eugene F. *The Medical Annals of Maryland, 1799–1899.* Baltimore, Md.: Williams and Wilkins, 1903.

Coulter, E. Merton. *The Civil War and Readjustment in Kentucky.* Chapel Hill: Univ. of North Carolina Press, 1926.

Cowan, Walter G., and Jack B. McGuire. *Louisiana Governors: Rulers, Rascals, and Reformers.* Jackson: Univ. Press of Mississippi, 2008.

Crimmins, M. L. "Leonard Waller Groce, the Cofounder of Texas' Main Cash Crop—Cotton." *West Texas Historical Association Yearbook* 27 (1951): 99–110.

Cumpston, Mike, and Johnny Bates. *Percussion Pistols and Revolvers: History, Performance and Practical Use.* New York: iUniverse, 2005.

Cunningham, Edward. *The Port Hudson Campaign, 1862–1862.* Baton Rouge: Louisiana State Univ. Press, 1994.

Cunningham, E. Patrick, John J. Dooley, Rebecca K. Splan, and Daniel G. Bradley. "Microsatellite Diversity, Pedigree Relatedness, and the Contributions of Founder Lineages to Thoroughbred Horses." *Animal Genetics* 32 (December 2001): 360–64.

Custance, Henry. *Riding Recollections and Turf Stories.* London: Edward Arnold, 1894.

Cutter, William L., ed. "Kilgour, John." In *American Biography: A New Cyclopedia,* vol. 7. New York: American Historical Society, 1920.

Daigle, J. J., G. E. Griffith, J. M. Omernik, P. L. Faulkner, R. P. McCulloh, L. R. Handley, L. M. Smith, and S. S. Chapman. *Ecoregions of Louisiana.* Map. Reston, Va.: U.S. Geological Survey, 2006.

Daniel, Larry J. *Battle of Stones River: The Nearly Forgotten Conflict Between the Confederate Army of Tennessee and the Union Army of the Cumberland.* Baton Rouge: Louisiana State Univ. Press, 2012.

———. *Days of Glory: The Army of the Cumberland, 1861–1865.* Baton Rouge: Louisiana State Univ. Press, 2004.

Danielle, L. E. "Dr. Geo. A. Feris." In *Types of Successful Men of Texas.* Austin, Tex.: Eugene Von Boeckmann, 1890.

Davis, John H. *The American Turf.* New York: John Polhemus, 1907.

Davis, William C. *Breckinridge: Statesman, Soldier, Symbol.* Baton Rouge: Louisiana State Univ. Press, 1974.

Delaney, Robert W. "Matamoros, Port for Texas During the Civil War." *Southwestern Historical Quarterly* 58 (April 1955): 473–87.

Delcourt, Hazel R. "Presettlement Vegetation of the North of Red River Land District, Louisiana." *Castenea* 41 (June 1976): 122–39.

Denbo, Bruce, and Mary Wharton, eds. *The Horse World of the Bluegrass.* Lexington, Ky.: John Bradford Press, 1980.

Denhardt, Robert M. *Foundation Dams of the American Quarter Horse.* Norman: Univ. of Oklahoma Press, 1995.

Derry, Margaret E. *Bred for Perfection: Shorthorn Cattle, Collies, and Arabian Horses Since 1800.* Baltimore, Md.: Johns Hopkins Univ. Press, 2003.

Deyle, Steven. *Carry Me Back: The Domestic Slave Trade in American Life.* Oxford: Oxford Univ. Press, 2005.

Diamond, William. "Imports of the Confederate Government from Europe and Mexico." *Southern History* 6 (November 1940): 470–503.

Di Brino, Nicholas. *History of the Morris Park Racecourse and the Morris Family.* Bronx, N.Y.: Bronx Historical Society, 1977.

Dieffenbach, Emory M., and Roy B. Gray. "The Development of the Tractor." In *Power to Produce: The Yearbook of Agriculture, 1960.* Edited by Alfred Stefferud. Washington, D.C.: Government Printing Office, 1960: 25–45.

Dizikes, John. *Sportsmen and Gamesmen.* Boston: Houghton Mifflin, 1981.

Drape, Joe *Black Maestro: The Epic Life of an American Legend.* New York: William Morrow, 2006.

DuBose, Joel C. *Notable Men of Alabama.* Atlanta: Southern Historical Society, 1904.

Duckers, Peter. *British Military Rifles 1800–2000.* Princes Risborough, England: Shire, 2005.

Dufour, Charles L. *Gentle Tiger: The Gallant Life of Roberdeau Wheat.* Baton Rouge: Louisiana State Univ. Press, 1957.

Dugatkin, Lee Alan. *Mr. Jefferson and the Giant Moose: Natural History in Early America.* Chicago: Univ. of Chicago Press, 2009.

Dupree, Stephen A. *Planting the Union Flag in Texas: The Campaigns of Major General Nathaniel P. Banks in the West.* College Station: Texas A&M Univ. Press, 2008.

Eakin, Sue L. *Lecompte: Plantation Town in Transition.* Baton Rouge: Venture Publications, 1982.

Eakin, Sue L., and Patsy K. Barber. *Rapides Parish: An Illustrated History.* Northridge, Calif.: Windsor Publications, 1987.

Eaton, John. *Grant, Lincoln, and the Freedmen: Reminiscences of the Civil War.* New York: Longmans, Green, 1907.

Edgerton, Robert B. *Death or Glory: The Legacy of the Crimean War.* Boulder, Colo.: Westview Press, 1999.

Eicher, David J. *Civil War High Commands.* Stanford, Calif.: Stanford Univ. Press, 2001.

Eisenburg, John. *The Great Match Race: When North Met South in America's First Sports Spectacle.* Boston: Houghton Mifflin, 2006.

Ellis, L. Tuffly. "Maritime Commerce on the Far Western Gulf, 1861–1865." *Southwestern Historical Quarterly* 77 (October 1973): 167–226.

Engle, Stephen D. *Don Carlos Buell: Most Promising of All.* Chapel Hill: Univ. of North Carolina Press, 1999.

Epstein, Helmut, and Ian L. Mason. *The Origin of the Domesticated Animals of Africa.* 2 vols. New York: Africana Publishing, 1971.

Ernst, Carl W. *Following Muhammad: Rethinking Islam in the Contemporary World.* Chapel Hill: Univ. of North Carolina Press, 2003.

Fahmy, Khaled. *All the Pasha's Men: Mehmed Ali, His Army and the Making of Modern Egypt.* Cambridge: Cambridge Univ. Press, 1997.

Federal Writers' Project for the Works Progress Administration for the State of Kentucky. *Military History of Kentucky.* Frankfort: State Journal, 1939.

Field, Ron, and Robin Smith. *Uniforms of the Civil War.* Guilford, Conn.: Lyons Press, 2005.

Fife, Robert O. "Alexander Campbell and the Christian Church in the Slavery Controversy." Ph.D. diss., Indiana Univ., 1960.

Finkel, Caroline. *Osman's Dream: The History of the Ottoman Empire.* New York: Basic Books, 2005.

Fletcher, William. *The History and Development of Steam Locomotion on Common Roads.* London: E. and F. N. Spon, 1891.

Forbis, Judith. *The Classic Arabian Horse.* New York: Liveright, 1974.

Foster, Douglas A. *A Life of Alexander Campbell.* Grand Rapids, Mich.: William B. Eerdmans, 2020.

Fowler, William M. *Under Two Flags: The American Navy in the Civil War.* Annapolis, Md.: Naval Institute Press, 2001.

Fry, Anna M. G. *Memories of Old Cahaba.* Nashville, Tenn.: Publishing House of the Methodist Episcopal Church, South, 1908.

Gaines, Bill. *History of Scott County.* 2 vols. Georgetown, Ky.: B. O. Gaines, 1905.

General Catalogue of Princeton University 1746–1906. Princeton, N.J.: Princeton University, 1908.

Golshan, Ali. *Introduction to the Turkmen Horse in Iran.* Tehran, Iran: Pejvake Keyvan, 2005.

Gray, Lewis C. *History of Agriculture in the Southern United States to 1860.* 2 vols. Washington, D.C.: Carnegie Institute, 1933.

Grenville, John A. S. *Europe Reshaped, 1848–1878,* 2nd ed. Oxford, UK: Blackwell Publishing, 2000.

Harris, Sheldon L. "John L. O'Sullivan Serves the Confederacy." *Civil War History* 10 (September 1964): 275–90.

Harrison, Fairfax. *The Belair Stud 1747–1761.* Richmond, Va.: Old Dominion Press, 1929.

———. *The John's Island Stud (South Carolina) 1750–1788.* Richmond, Va.: Old Dominion Press, 1931.

———. *Mares.* Vol. 1 of *Early American Turf Stock 1730–1830.* Richmond: Old Dominion Press, 1934.

———. *The Roanoke Stud 1795–1883.* Richmond, Va.: Old Dominion Press, 1930.

Harrison, Lowell H. *The Civil War in Kentucky.* Lexington: Univ. Press of Kentucky, 1975.

———. "George W. Johnson and Richard Hawes: The Governors of Confederate Kentucky." *Register of the Kentucky Historical Society* 79 (winter 1981): 3–39.

———. "The Government of Confederate Kentucky." In *The Civil War in Kentucky: Battle for the Bluegrass State,* edited by Kent M. Brown, 79–102. Mason City, Iowa: Savas Publishing, 2000.

———. *Kentucky's Road to Statehood.* Lexington: Univ. Press of Kentucky, 1992.

———, and James C. Klotter. *A New History of Kentucky.* Lexington: Univ. Press of Kentucky, 1997.

Harrell, David A., Jr. "Disciples of Christ." In *Dictionary of Afro-American Slavery,* edited by Randall M. Miller and John D. Smith, 191–92. Westport, Conn.: Praeger, 1997.

Harter, Jim. *World Railways of the Nineteenth Century: A Pictorial History in Victorian Engravings.* Baltimore: Johns Hopkins Univ. Press, 2005.

Hazlett, James C., Edwin Olmstead, and M. Hume Parks. *Field Artillery Weapons of the Civil War,* rev. ed. Chicago: Univ. of Illinois Press, 2004.

Henderson, Robert W. *Early American Sport: A Checklist of Books by American and Foreign Authors Published in America Prior to 1860, Including Sporting Songs.* Rutherford, N.J.: Fairleigh Dickinson Univ. Press, 1977.

Hendricks, Bonnie L. *International Encyclopedia of Horse Breeds.* Norman: Univ. of Oklahoma Press, 1995.

Henson, Margaret S. *McKinney Falls: The Ranch Home of Thomas F. McKinney, Pioneer Texas Entrepreneur.* Austin: Texas State Historical Association, 1999.

———. *The Samuel May Williams Home: The Life and Neighborhood of an Early Galveston Entrepreneur.* Austin: Texas State Historical Association, 1992.

Herndon, William H., and Jesse W. Weik. *Herndon's Lincoln: The True Story of a Great Life.* 3 vols. Chicago: Belford, Clarke, 1889.

Hervey, John. *Racing in America, 1665–1865.* 2 vols. New York: The Jockey Club, 1944.

Hill, Emmeline W., Daniel G. Bradly, Mahomed Al-Barody, Okan Ertugrul, Rebecca K. Splan, Il'ya Zakharov, and E. Patrick Cunningham. "History and Integrity of Thoroughbred Dam Lines Revealed in Equine mtDNA Variation." *Animal Genetics* 33 (August 2002): 287–94.

Hillenbrand, Laura. *Seabiscuit: An American Legend.* New York: Ballantine Books, 2003.

History of Education in Kentucky. Bulletin of Kentucky Department of Education 7. Frankfort: Kentucky Department of Education, 1914.

Hogan, William R. "Amusements in the Republic of Texas." *Journal of Southern History* 3 (November 1937): 397–421.

Hollandsworth, James G., Jr. *Pretense of Glory: The Life of General Nathaniel Banks.* Baton Rouge: Louisiana State Univ. Press, 2005.

Holley, Donald. *The Second Great Emancipation: Mechanical Cottonpicker, Black Migration and How They Shaped the Modern South.* Fayetteville: Univ. of Arkansas Press, 2000.

Hollingsworth, Kent. *The Kentucky Thoroughbred.* Lexington: Univ. Press of Kentucky, 1985.

Hotaling, Edward. *The Great Black Jockeys: The Lives and Times of the Men Who Dominated America's First National Sport.* Rocklin, Calif.: Forum, 1999.

———. *Wink: The Incredible Journey and Epic Journey of Jimmy Winkfield.* New York: McGraw-Hill, 2004.

Hubbard, Charles M. *The Burden of Confederate Diplomacy.* Knoxville: Univ. of Tennessee Press, 2000.

Hulbert, Richard C., Jr. "The Ancestry of the Horse." In *Horses Through Time,* edited by Sandra L. Olsen, 11–34. Boulder, Colo.: Roberts Rhinehart for Carnegie Museum of Natural History, 1996.

Hunter, Avalyn. *American Classic Pedigrees (1914–2002).* Lexington: Blood-Horse Publications, 2003.

Hyland, Ann. *The Horse in the Ancient World.* Westport, Conn.: Praeger, 2003.

Jansen, Thomas, Peter Forster, Marsha A. Levine, Hardy Oelk, Matthew Hurles, Colin Renfrew, Jürgen Weber, and Klaus Olek. "Mitochondrial DNA and the Origins of the Domestic Horse." *Proceedings of the National Academy of Sciences* 99 (6 August 2002): 10905–10910.

Jennings, Walter W. *Origin and Early History of the Disciples of Christ.* Cincinnati, Ohio: Standard Publishing, 1919.

Jensen, Christian E. *Lives of Caroline County Maryland Physicians 1774–1984.* Denton, Md.: Baker Printing, 1986.

Johnson, David. *John Randolph of Roanoke.* Baton Rouge: Louisiana State Univ. Press, 2012.

Johnson, Viginia C., and Barbara Crookshanks. *Virginia Horse Racing: Triumphs of the Turf.* Charleston, S.C.: History Press, 2008.

Johnston, William P. *Life of Gen. Albert Sydney Johnston.* New York: Appleton, 1878.

Jones, Elias. *History of Dorchester County, Maryland.* Baltimore, Md.: Williams and Wilkins, 1903.

———. *Keene Family History and Genealogy.* Baltimore, Md.: Kohn and Pollock, 1923.

Judd, David W. *Life and Writings of Frank Forester (Henry William Herbert).* London: Frederick Warne, 1882.

Kamoie, Laura C. *Irons in the Fire: The Business History of the Tayloe Family and Virginia's Gentry, 1700–1860.* Charlottesville: Univ. of Virginia Press, 2007.

Karpat, Kemal H. "The Social and Economic Transformation of Istanbul in the Nineteenth Century." In *Studies on Ottoman Social and Political History: Selected Articles and Essays,* edited by Kemal H. Karpat. Boston, Mass.: Brill, 2002.

Kavar, Tatjana, and Peter Dovč. "Domestication of the Horse: Genetic Relationships Between Domestic and Wild Horses." *Livestock Science* 116 (July 2008): 1–14.

Kilbride, Daniel. *Being American in Europe, 1750–1860.* Baltimore, Md.: Johns Hopkins Univ. Press, 2013.

Kirsan, Kathleen H. *American Running Horse: A Forgotten Breed.* Wheatland, Calif.: Privately published, 2023.

———. *Legacy of Lexington.* Wheatland, Calif.: Privately published, 2014.

———. *North American Sport Horse Breeder.* Wheatland, Calif.: Privately published, 2013.

Klynstra, Foppe B. *Nobility of the Desert: The Arab Horse of the Bedouins.* Translated by K. Schmitt and S. Eicher. Hildesheim, Germany: Olms Presse, 1990.

Kulling, Peggy, and A. Vasudevan. "Gadara." In *International Dictionary of Historic Places,* vol. 4, *Middle East and Africa,* edited by Noelle Watson. Chicago: Fittzroy Dearborn Publishers, 1996).

Lacy, Lisa M. *Lady Anne Blunt in the Middle East: Travel, Politics and the Idea of Empire.* London: Bloomsbury Publishing, 2020.

Lancaster, William. *The Rwala Bedouin Today,* 2nd ed. Prospect Heights, Ill.: Waveland Press, 1997.

Levine, Marsha A. "Domestication and Early History of the Horse." In *The Domestic Horse: The Origins, Development and Management of Its Behavior,* edited by Daniel S. Mills and S. M. McDonnell. Cambridge: Cambridge Univ. Press, 2005.

Lewis, Jack P. "James Turner Barclay: Explorer of Nineteenth-Century Jerusalem." *Biblical Archeologist* 51 (September 1988): 163–70.

Lovell, Mary S. *Rebel Heart: The Scandalous Life of Jane Digby.* New York: Norton, 1995.

Lynghaug, Fran. *The Official Horse Breeds Standards Book.* Minneapolis, Minn.: Voyageur Press, 2009.

Mackay-Smith, Alexander. *The Colonial Quarter Race Horse.* Richmond, Va.: Whitter and Shepperson, 1983.

———. *The Race Horses of America, 1832–1872: Portraits and Other Paintings by Edward Troye.* Saratoga Springs, N.Y.: The National Museum of Racing, 1981.

———. *Speed and the Thoroughbred: The Complete History.* Lanham, Md.: Derrydale Press, 2000.

Maltby, Mary Breckinridge. *Mary Cyrene Breckinridge.* Georgetown, Ky.: Self-published, 1910.

———. "Recollections of Civil War Times in Kentucky." *Register of the Kentucky Historical Society* 45 (July 1947): 225–34.

Mangum, William P., II. *A Kingdom for the Horse: The Legacy of R.A. Alexander and Woodburn Farms.* Louisville: Harmony House, 1999.

Marshall, Anne E. *Creating a Confederate Kentucky: The Lost Cause and Civil War Memory in a Border State.* Chapel Hill: Univ. of North Carolina Press, 2010.

McAllister, Lester G. *Bethany: The First 150 Years.* Bethany, W.Va.: Bethany College Press, 1991.

McCrary, Peyton. *Abraham Lincoln and Reconstruction: The Louisiana Experiment.* Princeton, N.J.: Princeton Univ. Press, 1978.

McDaniels, Pellom, III. *Prince of Jockeys: The Life of Isaac Burns Murphy.* Lexington: Univ. Press of Kentucky, 2013.

McPherson, James M. *Abraham Lincoln and the Second American Revolution.* New York: Oxford Univ. Press, 1991.

———. *Battle Cry of Freedom: The Civil War Era.* New York: Oxford Univ. Press, 1988.

McWhiney, Grady. *Braxton Bragg and Confederate Defeat. Vol. 1, Field Command.* New York: Columbia Univ. Press, 1969.

Menn, Joseph K. *The Large Slaveholders of Louisiana, 1860.* New Orleans, La.: Pelican Publishing, 1964.

Merry, Thomas B. *The American Thoroughbred.* Los Angeles: Commercial Printing House, 1905.

Mooney, Katherine C. *Isaac Murphy: The Rise and Fall of a Black Jockey.* New Haven: Yale Univ. Press, 2023.

———. *Race Horse Men: How Slavery and Freedom Were Made at the Racetrack.* Cambridge, Mass.: Harvard Univ. Press, 2014.

Mowery, David L. *Morgan's Great Raid: The Remarkable Expedition from Kentucky to Ohio.* Charleston, S.C.: History Press, 2013.

Moyse-Bartlett, Hubert. *Louis Edward Nolan and His Influence on the British Cavalry.* London: Leo Cooper, 1971.

Nicholas, Ron. "Mill Springs: The First Battle for Kentucky." In *The Civil War in Kentucky: Battle for the Bluegrass State,* edited by Kent M. Brown, 48–73. Mason City, Iowa: Savas Publishing, 2000.

Nicholson, James C. *The Notorious John Morrissey: How a Bare-Knuckle Brawler Be-*

came a Congressman and Founded Saratoga Race Course. Lexington: Univ. Press of Kentucky, 2016.

Noe, Kenneth W. *Perryville: This Grand Havoc of Battle.* Lexington: Univ. Press of Kentucky, 2001.

Nosworthy, Brent. *Bloody Crucible of Courage: Fighting Methods and Combat Experience of the Civil War.* New York: Carroll and Graf, 2005.

Oates, Stephen B. "Henry Hotze: Confederate Agent Abroad." *The Historian* 27 (February 1965): 131–50.

O'Dell, Gary A. "At the Starting Post: Racing Venues and the Origins of Thoroughbred Racing in Kentucky, 1783–1865." *Register of the Kentucky Historical Society* 116 (winter 2018): 29–78.

———. "Denton Offutt: America's First 'Horse Whisperer'?" *Register of the Kentucky Historical Society* 108 (summer 2010): 173–212.

———. "Under Siege: Kentucky and the Transformation of American Thoroughbred Racing, 1865–1936." *Register of the Kentucky Historical Society* 118 (summer 2020): 389–446.

Oliver, Floyd. "The Breeding Behind Domino." Bloodhorse, https://www.bloodhorse.com/horse-racing/articles/154278/the-breeding-behind-domino.

Olsen, Sandra L. "Early Horse Domestication on the Eurasian Steppe." In *Documenting Domestication: New Genetic and Archaeological Paradigms,* edited by Melinda A. Zeder, Daniel G. Bradley, Eve Emshwiller, and Bruce D. Smith. Berkely: Univ. of California Press, 2006.

On the Deteriorated Condition of Our Saddle-Horses. London: T. Hatchard, 1853.

Owen, Thomas M. *History of Alabama and Dictionary of Alabama Biography.* 4 vols. Chicago: S. J. Clarke Publishing, 1921.

Owsley, Frank L. *King Cotton Diplomacy: Foreign Relations of the Confederate States of America,* 2nd ed. Chicago: Univ. of Chicago Press, 1959.

Parker, S. Thomas. "The Decapolis Reviewed." *Journal of Biblical Literature* 94 (September 1975): 437–41.

Parks, Joseph H. *Edmund Kirby Smith, C.S.A.* Baton Rouge: Louisiana State Univ. Press, 1954.

Paskoff, Paul F. "Measures of War: A Quantitative Examination of the Civil War's Destructiveness in the Confederacy." *Civil War History* 54 (March 2008): 35–62.

Passell, Peter. "The Impact of Cotton Land Distribution on the Antebellum Economy." *Journal of Economic History* 31 (December 1971): 917–37.

"Pickett's Administration, 1879–1887." *History of Education in Kentucky.* Bulletin of Kentucky Department of Education 7 (July 1914): 149–69.

Pinkston, Georgia P. D. *A Place to Remember: East Carroll Parish, La. 1832–1976.* Baton Rouge: Claitor's Publishing Division, 1977.

Poret, Ory G. *History of Land Titles in the State of Louisiana.* Baton Rouge: State Land Office, 1972.

Porter, Ed Thompson. "Letters of George W. Johnson: Provisional Governor of Kentucky Under the Confederacy." *Register of the Kentucky Historical Society* 40 (October 1942): 337–52.

Power, Frederick D. *Life of William Kimbrough Pendleton, LL.D., President of Bethany College.* St. Louis: Christian Publishing Company, 1902.

Prior, Charles M. *The Royal Studs of the Sixteenth and Seventeenth Centuries: Together with a Reproduction of the Second Earl of Godolphin's Stud Book and Sundry Other Papers Relating to the Thoroughbred Horse.* London: Horse and Hound Publications, 1935.

Prushankin, Jeffery S. *A Crisis in Confederate Command: Edmund Kirby Smith, Richard Taylor, and the Army of the Trans-Mississippi.* Baton Rouge: Louisiana State Univ. Press, 2005.

Ramage, James A. *John Wesley Hunt: Pioneer Merchant, Manufacturer and Financier.* Lexington: Univ. Press of Kentucky, 1974.

———. *Rebel Raider: The Life of General John Hunt Morgan.* Lexington: Univ. Press of Kentucky, 1995.

Randall, James G. "Captured and Abandoned Property During the Civil War." *American Historical Review* 19 (October 1913): 65–79.

Raswan, Carl R. "Tribal Areas and Migration Lines of the North Arabian Bedouins." *Geographical Review* 20 (July 1930): 494–502.

Rice, James. *History of the British Turf, from the Earliest Times to the Present Day.* 2 vols. London: Samson Low, Marston, Searle, and Rivington, 1879.

Richardson, Charles. *The English Turf: A Record of Horses and Courses.* Edited by E. T. Sachs. London: Methuen, 1901.

Richardson, Clive. *British Horse and Pony Breeds and Their Future.* London: J. A. Allen, 2008.

Richey, Alexander G. *Lectures on the History of Ireland, From A.D. 1534 to the Date of the Plantation of Ulster.* London: Longmans, Green, 1870.

Ridgeway, William. *The Origin and Influence of the Thoroughbred Horse.* Cambridge: Cambridge Univ. Press, 1905.

Riess, Steven A. "The Cyclical History of Horse Racing: The USA's Oldest and (Sometimes) Most Popular Spectator Sport." *International Journal of the History of Sport* 31, nos. 1 and 2 (March 2014): 29–54.

———. *The Sport of Kings and the Kings of Crime: Horse Racing, Politics, and Organized Crime in New York, 1865–1913.* Syracuse, N.Y.: Syracuse Univ. Press, 2011.

Robertson, William H. P. *The History of Thoroughbred Racing in America.* New York: Bonanza Books, 1964.

Rodinson, Maxime. *Europe and the Mystique of Islam.* Seattle: Univ. of Washington Press, 1987.

Roland, Charles P. *An American Iliad: The Story of the Civil War,* 2nd ed. Lexington: Univ. Press of Kentucky, 2002.
Rollins, Robert. *A History of the Hurstbourne Country Club.* Louisville: Power Creative, 2000.
Royle, Trevor. *Crimea: The Great Crimean War.* New York: Palgrave Macmillan, 2004.
Schofler, Patti. *Flight Without Wings: The Arabian Horse and the Show World.* Guilford, Conn.: Lyons Press, 2006.
Schreckengost, Gary. *The First Louisiana Special Battalion: Wheat's Tigers in the Civil War.* Jefferson, N.C.: McFarland, 2008.
Sehlinger, Peter J. *Kentucky's Last Cavalier, General William Preston 1816–1887.* Lexington: Kentucky Historical Society, 2004.
Sigaud, Louis A. *Belle Boyd: Confederate Spy.* Richmond, Va: Dietz Press, 1944.
Silberman, Neil A. "Desolation and Restoration: The Impact of a Biblical Concept on Near Eastern Archaeology." *Biblical Archaeologist* 54 (June 1991): 76–87.
Silverstone, Paul H. *Civil War Navies.* New York: Routledge, 2006.
Simon, John Y. "Lincoln, Grant, and Kentucky in 1861." In *The Civil War in Kentucky: Battle for the Bluegrass State,* edited by Kent M. Brown, 1–22. Mason City, Iowa: Savas Publishing, 2000.
Smith, Andrew F. *Starving the South: How the North Won the Civil War.* New York: St. Martin's, 2011.
Smith, Timothy B. *The Untold Story of Shiloh: The Battle and the Battlefield.* Knoxville: Univ. of Tennessee Press, 2006.
Smith, Zachariah F. *History of Kentucky.* Louisville, Ky.: Courier-Journal Job Printing, 1892.
Somers, Dale A. *The Rise of Sports in New Orleans 1850–1900.* Baton Rouge: Louisiana State Univ. Press, 1972.
Speed, John G. *The Horse in America.* New York: McClure, Phillips, 1905.
Spencer, John H., and Burilla B. Spencer. *A History of Kentucky Baptists.* 2 vols. Cincinnati, Ohio: J. R. Baumes, 1886.
Stafford, George M. G. *The Wells Family of Louisiana and Allied Families.* Alexandria, La.: Standard Printing, 1941.
Stephenson, Wendell H. "Ante-Bellum New Orleans as an Agricultural Focus." *Agricultural History* 15 (October 1941): 161–74.
Stevenson, Dwight E. *The Bacon College Story: 1836–1865.* Lexington: College of the Bible, 1962.
Stickles, Arndt M. *Simon Bolivar Buckner: Borderland Knight.* Chapel Hill: Univ. of North Carolina Press, 1940.
Struna, Nancy L. "The North-South Races: American Thoroughbred Racing in Transition, 1823–1850." *Journal of Sport History* 8 (summer 1981): 28–57.
Surdam, David G. "The Union Navy's Blockade Reconsidered." *Naval War College Review* 51 (autumn 1998): 85–107.

"Swartz [sic], Edward George." *National Cyclopedia of American Biography*, vol. 27 (New York: James T. White, 1927), 8.

Taffin, John. *Gun Digest Book of the 44*. Northfield, Ill.: Gun Digest Books, 2006.

Taylor, Joe Gray. *Louisiana: A History*. New York: Norton, 1984.

Townsend, William H. *Lincoln and the Bluegrass: Slavery and Civil War in Kentucky*. Lexington: Univ. Press of Kentucky, 1955.

Treat, Payne J. *The National Land System 1785–1820*. New York: E. B. Treat, 1910.

Upton, Peter, and Hossein Amirsadeghi. *Arabians*. San Francisco, Calif.: Chronicle Books, 1999.

Vosburgh, Walter S. *Cherry and Black: The Career of Mr. Pierre Lorillard on the Turf*. New York: Printed for the author, 1916.

———. *Racing in America, 1866–1921*. New York: Jockey Club, 1922.

Wagoner, Don M. *Equine Genetics and Selection Procedures*. Dallas, Tex.: Equine Research Publications, 1978.

Wall, Maryjean. *How Kentucky Became Southern: A Tale of Outlaws, Horse Thieves, Gamblers, and Breeders*. Lexington: Univ. Press of Kentucky, 2010.

Wallace, John H. *The Horse of America in his Derivation, History, and Development*. New York: Self-published, 1897.

Wallner, Barbara, Nicola Palmieri, Claus Vogl, Doris Rigler, Elif Bozlak, Thomas Druml, and Vidhya Jagannathan. "Y Chromosome Uncovers the Recent Oriental Origin of Modern Stallions." *Current Biology* 27 (July 10, 2017): 2029–35.

Wallner, Barbara, Claus Vogl, Priyank Shukla, Joerg P. Burgstaller, Thomas Druml, and Gottfried Brem. "Identification of Genetic Variation on the Horse Y Chromosome and the Tracing of Male Founder Lineages in Modern Breeds." *PLOS One* 8 (2013): e60015.

Walther, Eric H. *William Lowndes Yancey and the Coming of the Civil War*. Chapel Hill: Univ. of North Carolina Press, 2006.

Weeks, Lyman H. *The American Turf: An Historical Account of Racing in the United States*. New York: Historical Co., 1898.

Welch, Ned. *Who's Who in Thoroughbred Racing*, 2 vols. Washington, D.C.: Who's Who in Thoroughbred Racing, 1947.

Weller, Jac. "The Confederate Use of British Cannon." *Civil War History* 3 (June 1, 1957): 135–52.

Wentworth, Judith Blunt-Lytton. *The Authentic Arabian Horse and His Descendants*. London: G. Allen and Unwin, 1945.

Wharton, Clarence R. *History of Fort Bend County*. San Antonio, Tex.: Naylor Co., 1939.

Whayne, Jeannie C., Thomas A. Deblack, and George Sabo. *Arkansas: A Narrative History*. Fayetteville: Univ. of Arkansas Press, 2002.

Wheat, Leo. "Memoir of Gen. C. R. Wheat, Commander of the Louisiana Tiger Battalion." *Southern Historical Society Papers* 17 (1889): 47–60.

Wickens, Kim. *Lexington: The Extraordinary Life and Turbulent Times of America's Legendary Racehorse.* New York Ballentine Books, 2023.

Whitehair, C. W. *Belle Boyd: The Rebel Spy.* Summerfield, Fla.: CW Whitehair, 2017.

Whitley, Edna T. *Kentucky Ante-Bellum Portraiture.* Paris, Ky.: National Society of the Colonial Dames of America in the Commonwealth of Kentucky, 1956.

Wik, Reynold M. *Steam Power on the American Farm.* Philadelphia: Univ. of Pennsylvania Press, 1953.

Willett, Peter. *The Classic Racehorse.* Lexington: Univ. Press of Kentucky, 1961.

Williams, Thomas H. *P.G.T. Beauregard: Napoleon in Gray.* Baton Rouge: Louisiana State Univ. Press, 1955.

Winants, Peter. *Steeplechasing: A Complete History of the Sport in North America.* Lanham, Md.: Derridale Press, 2000.

Winters, John D. *The Civil War in Louisiana.* Baton Rouge: Louisiana State Univ. Press, 1963.

Wishart, David J. *The Fur Trade of the American West, 1807–1840: A Geographical Synthesis.* Lincoln: Univ. of Nebraska Press, 1979.

Woodman, Harold D. *King Cotton and His Retainers.* Lexington: Univ. of Kentucky Press, 1968.

Yarema, Alan E. *American Colonization Society: An Avenue to Freedom?* Lanham, Md.: Univ. Press of America, 2006.

INDEX

Note: Page numbers in italic denote illustrations.